AMERICAN BOOK COMPANY'S

PASSING THE LOUISIANA LEAP 8

IN

ENGLISH/LANGUAGE ARTS

May 2005

Teresa Valentine
Kate McElvaney

Dr. Frank Pintozzi
Executive Editor

American Book Company
PO Box 2638
Woodstock, GA 30188-1383
Toll Free: 1 (888) 264-5877   Phone: (770) 928-2834 Fax: (770) 928-7483
Web Site: www.americanbookcompany.com

ACKNOWLEDGEMENTS

The authors would like to acknowledge the technical and editing assistance of Marsha Torrens.

The Formatting Department is especially grateful to Mary Stoddard for going above and beyond in the preparation of this book for publication.

All the characters, places, and events portrayed in this book are fictitious, and any resemblance to real people, places, or events is purely coincidental.

This product/publication includes images from CorelDRAW 9 and 11 which are protected by the copyright laws of the United States, Canada, and elsewhere. Used under license.

Copyright© 2005
by American Book Company
PO Box 2638
Woodstock, GA 30188-1318

ALL RIGHTS RESERVED

The text of this publication, or any part thereof, may not be reproduced or transmitted in any form or by any means, electronic or mechanical, including photocopying, recording, storage in an information retrieval system, or otherwise, without the prior written permission of the publisher.

Printed in the United States of America
05/05

LEAP 8 Language Arts
Table of Contents

Preface 5
   Test-Taking Tips 6
Pretest 1
   General Directions 1
   Session 1—Writing 2
   Essay 13
   Session 3–Using Information Resources 13
   Evaluation Chart for LEAP 21 Grade 8 English Language Arts 25

Chapter 1 Capitalization, Punctuation, and Spelling 27
   Capitalization Rules 27
   Punctuation Rules 30
   Root Words with Suffixes and Prefixes 37
   Chapter 1 Review: 41

Chapter 2 Parts of Speech 43
   Nouns 43
   Pronouns 46
   Verbs 51
   Misplaced Modifiers 55
   Adjectives 55
   Adverbs 57
   Common Mistakes with Adverbs and Adjectives 58
   Absolute Concepts 58
   Prepositions 60
   Interjections 60
   Conjunctions 61
   Chapter 2 Review: Identifying the Parts of Speech 63

Chapter 3 Planning the Composition 65
   The Writing Process 65
   The Writing Prompt 65
   Organizing Ideas 69
   Focusing Ideas 70
   Chapter 3 Review: Planning the Composition 75

Table of Contents

Chapter 4 Writing the Composition — 77
Drafting the Composition 77
Writing Conclusions 85
Sentence Structure Variety 86
Chapter 4 Review: 91

Chapter 5 Descriptive and Narrative Writing — 95
Descriptive Writing..96
Narrative Compositions 103
Chapter 5 Review...111

Chapter 6 Expository and Persuasive Composition — 115
Expository Compositions 115
Cause-Effect Extended Response 119
Persuasive Writing 122
Chapter 6 Review 129

Chapter 7 Using the Writer's Checklist — 133
Sentence Usage 138
Commas and End Punctuation..139
Capitalization 139
Formatting 140
Spelling 140
Penmanship 140
Chapter 7 Review 141

Chapter 8 Word Meaning and Analysis — 143
Word Derivation and Analysis 143
Context Clues... 149
Idioms 152
Chapter 8 Review: 153

Chapter 9 Main Ideas, Summarizing, and Paraphrasing — 155
Detail..155
Main Ideas..156
Summarizing 163
Paraphrasing 166
Chapter 9 Review 168

Chapter 10 Inferences, Predictions, and Conclusions — 171
Inferences...172
Predictions 175
Conclusions 180
Chapter 10 Review 183

Chapter 11 Organizational Patterns for Information   187

Chronological Order 188
Time Order 191
Spatial Order 191
Inductive and Deductive Reasoning 193
Chapter 11 Review: 197

Chapter 12 Fact, Opinion, and Probability   201

Finding Facts and Opinions 202
Probability 204
Chapter 12 Review 208

Chapter 13 Author's Viewpoint   211

Author's Viewpoint 211
Evidence: Supporting a Viewpoint 217
Persuasive Techniques 218
Persuasive Techniques in Advertising and Nonfiction 218
Chapter 13 Review 223

Chapter 14 Using Information Resources   225

Organization of Information Resources 226
Types of Resource Materials 227
Business letters 237
E-Mail 238
Memos 238
Chapter 14 Review 241

Chapter 15 Electronic Information Sources   243

Finding Resources With the Electronic Library Information System 243
Computer Research 245
Validating Internet Sources 247
Electronic Storage 250
Safety 251
Electronic Media Research 252
Chapter 15 Review 254

Chapter 16 Evaluating and Citing Information Sources   255

Using Information in Research 255
Primary Sources of Information 255
Secondary Sources of Information 259
Quoting Sources in Text 261
Citing Sources 262
Chapter 16 Review: Evaluating and Citing Resources 266

Chapter 17 Graphic Aids and Organizers   269

Tables 269
Graphs 270

Table of Contents

Graphic Organizer...274
Timelines 280
Maps..282
Chapter 17 Review: Graphic Aids 285

Chapter 18 Literary Genres and Story Structure   287

Literary Genres 287
Fiction 288
Drama 290
Epic 290
Plot Structure 294
Setting 296
Literary Characters 297
Theme 300
Chapter 18 Review 301

Chapter 19 Literary Elements and Devices   305

Figurative Language 308
Creating Mood 312
Author's Tone 314
Point of View 317
Literary Style 318
Syntax 320
Chapter 19 Review: Literary Elements and Devices 321

Chapter 20 Comparing and Contrasting   323

Introduction To Comparing and Contrasting 323
Comparing and Contrasting in a Reading Passage 324
Comparing and Contrasting Language and Tone 326
Comparing and Contrasting Author's Word Choice and Syntax
   Within a Text and in Two or More Texts 329
Comparing and Contrasting Universal Themes Within
   and Between Texts 331
Comparing Contrasting Conflict in Two or More Texts 331
Comparing and Contrasting Characters in Fiction 332
Chapter 20 Review: Comparing and Contrasting 336

Chapter 21 Writing About Literature   339

Forms of Literature 340
Chapter 21 Review 345

Post Test 1   349
Post Test 2   373

PREFACE

Passing the LEAP 21 Grade 8 in English/Language Arts will help students who are learning or reviewing standards for the eighth grage English Language Arts Test. The materials in this book are based on the LEAP 21 assessment standards as published by the Louisiana Department of Education.

This book contains several sections. These sections are as follows: 1) General information about the book; 2) A Pretest; 3) An Evaluation Chart; 4) Chapters that teach the concepts and skills that teach the standards and test readiness; 5) Two Post Tests. Standards are posted at the beginning of each chapter as well as in the chart of standards in the answer manual.

We welcome comments and suggestions about the book. Please contact the authors at

American Book Company
PO Box 2638
Woodstock, GA 30188-1383

Toll Free: 1 (888) 264-5877
Phone: (770) 928-2834
Fax: (770) 928-7483
web site: www.americanbookcompany.com

ABOUT THE AUTHORS

Teresa Valentine

is currently enrolled in the Masters of Arts in Professional Writing Program at Kennesaw State University, Kennesaw, GA. She has worked as a writing consultant to graduate students in the Bagwell College of Education at Kennesaw, and coached undergraduates from all disciplines in composition writing. Teresa graduated Suma Cum Laude from Kennesaw with a degree in English.

Kate McElvaney

graduated Magna Cum Laude from the University of Hawaii at Manoa with a Bachelor of Education degree in English. She has worked as both a middle and high school Language Arts teacher. Kate has also worked as a reading specialist to at-risk students at the elementary level.

About the Executive Editor

Dr. Frank J. Pintozzi is an adjunct Professor of Education at Kennesaw (GA) State University. For over 28 years, he has taught English and reading at the high school and college levels as well as in teacher preparation courses in language arts and social studies. In addition to writing and editing state standard specific texts for high school and middle school exams, he has edited and written numerous college textbooks.

TEST-TAKING TIPS

1. **Complete the chapters and practice tests in this book.** This text will help you review the skills for English/Language Arts: Reading. The book also contains materials for reviewing skills under the Research standards.

2. **Be prepared.** Get a good night's sleep the day before your exam. Eat a well-balanced meal, one that contains plenty of proteins and carbohydrates, prior to your exam.

3. **Arrive early.** Allow yourself at least 15–20 minutes to find your room and get settled. Then you can relax before the exam, so you won't feel rushed.

4. **Think success.** Keep your thoughts positive. Turn negative thoughts into positive ones. Tell yourself you will do well on the exam.

5. **Practice relaxation techniques.** Some students become overly worried about exams. Before or during the test, they may perspire heavily, experience an upset stomach, or have shortness of breath. If you feel any of these symptoms, talk to a close friend or see a counselor. They will suggest ways to deal with test anxiety. **Here are some quick ways to relieve test anxiety:**

   - Imagine yourself in your most favorite place. Let yourself sit there and relax.
   - Do a body scan. Tense and relax each part of your body starting with your toes and ending with your forehead.
   - Use the 3-12-6 method of relaxation when you feel stress. Inhale slowly for 3 seconds. Hold your breath for 12 seconds, and then exhale slowly for 6 seconds.

6. **Read directions carefully.** If you don't understand them, ask the proctor for further explanation before the exam starts.

7. **Use your best approach for answering the questions.** Some test-takers like to skim the questions and answers before reading the problem or passage. Others prefer to work the problem or read the passage before looking at the answers. Decide which approach works best for you.

8. **Answer each question on the exam.** Unless you are instructed not to, make sure you answer every question. If you are not sure of an answer, take an educated guess. Eliminate choices that are definitely wrong, and then choose from the remaining answers.

9. **Use your answer sheet correctly.** Make sure the number on your question matches the number on your answer sheet. In this way, you will record your answers correctly. If you need to change your answer, erase it completely. Smudges or stray marks may affect the grading of your exams, particularly if they are scored by a computer. If your answers are on a computerized grading sheet, make sure the answers are dark. The computerized scanner may skip over answers that are too light.

10. **Check your answers.** Review your exam to make sure you have chosen the best responses. Change answers only if you are sure they are wrong.

LEAP 21 Grade 8 Language Arts Pretest

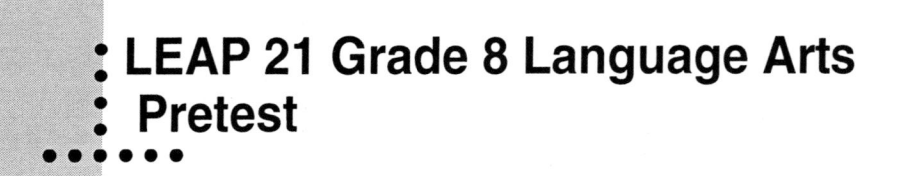

The purpose of this pretest is to measure your skills in English Language Arts. The pretest is based on the Louisiana LEAP 21 standards for English Language Arts. Competency in these standards is required for promotion to ninth grade.

GENERAL DIRECTIONS

- Read all directions carefully.
- Read each question or example. Then choose the best answer.
- Choose only one answer for each question. If you change an answer, be sure to erase the answer completely.
- At the end of the test, you or your instructor should score your test. Then determine whether or not you are prepared to be tested on the LEAP 21 Grade 8 in English Language Arts.

Pretest

SESSION 1—WRITING

On the real test, you will have extra pages for your prewriting and your rough draft. You will also have an answer document with two pages labeled for the final draft. In the real test, write your final draft only in the answer document.

For this pretest, however, you will use your own paper for each step. First, you may take a few minutes to brainstorm or create an outline. Then write a rough draft. Be sure to label each page, identifying the steps. Then write your final draft on two pages.

WRITING TOPIC

Read the topic in the box below. Write a well organized composition of at least 150–200 words. Be sure to follow the suggestions listed under the box.

> Your school newspaper has asked for writing submissions for the next issue. You decide to submit a story about the following:
>
> Write about how, if given the power, you would change the world to make it better.
>
> Before you begin to write, think about the problems in the world today. They could be large problems or small problems. What would solve these problems? How could you improve the world?
>
> Now write a **multi-paragraph** composition for the newspaper **telling** what you would do to change the world.

- Give specific details and explain why you think the way you do so that your readers will understand what you mean.
- Remember that the people in your audience are your fellow students; use appropriate language and explain your ideas clearly.
- Be sure to write clearly and to check your composition for correct spelling, punctuation, and grammar.

NOTE: *On the real test, your teacher will read instructions to you and will hand out the answer documents. You will also be told that for this session, and this session only, you will be allowed to use a dictionary and a thesaurus, along with a Writer's Checklist.*

ENGLISH LANGUAGE ARTS WRITER'S CHECKLIST

As you write your composition, remember these important points.

Composing:

☐ Write on the assigned topic.

☐ Present a clear main idea.

☐ Give enough details to support and elaborate your main idea.

☐ Present your ideas in a logical order.

Style/Audience Awareness

☐ Write with your audience (the person or group identified by the topic) in mind.

☐ Use vocabulary (words) that expresses your meaning well.

☐ Use sentences that make your main idea interesting to your audience.

Sentence Formation:

☐ Write in complete sentences and use a variety of sentence patterns.

Usage:

☐ Write using appropriate subject-verb agreement, verb tenses, word meaning, and word endings.

Mechanics:

☐ Write using correct punctuation.

☐ Write using correct capitalization.

☐ Write using appropriate formatting (e.g., indentations, margins).

Spelling:

☐ Write using correct spelling.

Remember to print or write neatly.

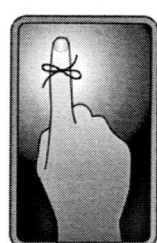

Pretest

SESSION 2—READING AND RESPONDING

In this section of the test, you will read three passages and a poem. Then you will answer questions about what you read. This part of the test contains both multiple-choice and constructed-response questions. Answer these questions on the lines provided.

The following article explains why hunters in Africa poach elephants. Read this article. Then answer questions 1 through 8.

Ivory Trade in Africa

1   The sun blazed relentlessly. In the steaming heat of the African summer afternoon, the herd of 11 female elephants browsed lazily. They had been awake much of the night before, eating grass and leaves in the Eastern savannas of Senegal, on the west coast of the great continent. Elephants spend 16 hours a day eating, and only 4–5 hours sleeping.

2   A 9-month-old calf nestled in the shade of her private "tent," formed by her mother's four legs and belly. The baby rarely left her mother's side. Elephant calves remain within yards of their mothers for the first nine years of their lives. If they stray further away, their mothers are quick to find them. Every day the mother deftly bathes her baby by sucking water into her trunk and spraying the refreshing shower over the baby. Then she makes mud for the baby to roll in. Mud relieves elephants from the heat of the sun.

3   The Senegal calf's mother seemed to have infinite patience with her. She was always close by, ready to affectionately entwine trunks, playfully nudge her, or gently support her over difficult terrain. Elephants are known to be family-oriented animals who lavish tender, loving care on their young and maintain close ties with them. While young males leave the herd at around 12 years of age, the bond between mother and daughter elephants can last up to 50 years.

4   The calf, lounging under her mother's belly, felt sleepy. Lulled by the sounds of the savanna and the comforting presence of the herd around her, she felt relaxed and safe. She knew that the herd's matriarch was close by. As the oldest female in the family group, the matriarch provided the leadership for the herd. All members of the herd looked to the "grandmother" for direction. When she fed, they fed. When she began to move on, the herd regrouped and followed her. The matriarch provided security and order for her herd.

5   A shrill trumpeting sound suddenly splintered the tranquility of the afternoon. The calf pulled herself up to a standing position as her mother raised her head to study the commotion around her. Other adults moved towards her, herding their young ahead of them. The group quickly formed a circle with three calves in the middle. The matriarch stood with her head raised, trunk straight up in the air, sniffing. Her ears spread out in a position of alarm.

6   The shots were heard before any of the elephants perceived human presence. The elephants began to panic, but they stood by their young. No one had been hurt. The matriarch began to flee in the opposite direction from the shots. The rest of the group followed,

herding their young ahead of them. Elephants can stride up to 25 miles per hour, a speed much faster than humans on foot can keep pace with. The herd was able to put distance between themselves and their only real predator.

7   Later, as night fell, the herd settled in a new area. The poacher was obviously inexperienced. None of the herd was killed. A more skilled hunter would have possibly slaughtered the entire herd. He would have come closer to the peaceful animals before firing. He may have used a more powerful gun. Even if the herd had circled, he would have targeted the matriarch and felled her first.

8   Skilled poachers know that elephants are some of the most social animals in the world. They are loyal to their herd, their young, and their leader. If a matriarch falls, the others will not leave her. Even in the face of death, they will surround their fallen companion. Elephants on either side of her would use their trunks and feet in an effort to get her to stand. This refusal to leave a downed relative, however, makes the elephants "sitting ducks." The poacher is able to kill one after the other. Entire herds are wiped out in this way.

9   What do poachers want with a herd of elephants? They only want their tusks. The tusks provide ivory, a valuable material that can be sold illegally in many countries, including the United States. Ivory is used to make craftwork such as statues, jewelry, and carvings. For this ivory, poachers saw off the tusks of the ambushed elephants and leave the dead animals where they lay.

10   Because of people's desire for ivory, African elephants are now on the list of endangered species. This list was created by a 1973 U.S. law to identify animals that are in need of human protection. Still, it was during the 1970s and 1980s that the most catastrophic loss of elephants to ivory hunters took place. Many countries in Africa lost up to 80% of their elephant population during that time.

11   In 1989, the Convention of International Trade in Endangered Species (CITES) imposed a world-wide ivory ban and recommended the most stringent protection possible for the African elephant. Since that time, the elephant population has rebounded somewhat, but illegal slaughter still continues in some African countries. As long as there is a market for ivory somewhere in the world, poachers will continue to hunt for their cash reward.

12   The elephant calf and her herd grazed and slept through the night. She forgot about the terror of the previous day. She was once again cradled in the safety of her family. She had no way of knowing that her chances for survival, for another year or for many years to come, depended on the will of international agencies and on people's decision to shun all products made from the tusks of her beloved family.

For questions 1 and 2, choose the correct answer.

1. The passage says that "In 1989, the Convention of International Trade in Endangered Species (CITES) . . . recommended the most stringent protection possible for the African elephant." What does stringent mean?

   A. demanding   B. shocking   C. official   D. unfair

Pretest

2. How does the author organize paragraphs 5 through 7 to make them easier to understand?
    A. The author uses a cause/effect pattern.
    B. The author gives a problem and then its solution.
    C. The author compares and contrasts.
    D. The author uses chronological order.

Write your answer to question 3 on the lines provided below.

3. What is the author's main purpose in this selection and why is it effective or ineffective?

_____
_____
_____

For questions 4 through 7, choose the correct answer.

4. Which of the following best summarizes why the matriarch is so important to the elephant family?
    A. She is patient with her calves.
    B. She is the oldest member in the family.
    C. She provides guidance and safety for the herd.
    D. She forms a long-lasting bond with her daughters.

5. The matriarch indicates there is danger by all of the following except
    A. sniffing the air.
    B. raising her head.
    C. spreading her ears.
    D. herding the young.

6. What is the main idea of paragraphs 10 and 11?
    A. Many elephants were killed in the 1970s.
    B. The elephant population is still in danger.
    C. CITES has been effective in saving elephants.
    D. Poachers hunt and kill elephants for their tusks.

7. To learn about endangered species that are not hunted by humans, which of the following resources would be most helpful?
    A. the author of this article
    B. the CITES report for 2004
    C. a Web site on endangered species
    D. a book on Senegalese poachers

Write your answer to question 8 on the lines provided below.

8. To help spread the word about the African elephant's problem, what are two things you could do in your community?

_____
_____

Elephants are not the only animals hunted by poachers. Read this article about other animals that are in demand and what is being done about it. Then answer questions 9 through 14.

Wildlife Trade

1   Elephants are killed for their tusks. Other wild animals are hunted for other parts of their bodies. Have you ever seen a rug made of zebra skin, or a piece of jewelry made of a lion's tooth? These are some of the thousands of wild animal body parts that are traded throughout the world every year.

2   Many international agencies try to have some control over the trade in wildlife. One of these agencies is the Convention on International Trade in Endangered Species (CITES). The CITES Animals Committee meets regularly. At each meeting, the committee receives reports about the trading of different wild animals. Below is a chart from one of these reports. This chart was part of a report submitted to the CITES Animals Committee meeting that took place in South Africa in 2004.

3   The chart shows the trade activity in narwhals over a period of ten years. Narwhals are a species of whale that lives in the Arctic Ocean. Like elephants, narwhals also produce ivory. They each have a single tusk that can be as long as eight feet. Narwhals are also hunted and traded for their bones, teeth, skin, and meat.

4   The chart is followed by a comment, which is part of the report to the committee. The comment is written by the researchers who prepared the report for the committee. It tells the committee whether or not they are concerned about this animal. If they are concerned, then they recommend a closer review by the committee. If, however, they find that the trade is within legal limits or if the animal is not endangered, then they do not recommend a closer review.

Look carefully at the chart about trade in narwhals, read the comment, and then answer the questions that follow.

Pretest

Gross Exports of Monodon Monoceros (Narwhals)

	Exporter	Term	1993	1994	1995	1996	1997	1998	1999	2000	2001	2002
1	Canada	Bodies	0	0	0	0	10	0	0	0	3	0
2	Canada	Ivory Carvings	0	0	0	5	0	0	0	0	0	0
3	Canada	Ivory pieces	0	0	0	0	0	0	0	0	4	0
4	Canada	Live	0	0	0	0	0	0	0	0	6	0
5	Canada	Meat (kg)	0	0	0	0	0	0	0	0	30	0
6	Canada	Skull	0	0	0	0	3	1	5	0	0	0
7	Canada	Teeth	4	0	0	0	0	0	4	0	4	0
8	Canada	Tusks	45	35	75	76	123	78	77	37	162	94
9	Denmark	Live	0	0	1	0	0	0	0	0	0	0
10	Georgia	Carvings	10	0	0	0	0	0	0	0	0	0
11	Georgia	Teeth	42	0	0	0	0	0	0	0	0	0
12	Georgia	Tusks	8	0	0	0	0	0	0	0	0	0
13	Germany	Ivory Carvings	0	0	1	0	0	0	0	0	0	0
14	Greenland	Bones	168	166	1	5	8	6	3	1	0	0
15	Greenland	Carvings	572	499	740	740	544	248	748	34	21	193
16	Greenland	Ivory Carvings	0	0	0	0	0	3	0	0	0	0
17	Greenland	Ivory pieces/scraps	5	6	18	16	10	9	41	0	0	0
18	Greenland	Meat (kg)	0	353	387	1023	618	2558	0	0	0	636
19	Greenland	Skin pieces	158	208	0	0	0	0	0	0	0	0
20	Greenland	Teeth	208	85	99	54	28	25	767	675	9	30
21	Greenland	Tusks	267	258	208	240	211	116	106	68	25	45
22	Norway	Tusks	0	0	0	0	0	0	0	0	0	1
23	United Kingdom	Bone Carvings	0	0	1	0	0	0	0	0	0	0
24	United Kingdom	Tusks	0	0	0	2	0	0	0	0	2	1
25	United States	Skin	0	0	0	61	0	0	0	0	0	0

Comment: Levels of trade from Canada and Greenland appear to be stable. However, despite the Animals Committee's recommendation in 1995, a comprehensive survey has still not been done, and the impact of current levels of trade on populations is uncertain. Therefore, it is recommended that this species should be reviewed.

Write your answer to question 9 on the lines provided below.

9. What is the strongest evidence to suggest that "Wildlife Trade" is a work of nonfiction?

_____

_____

_____

For questions 10 through 12, choose the correct answer.

10. According to the information in the chart, which country exported the greatest number of Narwhal carvings between 1993 and 2002?
    A. Canada
    B. Greenland
    C. Georgia
    D. United Kingdom

11. Which sentence in the selection best supports the idea that Narwhals are distinctive?
    A. Like elephants, narwhals also produce ivory.
    B. They each have a single tusk that can be as long as eight feet.
    C. Narwhals are a species of whale that lives in the Arctic Ocean.
    D. Narwhals are also hunted and traded for their bones, teeth, skin, and meat.

12. Based on information from the passage and the chart, which is the best description of the current Narwhal population?

    A. They are being overhunted.
    B. The population is booming.
    C. Narwhal population is stabilized.
    D. The population status is not known.

Write your answer to question 13 on the lines provided below.

13. How effective is the work that CITES is doing in controlling the trading of wildlife products?

_____

_____

For question 14, choose the correct answer.

14. What conclusion can be made from the narwhal chart and the comment that follows?

    A. Greenland and Canada have passed anti-narwhal trading laws.
    B. Narwhals will be extinct by the year 2010.
    C. The advice CITES gives is not always taken.
    D. The Animal Committee meets every month.

The following poem by William Blake is from a book of poems entitled **Songs of Innocence and Experience**. This poem is among the "Songs of Experience." Read the poem, and then answer questions 15 through 20.

Ah Sunflower

by William Blake

Ah Sunflower, weary of time,
Who countest the steps of the sun;
Seeking after that sweet golden clime
Where the traveller's journey is done;

Where the Youth pined away with desire,
And the pale virgin shrouded in snow,
Arise from their graves, and aspire
Where my sunflower wishes to go!

Write your answer to question 15 on the lines provided below.

15. In your own words, explain how the sunflower in the poem feels. Give an example of why the sunflower might feel that way.

_____

_____

For questions 16 through 20, choose the correct answer.

Pretest

16. What does "countest the steps of the sun" in the second line of the poem mean?
    A. watched the sun walk
    B. strolled in a hot climate
    C. measured the hours
    D. climbed towards the sky

17. How does the narrator feel about the sunflower?
    A. He feels sorry for the sunflower.
    B. He thinks the sunflower is overreacting.
    C. He thinks the sunflower is funny.
    D. He feels happy for the sunflower.

18. Considering that Blake included this poem as a "Song of Experience," which universal theme does it best express?
    A. love is not only for the young
    B. truth is more precious than gold
    C. every situation has its positives
    D. sometimes experience is painful

19. Which feature of the selection most strongly indicates that it is a poem?
    A. It is divided into lines and stanzas.
    B. It is told in third person.
    C. It appeals to the senses.
    D. It has a title.

20. How are the word choice and imagery in the first stanza different from that in the second stanza?
    A. The words and images in the first stanza are harsh while those in the second stanza are calming.
    B. The word choice and imagery in the first stanza are depressing while those in the second are uplifting.
    C. The words and images in the first stanza are warm while those in the second are cold.
    D. The word choice and imagery in the first stanza are of love while those in the second stanza are of hate.

Many cultures have traditional folk tales that attempt to explain why things in the world are the way they are. Read this Liberian folk tale about why spiders have small waists. Then answer questions 21 through 28.

Why Spider Has a Small Waist

1   Once upon a time, Spider's body was not the way it is today. Spider had a body like most animals and human beings: well shaped with a broad waist. Spider was very popular among the people in all the surrounding towns. He was known as a trickster—someone who is sly and mischievous and plays pranks on people— but everyone enjoyed his company because he was also very amusing and gregarious. Whenever there was a wedding, baby shower, or any such social function, the organizers were sure to invite Spider.

2   It so happened that one day, two feasts were to take place in two different sections of the town. One feast was taking place on the east side of town, and the other feast was taking place on the west side of town. The organizers of both events decided to invite Spider. When the representative from the residents on the east side of town met with Spider, he informed him that their feast would take place on Friday evening. After asking several questions about the nature of the feast, Spider agreed to attend.

3   Shortly after the east side representative left Spider's residence, the representative of the residents on the west side of town arrived and gave Spider an invitation to their feast. Like the festivity on the east side, the west side party would take place on Friday evening. Spider asked the west side representative the same questions he had asked the east side representative and then expressed his willingness to attend.

4   Whether he recognized it or not, Spider was faced with a dilemma. He had accepted invitations from both sides of town, and both feasts were to take place at approximately the same time on the same day. Now, at that time, there were no clocks, telephones, fax machines, or e-mail to tell Spider the time of the feast. He mistakenly thought that it was impossible for both feasts to start at the same time. His plan was to go to the feast that started first, eat all he could eat, and then go to the second feast. To put his plan into effect, he came up with a scheme.

5   On the day of feasts, Spider got himself a very long and sturdy rope. He tied the rope around his waist, and took one end of it to his friends on the east side of town. He told them to pull on the rope when the feast was about to begin. He took the other end of the rope, gave it to his friends on the west side of town, and told them to pull on the rope when it was time for the feast. When he felt a tug, he would head for the feast on that side of town.

6   After giving his friends the two ends of the rope, Spider stood in the town center waiting for a pull on the rope. He waited and waited, but no one pulled the rope. Finally, the time arrived! Spider felt a tug from the east side. He quickly started heading in the direction of the east side festival, happily imagining the delicious banquet that awaited him. Suddenly, he felt another jerk from the west side, and he was pulled back to the center of town, right back where he had started!

7   Spider soon became the object of a tug-of-war. His friends on both sides of town kept pulling on the rope because they did not understand why he was not coming. The rope began to get tighter and tighter around his waist as his friends pulled from both directions. They pulled and pulled, but Spider did not show up. Harder and harder they pulled, but still no Spider!

8   The harder Spider's friends pulled, the tighter the rope around his waist became. His waist got smaller—and smaller—and smaller. He tried fruitlessly to call for help, but none came, since everyone had gone to one feast or the other. He just sat in the middle of town feeling sorry for himself. As he looked at his waist, he could see it shrinking. In fact, he had come to look like a big figure eight. He realized that trying to attend two feasts on the same day was a bad idea.

9   Eventually, Spider fainted in the town center. He did not get to go to either of the feasts, and his waist had shrunk from its broad shape to a tiny little band. That is the reason why today spiders have small waists.

Read this sentence from the story.

> He tried <u>fruitlessly</u> to call for help, but none came, since everyone had gone to one feast or the other.

21. In this sentence, <u>fruitlessly</u> is closest in meaning to

A. without hope.
B. without success.
C. without fear.
D. without assistance.

Pretest

22. Why is paragraph 4 important in this selection? 1-M2
    A. It introduces the conflict.
    B. It describes the setting of the story.
    C. It shows a contrast between two feasts.
    D. It shows the traits of the main character.

23. Which statement best explains why Spider used a rope for his scheme? 7-M4
    A. He wanted a smaller waist.
    B. He liked to play tug-of-war.
    C. He wanted to go to both feasts.
    D. He liked the feeling of being pulled.

24. What conclusion can the reader draw about Spider in this story? 1-M2
    A. He is curious and ill.
    B. He is proud and dazed.
    C. He is excited and cunning.
    D. He is confused and sorry.

25. Which sentence in the passage best supports the idea that Spider's plan will fail? 7-M1
    A. He mistakenly thought that it was impossible for both feasts to start at the same time.
    B. He tried fruitlessly to call for help, but none came, since everyone had gone to one feast or the other.
    C. His plan was to go to the feast that started first, eat all he could eat, and then go to the second feast.
    D. His friends on both sides of town kept pulling on the rope because they did not understand why he was not coming.

26. Which of the following could Spider have done to solve his problem instead of tying the rope to his waist? 7-M2
    A. tied a rope to his wrists
    B. only accepted one invitation
    C. used a chain instead of a rope
    D. climbed a tree and waited for a signal

Write your answers to questions 27 and 28 on the lines provided below.

27. What real-life lesson can be learned from this passage? Give a detail from the passage to support your answer. 6-M1

   _____

   _____

28. Give two examples of how a folk tale is different from other works of fiction. 6-M2

   _____

   _____

   _____

Essay

> **29.** In both "Ah Sunflower" and "Why Spider has a Small Waist," the characters want something that they do not get. Identify what each character wants, and how not getting it affects them. Use a detail from each passage to support your explanation.

Session 3–Using Information Resources

Introduction: In this section of the test, you are asked to look at some reference materials and then use the materials to answer the questions on pages 21 and 22.

Topic: Suppose you want to write a report about the role wind plays in people's lives. You will need to learn about how wind affects people's jobs, their day-to-day lives, as well as their leisure activities. Four different sources of information about wind are included in this section of the test. The information sources and the page numbers where you can find them are listed below.

> 1. Encyclopedia Entry
>   "Prevailing Winds" (pages 14 and 15)

> 2. Excerpts from a book, *Storm Chasers*
>   A. Excerpt from the Preface (page 16)
>   B. Table of Contents (page 17)

> 3. Article from a Magazine
>   "Origin of the Winds" (pages 18 and 19)

> 4. Internet Web Site Information
>   "How to Make and Fly Your Own Kite" (page 20)

Model bibliographic entries for the different types of references are on page 21. These show acceptable formats for entries.

Pretest

Directions: Skim pages 14 through 20 to become familiar with the information contained in these sources. Remember that these are reference sources, so you should not read every word in each source. Once you have skimmed these sources, answer the questions on pages 21 and 22. Use the information sources to help you answer the questions. As you work through the questions, go back and read the parts that will give you the information that you need.

> 1. Encyclopedia Entry
> "Prevailing Winds"

BANDS OF PREVAILING WINDS

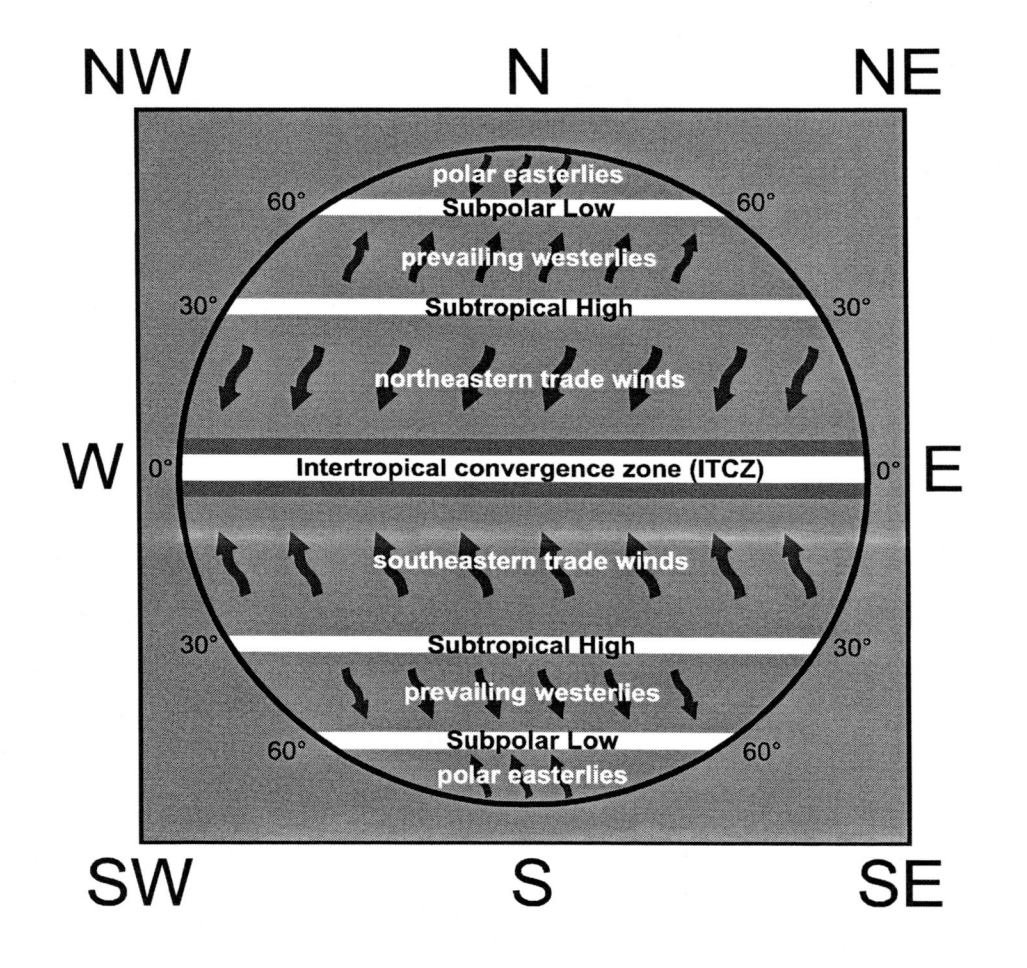

NW   N   NE

polar easterlies
60°   Subpolar Low   60°
prevailing westerlies
30°   Subtropical High   30°
northeastern trade winds
W   0°   Intertropical convergence zone (ITCZ)   0°   E
southeastern trade winds
30°   Subtropical High   30°
prevailing westerlies
60°   Subpolar Low   60°
polar easterlies

SW   S   SE

1 The globe can be divided into six belts by latitude. In each of these belts, there are winds that blow most often. These are called the **"prevailing winds"** of that latitudinal belt. These belts are marked by their distance—in degrees—from the equator. For instance, one belt extends from the equator—which is 0 degrees—to 30 degrees north of the equator

2 If you look closely at the diagram of the bands of the prevailing winds around the world, you will see a pattern in the directions these winds take. If you start at the equator and go north, you will notice that in the first belt, the winds blow from upper right to lower left (or, from northeast to southwest). In the next band to the north, the winds reverse, blowing from southwest to northeast. In the top band, which includes the North Pole, the winds again reverse direction.

3 Now, if you look at the wind belts from the equator going south, the same reversals occur. This time, however, they start with winds that blow from southeast to northwest.

4 Winds are named for the direction **from which they come.** For instance, if winds are called northeastern winds, or **"north easterlies,"** it means that the winds are traveling **from** the northeast.

5 From the diagram on the previous page, you will notice that between 30° north and 30° south of the equator, the prevailing winds are called **trade winds**. Above the equator they are the **Northeast Trade Winds,** and below the equator they are the **Southeast Trade Winds**. If you understand what causes the trade winds, you will understand the basic causes of all prevailing winds.

6 As has been stated, the trade winds occur near the equator. As the hottest latitude on earth, the equator produces very warm air. Warm air rises and expands. At the equator, the air rises and expands, moving away from the equator. As it flows away from the equator, it cools down. Cool air sinks. Now we have a warm area near the equator, from which the air is leaving, and a cool area about 30° away from the equator, in which there is a lot of cool air. Air always moves from cool to warm. That is why the cooled winds blow back to the equator from the cooler zones around 30° north and 30° south of the equator. This movement of air is the trade winds.

7 Why are the arrows in the diagram slanted? Why do the Northeast Trades travel back to the equator from the northeast, moving southwest, and not directly due south to the equator? The reason why the prevailing winds do not travel directly north and south is because they are not only influenced by the heat and coolness of the planet, they are also influenced by the motion of the planet. The earth is spinning around, and this makes the winds move in diagonal directions of the compass. The force that the earth's spinning has on prevailing winds is called the **Coriolis force**.

> 2. Excerpts from a Book, *Storm Chasers*
>   A. Excerpt from the Preface

PREFACE

1   The sky looks ominous. In the Texas panhandle, a severe storm is forming, as a moving mass of warm, moist air from the Gulf of Mexico collides head-on with a wall of cooler air veering off the Rocky Mountains. Warm air shoots upwards in the face of the cool barrier, only to slam into shearing winds high in the atmosphere. The shearing winds—now from one direction, now, higher up, from another—bend and bully the column of warm air until the whole mass becomes a twisting whirlpool of wind.

2   The severe weather specialists at the National Weather Service in Austin, Texas, watch the developing storm's every move. It is May in Tornado Alley. Spring always means high tornado alert in this stretch of continent between South Dakota and Texas. And the panhandle storm is exactly the kind that can produce these lashing tails of Nature. It is time to warn residents in the area. It may be necessary to evacuate, and they will need as much warning time as possible. Unfortunately, they can't always have as much as they need.

3   Outside of Elk City, Oklahoma, a different team of specialists monitors the same storm on their weather tracking instruments. This team is not interested in warnings to avoid the storm. They are already in their vehicle heading straight for it. They are called **storm chasers**, and they do the field work in the science of tornado research.

4   Even as they head towards the Texas panhandle, the chase team studies the latest data on the gathering storm. Their vehicle is equipped with the same Doppler radar devices used by National Weather Service meteorologists. On-board television screens link them to the Weather Channel. The Internet provides data, and satellite feeds send images of the storm from space.

5   In Texas, the storm builds. The "mezocyclone," the whirlpool of wind that has formed high in the storm cloud, threatens to spawn a tornado. Winds on the ground approach 70 miles per hour. The sky darkens to almost night as a sagging ceiling of black cloud bears down upon the earth. Warnings have gone out, and residents have headed for shelter.

6   Hail the size of walnuts flung from uneasy skies creates an alarming pinging sound on rooftops, a natural Morse code spelling out, *Alert! Storm approaching*! The hail comes from miles up within the storm. The rising warm air has brought its moisture so high into the atmosphere that it has frozen into pellets. Then, like a child keeping a beach ball airborne, the strong updraft keeps bouncing the pellets upwards where they collect more ice and become larger. Finally, too heavy for the updraft to support anymore. . .

> 2. Excerpts from a Book, *Storm Chasers*
>
>   B. Table of Contents

CONTENTS

Preface

A glimpse into the Storm Chaser's life 4

Chapter One

How a Gentle Breeze Becomes a Storm 12
Tornados 20
Tropical storms 28
Hurricanes 37
Cyclones 45
Other storms 55

Chapter Two

Reading the Weather 66
How Experts see a Storm. 78
Experiencing a Storm. 90

Chapter Three

Who Chases Storms? 101
Organizations Involved in Storm Information 105
What do They Learn? 137
What Dangers do They Face? 145
How to get Involved 152

Chapter Four

Storm Chaser Survival Strategies. 166
Outfitting the Storm Chaser Vehicle 178
Interviews with Storm Chasers 182

Bibliography 89

List of Organizations 195

Acknowledgements. 197

Credits 198

Index 199

3. Article from a Magazine:
"Origin of the Winds"

Origin of the Winds
by Carla Harrison

1   According to Native American folklore, there was a time, long ago, when there were no winds. Without winds, snow dropped directly and unattractively to Earth, no breezes lightened the heat of summer, and no gales stirred up the ocean waters into lively and beautiful waves. At that time, in the frigid lands of the north, lived a husband and wife who had no children.

2   Without children, the husband and wife were despondent. They dreamed of having a son or a daughter to help them in their old age: someone they could teach the many things they had learned throughout life.

3   "I would teach my son to hunt and to trap," said the husband. "We would make weapons and we would stalk bears and trap seals for food to last us through the long winter."

4.   "I would teach my daughter to make clothes from bearskin and to prepare meat for storage, and I would tell her all the stories my mother told me," dreamed the wife.

5   One night, the wife had an extraordinary dream. In the dream, a dog sled arrived at her door. The driver beckoned her to come into the sled, and the wife obeyed. She knew, somehow, that the driver was *Igaluk*, the Moon Spirit, who comforted sad people. The kind driver of the dogsled brought the wife beyond her village, and beyond, beyond her land. Finally, they stopped in a sky-world of glistening ice and snow that sparkled like stars. In all directions, the wife could see only ice. Then she saw a small tree.

6   "You must cut down that tree and whittle a doll out of it," said the Moon Spirit. "It will bring you happiness."

7   But then the wife woke up. How was she to find the tree that the Moon Spirit had shown her? She told her husband of the dream, and although he was skeptical at first, she pleaded with him so much that, to appease her, he set out to he knew not where. He only knew he had to try and find the tree.

8   At the edge of the village, the husband noticed a path through the snow that was bathed in light. He knew that this was the path he was to take. For many hours he walked, until finally he saw the tree. He immediately recognized it as the tree his wife had described to him, and he cut it down and took it home. The husband was a master carver, and he carved a life-like boy out of the trunk of the tree. The wife clothed the doll in seal skins. They were happy and full of hope for the first time in many years. They left food out for the doll and went to bed.

9   In the morning, a heartbreaking surprise awaited them: the doll had vanished. The couple found footprints and anxiously followed them, but they led only to the edge of the village. Then they stopped. The couple returned home with heavy hearts.

10 The sad husband and wife did not know that their "son" had followed the same radiant path the husband had followed when searching for the tree. They did not know that he also had a mission for the well-being of the earth and its people. The doll-boy walked east to the edge of the earth. He saw how the sky-dome came down and met the earth on the eastern horizon. He also saw a hole in the wall of the sky-dome. An animal skin covered the hole, and something was pushing against it from outside. The doll-boy untied the lashing that held the animal skins in place. The skins drew apart, and a great rush of wind blew in. Many beautiful birds and animals blew in along with it.

11 When the wind had gusted enough, the doll-boy tied up the skins again, blocking the wind out. He spoke to the wind, giving it clear instructions: "Wind, you are to blow hard sometimes, and sometimes blow softly. And, at times, you are to remain calm and refrain from blowing."

12 The doll-boy continued his journey. This time, he walked until he came to the southern wall of the great sky-dome and saw where the sky met the earth on the southern horizon. He also saw another hole in the sky, covered by animal skins. As in the east, it looked as if a force was pushing against the skins from outside the sky-dome. The doll-boy again untied the lashings that held the skins in place, and again, a wind blustered onto the earth, bringing with it birds, animals, and trees.

13 After closing up the hole in the southern sky-wall again, the doll-boy gave the same instructions to the southern winds that he had given to the eastern winds. Then he proceeded to the western edge of the earth. There, he opened the same kind of hole in the sky, this time unleashing torrents of winds and rains and sprays of ocean waves. Again he closed up the hole and gave the same orders to the western winds.

14 In the north, the icy winds that raged through the hole in the sky-wall were so bitter that the doll-boy was almost frozen in his tracks. He quickly closed up the hole and gave the same directive to the frigid northern winds that he had given to their brothers and sisters in the other three corners of the earth. Then, he commenced his journey homeward.

15 The husband and wife were overjoyed to see their son, and the villagers were enthralled with his stories of the edges of the earth. Winds and breezes blew, birds filled the air, and the people breathed deeply. The doll-boy had brought good fortune to the people of the earth, and for this, he was honored and loved by all, especially his parents, who were never lonely again.

4. Internet Web site Information
   "How to Make and Fly Your Own Kite"

How to Make and Fly Your Own Kite

The serene look of a colorful kite floating in the blue sky above one's head is an experience beloved by children and adults alike! If you've never made or flown a kite before, this is the site for you! If you have, explore our links to information even the most experienced kite-flyer can use!

- Basic Kite Flying
- Buy a Kite Kit
- How to Make a Kite
- Types of Kites
- Sale Kites
- Read the Wind

Bibliographic Entries

The following five sample entries are based on formats from the *Modern Language Association (MLA) Handbook for Writers of Research Papers*. They show some acceptable formats for bibliographic entries.

A Book by a Single Author

Levy, Ellen. Bird Habitats. New York: Bunting Press, 1997.

A Book by More than One Author

Varick, William M., and Geraldine Abernathy. Endangered Birds of California. San Francisco: Wild World Publications, 1996.

An Encyclopedia Entry

"Extinct Birds." Encyclopedia Americana. 1998.

A Magazine Article

Alfaro, Lorenzo. "Exploring Off the Beaten Path." Natural Life 25 August 1997: 21-28.

Book Issued by Organization Identifying No Author

American Birding Association. Warbler Identification Guide. Chicago: American Birding Association, 1995.

For questions 30 through 34, choose the correct answer.
Use the model bibliographic entries to answer this question.

30. Which of the entries below is an example of a correct bibliographic entry for a book by more than one author?

    A. Kessler, Greta, and Marcus P. Smith. How Sailors Read the Winds. New York: Sporting Life Publications, 2000.
    B. Kessler, Greta, and others. "How Sailors Read the Winds." New York, Sporting Life Publications, 2000.
    C. How Sailors Read the Winds. By Greta Kessler and Marcus P. Smith, New York: Sporting Life Publications, 2000.
    D. Smith, Marcus P., and Kessler, Greta. How Sailors Read the Winds. Sporting Life Publications: New York, 2000.

31. Winds blow in all of the following directions except

    A. southeast to northwest.
    B. southwest to northeast.
    C. northwest to southeast.
    D. northwest to southwest.

32. The article from the magazine would be most useful for finding information about

    A. how wind is categorized.
    B. ways that wind lifts kites into the air.
    C. ways that wind fits into the customs of different people.
    D. how wind combines with weather changes to produce storms.

Pretest

33. On which page of the book about storm chasers would you begin to look for an interview with storm chaser Mitch Frame? 5-M1

   A. 45 B. 105 C. 182 D. 197

34. To locate more resources on storm chasers, where should you look? 5-M3

   A. chapter three in the storm chasers book
   B. the bibliography of the book on storm chasers
   C. the encyclopedia entry
   D. the magazine article

Write your answer to questions 35 and 36 on the lines provided below.

35. What are winds that blow from the southeast to the northwest known as? In what source did you find this information? 5-M2

   _____
   _____
   _____

36. In a few sentences, summarize the kind of information given on the Web site and explain how it relates to your research on wind. 5-M2

   _____
   _____
   _____

Session 4—Proofreading

Read the rough draft of a student's letter. The student, is asking for information on careers in designing video games. After reading the letter addressed to Biohazard Games, Inc., answer questions 37 through 44.

---

401 West Northern Ave.
Crowley, LA 70526

Biohazard Games, Inc.
2607 Eastwood Drive, #61
Colombia, MO 65202

September 12, 2004

(1) Dear Director:

    I am a student at Crowley Middle School in Crowley, Louisiana. For my **(2)** <u>Social Studies</u> class, I am working on a research paper about job opportunities in the gaming industry. **(3)** <u>Video games are very interesting. They are cool</u>. **(4)** <u>I'd</u> love to have a job designing new video games.

    (5) <u>In my paper I am</u> explaining the different careers available in the gaming industry. Because your business creates many of the new high-tech computer games, I thought that you could provide the information I need. Please send me any **(6)** <u>broshures</u> or informational pamphlets you can.

    I would appreciate **(7)** <u>your</u> sending of the information requested as soon as possible. I have a paper deadline on November 1.

    Thank you for considering **(8)** <u>my request I look forward</u> to hearing from you.

Sincerely,

Alexander du Monde

Choose the correct answers to questions 37 through 44. Mark only one answer for each question.

37. How should you correct the error in number 1?

    A. change **Dear Director:** to **Dear Personnel Officer:**

    B. change **Dear Director:** to **Dear Director,**

    C. change **Dear Director:** to **Dear Sir:**

    D. There is no error.

38. How should you correct the error in number 2?

    A. change **Social Studies class,** to **Social Studys class,**

    B. change **Social Studies class,** to **Social Studies Class,**

    C. change **Social Studies class,** to **social studies class,**

    D. There is no error.

Pretest

39. How should you correct the error in number 3?

    A. change **Video games are very interesting. They are cool.** to **Video games are very interesting, they are cool.**

    B. change **Video games are very interesting. They are cool.** to **Video games are cool and very interesting.**

    C. change **Video games are very interesting. They are cool.** to **Video games are very interesting and they are cool.**

    D. There is no error.

40. How should you correct the error in number 4?

    A. change **I'd** to **I'ld**   C. change **I'd** to **I'ed**
    B. change **I'd** to **I should**   D. There is no error.

41. How should you correct the error in number 5?

    A. change **In my paper I am** to **In my paper I'm**

    B. change **In my paper I am** to **In my paper, I am**

    C. change **In my paper I am** to **In my paper; I am**

    D. There is no error.

42. How should you correct the error in number 6?

    A. change **broshures** to **brossures**   C. change **broshures** to **brochures**
    B. change **broshures** to **brosures**   D. There is no error.

43. How should you correct the error in number 7?

    A. change **your** to **you**   C. change **your** to **your's**
    B. change **your** to **you're**   D. There is no error.

44. How should you correct the error in number 8?

    A. change **my request_I look forward** to **my request; I look forward**

    B. change **my request_I look forward** to **my request, I look forward**

    C. change **my request_I look forward** to **my request and I look forward**

    D. There is no error.

EVALUATION CHART FOR LEAP 21 GRADE 8 ENGLISH LANGUAGE ARTS

Directions: On the following chart, circle the question numbers that you answered incorrectly, and evaluate the results. These questions are based on the LEAP 21 assessment standards. Then turn to the appropriate topics (listed by chapters), read the explanations, and complete the exercises. Review other chapters as needed. Finally, complete the practice test to assess your progress and further prepare you for the eighth grade language arts test.

*Note: Some question numbers may appear under multiple chapters because those questions require demonstration of multiple skills.

Chapters	Diagnostic Test Question
Chapter 1: Capitalization, Punctuation, Spelling	37, 38, 44
Chapter 2: Parts of Speech	43
Chapter 3: Planning the Composition	29,
Chapter 4: IWriting the Composition	29
Chapter 5: Descriptive and Narrative Writing	29
Chapter 6: Expository and Persuasive Composition	29
Chapter 7: Using the Writer's Checklist	29, 37, 38, 44, 39, 41, 43
Chapter 8: Word Meaning and Analysis	1, 21
Chapter 9: Main Ideas, Summarizing, and Paraphrasing	4, 6, 14, 20, 25
Chapter 10: Inferences, Predictions, and Conclusions	4, 6, 14, 20, 25
Chapter 11: Organization Patterns	4, 6, 14, 20, 25, 5, 11, 23
Chapter 12: Fact, Opinion, Probability	5, 11, 23
Chapter 13: Author's Viewpoint	2, 3, 17
Chapter 14: Using Information Resources	33, 35, 32
Chapter 15: Electronic Information Sources	33, 35, 32
Chapter 16: Evaluating and Citing Information Sources	7, 8, 26, 35, 32, 34, 7, 30
Chapter 17: Graphic Aids	31
Chapter 18: Literary Genres and Story Structure	15, 28, 29, 9, 19, 22, 24

Pretest

Chapters	Diagnostic Test Question
Chapter 19: Literary Elements and Devices	22, 24
Chapter 20: Comparing and Contrasting	18, 27, 29
Chapter 21: Writing About Literature	29

Chapter 1
Capitalization, Punctuation, and Spelling

LOUISIANA READING BENCHMARKS ADDRESSED IN THIS CHAPTER INCLUDE:	
ELA-3-M2	Demonstrating use of punctuation (e.g., colon, semicolon, quotation marks, dashes, parentheses), capitalization, and abbreviations (1, 4)
ELA-3-M5	Spelling accurately using strategies and resources (e.g., glossary, dictionary, thesaurus, spell check) when necessary

Writing is an important skill for sharing ideas and feelings. To share your ideas well, your writing needs to be free of capitalization, punctuation, and spelling errors. This chapter offers teaching sections and reviewing practices. It will cover the basic rules of capitalization, punctuation and spelling. Each section has an explanation of the rules followed by practice exercises. The work in this chapter will help you get ready for taking the writing/proofreading portions of the LEAP 21 Grade 8. For more information on these writing skills, please refer to the companion text *Basics Made Easy: Grammar and Usage Review* by American Book Company.

CAPITALIZATION RULES

1. **Capitalize the first word of a sentence.**

    Example 1: My new hobby is skateboarding.

    Example 2: Good balance is an important part of skateboarding.

2. **Capitalize the first word of a direct quotation.**

    Example 1: My trainer said, "Keep your head up as you climb the ramp."

    Example 2: "The correct stance," she said, "allows you to change directions quickly."

3. **Capitalize proper nouns, names of specific people, places, things, or ideas.**

    Capitalize proper adjectives, adjectives formed from proper nouns.

    - **Names and Personal Titles:** Capitalize the name and title of a person, including initials and abbreviations of titles.

        Example: The skatepark owner, Mr. King, has worked with skaters for 16 years.

Capitalization, Punctuation, and Spelling

4. Capitalize a word that shows a family relationship only when it is used as someone's name.

    Example 1: Sam's uncle builds skateboarding ramps and grind rails.

    Example 2: We can count on Grandpa Frank to take us skating on Saturdays.

5. Listing of Capitalization Issues

    - **Languages, Nationalities, and Religious Terms**

        Example: I have a Spanish language skateboarding CD.

    - **School Subjects**

        Capitalize the name of a specific school course (Chemistry 1), but not a general reference to a school subject (science, math).

        Example 1: Our physical education class is offering credit for skateboarding.

        Example 2: We learned about muscles people use in skateboarding in Biology I.

    - **Organizations and Institutions**

        Capitalize the important words in the official names of organizations (Southeastern Louisiana University), but not words that refer to kinds of organizations (school, university).

        Example 1: Mary Wenig, a student at Blackwell Middle School, began a club called Girls Skate Out.

        Example 2: The best skatepark is located next to the university.

    - **Geographical Names**

        Capitalize continents, countries, states, cities, towns, villages, streets, roads, highways, sections of a country or continent, landforms, bodies of water, planets, and public areas. Do not capitalize the names of seasons or directions.

Names	Examples
Continents	North America, Australia, Africa, Europe
Political units	Canada, United States, Louisiana, New Orleans
Sections of a country	the Midwest, the West Coast, the South
Roads	Main Street, Interstate 10, Highway 92
Landforms	the Rocky Mountains, the Sahara Desert
Bodies of Water	Gulf of Mexico, Lake Pontchartrain, First Creek
Public Areas	Civic Plaza, Lafayette Square, Central Park
Seasons	winter, spring, summer, fall
Directions	east, west, north, south

    - **Events and Time Periods**

        Capitalize the names of events, historical periods and documents, holidays, months and days.

Names	Examples
Historical events	the Louisiana Purchase, Gettysburg Address
Periods of history	the Renaissance, Middle Ages, Reconstruction
Holidays	Fourth of July, Thanksgiving, Presidents' Day
Months and days	June, July, August, Saturday, Sunday, Monday
Documents	the Constitution, Declaration of Independence

4. Capitalize the titles of created works.

Capitalize the first word, the last word, and all other important words in the titles of books, plays, magazines, newspapers, movies, poems, stories, and articles. Within a title, don't capitalize articles, conjunctions, and prepositions of fewer than five letters.

> **Example 1:** The movie *Shrek 2* is a parody of well-known stories from *Grimm's Fairy Tales*.
>
> **Example 2:** *The Shreveport Times* ran an article called "Teens for Hire" that discusses job choices teenagers have today.

5. Capitalize salutations, or greetings, and closings of letters.

> **Example 1:** To Whom It May Concern:
>
> **Example 2:** Sincerely,

6. Capitalize abbreviations of titles, names, and organizations.

> **Example 1:** CEO - chief executive officer
>
> **Example 2:** AAA - American Automotive Association
>
> **Example 3:** My doctor's name is T. J. McIntire, M.D.

7. Capitalize some common computer terms.

> **Example:** Web site, Web page, Internet, URL

Practice 1: Capitalization

Review rules 1–6. Read the following sentences. On your own paper, rewrite the sentence to correct any capitalization mistakes, or write C if the sentence is correctly capitalized.

1. The word "hurricane" comes from Huracan, the god of big winds and evil spirits once worshiped by the maya people of central america.
2. In the atlantic and eastern pacific oceans "hurricane" is the word used to describe tropical cyclones.
3. a hurricane can last more than two weeks as it travels up a coastline.
4. Scientists at the national hurricane center in miami track storms using satellite images.
5. The National Oceanic and Atmospheric Administration, noaa, has planes with computers to measure how fast the winds are inside hurricanes.
6. The deadliest hurricane in the United States struck galveston, texas in 1900.
7. The costliest hurricane was andrew in 1992.

Capitalization, Punctuation, and Spelling

8. Hurricanes are most likely to form from june through november.

9. Hurricanes rarely occur during the Winter and Spring.

10. The web site for USA today has charts showing the probabilities of hurricanes by month and by state.

11. Read the passage below. On your own paper, write a C if the sentence is correctly capitalized. Revise the sentence if the capitalization is incorrect.

   D. To: James Rivel, ph.d.

   E. From: Sally Robertsen

   F. Dear dr. Rivel:

   G. For my final paper in English, I would like to write about how Langston Hughes influenced the Harlem Renaissance.

   H. I will address how this famous Author and Poet added to the movement in the following ways:

   I. Hughes expressed the hopes, fears, and dreams of blacks

      I. called attention to black culture

      II. helped pave way for the civil rights movement

      III. provided literary roots for future generations

   J. yours truly,

   K. Sally Robertsen

PUNCTUATION RULES

COMMA RULES

1. Compound Sentences

Use a comma before any conjunction that joins the clauses of a compound sentence. The list of conjunctions is known as FANBOYS: <u>f</u>or, <u>a</u>nd, <u>n</u>or, <u>b</u>ut, <u>o</u>r, <u>y</u>et, <u>s</u>o.

> **Example 1:** Every state has a state song, but Louisiana has two.
>
> **Example 2:** "Give Me Louisiana" and "You Are My Sunshine" are the state songs, and they both describe the beauty of Louisiana.

2. Introductory Words

Use a comma to separate an introductory (opening) word or phrase from the rest of the sentence.

> **Example 1:** Written in 1940, "You Are My Sunshine" has become a national favorite.
>
> **Example 2:** Although originally written by a former Louisiana governor, the song is now a children's classic.

3. Dates, Addresses, and Letters

- Dates

Use a comma between the day of the month and the year. If the date falls in the middle of a sentence, use another comma after the year. Do not use a comma between a month and a year.

Example 1: July 4, 2005

Example 2: July 2005

- **Addresses**

    Use a comma to separate the city and the state in an address. If the address falls in the middle of a sentence, use another comma after the state.

    Example 1: Baton Rouge, Louisiana

    Example 2: When you visit Monroe, Louisiana, be sure to see the Biedenharn Museum and Gardens.

- **Parts of a Letter**

    Use a comma after the greeting in a friendly letter and after the closing in a letter.

    Example 1: Dear Rachel,

    Example 2: Sincerely,

Practice 2: Punctuation with Commas

Review rules 1–3. Read the passage below. On a separate piece of paper, rewrite the sentences to correct any punctuation mistakes, or write C if the sentence is correctly punctuated.

(1) January 12 2005

(2) Dear Amanda

(3) I am so glad you are going to be my pen pal. (4) I have never met anyone from Louisiana and I have never been there. (5) I have lived in Marietta Georgia my whole life. (6) In the almanac in my class I looked up information about your state. (7) I didn't know there was so much water there but now I do. (8) I was hoping to learn more about your state. (9) My teacher asked us to find out different things. (10) What is your state symbol? (11) Do you have a state bird? (12) Honestly I would rather learn about you. (13) Please write me back soon. (14) In the meantime I will read more about Louisiana in my almanac.

(15) Sincerely

Elizabeth Ward

COMMA RULES CONTINUED

4. **Elements Set Off in a Sentence**

    Use commas to separate elements that are not essential to a sentence. This helps to highlight the main ideas of a sentence.

    - **Nouns of address**

        Use commas to set off a name or a noun in direct address.

Capitalization, Punctuation, and Spelling

Example: You must save your allowance, Jeanette, if you want to rent that video.

- **Appositives**

    Use commas to set off some appositives, a noun or phrase that explains a word in a sentence.

    Example: Jeanette, a student at Madison Middle School, began a video review column.

- **Clauses and Phrases**

    Use commas to set off a phrase that interrupts the flow of a sentence.

    Example 1: Jeanette, because of her hard work, won coupons from a video store.

    Example 2: Jeanette, because she was generous, offered to rent a video for the school newspaper staff.

    Example 3: Mr. Garret, who had read all the new columns, praised the students for their great writing.

> **HINT:** In writing, you have to put in stops and pauses so the reader can understand your thoughts. Commas are the pauses. When you read a sentence aloud, listen for the pauses, check the comma rules, and insert a comma when needed

5. Elements in a Series

Use commas to separate three or more items in a series and to separate adjectives that come before a noun.

- **Subjects, Verbs, Objects**

    Example 1: Use a comma after every item except the last in a series of three or more items.Sam, Noah, Sara, and Steve start soccer this Saturday.

    Example 2: Sam can already dribble, pull-back, and shoot.

    Example 3: Sara will bring soda, snacks, and soccer balls to the first practice.

- **Phrases and Clauses in a Series**

    Example 1: Noah called the other players, gathered the equipment, and reserved the field for Saturday's practice.Before we can practice, before we can play, and before we can win, we have to work as a team to prepare mentally.

- **Two or More Adjectives**

    In most sentences, use a comma after each, except the last, of two or more adjectives that come before a noun. (See hint following.)

    Example 1: Soccer is a safe, aerobic sport for everyone to play.

    Example 2: Steve found a community soccer rule book

> **HINT:** If you can reverse the order of the adjectives without changing the meaning of the sentence, separate them with commas. Or, if you can use *and* between the adjectives, separate them with commas.

6. Quotations

Use commas before and after direct quotations. Commas are not used when a quotation is an exclamatory statement or a question.

> **Example:** "Use your left foot," Coach Shelby instructed, "when you're on the left side of the goal."
>
> **Example:** "Shoot!" yelled Coach Shelby.
>
> **Example:** "Who are you covering?" asked Coach Shelby.

Practice 3: Punctuation with Commas

Review rules 4–6. Read the following sentences. On your own paper, rewrite the sentence to correct any punctuation mistakes, or write C if the sentence is correctly punctuated.

1. The Pelican State The Bayou State and Sportsman's Paradise are all nicknames for Louisiana.
2. Louisiana has a state insect bird dog tree and flower.
3. Louisiana sends honeybees the official Louisiana state insect all over the United States.
4. The Eastern Brown pelican which can be found on the state's flag and seal lives in the Gulf Coast region of Louisiana.

SEMICOLON RULES

1. Compound Sentences

Use a semicolon between the clauses of a compound sentence when no conjunction (FANBOYS) is used. Also, instead of using a period, you can use semicolons to join two separate, but related sentences.

> **Example:** The trip to the beach was a blast; everyone had a great time.
>
> **Example:** Sunny skies and cool breezes greeted us every day; we couldn't ask for better.

2. Compound Sentences with Conjunctive Adverbs

Use a <u>semicolon</u> before and a <u>comma</u> after a conjunctive adverb that joins clauses of a compound sentence. Some conjunctive adverbs are *therefore, however, so, then, consequently, for instance, nevertheless, besides, moreover, instead,* and *besides.*

> **Example:** Andrew did not know how to swim; nevertheless, he had fun on the beach.
>
> **Example:** We played all kinds of games; for instance, we played an extreme Marco Polo!

3. Items in a Series

Use a semicolon to separate items in a series that contain commas.

> **Example:** Alicia found a rough, glittery stone; an echoing, brittle brown shell; and a smelly, slimly kelp strip.

Practice 4: Punctuation with Semicolons

Read the following passage. Look for semicolon use. On your own paper, rewrite each numbered sentence to correct any punctuation errors. If the sentence punctuation is correct, write C.

Capitalization, Punctuation, and Spelling

(1) Origami is the ancient art of paper folding. (2) Origami comes from two Japanese terms. (3) *Oru* is the Japanese word for folding, *kami* is the Japanese word for paper. (4) For centuries, there were no written directions for folding origami models the directions were taught by hand. (5) These models were passed down from generation to generation, consequently the models changed their shapes and titles often. (6)Today, you can learn different models by following a sequence of folding techniques found in books or on the Internet. (7) The more common patterns include the peaceful, swimming swan, the jumping, traditional frog, and the lucky, peaceful crane. (8) Origami is an easy hobby to begin it requires only one material, paper. (9) There are very few rules in origami however, one rule is that you fold one sheet of square paper without cutting or gluing. (10) The creativity in origami comes in adapting the patterns or in creating your own new pattern.

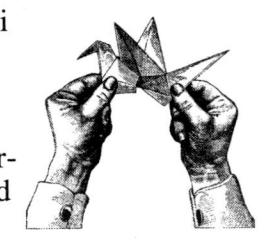

QUOTATION MARK RULES

1. Direct Quotations

Use quotation marks ("") at the beginning and the end of direct quotations. Quotation marks let readers know exactly who said what. Indirect quotations do not contain a person's exact words and do not use quotation marks. You can usually tell an indirect quotation because of the use of conjunctions (*that*, *if*, *who*, *what*, and *why*).

Example 1: "I wish I were successful," sighed Carmella. "I just want to be good at something."

Example 2: Maya Angelou said, "Success is liking yourself, liking what you do, and liking how you do it."

Example 3: Spencer thought that success was shown by your accomplishments.

2. Title of Short Works

Use quotation marks to set off the title of short works, such as songs, poems, short stories, and articles.

Example 1: "Crazy in Love" (song)

Example 2: "The Gift of the Magi" (short story)

3. Other Punctuation with Quotations

Using quotation marks affects the use of other punctuation. Follow these rules to use other punctuation correctly with quotation marks.

- **Place periods inside quotation marks.**

    Example: Miller said, "I am a successful baseball player."

- **Place question marks and exclamation points inside quotation marks if they belong to the quotation. But place questions marks and exclamation points outside the quotation marks if they belong to the whole sentence.**

    Example 1: "What is your definition of success?" Samantha asked.

    Example 2: Did she hear him say, "Success is unknowable"?

- **Use a comma to end a quotation that is a complete sentence but is followed by explanatory words.**

    Example: "I think success is achieving your goals," said Maria.
- **Place semicolons outside quotation marks.**

    Example: Simon said, "I agree"; then he smiled.

Practice 5: Punctuation with Quotation Marks

Read the following sentences. Add quotation marks and other punctuation where needed. Write C if the sentence is correct.

1. The reviewer said that the movie was a great film for the whole family.

2. I wouldn't take my little sister to see it Marissa said it can be scary.

3. Lance said I loved Lord of the Rings; it's a fantastic movie.

4. Enya performed the song May It Be for the movie soundtrack.

5. Lord of the Rings: Does it Work? is an article that compares the book with the movie.

APOSTROPHE RULES

1. **Possession**

Use an apostrophe (') to show possession or ownership.

To make a singular noun possessive, add an apostrophe and –s

   Example: The cat's hair was standing on end.
- **To make a plural noun ending in *s* possessive, add an apostrophe**

    Example: Cats' reactions can scare off even big dogs.
- To make a plural noun not ending in *s* possessive, add an apostrophe and –s

    Example: The children's librarian read a book about cats to them.

NOTE: Some words are already possessive by definition. These include *yours, his, hers, ours,* and *theirs*. They do not use apostrophes at all, even though they end in *s*.

2. **Contractions**

Use an apostrophe to combine two words. The apostrophe takes the place of the missing letters.

Capitalization, Punctuation, and Spelling

Common Contractions		
I am / I'm	you are / you're	she is, she has / she's
would not / wouldn't	it is / it's	you will, you shall / you'll
all is / all's	do not / don't	who is, who has / who's
I would, I had / I'd	can not / can't	we will / we'll
let us / let's	will not / won't	is not / isn't
did not / didn't	I have / i've	who will / who'll
are not / aren't	there is / there's	we would, we had / we'd
they are / they're	he will / he'll	she will / she'll
would have / would've	should have / should've	could have / could've
should not / shouldn't	could not / couldn't	we are / we're

NOTE: There is a difference between it's and its. It's is the contraction made by joining it and is. Its is the possessive pronoun showing ownership; notice that it does not use an apostrophe.

Practice 6: Punctuation with Apostrophes

Read the following passage. Look for apostrophe use. On your own paper, rewrite the sentence to correct any apostrophe errors. If the sentence is correctly punctuated, write C.

(1) Theres great diversity in a rainforest. (2) Anyone whos interested in insects and frogs should try hiking in a rainforest. (3) Rainforests have many places for creatures to hide. (4) The falling leaves bring nutrients to the forests top soil. (5) The trees shouldnt be cleared from the rainforest. (6) The damage that is caused by clear-cutting cant be undone. (7) One creature that suffers from removing trees is the tree frog. (8) Its skin must stay moist. (9) The trees provide the frog water and protection. (10) Its important for the rainforest creatures to have the trees for food and homes.

END PUNCTUATION RULES

1. **End a complete statement with a period (.).**

    Example: I will pass the test.

   - **Periods are also used with abbreviations.**

        Example: The American Book Co. will help me pass the test.

        Example: Infotek, Inc. has a new phone number.

2. **End a question with a question mark (?).**

    Example: Do you know what information will be on the test?

3. **End a statement that expresses strong feelings with an exclamation point (!).**

    Example: I passed the test!

Practice 7: Punctuation with End Punctuation

Read the following sentences. Add the correct end punctuation.

1. Mars is the closest planet to Earth
2. Do you think there is life on Mars
3. People often call Mars the "red planet"
4. We sent a rover to Mars to investigate its rocky, barren terrain
5. The images the rover sent back were amazing
6. Will we send Earthlings to explore Mars

SPELLING RULES

Write *i* Before *e*

Use *i* before *e* except after *c*, or when the letters sound like *a* as in *neighbor* and *sleigh*.

> **Example:** relief, friend, perceive, eight, weight
>
> **Exceptions:** financier, foreigner, forfeit, height, leisure, neither, seize, science, scientific, sheik, species, weird

Practice 8: Spelling

Read the following sentences. On your own paper, correct any spelling mistakes, or write C if the sentence is correct.

1. I don't beleive the casheir gave me a reciept.
2. The leiutenant argued with the police cheif.
3. They felt so much releif when the science test was over.
4. The beleif that deciet is wrong is universal.
5. The shipyard wieghs all frieght before loading the containers.

ROOT WORDS WITH SUFFIXES AND PREFIXES

A **root word** is the basic part of a word, and it is the building block on which the meanings of new words are built. Many roots are real words themselves: *graph* (a diagram), for example. To build new words from roots we may add prefixes or suffixes.

> **Example:** *holo* + *graph* = holograph (3-dimensional image)

A **prefix** is a group of letters that is placed **before** a root word to change the meaning.

A **suffix** is a group of letters that is placed **after** a root word to change the meaning.

You will learn more about roots, suffixes, and prefixes in Chapter 8

Capitalization, Punctuation, and Spelling

1. Words with Prefixes

When adding a prefix to a word, do not change the spelling of the root word even when the last letter of the prefix and the first letter of the word are the same.

Example: dissatisfied, unnoticed, preemptive, dissolve, nonnegotiable

2. Words with Consonant Endings

Double the final consonant before a suffix beginning with a vowel if the word

- has only one syllable (wit – witty),
- or is stressed on the final syllable (
- or the word ends in one consonant preceded by one vowel.

Example: admit – admittance, begin – beginning, control – controlling
forget – forgettable, god – goddess, prefer – preferred
stop – stopper, sum – summary, stun – stunned

3. Words with a Silent *e*

When adding a suffix to a word with a silent *e*, drop the *e* before adding a suffix that begins with a vowel. Do not drop the *e* when the suffix begins with a consonant.

Example: use – using – useful, like – liking - likeness
love – loving – lovely,   state – stating - statement
smile – smiling – smiled, brave – bravely – braveness

Exceptions: argument, ninth, truly, awful

- Don't drop the *e* if it changes the meaning of the root word.

    dye + ing = dyeing (not dying), singe + ing = singeing (not singing)

- Don't drop the *e* if the *e* clarifies pronunciation.

    flee + ing = fleeing (not fleing)

- Don't drop the *e* if the sound *c* or *g* must be kept soft.

    notice + able = noticeable (not noticable)

    courage + ous = courageous (not couragous)

    judge + ment = judgment (not judgement)

4. Words Ending in *y*

When adding a suffix to a word ending in a consonant followed by *y*, change the *y* to an *i*.

Example: beauty – beautiful, happy – happiness, ply – pliable

Exceptions: Keep the *y* when the suffix being added is *–ing*. flying, hurrying, trying
Keep the *y* in some one-syllable base words. dryness, shyness

Practice 9: Spelling

Combine the following prefixes, suffixes, and root words correctly.

1. care + fully _____
2. semi + sweet _____
3. manual + ly _____
4. odor + less _____
5. happen + ing _____
6. easy + ly _____
7. swim + ing _____
8. beauty + ful _____
9. occur + ed _____
10. un + fortunate + ly _____

PLURALS

1. **Form the plural for most nouns by adding *s*. Form the plural for nouns that end in *-ch*, *-s*, *-sh*, *-x*, or *–z* by adding *–es*.**

   Example: trees, nights, books; *-x*, boxes; *-sh*, splashes; *-ch*, patches

2. **Form the plural for common nouns ending in a *consonant* and *y*, by changing the *y* to *i* and add *-es*.**

   Example: flies, studies

3. **Form the plural for common nouns that end in a *vowel* and a *y* by adding only an *-s*.**

   Example: donkeys, monkeys, Tuesdays

4. **Form the plural of nouns that end in a *vowel* and an *o* by adding an *-s*.**

   Example: radios, rodeos, studios

5. **Form the plural of nouns that end in a *consonant* and an *o* by adding *-es*.**

   Example: echoes, heroes, dominoes

6. **Form the plurals of nouns that end in *f* or *fe* two ways:**

   - If the final *f* sound is still heard in the plural form of the word, add *-s*.
     Example: roofs, chiefs
   - If the final *f* sound becomes a *v* sound, change the *f* to *ve* and add *-s*.
     Example: wives, loaves

Capitalization, Punctuation, and Spelling

HOMONYMS

Homonyms are words that sound alike but have different meanings and spellings. There are many homonyms in the English language and they usually come in pairs or trios. Some commonly confused homonyms are listed below. Practice writing these homonyms in sentences. Your teacher or other students can then check to see if you are using them correctly.

Common Problem Homonyms				
a lot	(a set of things; a piece of land)		**our**	(belonging to us)
allot	(to distribute)		**hour**	(60 minutes; time of day)
cite	(to refer to)		**pour**	(to flow; transfer liquid)
site	(a location)		**pore**	(tiny opening in the skin)
sight	(vision; to see; a noteworthy place)			
coarse	(rough)		**road**	(a route, street, or highway)
course	(path of travel; class)		**rode**	(past tense of *ride*)
			rowed	(propelled a boat with oars)
for	(in place of, in regard to)		**stare**	(gaze fixedly)
four	(number after three)		**stair**	(one of a flight of steps)
heal	(to make well; regain health)		**tale**	(a story)
heel	(back part of foot; OR stay at one's side)		**tail**	(protruding end of animal's spine)
he'll	(contraction of *he will*)			
hear	(to perceive sound)		**than**	(introduces second element in a comparison)
here	(in this place)		**then**	(after that time; next)
him	(pronoun, objective case, for *he*)		**very**	(extremely; exactly)
hymn	(song of praise to God)		**vary**	(to make or become different)
knew	(past tense of *know*)		**would**	(conditional form of *will*)
new	(recent; not old)		**wood**	(fibrous substance of a tree)
morning	(part of day before noon)			
mourning	(grieving)			

> **HINT:** The spell checker on a computer is a great tool for proofreading your writing. However, you should never trust it completely. Carefully proofread your writing, and use a dictionary for words you are not sure that your spell checker will catch, such as the homonyms listed above.

Practice 10: Spelling

Read the following sentences. Correct any spelling mistakes you find by writing the word correctly above the mistake. The first one is done for you.

    A lot
1. Allot of guests have arrived at the convention.
2. Their hear to listen to the candidate's speechs.
3. The speaker has asked that all radioes and phones be turned off.
4. Some of the guests are local disc jockies hoping for an interview.
5. The success of they're speeches can effect the elections.
6. Too people will introduce each candidate.
7. It was quite moving to here the heros from September 11 speak.
8. The candidates very in there approach to improving the economy.
9. The echos of applause could be herd long after the convention had ended.
10. Lunchs were distributed after the major speakers.

CHAPTER 1 REVIEW:

Read the following letter. Answer the questions that follow.

    (1) Dear mr. spielberg:

    (2) I am a student at Albany middle school in Louisiana. (3) I think you are a fantastic filmmaker, my favorite movie is *E.T.* (4) I have been very interested in making movies ever since I recieved a video camera for Christmas last year. (5) I read somewhere that you began making movies when you were young and that is what I hope to do. (6) I was wondering if you had any advice to offer me about writing filming and directing. (7) What kinds of decisions do you think are the most important for a filmmaker. (8) I think location can be very important to a film's meaning. (9) Louisianas landscape has inspired me to create a film. (10) I am planning to film a short movie based on a short story I wrote called, The Wild Water.

Sincerely,

Thomas Selenas

1. How should you correct the error in sentence 1?
    A.   change **mr. spielberg:** to **Mr. Spielberg,**
    B.   change **mr. spielberg:** to **Mr. Spielberg:**
    C.   change **mr. spielberg:** to **Mr. Speilburg:**
    D.   There is no error.

Capitalization, Punctuation, and Spelling

2. How should you correct the error in sentence 2?
    A. change **Louisiana** to **louisiana**
    B. change **Albany middle school** to **Albany Middle school**
    C. change **Albany middle school** to **Albany Middle School**
    D. There is no error.

3. How should you correct the error in sentence 3?
    A. change **filmmaker,** to **filmmaker;**
    B. change **filmmaker,** to **film maker,**
    C. change *E.T.* to **"E.T."**
    D. There is no error.

4. How should you correct the error in sentence 4?
    A. change **interested** to **intrested**
    B. change **very** to **vary**
    C. change **recieved** to **received**
    D. There is no error.

5. How should you correct the error in sentence 5?
    A. change **you began making movies when you were young** to **"you began making movies when you were very young"**
    B. change **young and that** to **young, and that**
    C. change **read somewhere that** to **read somewhere, that**
    D. There is no error.

6. How should you correct the error in sentence 6?
    A. change **directing.** to **directing?**
    B. change **writing filming and directing.** to **writing, filming, and directing.**
    C. change **writing filming and direction.** to **writing; filming; and directing.**
    D. There is no error.

7. How should you correct the error in sentence 7?
    A. change **decisions** to **decissions**
    B. change **important** to **importent**
    C. change **filmmaker.** to **filmmaker?**
    D. There is no error.

8. How should you correct the error in sentence 8?
    A. change **film's** to **films**
    B. change **can be** to **could be**
    C. change **location** to **locasion**
    D. There is no error.

9. How should you correct the error in sentence 9?
    A. change **Louisianas** to **Louisiana's**
    B. change **inspired** to **enspired**
    C. change **inspired me** to **inspired me,**
    D. There is no error.

10. How should you correct the error in sentence 10?
    A. change **short movie based** to **short movie; based**
    B. change **I am** to **I'm**
    C. change **The Wild Water** to **"The Wild Water"**
    D. There is no error.

Chapter 2
Parts of Speech

LOUISIANA READING BENCHMARKS ADRESSED IN THIS CHAPTER INCLUDE:	
ELA 3-M4	Demonstrating understanding of the parts of speech to make choices for writing (1, 4).

Parts of speech refers to the eight different types of words: **nouns**, **pronouns**, **verbs**, **adjectives**, **adverbs**, **prepositions**, **conjunctions**, and **interjections**. This chapter will provide lessons and review for the eight parts of speech. Each section contains a definition of the part of speech followed by practice exercises.

NOUNS

A **noun** is a word that names a person, a place, a thing, or an idea. Nouns have a *number*, meaning they can be either *singular* (one) or *plural* (more than one).

CLASSES OF NOUNS

- Common Nouns: A **common noun** refers to general people, places, things, or ideas.
    Examples: girl, computer, apple, religion

- Proper Nouns: A **proper noun** names a particular person, place, thing or idea. Proper nouns are always capitalized.
    Examples: Sara, Compac™, Macintosh™, Christianity

- **Collective Nouns:** A **collective noun** names a group or unit. Collective nouns can be either common or proper.
    Examples: House of Representatives, herd, band, family

- **Concrete Nouns:** A **concrete noun** names a thing that can be seen, touched, heard, smelled or tasted. Concrete nouns can be either proper or common.
    Examples: car, song, perfume, chocolate
    Examples: Ford Mustang, "Red River Valley," Glow, Hershey's™

- **Abstract Nouns:** An abstract noun names an idea, condition, or feeling. These are things that *cannot* be seen, touched, heard, smelled, or tasted. Abstract nouns can be either proper or common.

    Examples: hope, freedom, faith, compassion, Swedish

Practice 1: Common and Proper Nouns

For each of the following sentences, underline the common nouns once and the proper nouns twice.

1. Louisiana is the only state that was once a royal colony of France.
2. New Orleans was founded in 1718.
3. The Union Army occupied the city for three years during the Civil War.
4. New Orleans's crescent shape comes from being founded on the bend of the Mississippi River.
5. Because of the city's unusual shape, confusion for visitors is common.

Practice 2: Abstract, Concrete, and Collective Nouns

On a separate piece of paper, make three lists of nouns: abstract, concrete and collective nouns. Each list should have at least seven items. When you are done with your lists, share them with your class or teacher. When discovering what others have listed, keep a note of any nouns which surprise you, if any—some you would not have thought of.

CASE AND FUNCTION OF NOUNS

The case of a noun tells how the noun is used in a sentence in relation to the other words in a sentence. There are three cases:

- Nominative Case: A **nominative case** noun acts as the **subject** of a clause. Nominative case nouns *usually* come before the verb in a sentence.

    Example: The **car** raced down the speedway.

    A nominative case noun can also act as a **predicate noun**, which is a noun that renames the subject after following the verbs *am, is, are, was, were, be, being, been.*

    Example: The car was a different **model** of racecar. The predicate noun, *model*, renames the subject, *car*.

- Possessive Case: A **possessive case** noun shows **ownership** or possession.

    Example: The *car's* engine ran on hydrogen.

- Objective Case: An **objective case** noun acts as a **direct object**, an **indirect object**, or an **object of a preposition**. Objective case nouns *usually* come after the subject and verb in a sentence.

    Direct objects receive the action of a verb. They answer the question "what?" or "whom?"

    Example: The driver prepared the **car**.

Chapter 2

Indirect objects tell to or for whom something is done. They answer the question "for whom?" or "to whom?" The indirect object comes before the direct object in a sentence. There must be a direct object in a sentence in order to have an indirect object.

Example: The driver told the **mechanics** the problems.

Objects of the preposition are the nouns after prepositions.

Example 1: The driver pulled the car into the **garage**.

Example 2: The *car's driver* gave the *audience* a *tour* of the *production shed*.

> Who *gave*? – **subject** – driver
>
> Whose *driver*? – **possessive** – car's
>
> *Gave* what? – **direct object** - tour
>
> *Gave* to whom? - **indirect object** – audience
>
> *Of* what? - **object of preposition** *of* – production shed

CASE	FUNCTION	SYMBOL
Nominative	Subject	S
	Predicate Noun	PN
Objective	Direct Object	DO
	Indirect Object	IO
	Object of a Preposition	OP
Possessive	Possessive Noun	POS

Practice 3: Function of Nouns

For the following sentences, underline and label each noun, using the symbols from the chart above.

1. The Marianas Trench is located in the Pacific Ocean, just east of the Philippines.
2. The British Royal Navy discovered the trench in 1951.
3. The Marianas Trench is the deepest spot in any ocean of the world.
4. The Marianas Trench is almost 7 miles deep.
5. The trench's depth is greater than the height of any mountain on the surface of the earth.
6. The U.S. Navy sent a mini-submarine to the bottom of the trench in 1960.
7. The deepest recorded fish was found in the Marianas Trench at 5.2 miles below the surface of the ocean.
8. Many species of fish have adapted to living in the high pressure and low light of the trench.
9. Viper fish are good examples of environmental adaptation.
10. These fish have enlarged eyes and light organs on their bodies to attract prey.

Parts of Speech

PRONOUNS

A **pronoun** is a word used in place of a noun. Words such as **I, you, me, she, he, it, which, they, mine, ours, their** are all pronouns. In writing, it is useful to use pronouns to replace nouns. The general rule is that if a name is repeated often this helps avoid repetition and creates sentences which flow smoothly and are easy to read.

FORMS OF PERSONAL PRONOUNS

As with nouns, a pronoun has a **case**, which tells how it functions in the sentence. A pronoun also has a **number**, meaning it can be either *singular* (one) or *plural* (more than one). A pronoun also has a **person**, which tells if the pronoun is speaking, is spoken to, or is spoken about.

- Nominative Case: A **nominative case** pronoun is used when the pronoun is the **subject** of a sentence.

    Example: **We** were late to the party.

- Possessive Case: A **possessive case** pronoun is used to show ownership. Unlike other possessives, apostrophes are **NOT** used with possessive pronouns, which already show ownership.

    Example: We took **our** two children with us.

- **Objective Case:** An objective case pronoun is used when the pronoun is a **direct object, indirect object**, or **object of a preposition**.

    Example: We took **them** with **us** to the party.

    Example: The guests gave **her** some great gifts.

Case, Number, and Person of Personal Pronouns			
	Nominative	Possessive	Objective
1st person singular	I	my, mine	me
2nd person singular	you	your, yours	you
3rd person singular	he, she, it	his, her, hers, its	him, her, it
1st person plural	we	our, ours	us
2nd person plural	you	your, yours	you
3rd person plural	they	their, theirs	them

Chapter 2

REFLEXIVE PRONOUNS

Reflexive pronouns are formed by adding *–self* or *–selves* to a personal pronoun. These pronouns reflect back on an earlier noun or pronoun. In other words, whenever there is a reflexive pronoun in a sentence there must be a person to whom that pronoun can "reflect." Reflexive pronouns indicate that the subject is not only doing the action of the verb, but also receives the action of the verb. Reflexive pronouns can be direct objects, indirect objects, objects of prepositions or predicate nominatives.

Examples: Dennis got home late; **he** fixed **himself** a snack after band practice. (Antecedent is Dennis)

I am giving **myself** the gift of time this summer. (Antecedent is I)

You excused **yourself** from the competition to be generous. (Antecedent is you)

One should help **oneself** to the simple things in life.

Reflexive Pronouns		
myself	himself	themselves
yourself	herself	itself
yourselves	oneself	ourselves

Practice 4: Pronouns

Use a separate sheet of paper for this practice. Rewrite the sentences in the following paragraph to correct pronoun use and improve the sentences. If a sentence is correct, make no changes.

(1) Tony Hawk has won hundreds of skate competitions. **(2)** Tony even had a video game named after himself. **(3)** Soon after Tony made your first money skating professionally, he built a skate park in its own backyard. **(4)** So how did he all begin for Tony Hawk? **(5)** When Tony was nine years old, him received his first skateboard. **(6)** By the age of 14, Tony Hawk had turned professional, and it began to win almost every competition his entered. **(7)** His has invented dozens of skateboard tricks and a professional style. **(8)** Their accomplishments have changed the face of skating. **(9)** Skating is no longer seen as a rebel sport for juvenile delinquents. **(10)** I can discover the joy of skating too; just pick up a board and go!

> **HINT**: A common writing mistake involves confusion between the pronouns *I* and *me*. When trying to decide whether to use the pronoun *I* or *me*, remember to look at how the pronoun is being used in the sentence. *I* is used for nominative case and *me* is used for objective case.

Examples: Xavier and *I* studied together for the test.

The test took *me* a long time to finish.

My mom took *Xavier and me* to the library.

Practice 5: Pronouns I and Me

Circle the correct pronouns in the sentences below. Use what you know about nominative case (subjects) and objective case (objects) to choose the correct pronoun.

1. Both my sister and (I, me) play piano.
2. My sister plays piano better than (I, me).
3. Thank you for giving my sister and (I, me) piano lessons.
4. Do you want to go to a piano concert with (I, me)?
5. Just between you and (I, me), I would rather play guitar.

PRONOUN ANTECEDENTS

An **antecedent** of a pronoun is the noun that the pronoun refers to or replaces. All pronouns have antecedents. Each pronoun must agree in number, gender, and person with its antecedent. Use a singular pronoun to refer to a singular antecedent. Use a plural pronoun to refer to a plural antecedent.

Examples: **Winners** can claim **their** prizes at the counter.

Michelle won **her** very first airplane ride on *The Spirit*.

The **airplane** got **its** name from Charles Lindberg.

Paul said **he** enjoyed **his** airplane ride last year.

Practice 6: Pronouns and Antecedents

A. In each sentence, underline the pronoun once and the antecedent twice.

1. Javier visited his grandmother by himself.
2. Javier's plane trip to Brazil was so long, he slept most of the way.
3. Grandmother Ferreiro hugged Javier tightly when she met him at the airport.
4. Javier and Grandmother's first outing took them on a tour of a rainforest.
5. Javier discovered that some tree frogs change their color to match the environment.

B. Circle the pronoun that correctly completes each sentence. Be sure that the pronoun agrees with its antecedent.

6. Most rainforest creatures have adapted (its, their) appearance to match (its, their) environment.
7. Javier took many photos of (his, its) adventures in Brazil.
8. Brazilians celebrate (its, their) independence day on September 7.
9. Many directors have shot (his, their) films in Brazil.
10. Because Brazil is so beautiful, (its, their) rainforests have been used in many films.

INDEFINITE PRONOUNS

Indefinite pronouns take the place of unnamed or unknown people or things. The pronoun is used when the meaning or quantity of what is being replaced is indefinite. Sometimes indefinite pronouns are used as indefinite adjectives when they are followed by the noun they describe.

Examples: **Few** arrived to help with the gardening project.

Few flowers bloom throughout the winter. (indefinite adjective)

Indefinite Pronouns					
all	both	everything	nobody	several
another	each	few	none	some
any	many	no	one	somebody
each	either	most	someone	nothing
anybody	everybody	something	much	one
anyone	everyone	other	such	neither
anything				

DEMONSTRATIVE PRONOUNS

Demonstrative pronouns point out specific people, places, or things without naming them. Sometimes demonstrative pronouns are used as demonstrative adjectives when they are followed by the noun they describe.

Examples: **These** were the best I could find at the garden center.

These flowers bloom all winter long. (demonstrative adjective)

Demonstrative Pronouns
this   that   these   those

Parts of Speech

RELATIVE PRONOUNS

Relative pronouns are words that act as a connection in a sentence, relating an adjective clause to the noun or pronoun it modifies.

> **Examples:** People **who** exercise regularly live longer lives.
>
> The gym, **which** we had been going to weekly, closed down.

Relative Pronouns					
what	whom	who	which	whose	that

INTERROGATIVE PRONOUNS

Interrogative pronouns ask questions.

> **Examples:** **Who** suggested that we go out to dinner?
>
> **Which** restaurant should we choose?

Interrogative Pronouns				
who	whose	whom	which	what

Practice 7: Pronouns

Underline the pronouns in the passage below. Identify the pronouns by labeling them **PER** for personal, **IND** for indefinite, **DEM** for demonstrative, **REL** for relative, and **INT** for interrogative.

"We must become the change we want to see." Do you know who said this? These words were spoken by a very famous man, Mahatma Ghandi. Ghandi wanted to change a lot about his world, and he did. He brought freedom to everyone in India through non-violent protest. Ghandi, who Indians call "father of the nation," was born in 1869 when India was still under the control of the British government. He created a method of social action based on courage, nonviolence, and truth. This he called Satyagraha. Satyagraha encouraged nonviolence and civil disobedience to reach political and social goals. Ghandi believed that the way people behave is more important than what they achieve. Through his behavior, he achieved greatness, and his beliefs encouraged others to do the same. Nothing could change his beliefs. We could all be inspired by this man.

Verbs

A **verb** is a word that expresses a physical action (run, jump, read) or mental action (think, know). Verbs also express a state of being (is, are, appears). Verbs are a necessary part of every sentence. Verbs are what the sentence subject is doing or being. There are three types of verbs: **action**, **linking**, and **helping**.

Action Verbs

An **action verb** tells that something is happening, has happened, or will happen. It can show a physical or mental action.

Examples: The cat **clawed** at the screen.

Apparently, she **wanted** to come inside.

Linking Verbs

A **linking verb** connects the subject with a word or words that describe it, predicate nouns or adjectives. Linking verbs can also be used to express a state of being.

Examples: The cat's fur **feels** soft. (predicate adjective)

The cat **is** a domesticated animal. (predicate noun)

The cat **is** on the couch. (state-of-being)

Common Linking Verbs			
am	become	appear	been
is	became	smell	seem
are	sound	feel	look
be	were	was	get
will be	stay	did	remain
being	grow	got	taste

Helping Verbs

A **helping verb** is a word or group of words that join with a main verb to help the meaning by creating a verb phrase. A **verb phrase** is a group of words all working together to act as the verb. The following examples show the entire verb phrase underlined and the helping verb in bold.

Examples: The cat **has** scratched the furniture before.

We **could have** removed her claws.

The procedure **would** hurt her too much.

Parts of Speech

Common Helping Verbs				
is	may	have	did	will
was	can	should	been	being
do	am	might	had	could
be	were	shall	would	
has	does	are	must	

Sometimes parts of the verb phrase are separated. The words that come between them are not part of the verb.

    Examples: My mother **has** never **liked** cats.

                Do you **own** a cat?

Practice 8: Verbs

Underline the verbs or verb phrases in following passage. Label each verb either as action (**A**), linking (**L**), or helping (**H**).

Cats and humans have lived together since ancient times. Cats are important to many cultures because of their helpful hunting skills, cleanliness, and beauty. The Egyptians had cats as pets around 2000 BC. From 1000-350 BC, however, cats were also seen as gods. The Egyptians worshipped and honored cats in life and death. Golden cat statues have been discovered in Egyptian tombs. Laws protected cats from harm. The punishment for harming or killing a cat was harsh. Cats are valuable, then and now.

VERB TENSES

Verb tense shows the time of an action or condition. Verbs indicate whether an event took place in the past, present, or future. There are six verb tenses:

- **Present Tense** is used to express action that is happening now, or an action that happens continually or regularly.

    Example: He walks to school every day.

- **Past Tense** is used to express action that has already happened.

    Example: He walked to school last year.

- **Future Tense** is used to express action that will happen in the future.

    Example: He will walk to school next year.

- **Present Perfect Tense** is used to express an action that began in the past but continues in the present or is completed in the present.

    Example: He has walked to school since kindergarten.

- **Past Perfect Tense** is used to express an action in the past that happens before another past action.

    Example: His father had walked to school as a boy.

- **Future Perfect Tense** is used to express an action that will begin in the future and will be completed by a certain time in the future.

    Example: He will have walked many miles by the time he graduates.

Tense	Verb Form
Present	live
Past	lived
Future	will live
Present perfect	have/has lived
Past perfect	had lived
Future perfect	will/shall have lived

Writing can be confusing when different verb tenses are used to describe actions that happen at the same time. When two or more actions occur at the same time or in a sequence, use the same verb tense to describe the action. Avoid changing the verb tense between sentences or within paragraphs.

Example: Jorge **was laughing** while Marcus **tells** a joke.

Corrected example: Jorge **is laughing** while Marcus **tells** a joke.

OR

Jorge **was laughing** while Marcus **told** a joke.

Practice 9: Verb Tenses

Identify the tense of the bold-faced verbs in the following sentences. On a separate sheet of paper, rewrite the sentences to correct the change in tense.

1. Rita **likes** swimming and **swam** laps at the pool every day.
2. We **will play** games now, and we **are having** cake later.
3. Omar **takes** auto mechanics and **fixed** cars on the weekend.
4. Joanne **danced** while William **sings** a song.
5. I **am learning** to play guitar, and it **hurt** my fingers.

Parts of Speech

COMMONLY CONFUSED VERBS

The following verb pairs are often confused. Learn the definitions of each in order to use the correct verb in your writing. Other tense forms of the verbs are in parentheses.

LIE AND LAY

Lie means to rest in a flat position or to be in a certain place. (lay, lain)

Lay means to put something down. (laid)

SIT AND SET

Sit means to be in a seated position. (sat)

Set means to put or place. (set)

LEARN AND TEACH

Learn means to gain knowledge or skill. (learned)

Teach means to help someone learn. (taught)

BRING AND TAKE

Bring refers to movement toward the speaker. (brought)

Take refers to movement away from the speaker. (took, taken)

Practice 10: Using the Correct Verb

Underline the correct verb in each of the following sentences.

1. Susan (learned, taught) her little sister how to tie her shoes.
2. When you go to the store, please (bring, take) these apples back.
3. I (lay, laid) my coat over the back of the chair.
4. Michelle (sat, set) down and started writing.
5. Many barriers (lay, laid) in the path of her success.
6. Please (bring, take) me dinner on your way home.
7. (Learn, Teach) children to never talk to strangers.
8. What states (lie, lay) along the Mississippi?
9. I can't remember where I (sat, set) down my math book.
10. My roller blades have (lain, laid) in the downstairs closet all summer.

MISPLACED MODIFIERS

A **modifier** is a phrase or clause that describes or adds meaning to another word. Verbals are often used as modifiers in sentences. A verbal or verbal phrase (the verbal and its modifiers all acting as a single part of speech) should be placed as close as possible to the word it is describing. Misplaced verbal phrases can confuse readers.

> **Example: Snapping dangerously**, the hunter pulled the alligator from the water.

In this example, the gerund phrase seems to be describing the hunter. To describe the alligator, the sentence should read as follows.

> **Corrected Example**: The hunter pulled the alligator, **snapping furiously**, from the water.

Practice 11:   Misplaced Modifiers

Underline the misplaced modifier in each of the following sentences. On a separate sheet of paper, rewrite the sentences to correct the misplaced modifier.

1. We heard the storm approaching sitting on the front porch.
2. To keep from getting wet the storm moved us inside.
3. While watering the flowers, a caterpillar cocoon was spotted by Louisa.
4. Louisa shouted to come see jumping excitedly.
5. Breaking open the cocoon, Louisa saw the butterfly emerge.

ADJECTIVES

An **adjective** is a word that describes a noun or a pronoun. An adjective tells *what kind*, *which one or ones*, *how many*, or *how much* about the word it is describing. The **articles** *a*, *an*, and *the* are also adjectives. Adjectives help writing become more vivid.

> **Examples: The talented** singer performed **favorite** tunes.
>
> **Several** songs reminded me of **a different** singer.

PREDICATE ADJECTIVES

Predicate adjectives are used after linking verbs to describe the subject.
> **Examples:** Her voice sounded **wonderful**.
>
> The costume she wore on stage was **beautiful**.

PROPER ADJECTIVES

Proper adjectives formed from proper nouns. They are always capitalized.
> **Examples: Italian** opera singers are known for their incredible voices.
>
> The most famous pop stars are **American**.

Parts of Speech

NOTE: Some pronouns act as adjectives when they come before the nouns they are describing. That, these, those, all, each, both, many etc.

Examples: **Many** performers try singing and acting.

Their talents are usually stronger in one area.

COMPARATIVE ADJECTIVES

Comparative forms of adjectives are used when comparing two things. Comparative adjectives are formed by adding –*er* to a short adjective, or by using the *word* more with a longer adjective.

Examples: The **prettier** actresses are often **more famous**.

Jennifer Lopez is **more talented** than Jennifer Love Hewitt.

SUPERLATIVE ADJECTIVES

Superlative forms of adjectives are used when comparing three or more things. Superlative adjectives are formed by adding –*est* to a short adjective, or by using the word *most* with a longer adjective.

Examples: I think J. Lo is the **most successful** actress turned singer.

She has the **coolest** dance moves of all.

Practice 12: Adjectives

A. Underline the adjectives in the following passage. Do not underline articles.

Growing up to ten feet long, Komodo dragons are the largest living reptiles in the world. They are agile climbers and can run very fast for short stretches. These voracious eaters love to dine on deer and wild boar. Even one bite is deadly, as Komodos carry poisonous bacteria in their mouths. Long forked tongues help them track fallen prey. Like all reptiles, though, they eat much less often than mammals of their size. The largest monitor lizards, they spend their days sunning and their nights in shallow burrows. Found on the islands of the Indonesian archipelago at the start of the 20th century, Komodos are endangered, with only a few thousand left. The islands of Padar and Rinca now serve as nature reserves to protect them.

B. The paragraph following contains no adjectives, except articles. Improve this paragraph by inserting adjectives. Share your improved paragraphs with your classmates.

The boy had hair and eyes. He was a boy. He had just woken up. He was going to school. He walked down the street looking at the ground. His mind thought about things. He knew school had started.

ADVERBS

An **adverb** is a word that describes a verb, an adjective, or another adverb. Adverbs often end in *–ly*, but not always. Adverbs improve writing by providing more description.

> **Examples:** Jennifer Lopez walked **slowly** into the room. (describes verb *walked*)
>
> The room was **really** quiet. (describes adjective *quiet*)
>
> Everyone turned **very** slowly to watch her. (describes adverb slowly)

Adverbs can be grouped into four categories:

- **Adverbs of Time** tell *when*, *how often*, and *how long*.
  > **Examples:** yesterday, today, tomorrow, daily, weekly, shortly, soon
- **Adverbs of Place** tell *where*.
  > **Examples:** here, there, backward, forward, out
- **Adverbs of Manner** tell *how* something is done.
  > **Examples:** well, carefully, quietly, loudly, honestly
- **Adverbs of Degree** tell *how much* or *how little*.
  > **Examples:** very, quite, too, greatly, really, more, partly, almost

COMPARATIVE AND SUPERLATIVE ADVERBS

The **comparative form** of an adverb compares two actions. Comparative adverbs are formed by adding *–er*, or the words *more* or *less* to an adverb. *Than* is used after a comparative adverb.

> **Examples:** Carl Lewis runs **faster** than Michael Johnson does.
>
> Decathlete Tom Pappas jumps **higher** than anyone I've ever seen.
>
> Olympic athletes train **more intensively** than other athletes do.

The **superlative form** of an adverb compares three or more actions. Superlative adverbs are formed by adding *–est*, or the words *most* or *least* to an adverb.

> **Examples:** Marion Jones spoke **most enthusiastically** about her performance.
>
> Our Olympic runners behaved **most honorably** in Athens.

NOTE: Avoid making double comparisons. Don't use *more* and *–er* or *most* and *–est* with the same adjective or adverb. It would be incorrect to say, "Gail Devers runs most fastest."

Parts of Speech

Some **comparative and superlative adjectives and adverbs** have irregular spellings. See the chart below.

Adjective/Adverb	Comparative	Superlative
bad	worse	worst
good	better	best
ill	worse	worst
little	less	least
many	more	most
much	more	most
some	more	most
well	better	best

COMMON MISTAKES WITH ADVERBS AND ADJECTIVES

GOOD AND WELL

Good is always an *adjective*, never an adverb. **Well** can be used as either an *adjective or an adverb*, depending on the sentence.

Example: The weather was **good**, so the outdoor concert went **well**.

FEW AND LITTLE, FEWER AND LESS

Few is used for numbers of things that can be counted; *little* is used for general amounts that can't be counted. *Fewer* is used when comparing number of things; *less* is used when comparing general amounts.

Examples: As the day went on, we had **less** energy and **fewer** events.

Few people turned out to watch the meet; a **little** rain kept them away.

BAD AND BADLY

Bad is always used as an *adjective*, either before a noun or after a linking verb. **Badly** is always used as an *adverb*.

Example: The athletes wanted so **badly** to win, so they felt **bad** when they lost.

ABSOLUTE CONCEPTS

Some adjectives and adverbs are not used in comparative or superlative forms because they already state an **absolute concept**. You cannot add more or most to these adverbs and adjectives because there is no better state.

Examples: It was the ~~most~~ perfect track meet ever.

I wish the ribbons were ~~more~~ equally distributed among the teams.

Absolute Concept Adjectives and Adverbs				
always	final	impossible	nothing	superior
complete	first	infinite	parallel	unanimous
equal	immortal	never	perfect	unique

DOUBLE NEGATIVES

A **double negative** is when two negative words are used together to express one negative idea. Avoid double negatives by using only one negative word in a clause. Not, no, *never*, *none*, and *nobody* are negative words. Compound words formed with *no* and the words *barely*, *hardly*, and *scarcely* also function as negative words.

Examples: There were hardly no penalties during the meet.

The losing team didn't have no hard feelings toward the winners.

In both cases, *no* should be replaced with *any* to avoid a double negative.

Practice 13: Adverbs

A. Underline the adverbs in the following sentences.

1. Athletes must breathe more deeply to supply their muscles with more oxygen.
2. The track meet ran smoothly despite the rainy weather.
3. The field here has good drainage.
4. The team has been practicing daily to prepare for the meet.
5. When an athlete collapsed on the field, the coaches rushed immediately to help.
6. He was very lucky; it was only dehydration.

B. Read the following sentences and notice the adverbs in bold. If the adverb is used correctly, write Correct. If the adverb is incorrect, rewrite it correctly.

7. Who on the team is **more likely** to win?_____
8. Juan throws **more farther** than Matt does._____
9. Who tried **hardest**, Juan or Matt?_____
10. Nico threw the javelin **farthest** in the meet. _____
11. Nico was **extremely** happy with his distance._____
12. The other team ran **gooder** than we expected._____
13. The meet lasted the **most longest** ever._____
14. I wanted so **bad** to come in 1st place. _____
15. The relay team raced **really good**._____

Parts of Speech

PREPOSITIONS

A **preposition** is a word or group of words that relates a word to another part of the sentence or to the whole sentence. Prepositions show relationships in time or space.

Prepositional phrases are phrases that include a preposition followed by a noun or pronoun acting as the object of the preposition. There may also be modifiers of the objects. In the following examples, the preposition is in bold, and the prepositional phrase is underlined.

Examples: Basketball season **at** school begins **in** three weeks.

We finally get to play **inside** the new gym.

They built the gym **behind** the school and **beside** the field.

Prepositions				
aboard	away from	down	like	through
above	because of	during	near	throughout
about	before	except	of	till
according to	behind	for	off	to
across	below	from	on	toward
after	beneath	in	onto	under
against	beside	in addition to	opposite	underneath
along	besides	in back of	out	until
alongside	between	in front of	outside of	unto
amid	beyond	in place of	over	up
among	by	in regard to	past	up to
apart from	by means of	inside	prior to	upon
around	concerning	in spite of	regarding	with
aside from	considering	instead of	since	within
at	despite	into	together with	without

INTERJECTIONS

An **interjection** is a word or phrase that is used to express strong feeling or surprise. Punctuation, usually a comma or an exclamation point, is used to set off an interjection form the rest of the sentence.

Examples: **Oh!** I had no idea I was so late.

Well, I guess there's no use complaining.

My goodness!

Practice 14: Prepositions and Interjections

In each sentence, circle the prepositions and underline the prepositional phrases. Underline any interjections twice.

1. Niagara Falls is divided by The Horseshoe Falls in Canada.
2. Except for one time, the Horseshoe Falls has never stopped flowing.
3. The water stopped for thirty hours in March of 1848.
4. Tons of ice became lodged at the source of the Niagara River, blocking the flow.
5. The people of the area were awakened by the strange silence.
6. Well, they didn't know what had happened and many panicked.
7. Some people walked across the rock floor of the channel. Unbelievable!
8. The ice pack broke up above the falls.
9. A solid wall of water rushed down the channel and crashed over the edge.
10. Whoosh! Niagara Falls was flowing again.

CONJUNCTIONS

A **conjunction** is a word that links other words or groups of words. There are three types of conjunctions:

- **Coordination conjunctions** connect related words, group of words, or sentences. Coordinating conjunctions connect things of equal importance. The list of coordinating conjunctions is known as FANBOYS: <u>f</u>or, <u>a</u>nd, <u>n</u>or, <u>b</u>ut, <u>o</u>r, <u>y</u>et, <u>s</u>o.

    Examples: Sam **and** Marcus tried out for the basketball team.

    The team is very competitive, **so** they practiced a lot.

    Basketball tryouts will be held on Tuesday, rain **or** shine.

Correlative conjunctions are pairs of conjunctions that work together to connect sentence parts.

    Examples: **If** Sam makes the team, **then** he'll be at practice after school

    Marcus hopes **not only** to make the team, **but also** to be team captain.

- **Subordinating conjunctions** connect two clauses that are not equally important. A subordinating conjunction connects a dependent clause to an independent clause.

    Examples: All players will have to pass a physical **before** they can play.

    Since they can dehydrate easily, the players take frequent water breaks.

Parts of Speech

Conjunctions				
Coordinating	**Correlative**	**Subordinating**		
and	either…or	after	before	though
but	neither…nor	although	if	till
or	not only…but also	as	in order that	unless
nor	both…and	as if	provided that	until
for	whether…or	as long as	since	when
yet	just as…so	as though	so that	where(as)
so	if…then	because	that	while

Practice 15: Conjunctions

Read the passage below, and underline all conjunctions. Try to notice whether the conjunction is coordinating, correlative, or subordinating.

Many foolhardy people have attempted stunts at Niagara Falls, but only one as daring as Charles Blondin. On June 30, 1859, Blondin crossed the Niagara Gorge on a tightrope and lived to tell about it. While halfway across the rope, he paused a moment before completing a backwards somersault. After his first crossing, Blondin was determined to beat his last performance. He again crossed the Niagara Gorge not only on his tightrope, but also while riding a bicycle. On August 19, Blondin crossed with a man upon his shoulders, but he barely made it. He was forced to stop six times during the crossing so the man on his back could dismount. The Great Blondin had done it again, but this time he had only just made it. Whether you believe him to be crazy or brave, Charles Blondin will remain a part of history.

CHAPTER 2 REVIEW: IDENTIFYING THE PARTS OF SPEECH

A. Write the part of speech of the boldfaced word or words above the word.

I have always **dreamed** of vacationing in **Hawaii**. **After** saving up my money for many years, I finally took that **trip**. It **was** the **best** vacation ever. **One** of the highlights of the trip was a **traditional** luau. **Wow! Listening** to Hawaiian music and sampling exotic foods took up most of the afternoon. Hula **dancers** performed for **us**. **Their** costumes were **very** beautiful. They moved **gracefully** to **the** music. **To vacation** in Hawaii was my dream, **and** I fulfilled it.

B. The fable below is the familiar tale, "The Ant and the Grasshopper." Fill in each blank with an appropriate word to complete the story. Above the word, write the part of speech you used to complete the sentence.

The Ant _____ the Grasshopper

In a field, one summer's _____ a Grasshopper was hopping about, chirping and singing to his heart's content. A _____ Ant _____ by, carrying along with great effort an ear of corn he was taking _____ his nest.

"Why not come and chat with _____," said the Grasshopper, "instead of working?"

"_____, I am helping _____ food for the winter," said the Ant, "and suggest you do the same."

"_____ bother about winter?" said the Grasshopper. "We have got plenty of _____ at present." But the Ant went _____ on its way and continued its work.

When the winter came, the Grasshopper had no food and found _____ dying of hunger. He saw the ants _____ corn from the stores they had collected in the summer. They _____ happy and healthy.

Then the Grasshopper knew: It is _____ to prepare.

Parts of Speech

Chapter 3
Planning the Composition

LOUISIANA READING BENCHMARKS ADDRESSED IN THIS CHAPTER INCLUDE:	
ELA-2-M1	Writing multi paragraph compositions (150–200 words) that clearly imply a central idea with supporting details in a logical, sequential order (1, 4)
ELA-2-M3	Identifying and applying the steps of the writing process (1, 4)

In this chapter, you will learn about the pre-writing stage of the **writing process**. The activities will help you read a **writing prompt**, **generate ideas**, **organize ideas**, and write a **central idea**. The chapter will also introduce the basic **structure of a composition**. The work in this chapter will help you get ready for taking the writing/proofreading portions of the LEAP 21 Grade 8.

THE WRITING PROCESS

Good home-cooked meals: We all know that creating a satisfying home-cooked meal which follows a hearty recipe and includes fresh ingredients takes time and effort. Just like with good cooking, good writing happens with time and effort. Also, just like good cooking follows a recipe and has the right ingredients, good writing follows a process and uses certain elements. The recipe for good writing is a three-step process: **Prewriting**, **Writing**, **and Post-Writing**. This chapter will discuss the first step in the process: prewriting.

Prewriting is the most important part of the process. It is what you do before you write your composition. Prewriting includes generating your ideas, organizing those ideas, and planning the writing.

THE WRITING PROMPT

The first step in good writing is understanding the directions. A **writing prompt** is a set of directions that present an idea or situation for students to write about. When you read a writing prompt, you need to look for clues about what to include in your composition. What

Planning the Composition

type of composition will it be? What details should be included? Who is the audience? **The writing prompt determines the topic and the structure of your response.** Read the following sample writing prompt carefully. As you read, notice the clues in boldface.

> Your school is sponsoring a composition contest, and you decide to enter. In your composition, you should **explain** the following: **What makes a person a hero?**
>
> Before you begin to write, think about your heroes. What **qualities** do they share? **Why** do you think they are heroes?
>
> Now write a **multi-paragraph** composition for the contest explaining what makes a person a hero.

What type of composition will you be writing?

The word *explain* shows that you will be writing a composition that defines, makes clear, or offers reasons. At this point, you would think about what you know about that type of composition. Think about how to structure the paragraphs of your composition. Think about what you need to explain.

What questions does the writing prompt ask?

The writing prompt asks, "*What makes a person a hero?*" Heroes are the general **topic** of the composition. It is generally what the composition is about. The answer to the writing prompt question will be the **central idea**, or the focus, of your composition: "*A hero is a person who...*" All your ideas should support your explanation of a hero. Think about what you know about heroes. Think about what you would include in your composition.

What supporting details does the writing prompt ask you to include?

The writing prompt asks you to think about the *qualities* a hero has. Think about people that you consider heroes, and ask yourself what traits or characteristics they have in common. These are your **sub-topics**: ideas which support your central idea. The writing prompt also asks *why*. It is asking you to provide reasons why some people are considered heroes. These are details which will support your sub-topics.

Who is the audience?

You should choose the language and tone of your composition based on your intended audience. The writing prompt mentions that this composition is for a school *contest*. You could assume that the **audience,** the people you are writing for, would be judges, perhaps teachers or students from your school. A composition entered in a contest and read by judges requires the use of more formal language.

What is the structure of your composition?

The writing prompt asks you to write a *multi-paragraph* composition. Think about how many paragraphs you need to write. A basic 3-paragraph format works here, but you may choose other formats. We will outline the basic format. The introductory paragraph usually has the **central idea** included. This can be written as the **topic sentence** of the introductory paragraph. In the hero example, the topic sentence could begin this way: "*A hero is someone who...*" The supporting paragraph would have **sub-topics**. In this example of heroes, the sub-topics could be one or two aspects of what you think a hero is. The next section has an example of how a student might structure this composition.

Chapter 3

> **SAMPLE COMPOSITION STRUCTURE**
>
> **Paragraph 1** – Introductory paragraph (introduction) including topic sentence and definition of hero.
>
> **Paragraph 2** – Supporting paragraph describing heroic qualities, or sub-topic(s), and why that makes someone a hero. Sentences providing an example of a hero with this quality should be included as well.
>
> **Paragraph 3** – Conclusion that summarizes the central idea. You should restate your topic sentence and summarize your information.

> **HINT:** Always read the writing prompt more than once. Reading the directions carefully will help you be clear about what you're writing.

Practice 1: Reading the Writing Prompt

Below are 5 questions. Following the five questions are two writing prompts. Read the writing prompts. Then, on a separate sheet of paper, answer the five questions for each writing prompt.

1. What type of composition will you be writing?
2. What questions does the writing prompt ask?
3. What supporting details should you include?
4. Who is the audience?
5. What is the structure of your composition?

A.

> Your local newspaper has asked for student article submissions, and you decide to write one. In your article, you should explore the following question: Does television affect young children positively or negatively?
>
> Before you begin to write, think about television and its effects on young children. What positive effects does TV have? What negative effects does TV have?
>
> Now write a multi-paragraph article for the newspaper discussing the effects of television of young children.

B.

> Your local school board is considering purchasing laptop computers for all students. You have decided to write a letter to your school board explaining how this purchase would affect student performance.
>
> Before you begin to write, think about the advantages and disadvantages of laptop computers for every student. In what ways would school be different? How would it affect student learning?
>
> Now write a multi-paragraph letter to your school board. Be sure to give specific details and to support those details with clear examples and evidence.

Planning the Composition

NOTE: Keep all of your papers from each of the practice sessions in this chapter. You will need to use them in later practices

GENERATING IDEAS

The second step in the prewriting process, after you understand what you need to write about, is to generate ideas. **Brainstorming** and **clustering** are two methods of gathering your ideas for writing. Remember that your purpose in this process is to get as many ideas as you can. No matter which method you choose, you should write down whatever comes into your head. Don't stop to judge, edit, or correct your writing. You want to keep your thoughts flowing. The more ideas you generate now, the better your composition will be.

BRAINSTORMING

Brainstorming is one way to gather ideas for your composition. When you brainstorm, you think about your topic and write down whatever thoughts come into your head. Don't worry about the value of the thoughts now. The goal of brainstorming is to let your thoughts flow freely onto the paper. When you are finished, you should have a list of ideas and details to use in writing your composition. For this reason, brainstorming is also called *listing*. For example, look at the following brainstorming list based on the writing prompt from earlier in the chapter:

What makes a person a hero?		
brave	selflessness	stepping up to the plate
courage	Mother Theresa	power used for good
dedication	helping others	defending freedom
overcoming fear	serving humanity	changing the world
doing what you need to	sense of purpose	Eleanor Roosevelt
overcoming obstacles	changing things	Marie Curie
Harriet Tubman	noticing what's wrong	Susan B. Anthony
can be ordinary people	work hard	make a difference
do extraordinary things	Sojourner Truth	help people
write books	Sally Ride	cure diseases
change laws	inspiring	fight for people's rights

Brainstorming can also help you focus your topic or form a particular opinion about a topic. This happens when you are finished brainstorming, and you look over your ideas and begin to organize them. You may notice that some of your ideas can be grouped together. For example, in the list above, many of the ideas focus on women as heroes. Another student's brainstorming list on the same topic may have generated ideas about war heroes or firefighters.

68

The brainstorming process can be done individually or in a group. Working with your peers to generate ideas can often be helpful for gathering many different ideas, since people have different opinions and experiences. Can you think of some other ways to develop different ideas or find new perspectives?

CLUSTERING

You can generate more ideas for your composition by using **clustering**. Clustering uses connected circles to show your thoughts and the connections they have to other thoughts. Start by writing your topic in a central circle: in this example, a hero. Think about how the topic might act, sound, feel, or appear. Think about what it means to be a hero. Think about examples and situations. Cluster these ideas around the center circle. Circle each idea you write and draw a line connecting it to a related idea. Let your mind wander as you are clustering to try to include as many ideas as you can. You want lots of details here, so write everything down. Look at the following example of clustering.

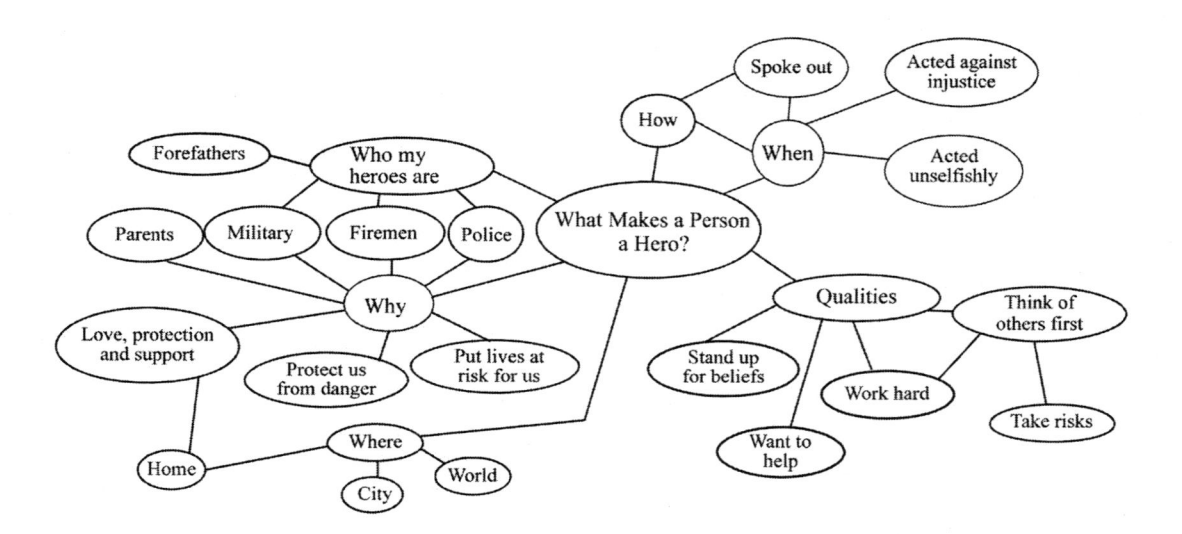

You might notice that this example of clustering has several different examples of heroes. The clustering process can continue many times until you've narrowed your ideas and thought of enough supporting details to write your composition. For example, the student who created this clustering might want to create another cluster about just one of the heroes. Based on the ideas already generated, which hero do you think would be a good choice?

Practice 2: Generating Ideas

Generate ideas for the two writing prompts from Practice 1. Try each of the following two methods: brainstorming and clustering.

ORGANIZING IDEAS

After you have generated your ideas, the third step in the prewriting process is to **organize** your best ideas. You won't use every thought that you wrote down during the generating ideas step in your final composition. Good writers know how to limit their ideas while providing lots of detailed support for those ideas.

Planning the Composition

Practice 3: Organizing Ideas

Look at the ideas that were generated during your brainstorming and clustering, and decide which of your ideas are most important. Underline the ideas that you like, or the ones that seem to be the most important. Cross out (cross out) any ideas that don't fit with your focused topic. You should be able to see a specific topic emerging from these thoughts. Getting them organized will help.

FOCUSING IDEAS

After exploring and organizing your information, the topic of your composition should be focused into a **central idea**. Instead of having a general topic for writing, you should have a very specific idea for your composition.

All of the examples in this chapter came from the same writing prompt:

> Your school is sponsoring a composition contest, and you decide to enter. In your composition, you should **explain** the following: **What makes a person a hero?**
>
> Before you begin to write, think about your heroes. What **qualities** do they share? **Why** do you think they are heroes?

Now write a **multi-paragraph** composition for the contest explaining what makes a person a hero.

Notice how the examples from the *Generating Ideas* section in this chapter were very different responses to the same prompt. These different responses became much more focused during the section on *Organizing Ideas*. Let's review the different focuses that arose from the same writing prompt:

General Topic	Focus	Supporting Details	
What makes a person a hero?	Women heroes	serve humanity fight for beliefs inspire us	Mother Teresa Marie Curie Susan B. Anthony Harriet Tubman Sojourner Truth Sally Ride
	African-American Civil Rights Leaders	fought for equal rights used non-violence to achieve results died for his beliefs	Martin Luther King, Jr.
	Firefighters	take risks to help people work hard dedicated to the community	

Now is the time to develop your focus into a central idea. A **central idea** explains the main idea of an entire composition, or can be formed into a **topic sentence** to explain the main idea of a particular paragraph; the central idea will always be part of the composition's introduction (most often) or conclusion (sometimes). Compositions need a clear central idea. The central idea lets the reader know what you will be writing about in your composition; it provides the topic and the purpose of your writing.

One technique for writing a central idea is to look at the information you've gathered and organized. You can take that information and create a chart such as the one above that breaks it into three sections. Look at the following sentences that state the central ideas for each of the three compositions from our chart. Notice how the sentences include the general topic, the focus, and supporting details.

> Women such as Harriet Tubman and Mother Teresa are heroes because they have served humanity and fought for their beliefs, inspiring people around the world.
>
> Martin Luther King, Jr. fought for equal rights for African-Americans using non-violent protest; he is a hero who died for his beliefs.
>
> Firefighters take risks to help people, and work hard, dedicated to serving others; this makes them heroes.

Before you write your central idea, it is a good idea to read the writing prompt again to be sure you understand the topic clearly and have covered all the ideas presented. In fact, another technique for writing the central idea is to turn the question from the writing prompt into a sentence. That will also give you the topic sentence for the introduction. Notice how the examples below answer questions presented in the prompt.

Writing Prompt:	*What makes a person a hero?*
Topic Sentence:	A person is a hero when she dedicates her time to improving the world
Writing Prompt:	*Write a composition that answers the following question: What is your favorite season? Why is it your favorite?*
Topic Sentence:	My favorite season is autumn when the temperature cools, and the trees glow with color.

Practice 4: Writing the Central Idea

A. **Look at the following writing prompt and possible topic sentences. Decide which sentence is the BEST choice for the central idea of a composition about the prompt. Support your response by discussing what makes each sentence correct or not.**

Planning the Composition

> The school newspaper needs personal student stories for a new column in the next issue. You decide to submit a story answering the question: What was your most embarrassing moment?
>
> Before you begin writing, think about an embarrassing experience you had. Where were you? What feelings did you experience?
>
> Now write a multi-paragraph story for the newspaper telling about your most embarrassing moment. Be sure to give detailed information so that your readers will understand what happened.

Possible Topic Sentences:
1. Embarrassing moments happen to us all.
2. I am going to write about my most embarrassing moment.
3. My most embarrassing moment happened when I was ten years old.
4. While vacationing with my family at the beach, I experienced an embarrassing moment that left me feeling awkward and foolish.

B. **Look at the following chart. On a separate sheet of paper, write a topic sentence for each of the focused topics.**

General Topic	Focus Topic	Supporting Details
Coral Reefs	1. Types of Reefs	Barrier reefs Coral Atolls
	2. Famous Reefs	Great Barrier Reef off Australian coast South Pacific ocean has the most reefs.
	3. Reefs in Danger	water pollution increased water temperature
	4. Life on the Reef	reef provides shelter for many animals interdependency

STRUCTURING YOUR COMPOSITION

The next step in the writing process is **structuring your composition**. For this, you take the following steps:

    1) Put all your words together to make sentences.

    2) Put the sentences together to make paragraphs.

    3) Put paragraphs together to make a composition.

As mentioned earlier in the chapter, a basic three-paragraph composition should include three main parts: **introduction**, **body**, and **conclusion**.

>The **introduction** is the first paragraph of your composition. This is where you introduce your topic by writing your central idea. A good introductory paragraph also captures the readers' attention, so that they will want to keep on reading.
>
>The **body** of this type of composition has one supporting paragraph. This paragraph has a topic sentence that focuses on a specific detail(s) related to your central idea. The paragraph is filled out with information and examples to support the detail(s).
>
>The **conclusion** is the last paragraph of your composition. This paragraph restates your central idea and summarizes your main points. No new information should be written in a conclusion.

ORGANIZATIONAL PATTERNS

A well-structured paragraph or composition is easy to read because the ideas are linked together, leading the reader from one idea to the next. The basic three-paragraph composition can be further organized into one of five **organizational patterns**: main idea and supporting detail, comparison and contrast, chronological order, cause and effect, or order of importance. The best structure for your composition depends on the topic, what point you want to make about the topic, what ideas you have to tell about the topic, and how those ideas are related to each other.

MAIN IDEA AND SUPPORTING DETAIL

This common pattern is probably similar to the writing you have done before. In this type of organization, details support a main idea just as the walls of a house support the roof. The main idea is stated first as a topic sentence or thesis statement. Then the rest of the paragraph or composition is spent developing that idea by giving details like facts, examples, and reasons. The following example of a paragraph begins with a topic sentence stating the main idea; the sentences within the paragraph provide examples, or supporting details.

> *Marie Curie is a hero. She is a hero to many scientists because of her ground breaking research into radioactivity. She is hero to many women because she was the first woman to win the Nobel Prize. Marie Curie was a brilliant physicist and researcher. She was a dedicated wife and mother. She helped injured soldiers during World War I with the use of X-ray machines. She used her fame to speak around the world about worthy causes. Marie Curie helped promote world peace by serving on the council of the League of Nations. Despite her great achievements, she was very modest and considered her life uneventful. Marie Curie's life may have been uneventful to her, but it was heroic to others.*

COMPARISON AND CONTRAST

This pattern is used when the writer wants to compare two subjects to show the similarities or differences. In the three-paragraph composition, there are two ways a writer can use this pattern.

Planning the Composition

One way to compare and contrast is to write about one subject completely before writing about the other. Using our example from earlier in the chapter about Civil Rights leaders, the student could write the first part of the body paragraph about Martin Luther King, Jr. and then write the second half of the paragraph about Malcolm X.

Another way to use this pattern is first to describe all the similarities between the subjects, and then to describe the differences. The following paragraph continues the comparison of Martin Luther King, Jr. and Malcolm X.

> *Martin Luther King Jr. and Malcolm X were both heroic leaders during the Civil Rights Movement. Both leaders had great speaking skills. Their ability to stir up emotion in their listeners helped them in their cause. Although both men believed in equality for African-Americans, they disagreed in how to get it. King believed in non-violent protest. Malcolm X believed that equal rights must be gained by any means necessary, including violence. Their different faiths gave them strength. King was a Baptist minister, while Malcolm X was a follower of Islam. Both displayed heroic traits, inspiring their followers to continue on with their work even after each of them was killed for his beliefs.*

CHRONOLOGICAL ORDER

This pattern structures the information in order of time. Narratives or stories are often organized with this pattern. A story makes more sense when the events are written in the order that they occur. The following paragraph also uses chronological order to explain a procedure.

> *Baking a pumpkin pie is a great holiday tradition that is easy to do. Begin with a unbaked pie shell. Preheat your oven to 350 degrees F. While your oven is heating, prepare the pumpkin filling. Add one can pumpkin filling, one can evaporated milk, two eggs, and two teaspoons cinnamon to a bowl. Stir ingredients until well combined. Pour into the unbaked pastry shell and bake for one hour. Sit back and enjoy as the aroma of a freshly-baked pie fills your home.*

CAUSE AND EFFECT

This organizational pattern helps you make connections between a result (effect) and the events (cause) that came before it. The usual structure of the cause and effect pattern begins with a statement giving the cause of something, and then you discuss the specific effects. Look at how the paragraph below shows the connection between a student's success and her hard work.

> *Nathan was thrilled to learn that he had been awarded the Principal's Honor Award. He had been working hard all semester. He had good grades in every subject. Nathan spent extra time studying after school. He often assisted other students in the tutoring center. He also had perfect attendance. It felt like all his efforts had been rewarded.*

ORDER OF IMPORTANCE

This is the most common organizational pattern. Every detail included in a paragraph should support the topic of that paragraph. However, some details and examples are more important than others. To give those details more emphasis, they are placed at the beginning of a paragraph. Newspaper articles, for example, are often written in this pattern to give readers the most important information first.

> *New England Patriots win Super Bowl 39! On a frigid Sunday night, they defeated the Eagles 24-21. Defense played a large role for both teams. But quarterback Brady and his wide receiver Branch played tag team with the football—piling up enough yards for Branch to break the super bowl record. Did you say Super Bowl? More like Super, Super Bowl. New England now has claim to having a legitimate football dynasty. Not to mention this year's sports event brought high class to the gridiron—Sir Paul McCartney performed well-loved hits and brought the crowd in under his spell.*

Practice 5: Structuring the Composition

Look at the two topics from Practice 1 and decide what organizational pattern each composition should follow. Explain your answers on a separate sheet of paper.

CHAPTER 3 REVIEW: PLANNING THE COMPOSITION

A. Read the sample writing prompts below. With a highlighter pen, go over the prompt and highlight the key words that provide clues to what type of composition you will be writing. Then, on a separate sheet of paper, answer the following questions for each prompt:

1. What type of composition will you be writing?

2. What questions does the writing prompt ask?

3. What supporting details should you include?

4. Who is the audience?

5. What is the structure of your composition?

a.

> Your English teacher has asked you to write a composition that describes your favorite holiday.
>
> Before you begin to write, think about all the different holidays. Which one do you like best? What do you like about this holiday? Are there specific traditions that make the holiday your favorite?
>
> Now write a multi-paragraph composition describing your favorite holiday. Be sure to give specific details and to support those details with clear examples.

Planning the Composition

b.

> As a class assignment, you need to write a composition that provides instructions about how to do something. Your composition could explain how to cook a favorite food, make something, play a sport, do an activity, or complete a specific job.
>
> Before you begin to write, think about something you know how to do well. What are the main steps a person should follow? How should you organize the instructions so that they are easy to follow?
>
> Now write a multi-paragraph explanation giving instructions about how to do something. Be sure to provide all the information needed for a person to complete the action you are describing.

B. Read the sample writing prompts from above again. Then, on separate sheets of paper, generate ideas for these topics using brainstorming or clustering.

C. Look at each of the writing prompts from Part A again. For each prompt, organize your ideas from Part B, underlining key ideas and crossing out unneeded ideas.

D. Using the ideas you generated and organized in Parts B and C, write topic sentences for each of the writing prompts on a separate sheet of paper.

E. Look at the topic sentences you wrote in Part D. Decide on the appropriate structure/organizational pattern for each of the compositions on those topics. Write that structure next to each topic sentence.

NOTE: Keep your papers from this Chapter Review for use in other chapters of this book.

Chapter 4
Writing the Composition

LOUISIANA READING BENCHMARKS ADDRESSED IN THIS CHAPTER INCLUDE:	
ELA-2-M1	Writing multi paragraph compositions (150–200 words) that clearly imply a central idea with supporting details in a logical, sequential order (1, 4)
ELA-3-M3	Demonstrating standard English structure and usage by using correct and varied sentence types (e.g., compound and compound-complex) and effective personal styles (1, 4, 5)

The second step in the writing process is writing. It may seem like an obvious step, but just as there are many ways to cook foods, there are many ways to go about writing compositions. There are also many individual skills involved in writing a composition. The more you practice, the easier writing will be. This is especially important with timed writing, like an in-class writing assignment or the LEAP 21 Grade 8.

DRAFTING THE COMPOSITION

In the previous chapter, you learned the prewriting stage of the writing process. You have read the writing prompt, generated topic ideas, organized your focused ideas, written a topic sentence, and planned the structure of your composition. Now it is time to write the **draft**. Writing a draft is a way of getting your ideas on paper so you can work with them. A draft is like the first pancake out of the pan—it can be messy or a little underdone. You will continue to improve a draft in the next stage of the writing process. When you write a draft, you want to focus on capturing the meaning from all of your planning in the prewriting stage. You already have a sense of where you are going; you just need to show it on paper. Using the women heroes' topic from page here is one method of drafting a basic three-paragraph composition:

Paragraph 1: For the **introduction**, write the topic sentence. Next, write one to two sentences that connect the topic to sub-topic(s). Make sure your sentences blend together to form a strong introduction.

Paragraph 2: For the **body**, use the subtopic(s) to form the paragraph, expanding the subtopic(s) with details. Write two to four sentences to explain and provide examples. Make sure that the sentences also support the main topic.

Writing the Composition

Paragraph 3: For the **conclusion**, reread the composition.
1. Choose two to three of the most important ideas.
2. Summarize the ideas in three sentences.
3. Restate your central idea using different words.

> [Mother Teresa and Harriet Tubman both <u>served humanity</u>.] Mother Teresa spen her entire life helping the sick and the poor. She founded The Missions of Charity in 1948, who [which] worked to treat the sick and dying people, especially children, in India. Harriet Tubman spent ten years leading escaped slaves to freedom. She was a nurse [also served as] during the Civil War. Both women helped make people's lives better.

> [Harriet Tubman and Mother Teresa had to <u>fight for their beliefs</u>.] Harriet Tubman believed that every human deserved freedom. She believed that slavery was wrong, and risked her own life to help free slaves. Bounty hunters were offered a lot of money to capture her ~~for these things~~, but she kept returning to the slave states anyway. Mother Teresa believed that every human should be able to die in peace and comfort. Mother Teresa founded many organisations and shelters to help people with illnesses such as leprosy and AIDS. These were the people no one wanted to help. She often had to convince governments to let her to set up these shelters. She spent a lot of time raising awareness and money to help those in need.

> [The lives of Mother Teresa and Harriet Tubman have <u>inspired many people</u> around the world to take action for their beliefs.] Mother Teresa was awarded the Nobel peace prize in 1979. After hearing of her good words, many people began to offer aid through her organizations around the world. Harriet Tubman was one of many people working the Underground Railroad. She encouraged others to take risks by courageously coming to the aid of escaped slaves.

As you can see in the sample draft composition, there are errors in writing. That is acceptable in a draft. The format, however, is in good shape. The **central idea** of the composition is clearly stated in the first paragraph, the **introduction**. The **sub-topics** *serving humanity and fighting for beliefs, which inspires people*, are also stated. They are explained more in the **body** paragraph of the composition.

The sub-topics in the second paragraph, the **body**, are <u>underlined</u>, and the topic sentence is in brackets [like this]. This sample shows how details support the sub-topics. The sub-topics now have complete paragraphs which support the central idea. Notice how the paragraph begins with a topic sentence and how the sub-topics are supported by explanation and examples.

In paragraph 3, the writer concludes the composition. This **conclusion** reminds readers of the most important ideas. The writer also restates the central idea, which is the kind of qualities heroes possess.

REMEMBER: A well-written composition responds to the writing prompt with

- a clear topic sentence
- an engaging introduction, supporting body, and conclusion
- a detailed discussion focused completely on the topic

Practice 1: Drafting the Composition

In Chapter 3, Practices 4 and 5, you wrote a topic sentence and chose an organizational pattern for the following writing prompt:

> The school newspaper needs personal student stories for a new column in the next issue. You decide to submit a story answering the question: What was your most embarrassing moment?
>
> Before you begin writing, think about an embarrassing experience you had. Where were you? What feelings did you experience?
>
> Now write a multi-paragraph story for the newspaper telling about your most embarrassing moment. Be sure to give detailed information so that your readers will understand what happened.

Using the prewriting activities you have completed on this topic, write a draft of the composition on a separate sheet of paper

NOTE: Keep all of your papers from each of the practice sessions in this chapter in a portfolio. You will need to use them in later practices.

A draft of a composition is not supposed to be perfect. It is your first attempt at getting all your ideas onto paper into an organized pattern. The rest of this chapter will help you improve your draft by providing practice in the following writing skills:

- Writing Introductions
- Elaboration of the Topic
- Writing Conclusions
- Using a Variety of Sentence Structures
- Using Transitional Words

WRITING INTRODUCTIONS

You learned how to write a basic introduction in the section before; however, a good writer develops the introduction to do more than just present the topic. A good **introduction** does three things:

- grabs the interest of the reader
- introduces the topic
- states the central idea

Writing the Composition

The introductory paragraph is one of the most important parts of a composition; it gives a first impression. The introduction sets up the composition's structure by introducing the topic and sub-topics. After reading an introduction, a reader should be able to name the author's purpose and tone. Use one of the following methods to begin your introductory paragraph. These methods will help get your readers' attention.

ASK A QUESTION

Asking a question at the beginning of a composition immediately forces your reader to start thinking. It sets up a curiosity that encourages the reader to keep reading. Read the following example:

> Can you imagine paying $2,500 for a family pet? Bulldogs are such valued pets that some people don't think twice about paying that much to own a prized puppy. However, a lot of money is wasted if you aren't able to keep the dog. Popularity of a dog is not a good enough reason to bring one into your family's home. Choosing a family pet is a difficult decision—one that should be based on knowledge, not emotion. Just because an animal is cute, does not mean it's the right pet for you. Before you choose a bulldog or any pet, you should consider the advantages and disadvantages of living with pets.

This introduction accomplishes all an introduction should. From the first sentence, the topic is clear. This composition will be discussing pets. The question draws readers in and encourages them to keep reading to find out more. The introduction clearly shows the writer's purpose is to educate the readers. The final sentence of the introduction states the central idea of the composition, the advantages and disadvantages of owning a pet.

USE A QUOTATION

A **well-chosen quote**, one that relates to your topic, can be a great way to capture the reader's attention. Quotes, especially from famous or respected people, add a sense of authority to a composition. Notice how the quote used in this introduction blends with the topic of this personal narrative.

> Henry David Thoreau said, "Go confidently in the direction of your dreams. Live the life you have imagined." Sometimes it's hard to be confident when you are working to make a dream come true. When I was ten, I decided I wanted to play soccer for a select, traveling soccer team. It seemed like all the other players on the team had more experience and better skills. However, this was my dream, and I was going to make it happen.

STATE A FACT

A **statistic** or **fact** that surprises or shocks readers will catch their attention and make them want to continue reading.

> More than 283,000 babies, sisters, brothers, mothers, fathers, aunts, uncles, cousins, and friends died together on December 26, 2004 because of the tsunamis that hit Indonesia. The tsunami was the result of a 9.0 earthquake, the largest worldwide in four decades.

It is hard to believe that an earthquake in the middle of the ocean caused so much death and disaster. Could the deaths from the tsunami have been prevented? Natural disasters happen all the time. Human life is lost. There are several things, however, that can be done to prevent the loss of life in future natural disasters.

This introduction begins with an alarming fact that engages the readers and gets them emotionally involved. When readers are emotionally moved, they are hooked. The introduction goes on to involve readers more by asking them what could have been done to prevent the deaths. This question leads them to the central idea of the composition, what can be done to prevent deaths from natural disasters.

GIVE A DESCRIPTION

A **vivid, detailed description** can make a fantastic introduction, setting the mood and exciting the reader's interest. Read the following example:

The aroma of freshly roasted peanuts and popcorn wafts through the ballpark. On the field, your team makes a triple play and the crowd goes wild! This is a regular weekend activity for many sports lovers today. But times are changing. You don't have to run around in the hot sun to play baseball anymore. Thanks to modern gaming technology, you can flip on your television and pop a game of video baseball into your game system. Will you head to the ballpark for a pick-up game or pick up your joystick and sit down in front of the TV? Before you decide, think about the differences between baseball and video baseball. Both require different equipment, build different skills, and have different dangers.

Notice how the opening line of this paragraph immediately leads the reader to topic of baseball. The description uses sensory images to help the reader experience the ballpark. The introduction presents the comparison/contrast structure of the composition and ends with the statement of the central idea. This idea is the differences between baseball and video baseball.

TELL A STORY

When you begin a composition with a story, it needs to be a brief story that connects to your topic. The goal is to interest your reader in what you have to say.

One afternoon last year, I was walking home from school when I heard a strange noise coming from the overgrown bushes by the playground. When I went to investigate, I discovered an abandoned kitten. He was thin and weak, and making a sad sound. Not sure what to do, I picked him up and rushed home with him. My mom and I nursed him back to health, and he became a treasured member of our family. This experience taught me a lot about responsibility.

Writing the Composition

The telling of the rescued kitten draws in the reader and introduces the topic at the same time. We can see by the last sentence that the central idea of the composition will be responsibility.

> **HINT:** Never begin your introduction with the words, "I am going to write about…" or "The purpose of my composition is…" You want to capture the attention of your readers, not bore them.

Practice 2: Writing Introductions

Write an introduction for each of the writing prompts below. Before you begin writing, be sure to use what you have learned in the previous chapter to generate ideas and form a central idea with three supporting details. Use a different type of lead for each introduction.

1. Recall a time when you felt proud of yourself. Write about the experience, what happened, and how it made you feel.
2. What are your feelings about war? Write a composition that explains your position.
3. Describe a favorite childhood pet or toy. What did it look like? How did it act? Why was it your favorite?
4. What is your definition of normal?
5. Many students have a difficult time in middle school because of bullying. What advice could you offer a student who has been the victim of a bully?

NOTE: Keep your introductory paragraphs for use in Practices 3 & 4.

ELABORATION AND SUPPORT IN THE BODY PARAGRAPH

During the prewriting stage of the writing process, you generate many ideas for a composition. However, once you begin writing the draft, you may find gaps in your composition, areas where you lack information. You may discover your topic needs more explanation. Now is the time for elaboration. **Elaboration** means to go into detail, explain, or say more about a topic. Once you have decided on your focus, written your introduction with a central idea, and chosen your sub-topics, how do you elaborate on those topics? Here are four methods of elaboration:

PROVIDE SPECIFIC DETAILS

Specific details provide answers to questions the reader might have about the topic. A good way to develop specific details is to think of questions a reader might ask about your topic and then write the answers. These answers can then be written into specific details to elaborate on your topic. Here is an example

Topic: Cats are Better Pets Than Dogs	
Questions	**Responses**
Why are cats better?	Cats are better behaved.
Is their behavior better?	They don't bark or jump.
How do they act?	They don't need to be trained as much.
Is there less responsibility?	They are cleaner creatures.
What kinds of responsibility do cats require?	They don't need as much entertainment.
	They don't need to be walked.
	They don't need as much supervision.

From this list, you can develop multiple paragraphs, including a paragraph like the following:

> A cat's behavior makes it a better choice for a pet than a dog. Cats can entertain themselves and spend much of their time on self-grooming. Dogs need lots of attention and entertainment. Cats are content to be left home, especially with a feline friend. Cats don't bark when they are disturbed, in need or happy. Their quiet meows and purrs let you know they are happy. A cat's gentle rubbing against your leg is much more pleasant than a drooling dog jumping in your face. Cats' calm behavior makes them great choices for pets.

INCLUDE RELEVANT FACTS

Facts are statements proven to be true. They help support your central idea and add validity to your composition. The following facts would be useful to elaborate on the comparison of cats and dogs:

- Both humans and cats have identical regions in the brain responsible for emotion.
- *A cat's brain is more similar to a person's brain than that of a dog.*
- It has been scientifically proven that stroking a cat can lower one's blood pressure.
- Tests done by the Behavioral Department of the Museum of Natural History conclude that while a dog's memory lasts about 5 minutes, a cat's recall can last as long as 16 hours.
- Abraham Lincoln loved cats. He had four of them while he lived in the White House.

GIVE EXAMPLES

Examples help show your ideas to readers. Rather then just telling them information, providing an example demonstrates an idea, making it clearer. Here is an example:

> When choosing a cat it is important to choose a breed that fits in with your household and lifestyle. Different households suit different cats. For example, a household with a large family would be a good choice for a Manx or Siberian cat. These cats are lively

Writing the Composition

and playful. They need only a little time and attention, but are loving and devoted. Manx and Siberian cats are also easy to handle, which is very important if you have small children. A household with older people would be a good choice for Birman or Maine Coon cats. These cats are relaxed to the point of being slothful, but are very loving. They are also more vocal than other breeds, which makes them good talkers.

SHARE AN EXPERIENCE

Can a story explain your topic? Sometime experiences, told as brief stories, are the best way to elaborate on a topic by providing a real-life occurrence to show your ideas. Here is an example of elaboration using an experience to support the topic about cats:

> Cats can be fantastic pets, especially for the elderly or homebound. I remember my grandmother and her cat Pepper. Pepper was her daily companion for many years. He would travel from room to room with her all day. Laundry day was their favorite. Grandma would rain the dirty laundry down on Pepper's head and laugh as he rolled and batted at the clothing. She loved having his loyal company in what could have been her lonely, daily chores.

GUIDELINES FOR ELABORATION AND SUPPORT:
- Elaboration is more than restating your topic sentence.
- Elaboration must be related to the topic.
- Elaboration should include specific details, not general statements.

> **HINT:** Remember that elaboration is a way to add details to the paragraphs in your composition's body that support your central idea.

Practice 3: Elaboration

A. Read the paragraphs below and decide if the topics have enough elaboration. Examine whether the elaboration follows the guidelines set above. Write your paragraph evaluations on a separate sheet of paper. Rewrite any paragraphs that need improvement on a separate sheet of paper.

1. Exercise is important for physical and mental health. Eating well gives your body energy. Complex-carbohydrates such as whole wheat bread and fruit are better for you than simple carbohydrates such as sugar and white flour. Vegetables are really good for you too; they provide important vitamins. If you don't eat well, then taking a multi-vitamin can help, but it is not a substitute for good eating and exercise. Exercising for an hour a day, five days a week will keep you healthy and strong.

2. All citizens should use their right to free speech. Free speech is an important part of the democratic process. This process began when our country was founded. This way citizens had a part in the governing of the nation. Elected officials represent the people, and should do what the people want. However, people have to speak up about what they want. Otherwise, their ideas are never

heard, and the elected officials do what they want. One important way citizens can use their free speech is by writing letters to their senators and representatives to express their opinions.

3. California is a great place to take a family vacation. California has many different climates that offer many different family activities. Families can visit the beach in sunny San Diego, or go skiing in Lake Tahoe. California coasts are home to scores of sea creatures from seals and sea lions to sharks and starfish. Many environmentalists have worked hard to protect the coastal life on California's shore, often coming into conflict with housing developers.

B. In Practice 2, you developed three supporting details for each of the writing topics. Use the methods described above to elaborate on those details for one or more of the topics.

WRITING CONCLUSIONS

The ending of a composition is just as important as the beginning. However, because it is the last part of a composition, it is often the most poorly written. You want your composition to end as strongly as it began. A well-written **conclusion** ties the main ideas in the composition together and leaves readers with a clear understanding of the importance of the topic. A good conclusion does three things:

- restates the central idea
- summarizes the main ideas
- gives readers something to think about

There are many ways to give your readers something to ponder. In the same way you captured the readers' attention in the introduction, you can continue to have their attention in the conclusion. A conclusion can end with a quotation, an anecdote, or one of the following:

CALL FOR ACTION

One effective way to end your composition is to urge the reader to **take some action**. Consider the following example that ends the composition on pets:

> If you want an animal to become a part of your family be sure to consider the advantages and disadvantages before making a purchase. A dog can be a great friend and protector. However, that same dog requires a great deal of responsibility and time. Spend some time at your local animal shelter or research animal types on the Internet; then you can be sure everyone will be happy.

This conclusion successfully completes the composition by restating the central idea and summarizing the most important advantages and disadvantage to pet ownership. Then it asks the readers to take action for themselves by researching.

MAKE A PREDICTION

A good conclusion does more than summarize; it also keeps your readers thinking about the topic. **Making a prediction** at the end of the composition is a good way to do this.

Read the conclusion to the comparison/contrast composition on baseball and video baseball:

Writing the Composition

> Baseball and video baseball are similar in many ways; they are both the same game. However, they are different in many ways. Baseball develops many physical skills, but requires a team and strength. Video baseball develops more mental skills, and it requires only a game system. Whichever you choose, baseball or video baseball, you are sure to have a good time playing.

This conclusion reminds readers of the main similarities and differences between the two forms of baseball. Then the prediction at the end makes a generalization. It predicts that readers will enjoy both forms of the game.

ASK A QUESTION

The conclusion summarizes the information already in the composition. It should leave your readers with enough information to consider your points. Leaving readers with a **question** lets them consider what they think and feel about your topic. Read the following example:

> I learned a lot about responsibility that year. Raising Cedar from kitten to cat taught me more than just how to care for another creature. I learned to give of my time and myself. I learned how much power I had. Who wouldn't want to experience that?

This reminds readers of why your topic is important. It also allows them an opportunity to keep thinking.

> **HINT:** Never introduce new or unrelated material in a conclusion. Conclusions should wrap things up!

Practice 4:   Writing Conclusions

Using your ideas from Practices 2 and 3, write conclusions to match the introductions and supporting paragraphs you wrote. Try out different types of conclusions.

SENTENCE STRUCTURE VARIETY

Another ingredient in the recipe for writing a good composition is mixing in different kinds of sentences. This is called **sentence variety;** it means using sentences of different lengths and structures. Simple sentences get your meaning across easily. More complicated, or complex sentences, add interest to your composition. Using both forms gives your composition sentence variety.

COMBINE SENTENCES

Combining sentences is a good way to add variety to your sentence structure. A paragraph with short, simple sentences may be easy to understand, but it is not very interesting to read. Read the following paragraph.

There was a hurricane. The hurricane struck the coast in Louisiana. The hurricane struck at night. The hurricane had high winds and rain. The hurricane caused major flooding. The hurricane caused a lot of damage. The hurricane destroyed many houses. The hurricane destroyed businesses. The hurricane caused many injuries. The hurricane caused a few deaths.

This paragraph has good, solid information. The sentences are short and so are easy to read, but the flow of the paragraph is choppy. This takes away from the impact of the information. Creating some longer sentences would improve the flow and the impact of the paragraph.

The hurricane struck the coastal Louisiana town in the middle of the night. The high winds and rains caused extensive flooding and damage as it swept through the town destroying homes and businesses. Numerous injuries were reported in addition to a few deaths.

Both paragraphs tell the same story, but the second one is more interesting to read. The sentence variety has added interest and impact. The writer created longer sentences by combining, or putting together, some of the short sentences. Sentence combining is done in many ways:

- **Use a semicolon** to combine two equally important, related sentences.
- The hurricane had high winds and rain; therefore, it caused extensive flooding and damage.
- **Use a conjunction** to compare or contrast two ideas in a sentence.
- The hurricane caused not only major property damage, but also numerous injuries.
- **Use a series** to combine three or more similar ideas.
- The hurricane struck the coastal town causing major flooding, extensive damage, multiple injuries, and a few deaths.
- **Use a relative pronoun** to introduce less important ideas.
- The hurricane, which struck in the middle of the night, left a path of destruction in the coastal Louisiana town.
- **Use an introductory phrase or clause** for less important ideas.
- Because it struck in the middle of the night, the horrible extent of the hurricane damage was not apparent until morning.

USE DIFFERENT BEGINNINGS

In the English language, the most common sentence structure includes subject, verb, and object, in that order. Adjectives, adverbs, and different phrases are often added to the middle or end of this structure. Using this same structure over and over can become boring and may even irritate readers. To add variety to sentences, start some with a part of speech other than the subject. Look at the following examples:

Begin with an adverb:

Replace "The hurricane's winds suddenly blew the roof off the house."

with "Suddenly, the hurricane's winds blew the roof off the house."

Writing the Composition

Begin with a prepositional phrase:

Replace "The governor saw many destroyed homes on a tour of the damage."

with "On a tour of the damage, the governor saw many destroyed homes."

Begin with a participial phrase:

Replace "The hurricane swept through the town, leaving a trail of destruction."

with "Leaving a trail of destruction, the hurricane swept through the town."

These examples show how to add a variety of sentence structures to your composition. The examples also show how a modifier is best understood when it is placed near the noun or verb it is modifying.

EXPAND WITH DETAILS

Expanding a sentence with details is a great way to add variety to your sentences. It will also improve your writing by making it more vibrant. You can add more details to a basic sentence in five ways:

Add adjectives or adverbs:
*The **high-speed** winds **effortlessly** tore off the roof.*

Add prepositional phrases:
*We sat **with our ears covered in the basement** until the storm passed.*

Add participial phrases:
***Holding our breath**, we hoped our home would endure the storm.*

Add subordinate clauses:
***When we finally came up from the basement**, we discovered what was left of our home.*

Add relative clauses:
*Our home, **which had been in our family for generations**, was in rubble.*

USE A QUESTION OR EXCLAMATION

Replacing a simple, quiet sentence with an explosive or questioning one will add emotion to your writing. Using an exclamation mark (!) adds excitement. Using a question mark (?) adds to a reader's curiosity. Sentence variety is part of the recipe for good writing. Compare the following examples:

Example: I didn't like it when my childhood home was destroyed by the hurricane. It was the worst feeling I've ever experienced.

Example: How would you like having your childhood home destroyed by a hurricane? It's the worst feeling I've ever experienced**!**

Practice 5: Sentence Variety

Rewrite the following paragraphs by varying the sentence structure. Share the results with the class or your teacher.

1. There are many uses for trees. Trees are practical. Chocolate, cinnamon, cloves, nutmeg, mace, olive oil, coconuts, rubber, turpentine, plastics, and cork are all products of trees. Other uses include lumber, mulch, paper, medicines, chemicals, maple sugar, fruits and nuts. The list goes on. Almost every part of the tree can be used. These products make our lives better.

2. Trees are versatile. We have to safeguard them. Many trees take many years to replace. The hardwoods take a long time. Hardwoods provide beautiful lumber for houses and furniture. Trees are a renewable resource. They will last for generations. We have to manage the forests properly.

3. We need to protect trees. Cities and counties nationwide now have tree ordinances. It is not enough just to replace the ones that are cut. We have to allow the trees with longer life spans to live as long as possible. The ordinances, or laws, provide protection for the existing trees. The laws require sufficient replanting when trees are cut down.

4. Dead trees serve a purpose too. Wild animals use dead wood for nesting. Woodpeckers dig holes in only dead, standing trees. They use the holes for nests. Rotted trees help replenish the soil. Dead trees provide food resources for many types of wildlife.

STYLE/AUDIENCE AWARENESS

- Write with your audience (the person or group identified by the topic) in mind.
- Use vocabulary (words) that expresses your meaning well.
- Use sentences that make your main idea interesting to your audience.

Once authors are clear about their purpose for writing, they must consider their audience—the person(s) who will read what they write. No matter what the piece of writing will be, there is always an audience of some type. It can be one particular person, a specific group of people, or a larger unknown audience. Knowing the audience gives authors information that is important to consider when making decisions about the way they will write. For instance, if an author is writing a book about the planets, it is very important to know whether he/she is writing for elementary school children or college students. Authors must use appropriate vocabulary and use sentences that keep the audience interested.

> **Example:** Topic: You're thinking about buying your first car and you research buyers' reviews about their new cars. Read the following two reviews written by the same person. Try to develop a picture of the audience that the writer had in mind.

Passage 1

Since you're in the market for a new car, I wanted to tell you about mine. My new car is cool! It's a 2004 Puma. It's got a 5-liter overhead cam engine with multi-port fuel injection. It can do 0–60 mph in 5 seconds. With that much engine, passing cars on the highway is a breeze, but handling corners on back roads is a little trickier than with my old truck. I love the rush I get when I'm cruising around with my new wheels. You should consider buying one, too.

Writing the Composition

Passage 2

Since you're in the market for a new car, I wanted to tell you about mine. My new car is the best one I've owned. It's a 2004 Puma. This sporty two-door is canary yellow with electric blue racing stripes and silver mag wheels. It has cordovan leather seats and a concert hall-quality sound system. The sunroof is the perfect finishing touch. You should see the looks I get when I'm cruising around with my new wheels. You should consider buying one, too.

In both paragraphs, the author is telling someone about a new car, but each paragraph includes very different details about the car. The passages differ because the author is writing for two different audiences with different interests, vocabulary, and knowledge. Passage 1 would most likely appeal to a person interested in the car's performance and speed. Passage 2 would most likely appeal to a person who is more interested in appearances and style.

Practice 1: Audience Awareness

1. Look at passage 1, what details about the car suggest it is written for an audience interested in speed and performance?
2. What descriptive words (vocabulary) in passage 2 suggest it is written for an audience interested in style and appearances?
3. How does the author capture and keep the interest of his audience?
4. Based on the differences in the passages, how would you describe the intended audience of each paragraph?
5. Write your own new car review for two different audiences. Write one for your friend and one for your parents or teacher.

SENTENCE FORMATION

- Write in complete sentences and use a variety of sentence patterns.

Sentence Formation or structure is an important part of writing style. Some authors write in a style that uses short, simple sentences (a single independent clause containing a subject and a verb). Others use complex sentences, or sentences that contain an independent clause as well as subordinate clause(s). The following examples describe the same event. Compare the two examples for sentence structure, and discuss how that structure contributes to the writer's style.

> **Example 1: Simple Sentences:** Swallows filled the trees. The noise was deafening.

> **Example 2: Complex Sentences:** Hundreds of migrating swallows dropped from the sky and blended into nearby trees, causing a din that had residents shouting at each other to be heard.

Both of these styles describe something clearly and express the event well. One way is not necessarily better than the other. However, it is a good idea to vary sentence structures in your essay for the writing test. Too many simple sentences can be boring and static and too many complex sentences can be too wordy and hard to follow. It's a good idea to incorporate both simple and complex sentences into your essay to keep it interesting. So mix it up!

The example below combines both simple and complex sentence structures. See if you can identify the simple and complex sentences.

Example 3: Simple and Complex Sentences: Hoping the disgust and dread he was feeling did not show on his face, Greg slowly stirred the glutinous green split pea soup his father had made. "Try it," his father gently commanded, watching him intently from across the small dining room table. Summoning all the courage he could muster, Greg held his breath and brought a small spoonful to his mouth. He took a bite. Swallowing hard, the soup slid down his throat like phlegm, coating it with a slimy film. "So, how is it?" his father asked. Ignoring the bitter aftertaste of the horrid soup, Greg smiled up at his father. "It's great, Dad."

Practice 2: Sentence Formation

A.) Read the following sentences. Write an S next to simple sentences and a C next to complex sentences.

1. He ate his lunch hungrily.
2. When the clock struck eight, she ran home to avoid being grounded.
3. After dinner, and before the movie, we stopped by the ice cream parlor.
4. The dog walked very slowly.
5. It feels good to exercise.
6. Write a simple sentence.
7. Write a complex sentence.

CHAPTER 4 REVIEW:

Part A For the Chapter Review in Chapter 3: Planning the Composition, you prepared brainstorming lists, freewriting samples, clustering diagrams, and questions for the four prompts below. You also wrote topic sentences to focus your central idea and chose an organizational pattern for your composition. Now, based on these prewriting activities and what you learned in this chapter, write a draft of a composition for one or more of the writing prompts. Use the skills you practiced in this chapter. You may also use the LEAP 21 ELA Writer's Checklist on **PAGE******.**

Writing the Composition

A.

> Your local community center is creating a youth position for its kindergarten after-school program. The position requires a written application including a descriptive composition that tells about yourself, your experiences with young children, and your educational goals.
>
> Before you begin to write, think about why you would be well suited for this position. What skills do you have? How would the children benefit from your presence? How would this position prepare you for your future?
>
> Now write a multi-paragraph composition for the job at the community center. Be sure to give specific details and to support those details with clear examples.

B.

> Your English teacher has asked you to write a composition that describes your favorite holiday or festival day.
>
> Before you begin to write, think about all the different holidays. Which one do you like best? What do you like about this holiday? Are there specific traditions that make the holiday your favorite?
>
> Now write a multi-paragraph composition describing your favorite holiday. Be sure to give specific details and to support those details with clear examples.

C.

> As a class assignment, you need to write a composition that provides instructions about how to do something. Your composition could explain how to cook a favorite food, make something, play a sport, do an activity, or complete a specific job.
>
> Before you begin to write, think about something you know how to do well. What are the main steps a person should follow? Organize your instructions in chronological order so they are easy to follow.
>
> Now write a multi-paragraph explanation giving instructions about how to do something. Be sure to provide all the information needed for a person to complete the action you are describing.

D.

> Your English teacher has asked you to write a composition that compares school now to what school might be like in the future.
>
> Before you begin to write, think about specific ways school may change in the next 50 years. In what ways will school be different? In what ways will school remain the same?
>
> Now write a multi-paragraph composition comparing school now to school in the future. Be sure to give specific details and to support those details with clear examples.

NOTE: **Keep your drafts from this Chapter Review for use in Chapter 5s Review.**

Writing the Composition

ENGLISH LANGUAGE ARTS WRITER'S CHECKLIST

As you write your composition, remember these important points.

Composing:

☐ Write on the assigned topic.

☐ Present a clear main idea.

☐ Give enough details to support and elaborate your main idea.

☐ Present your ideas in a logical order.

Style/Audience Awareness

☐ Write with your audience (the person or group identified by the topic) in mind.

☐ Use vocabulary (words) that expresses your meaning well.

☐ Use sentences that make your main idea interesting to your audience.

Sentence Formation:

☐ Write in complete sentences and use a variety of sentence patterns.

Usage:

☐ Write using appropriate subject-verb agreement, verb tenses, word meaning, and word endings.

Mechanics:

☐ Write using correct punctuation.

☐ Write using correct capitalization.

☐ Write using appropriate formatting (e.g., indentations, margins).

Spelling:

☐ Write using correct spelling.

Remember to print or write neatly.

Chapter 5
Descriptive and Narrative Writing

LOUISIANA READING BENCHMARKS ADDRESSED IN THIS CHAPTER INCLUDE:	
ELA-2-M1	Writing multi paragraph compositions (150–200 words) that clearly imply a central idea with supporting details in a logical, sequential order (1, 4)
ELA-2-M2	Using language, concepts, and ideas that show an awareness of the intended audience and/or purpose (e.g., classroom, real-life, workplace) in developing complex compositions
ELA-2-M3	Identifying and applying the steps of the writing process
ELA-2-M4	Using narration, description, exposition, and persuasion to develop various modes of writing (e.g., notes, stories, poems, letters, compositions, logs)

Do you like to hear a good story? People, all over the world, have loved stories: stories about nature, stories about themselves, and stories about lands and peoples they have never seen. What kinds of stories do you like to hear or to read? You may like mystery, fantasy, or humor. Your friends may like ghost stories or historical fiction. For all types of stories, you will see descriptive and narrative elements in the writing.

When you write a descriptive or a narrative composition you are telling a story. Your **audience** will be fellow students or your teachers; your purpose will be to entertain and share life's lessons. In a **descriptive composition**, you will be creating a scene or picture in your readers' minds. You will use the literary device of imagery to bring a brief insight to your audience. The insight, shown, not told, from a scene, will have sights and sounds and smells and tastes and textures. When you choose words to describe the scene, you will consider what tone or mood you want to bring to your audience. Description is a part of **narrative compositions** also. Narrative compositions use description and add a story line, usually with dialogue, people speaking. A story line is a series of events, ending with a message. Usually narratives end with the writer learning a lesson or gaining a new perspective. In this chapter, you will learn more about these two types of compositions.

Descriptive and Narrative Writing

DESCRIPTIVE WRITING

What does a descriptive composition look like?

The following paragraph <u>shows</u> how a descriptive paragraph may be written:

Alarm!

A piercing shriek tore through my dreams and blankets . . . Pushing a sleep-heavy hand through folds of a purple sheet, aiming for a tiny, blue "off" button and clapping my other hand over an ear, I twisted and fell off my narrow bed. Dust motes shot up from the unvacuumed carpet and into my mouth, stale and bitter, as I landed with a muffled thunk. The alarm's shrill warning grew louder with every second. As I struggled to untangle from the strangling, slick sheet, a glossy black leather shoe appeared, inches from my face. The fragrance of spring-fresh soap and aqua-minty toothpaste wafted down as the hollow click of a button silenced the morning's scream. They know; I am a night person.

This example of descriptive writing shares an event with readers. It is dramatic in its tone. The words which add to the drama are piercing, shriek, tore, clapping, shot up, twisted, shrill, warning, struggled, strangling, glossy, and scream. If the writer had wanted a calmer tone, the following words could be used: humming, signal, nudged, holding, drifted up, turned, lilting, whistle, wiggled, clinging, shiny, and call. When you write a descriptive composition, you will want to have a clear goal about how you want to communicate the tone. You may choose a tone that will appeal to your audience. Or you may choose a tone which adds to the description's insight. This writer, using a dramatic tone with vivid description, shows the message revealed at the end: this is a night person's exaggerated view of morning.

How is a descriptive composition organized?

This writer organized the "Alarm!" description in a **chronological** (time) **order**; that means one action happens right after the other. There is also another way to organize descriptions. You may write about the **most noticeable** parts of the scene **to the least noticeable**. This organizing style may be reversed too; you may want to write about the least noticeable parts to the most noticeable.

How many senses are written about in the paragraph above?

If you read carefully, you will notice that all the senses are addressed. Through the words written on the page, the writer shares what is seen, the glossy shoe; what is heard, the piercing shriek, the thunk, and shrill warning; what is smelled, the spring-fresh soap and minty toothpaste; what is touched, the slick sheet; and what is tasted, the stale dust motes. In this way, the writer keeps readers interested in the writing.

When you describe a person, place, thing, or event, think about the words that will appeal to several of the reader's five senses. To paint a scene, you will use nouns to give the reader something physical to sense and verbs to give the reader an action to experience. You will also want to add adjectives and adverbs to make the picture as lively or as filled with sensations as it can be.

For example, if you write about going to a either a county fair or a street carnival, you will most likely tell about what you see: brightly colored balloons: reds, blues, greens, yellows, and one shade of purple twisting and twirling in the sunshine at the end of white satin streamers and mounds of fluffy cotton candy trailing pink clouds from paper cones.

What are the other senses a writer will describe?

In addition to describing these sights, you will want to add other descriptions. These descriptions are listed below:

what you hear:	the hooting melody of a carousel and the friendly shouts of booth carnies, calling people to come play
what you smell:	the salty aroma of popcorn drifting from booth counters and the pungent sharp scent of pine shavings under foot
what you feel:	a cool breeze blowing your hair as you spin on the Ferris wheel and cold, slick coins that you count out for the next ride.
what you taste	the sweet sugar powder from a funnel cake as it clings to your lips and hands and the refreshing icy tartness of a frozen lemonade

By including words that speak to several of the five senses, you will give your readers a full sensory experience. In this chapter, you will develop your descriptive writing skills by using

- Sight Words
- taste words
- touch words
- smell words
- sound words

DESCRIPTIVE WORDS

SIGHT WORDS

Which sense do you refer to the most?

Most people refer to their sense of sight. Does the following dialogue sound familiar?

"I'll *see* you later after I've *seen* what Yvonne wants me to *look* at.

"OK. *Look* for me later by the gym. I'm going to *watch* the band march around."

We speak with sight words so often because we trust our eyes and our sense of sight more than any of our other senses. So you will want to have descriptions that speak to the "eye" of your reader. In picture books, there are no words; the pictures alone tell a story. But you will want to do the opposite: you will paint a picture using words. With some practice, you will become a skilled "painter" with words. To start, you can use sight words to describe **size, shape, color, surface appearance**, or **action**.

Descriptive and Narrative Writing

SIZE WORDS

broad	bottomless	enlarged	gigantic
wide	tiny	enormous	hulking
petite	bulky	shriveled	wizened
bloated	colossal	extended	towering

SHAPE WORDS

angular	crescent-shaped	crumpled	linear
arched	crooked	diamond-shaped	scalloped
bent	cube	flat	slanted
bowed	curved	horizontal	twisted

COLOR WORDS

arresting	colorless	faint	harsh
blinding	deep-hued	flashy	loud
blurred	discolored	gaudy	pale
brilliant	faded	glaring	vivid

SURFACE APPEARANCE WORDS

bumpy	gritty	powdery	slimy
damp	gummy	pitted	smooth
dry	moistened	rigid	studded
encrusted	parched	rough	velvety

ACTION WORDS

crawl	dawdle	hobble	slide
creep	gallop	leap	soar
gobble	glide	devour	sprint
dance	hike	plod	stagger

98

Practice 1: Sight Words

Choose one board game in your home or school, such as *Monopoly* or *Pictionary*, and describe it in one paragraph. Use the list of questions below to help you. Try using words listed in the box on the previous page

What size is it?

Does it have any playing cards or token cards with it?

What kinds of playing pieces does it have?

What sort of counting or direction device does it have and what does it look like? (such as dice or a spinner)

What kind of box is it in?

Does it have a picture on the box or playing board?

What action is taking place in the picture(s)?

What is the surface appearance of the objects in the game?

Practice 2: Sight Words

Think about your favorite writing tool. It may be a yellow No. 2 pencil, a glittery gel pen, a smooth-rolling ball point pen, a fine-tip marker, or even an old fashioned fountain pen. Whatever your favorite tool for writing is, think about the last time you wrote or drew with it. Write one paragraph to describe it looks like and what the image it puts on a page is like—a sharp image, a smoky graphite smear or a bright slash. Be sure to include specific words that describe its size, shape, color, surface appearance, and action.

TOUCH WORDS

Through the sense of touch, you can learn many qualities about an object. For example you can learn **texture, temperature, shape** (as in Sight section), **weight**, and **density**. If you close your eyes and reach into a bag of different candies, you can choose one piece of candy and describe its qualities. For example, if you chose a gummi-type candy the texture will be squishy and the surface powdery. Its temperature will likely be the same as the room temperature. And with your eyes still closed, you may be able to tell if the piece of candy's shape is worm-like or bear-like. The piece of gummi candy will most likely be light, as light as an earthworm but less dense—earthworm guts would be more solid than gummi sugar candy.

TEXTURE WORDS

rough	fuzzy	knobbed	silky
coarse	shaggy	pitted	delicate
granular	nubby	smooth	woven
nappy	studded	fluffy	rubbery

Descriptive and Narrative Writing

TEMPERATURE WORDS

arctic	broiling	frosty	scorching
blustery	hot	nippy	sweltering
chilly	humid	numbing	tepid
cold	lukewarm	raw	torrid

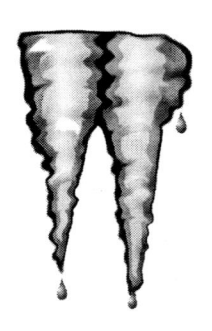

WEIGHT WORDS

airy	weightless	heavy	insubstantial
buoyant	wispy	immovable	unwieldy
feathery	bulky	massive	weighty
light	dense	tonnage	slight

DENSITY WORDS

closeness	congested	impenetrable	opaque
clustered	crowded	impermeable	solid
compact	dense	hardness	thick
condensed	firmness	jammed	viscosity

Practice 3: Touch Words

Find an object in your desk, backpack, or locker. Pair up with another student. With your partner's eyes closed, place the object in his or her hand. Your partner will then feel the object (with eyes still closed). Then take the object back, and hide it while your partner's eyes open again. Now, you close your eyes, and your partner will give you an object. Give the object back when you have thought of words to describe it to yourself. Finally, each of you will write a paragraph describing how the object felt. Use words that describe texture, temperature, weight, density, and shape.

Practice 4: Touch Words

Consider a favorite cluttered or organized place. Choose one to describe. Think about the way different parts of that place feel. How hot or cool is it? Write one paragraph describing the texture, temperature, shape, weight, density of this place, and/or objects in the place.

Sound Words

Sound can be a difficult sense to describe. One helpful way to describe sounds is to use other sense words or comparisons. For example, one car's engine may sound like a rainbowed hum, while another car's engine may make a sound like a screaming tuba. Or, a cat's purr may sound coarse or velvety, or a person may speak coolly or with warmth. Another helpful way to write about sound is to describe how the sound was made. For example, a laughing person may guffaw, giggle, snigger, chuckle, chortle, hoot, or cackle. Also, a singing bird may cheep, tweet, chirp, hoot, coo, caw, whistle, trill, warble, or chirrup. You can also describe sounds by volume, pitch, or quality (character).

Volume Words

bellow	deafening	hushed	shriek
blare	droning	murmur	thundering
blast	faint	racket	whisper
booming	holler	screech	yell

Pitch Words

alto	guttural	mellow	soprano
baritone	nasal	sharp	tenor
bass	piercing	shrieking	tonal
flat	rumble	shrill	low

Sound Quality Words

bang	buzz	fizz	sputter
barked	clang	hiss	squawk
beep	clatter	jangle	wheeze
bray	clink	purring	whoosh

Practice 5: Sound Words

Which type of music do you listen to? How would you describe the music and your favorite songs or arrangements? Think of all the different sound words you can use and write a paragraph describing your favorite music. Remember you may also use comparisons to describe music, such as *that drummer pounds out a beat like a sledgehammer driver working overtime.*

Descriptive and Narrative Writing

Practice 6: Sound Words

Choose two places to practice listening: one very quiet and one very loud. Your backyard or your local library may be quiet places and the school bus or your local store may be loud. Chose a time when the quiet place will be quiet and the loud will be loud. Sit down or lean against a wall or tree, close your eyes, and listen. Listen for a length of time to all the sounds you can hear. Think about how to describe their volume, pitch, and sound quality. Then, write a paragraph for each place that describes all the sounds you heard. Exchange papers with another student. See if each of you can guess where the other person heard the sounds that are described in the paragraph.

SMELL WORDS

How do we describe SMELL?

The average human nose can recognize over 2,000 different odors (animals know many times more). We cannot name them all, but we can give general descriptive words for the smells. You may use the word *spicy* to refer to the smell of Mexican food or *sweet* to describe the aroma of a candy shop. Some items have such unique odors that naming them gives enough information. Examples of these items include coffee, gasoline, ammonia, bleach, vinegar, jasmine, vanilla, cinnamon, and mint. You can use comparison to describe a smell; for example, old shoes may smell like composted grass. Study the list of words below to help you describe odors.

SMELL WORDS

acrid	earthy	lemony	scented
aromatic	flowery	musty	smoky
burnt	fragrant	perfumed	stale
dusty	fresh	rotten	sweet

Practice 7: Smell Words

Take a fifteen minute walk around your school or your home. Pay attention to the various smells in different parts of the area. Usually, the library will smell differently from the bus line, and your kitchen will smell different from the laundry area. Write a paragraph about either your school or home; describe the smells and compare them to one another.

Practice 8: More Smell Words

Think about your favorite place for smells. What did you smell the last time you were there? What about these smells are pleasing to you? Write a paragraph describing these smells and the effect they have on you.

TASTE WORDS

How do we describe TASTE WORDS?

Unlike our noses, our tongues can detect only four tastes: sweet, sour, salty, and bitter. But you can use other words to describe all the sensations of taste. Temperature, texture, and smell are all part of your sense of taste. This is really why a steaming mug of hot chocolate "tastes" so much better than hot chocolate that is left too long. This "old" hot chocolate has cooled and even thickened. When the hot chocolate is hot and fresh, its warm aroma, the silkiness of the liquid, and the foamy sweet marshmallows melting on top add to the taste sensations of the drinker. So, you can use a mixture of words, such as those listed below, to give the reader a good sense of what something tastes like.

TASTE WORDS

acidic	hot	salty	tart
bitter	juicy	spoiled	tasty
chocolaty	metallic	syrupy	tender
crunchy	mouth-watering	tangy	zesty

Practice 9:   Taste Words

As a homework assignment, eat your favorite food. As you eat it, close your eyes and pay attention to the flavors you taste. Remember that texture, temperature, and smell play an important role in your sense of taste. Take notes on the tastes you experience. Then, write a paragraph that describes the flavors of your favorite food and why you enjoy them. Use specific words so that the reader will want to run out and eat your favorite food.

Practice 10:   Taste Words

You have already described four sensory aspects of favorite places or things. The last sense is taste. Think of some way you experience taste in your favorite place. Maybe you eat your favorite food there. In this case, your paragraph is already written. Otherwise, write a paragraph that describes your experience of taste in your favorite place.

NARRATIVE COMPOSITIONS

Since forever, people have enjoyed hearing and telling stories. Narratives are stories. Someone who writes a narrative wants to share a personal story or stories their friends or families tell them about. They tell about and show (through descriptions) events that teach a lesson. True stories and documentaries on television bring narratives to a much bigger audience. People like to watch stories about real lives; they find these stories help them understand why humans behave as they do. A narrative may tell about an entire lifetime; autobiographies and biographies are this type of narrative. More commonly, though, narratives will tell stories of important or even unimportant experiences and events, in a person's life.

Descriptive and Narrative Writing

Your audience will learn from the experience you share in a narrative. This learning will happen in part because you will share what you learned in the experience. Narrative writers always include how the event(s) changed them. For instance, you might write about the first time you gave a power point presentation. You could describe the fun you had adding pictures, different fonts, and animation to the slides. You could then show the horror you felt when seeing that only half your slides saved to the floppy disk. You could write about how you also came to understand that "less is more" when using unusual fonts—half the slides are unreadable! You could include how you learned the hard way and in front of your class the wisdom of reading presentation guidelines. Another kind of lesson you could write about may be that you could see the humor of the errors and could laugh at yourself. You could also write about how your teacher was pretty easy on you—giving you complements on your creative strengths, so all is not lost. These are the kind of points that a narrative can make.

So, there are two features that identify a narrative: It is a story, and it is a story with a purpose. This can be a brief story with one small event, lasting only a few seconds. For example, you might write about a moment when you watch a new student drop his tray, splashing spaghetti sauce and how your best friend stood by him and helped him clean up. This is an example of an almost unnoticeable event, but one that has an effect on you. In a narrative such as this one, the "story" would consist more of your reflection on the event, and the way in which the event changed the you. Only a small part of the narrative would relate the actual "event."

In this chapter section, you will learn how to write a narrative composition about an event in your life. Writing a narrative involves learning the key steps for this type of writing. Applying and practicing what you learn in this chapter will help you improve your ability to write a successful narrative.

KEY STEPS FOR WRITING A NARRATIVE

When writing a narrative, follow these simple steps:

STEP I   Analyze the Writing Topic.

STEP II   Organize Your Narrative.

STEP III Write a Rough Draft of Your Narrative.

STEP IV   Edit and Proofread the Draft of Your Narrative.

STEP V   Write a Final Copy of the Narrative.

By studying these steps, you can gain a better understanding of how to write a narrative. They can also guide you in the writing process. In this way, you should be more prepared for your writing tests, and you should feel more confident about your ability to write a narrative.

STEP I: ANALYZE THE WRITING TOPIC

In the LEAP 21 Grade 8 in Writing, you will be given a writing prompt and asked to write a response to that prompt. Some of the prompts will require you to write a narrative composition. Analyzing the topic of that prompt is the first step in writing a narrative. The writing topic helps you think about what you will write. It creates a focus for your writing. You will want to read and reread the writing prompt carefully. In this way, you will respond only to the stated topic without turning from it.

To illustrate the steps in writing a narrative composition, we will follow the process through the story of Selena, a student in Mr. Bragg's English class. As a practice prompt, Mr. Bragg asked his class to write a narrative response to the following prompt.

Topic for a Narrative Composition

Write about the most embarrassing experience that you have had. Describe the experience and give reasons why it was an embarrassing and unpleasant experience. Include enough details so that the reader understands why the experience was embarrassing, how it affected you, and what you learned from it.

In analyzing the prompt, you can see that the main idea is an embarrassing experience. You will have to think of one that meant something to you. Then, you must decide how you were affected. You cannot just say that it was bad; you must give reasons for your statement. Your description of the event will provide these reasons. Make sure it has plenty of detail in it. Think about all the details about the event that you will include in the composition. Finally, what did you learn from it, and how did you change as a result of it? What can your readers learn from it?

Now that you have read the prompt carefully and analyzed each part of it, it is time to choose your specific topic. Notice that this writing topic requires you to think about an embarrassing experience. A good way to prepare for this writing topic is to brainstorm about some embarrassing experiences. Here is how a student named Selena brain stormed for this topic:

Embarrassing Experiences I Could Write About

- When I cooked spaghetti
- Time I had to go to the hospital
- My group presentation fiasco
- The day I found a map

After brainstorming, Selena eventually decided to write about one of these experiences for her narrative composition. She felt she could write a good narrative about her part in the group presentation fiasco.

When you write a narrative, you should choose a point of view, or perspective, from which the story is told. A point of view is the position or outlook from which a character tells the story. Establishing a clear and consistent point of view in your narrative helps your readers to follow the events and characters in your story more easily.

The typical points of view to select would be either a first-person point of view or a third-person point of view. When you tell a story about a personal experience, you would write from a first person point of view using words such as I, me, and my. When you write about events that happened to someone besides yourself, and you write as an observer rather than a participant, then you would use words such as he, she, her, him, his, they, their, and so on.

Selena needed to decide on a point of view for her narrative about the group presentation. Since she personally experienced the presentation fiasco, Selena chose the first-person point of view for her narrative.

Descriptive and Narrative Writing

Practice 11: Brainstorming and Establishing a Point of View

On your own or in a group, think about some of your most embarrassing experiences. If you cannot recall any, think about such things as foods, clothes, trips, sports, school, books, movies, or other topics that will trigger ideas. On a separate sheet of paper, make a list similar to Selena's. Discuss your lists with your group or with your teacher. Identify your audience. Then, choose the best topic for your narrative composition.

STEP II: ORGANIZE YOUR NARRATIVE

Selena was not sure about how she should proceed with the next step, "Organize Your Narrative." However, she took careful notes in Mr. Bragg's English class as he taught how to do this step. He said that a story should begin by establishing a setting. A setting is the time, place, and general background for a narrative. Selena knew her setting would be in her old school, in her history class. She would describe the room, the time of year, and the special presentation equipment

Mr. Bragg also explained that a narrative needs one or more characters (persons in the story). Selena thought about how she and her group and her teacher would be the characters. In addition, a story must contain a plot. A plot, he reminded them, is a series of related events. The plot includes a conflict (struggle between different forces in a story) and events that lead to a climax (turning point) in a story. A writer should also use suspense, so readers look forward to the next event in the narrative. Therefore, a narrative composition should have a setting, one or more characters, a clear plot with a beginning, a middle, and an end, and include a conflict, a turning point, and suspense.

Next, Mr. Bragg stressed that most narratives follow a chronological order, which is one event following another event as they happen. The reader can then experience each event as it happens in a logical time sequence. He recommended that his students create a plot diagram before writing their narrative compositions. This would provide a basic outline to follow as they list the main events in their stories. The following illustration is Selena's plot diagram for her group presentation fiasco. Notice how she labeled the events that show setting, suspense, conflict, and climax.

Plot Diagram for Group Presentation Fiasco in Chronological Order

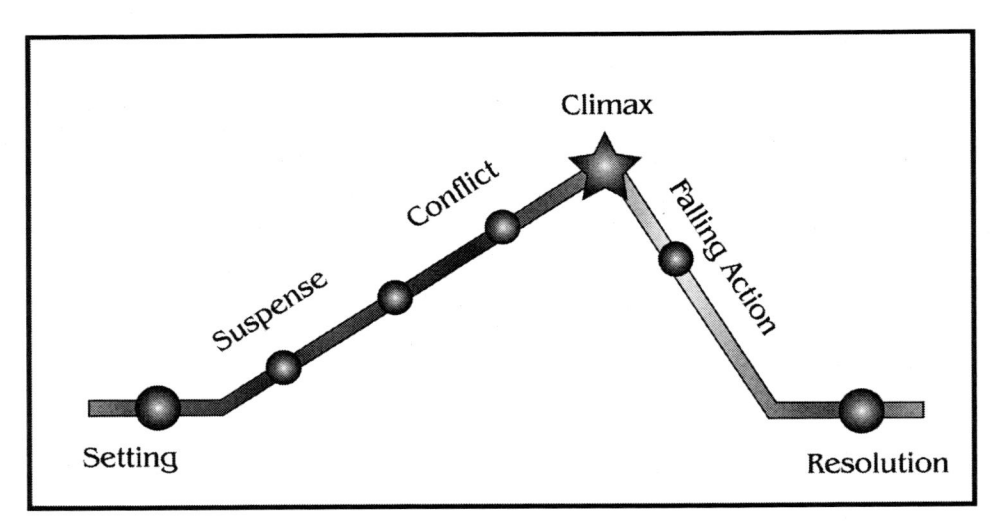

Practice 12: Organizing Your Narrative

Review Selena's plot diagram for her narrative composition. Using her example as a guide, create a plot diagram for the topic you chose for your narrative composition. Then, seek feedback by sharing the results with your class or with your teacher.

STEP III: WRITE A ROUGH DRAFT OF YOUR NARRATIVE

In class, Mr. Bragg told his students that they will be writing 3 paragraphs in their narrative composition. They may write 150 to 200 words; narratives may run longer with story line development but not much. In the first paragraph, the writer introduces the story by describing the setting and by stating the purpose of the narrative. In paragraph 2, the writer tells the main parts of the story. In the last paragraph, the writer ends the narrative. This ending is sometimes called the resolution because it wraps up the plot and comes to a conclusion or lesson learned from the story.

Mr. Bragg further explained that the rough draft will contain errors and will probably need some changes, but the reader should be able to read the entire narrative in the rough draft from beginning to end. The rough draft contains sentences and paragraphs, and therefore, is a big step forward toward a complete narrative composition.

Based on Mr. Bragg's guidelines, Selena writes a brief outline of her composition. That evening, Selena starts to write her rough draft. She follows the 3 paragraph format. Using her plot diagram as a guide, she writes in her first-person narrative point of view. She adds details to the plot and tries to connect the events together in chronological order. Read and evaluate Selena's rough draft.

Trial by Oil

I wished that I was sitting under the frigid waters of Lake Pontchatrain. But, no I was standing, I was waiting to start a class presentation. I remember gazing at Huey Long's old picture taped to the wall, next to the school calendar. September's photo featured the colors of red, orange, and yellow. That same color yellow ran in a stripe up my back giving me chills. I suffered from a fear: public speaking. I wished I could have fled like a yellow rabbit to the lake.

Matt was waving his hand at me to start. We were leading a talk about 1960s culture. Matt brought music and a CD player, and I brought sunflour cookies and a lava lamp. The power point was my idea. So I got the pointer. Our table was full with 60's stuff. It was also draped with wires. Folk rock music played softly. The lava lamp glowed dimly as Matt gave his speech, and then I was on. "The Rolling Stone's" music blared, making me ill. My throat closed in panic; my heart twisted fearfully. I looked down from Huey Long to real faces—they were looking back! I moved, accidentally stepping on a wire. The lava lamp leviated with a jerk and then crashed down, shattering clear glass and splashing thick oil. No one moved or breathed. I whispered: "Anybody got a mop?"

Descriptive and Narrative Writing

Matt went to fetch a mop while everyone sat still, I began my talk. I don't remember a word, and others said I was as white as a ghost. They sympathized with the disaster. But that was the cure for my phobia.

Practice 13: Evaluating Selena's Rough Draft for Content and Organization

Reread the rough draft of Selena's narrative composition, "Trial by Oil" Then, comment on the content and organization of her composition by analyzing its strengths and areas for improvement. As a guide, respond to the following questions.

1. What is the purpose of Selena's narrative?
2. Does Selena describe the setting well? Cite some examples.
3. List the key events in the narrative. Is the story chronological?
4. Briefly describe each character in the narrative.
5. Identify the main conflict(s) in the narrative.
6. List two examples of suspense in the story.
7. State the climax of the narrative.
8. Is there a clear resolution when the story ends? Explain.

Analysis of Content and Organization of Selena's Rough Draft

Selena states the purpose of "Trial by Oil" in the first paragraph of her rough draft:

"But, no I was standing, I was waiting to start a class presentation." As Mr. Bragg advised, she indicates the purpose of her story in the introduction. However, he has told her to strengthen how she states her purpose.

In the opening paragraph, Selena describes the story's setting: the school room. Her description is well developed, but a few words could be more specific.

The narrative follows chronological order. She has followed her plot diagram. Selena uses the first-person point of view as the narrator while the minor character is her friend, Matt.

Selena shows a simple event. She communicates her own fears. She includes suspense in the narrative, when she is about to speak. The climax of the narrative occurs when Selena steps on the wire, causing the lamp to jerk and fall.

Mr. Bragg felt that in Selena's rough draft, the resolution of the story is not clear. In her rush to finish, Selena forgot to include the final lesson or message of the story. When Selena and her teacher looked at the plot diagram, they found the lesson that Selena had left out. Mr. Bragg suggested that she add this. He praises Selena's use of writing **interior monologue**, what characters say silently to themselves. Readers will understand the narrator better.

Practice 14: Evaluating a Rough Draft for Content and Organization

Based on what you have learned about a rough draft from this section, write a rough draft of your narrative composition. Use your plot diagram to guide your writing. Then, comment on the content and organization of your rough draft by analyzing its strengths and areas that need corrections. Use the questions from Practice 3 to help you evaluate your work. Also seek feedback from your teacher or peer partners.

STEP IV: EDIT AND PROOFREAD YOUR NARRATIVE'S DRAFT

The next step in writing a narrative is to edit and proofread the rough draft. The goal is to find errors in language use, sentence variety, and writing conventions. **Writing conventions** means the correct use of spelling, punctuation, and grammar and usage. After finding any errors, the next goal is to correct them.

When she finished the rough draft of her narrative, Selena reread what she had written. Mr. Bragg gave his students the guide seen below to use when editing and proofreading their drafts. Selena will use this while she reads her rough draft to help her find errors in language and writing conventions.

Questions for language use, sentence variety, and writing conventions (spelling, punctuation, and grammar and usage).

1. Are there clear transitional words in your narrative that show the relationship between the events in the story? List them.
2. Could you strengthen your choice of words to improve the narrative? How?
3. Does the narrative include a variety of sentences? Explain.
4. What changes in spelling, punctuation, and grammar should you make in your narrative composition?

Analysis of Language and Writing Conventions

Mr. Bragg read Selena's rough draft for language and writing conventions, and they met in a conference. First, Mr. Bragg discussed transitions between events with her. When a narrative moves the reader from one event to another that is a **transition**. To make this transition flow smoothly and clearly, there needs to be a linking transitional word.

For example, there is a transition between Selena thinking about yellow and needing to start the presentation. Mr. Bragg gave Selena a list of transitional words to use in her narrative. This list is not complete but it is a good start: first, later, then, until, eventually, immediately, as, before, soon, suddenly, and meanwhile. For a different type of transition, Mr. Bragg noted that Selena could add dialogue for the transition to the last paragraph—an answer to her question would move the story along smoothly.

Working with Mr. Bragg, Selena has learned that she needs to use specific words in the narrative. Specific words are more effective than general or vague words. Selena looked at her class notes on descriptive writing and made changes. For example, read the following sentence with the specific words underlined, *"September's photo featured harvest hues of apple red, pumpkin orange, and summer squash yellow."* She is now using specific sight words. She also changed a cliché found in the last paragraph. Instead of *white as a ghost* she rewrote it to read, *"as white as a cave salamander..."*

Descriptive and Narrative Writing

Mr. Bragg also pointed out that Selena's sentences need more variety. Her rough draft contains many short, simple sentences. They make it sound choppy. He asked her to review her notes on "Developing Sentence Variety." Selena read that using different kinds of sentences improves the flow of the narrative; this and keeps the reader interested. Selena began to combine her simple sentences. She also worked on starting her sentences with something other than a subject.

For example, these four short simple sentences appear in the middle of the composition: *The power point was my idea. So I got the pointer. Our table was full with 60's stuff. It was also draped with wires.* Selena rewrote them this way: *The power point was my idea, so I got the pointer. Our table was crammed with 60's stuff and was draped with wires.* Notice how putting these sentences together creates a smoother flow of ideas; this spurs the reader's interest in the events to come. As she rewrote the final draft of her story, Selena continued combining some of her sentences.

Selena noticed the rough transition at the beginning of the first paragraph: *I wished that I was sitting under the frigid waters of Lake Pontchatrain.* To smooth the transition, Selena rewrote this sentence beginning it with an introductory phrase: "*On that day,*"

Selena then looked at her errors in writing conventions. She saw that her rough draft's capitalization, spelling, punctuation, and grammar needed corrections. For example, in the second paragraph, she misspelled *sunflour* and *leviated*.

Also in the first few lines, Selena saw this run-on sentence: *But, no I was standing, I was waiting to start a class presentation.* Selena rewrote this, blending ideas and adding an adjective: *But, no. I was standing and waiting to start another embarrassing class presentation.* Selena continued to make these types of changes throughout her draft.

Mr. Bragg praised Selena's use of a consistent past tense in her rough draft. He noted that the subject-verb agreements were mostly correct as well. She also used other parts of speech correctly: nouns, pronouns, adjectives, and adverbs.

Practice 15: Editing and Proofreading Your Rough Draft

Reread the rough draft of your narrative composition. Based on editing and proofreading hints you learned from Selena's work, what corrections should you make in your rough draft? As a guide, respond to the questions from Practice 5 about writing conventions. Discuss your findings with your peer partners or with your teacher.

STEP V: WRITE A FINAL COPY OF THE NARRATIVE

This is the fifth and last step of the writing process. After revising her composition, Selena has written the final draft. She has added the missing part of the story, about the lesson learned. Her composition now has:

- a setting;
- a plot;
- a clear beginning, middle, and end;
- characters and conflict,
- suspense, and
- resolution.

Selena has also added transitional words, so readers can follow the narrative more easily; added vivid and concrete words and expressions, to be more descriptive; varied her sentences, to improve the flow of the narrative, and corrected most of her errors in capitalization, spelling, punctuation, and grammar.

Now, read and evaluate Selena's final copy of her narrative.

Trial by Oil

On that day, I wished that I were sitting under the frigid waters of Lake Pontchartrain. But, no. I was standing and waiting to start another embarrassing class presentation. I remember gazing at Huey Long's tattered picture taped to the wall, next to the school calendar. September's photo featured harvest hues of apple red, pumpkin orange, and summer squash yellow. The same color yellow ran in a stripe up my back giving me chills. I suffered from a phobia: public speaking. If I'd known what the cure would be, I would have fled like a yellow rabbit to the lake.

"Time to start," Matt was waving his hands. We were about to lead a talk about 1960s culture. Matt brought music and a CD player, and I brought sunflower cookies, posters, and a lava lamp. The Power Point was my idea, so I got the pointer. Our table was crammed with 60's stuff and was draped with wires. Folk rock music played softly, and the lava lamp glowed dimly as Matt gave his speech. Then I was on. I looked down from Huey Long's face to real faces—they were looking back! My throat closed in panic; my heart twisted fearfully. I retreated, accidentally stepping on a wire. The lava lamp levitated with a jerk and then crashed down, shattering clear glass and splashing thick oil. No one moved or breathed. I whispered: "Anybody got a mop?"

"Groovy mess there, Selena. Like far out, outta sight!" Matt's humor soaked up some of the shock as he went to fetch a mop. Everyone laughed at his '60s slang while the oil spread gently and the glass glittered silently. Then, I began my talk. I don't remember a word, and others said I was as white as a cave salamander. But that was the cure for my phobia. Nothing more embarrassing can ever happen to me again—so why worry? So I don't.

Practice 16: Writing the Final Copy of Your Narrative

Based on the corrections in your rough draft, write a final copy of your narrative. Share your final copy with your teacher or peer group. Have them rate your rough draft compared with the final copy. Evaluate your strengths and challenges in narrative writing.

CHAPTER 5 REVIEW

A. Read the responses to the following two writing prompts. Then, circle any sight, smell, touch, sound, and taste words. Which sense is dominant in each description?

Describe one person you have met or known. Include details such as this person's appearance and mannerisms.

Descriptive and Narrative Writing

Response 1

Clown Time

Have you ever met a real clown—without his make-up? I have. This clown is my cousin Tommy, and he is the least likely clown I would never imagine.

Tommy, as BeJangles, wears a knobby fire-engine red nose over snow-white grease paint on his face. His brows are drawn as high arches on his forehead in a coal-black shade. BeJangles wears a white spandex cap to cover Tommy's hair and glues on a halo of flaming-orange frizz that gleams and shimmers under big-top lights. His maroon lips, painted in a plump bow-shape, spread to the middle of his cheeks. BeJangles' clothes are cut from a silky bright yellow, cherry-red checkered cloth. This costume has gold bells and cymbals sewn into it, so he jangles and pings as he moves. BeJangles juggles silver bells and rain sticks too! The noise of rattling *tat-tats* and sudden *clang, clangs* makes his juggling suspenseful and loud. As a finale, he flings himself into whooshing back-flips.

BeJangles, as Tommy, is an easy-going cousin. Tall and thin as a car antenna, his mannerisms are like a young sloth's. His clear hazel eyes and sticky-up raven hair disguise a quick mind. As BeJangles, Tommy loves to make adults and children laugh. As Tommy, he just loves everybody.

Response 2

My Friend

My friend, Brittany, is one of the most interesting persons I have ever met. Her long, flowing skirt swishes through the halls at school. People always stop and stare at her, but she does not care. She wears these multicolored clothes. Between the skirt and the loose fitting, ruffled blouses she wears, she looks like a gypsy.

She wears her hair long and curly, and it falls down her shoulders really thick like dark vines, and her earrings are very large, usually with vibrant images of delicious-looking fruit on them. Her makeup is very striking. Swirls of purple eye shadow and pink blush cover the upper part of the face, followed by a deep crimson lipstick and lip liner.

When she walks, she seems to careen effortlessly across the floor. Her pointed shoes sparkle in the sunshine of the skylight hall. People usually hear the rustle of her skirt before they see her. Everyone always turns around to notice what new accessory she's purchased for her outfits.

She wears a perfume on her hands which reminds me of almonds, and her skin is the color of cinnamon. She said she was born here, but her exotic appearance reminds me of another time and another place. Some people make fun of her, saying the fabric she wears in one outfit could easily make three dresses, but she does not care. The comments don't seem to bother her, and her appearance is memorable enough to make the cut for this composition.

Describe your favorite food. Include all aspects of the food which make it delicious to you.

Response 3

My favorite food would have to be the lasagna that my mother makes for me. The lasagna is memorable for its taste, feel, and smells.

The mozzarella cheese on the top of the lasagna has a gooey and juicy feel to it. As I bite into the noodles, my teeth easily slice through the moist noodles.

The inner layers of ricotta cheese are also very satisfying. The ricotta cheese has a grainy texture. Of course, the lasagna in the center areas is very hot. You can see steam rising more quickly out of the lasagna as your fork punctures the central layers. The round pieces of chopped Italian sausage and spiced hamburger meat make a delectable addition to the central layers.

Towards the bottom, the red tomato sauce mixes together with bits of the ricotta and the meats. The sauce tastes fresh because it comes from freshly diced tomatoes. You can almost smell the earth the tomatoes grew in, along with the aromas of sun-dried oregano and basil, as you bring the juicy bottom of the lasagna to your mouth.

All in all, the robust flavors and aromas of the lasagna, combined with its texture, make it a scrumptious dining opportunity worth repeating and a great addition to my list of favorite foods.

B. Think about someone you most admire. This person can be real or imaginary. In 3 paragraphs, describe this person, using several senses to create a detailed portrait of this individual.

C. In 3 paragraphs, create a scene of a real or imaginary place. Include specific details using several of the five senses.

To improve your proficiency in writing a story or narrative, complete these activities.

1. Using the five steps for writing a narrative from this chapter, write two or three more stories. Organize each story into 3 paragraphs. As a model, review Selena's final story about her presentation fiasco. Share each completed narrative with your teacher or class for feedback.

Choose your own narrative topics, or select some of the following topics:

- Tell a story about a time you were really afraid. What made your experience so frightening? How did you feel when it was over? Develop your story with details.

- Write an imaginary story about meeting an alien from another planet. Tell the reader about the experience. Develop your story with details.

- Write about an experience you had that taught you a valuable lesson about life. Tell about the main events of that experience. Develop your story with details.

- Tell a story about a friend or family member who made everyone laugh. Write a narrative about the experience. Develop your story with details.

- **Tell a story about your favorite or least favorite student at school. Create a real or imagined narrative about this person. Develop your story with details.**

2. Alex's assignment was to write a story about someone else. His topic was this:

Descriptive and Narrative Writing

Tell a story about someone you admire. Write a narrative about the first time you met this person. Develop your story with details.

Read and evaluate Alex's narrative. On your own or in a group, review the story and decide whether it needs to be revised or not. List the reasons for your decision. If the story needs revision, suggest ways that Alex could improve his narrative. If changes are needed, revise the story. Then, share the revision with your class or with your teacher.

The Real Hawk-Eye

Whenever I see a hawk swoop and dive over a fog-shrouded meadow, hunting dinner, I think of my first boss. He is the director for the nature center student volunteers, where I went to apply. Way over six-feet tall, dressed in muddy forest green coveralls and a floppy-brimmed camouflage hat, he looked to me like a giant poacher. His face was solemn as I asked for the director. Maybe his shaggy, silvered eyebrows twitched, but he led me to an office.

Abruptly, he traded the camo hat for a glossy black silk top hat and sat behind a canoe-sized desk. When he spoke, his voice rumbled low but had a melodious rhythm, like a calliope. We shook hands over my application; I will never forget that handshake. Two fingers were missing from his gnarled hand, which was crisscrossed with violet scars, and pitted with the wounds wild things cause; he clasped my hand carefully, lifting and dropping his arm with great deliberation. As I looked up, I caught a whiff of corn kernels, field mice, and bat guano from his clothes. Meeting my gaze, his face relaxed into his normal sunny expression. Suddenly, he was out the door with a crashing bang, hoarsely calling for me to start the next day.

His name is Mr. A. Travis. You may see Mr. Travis striding along cool, shaded paths with a hawk perched securely on one broad shoulder and his hands full of feed sacks. But you may not want to ask what is in them.

Chapter 6
Expository and Persuasive Composition

LOUISIANA READING BENCHMARKS ADDRESSED IN THIS CHAPTER INCLUDE:	
ELA-2-M1	Writing a composition that clearly implies a central idea with supporting details in a logical, sequential order.
ELA-2-M4	Using narration, description, exposition, and persuasion to develop various modes of writing (e.g., notes, stories, poems, letters, essays, logs) Use the various modes to write compositions including: • problem/solution essays • essays defending a stated position.

The purpose of **expository writing** is to explain or give information about a topic. Expository writing may describe a *process*, (how to play the position of soccer goalie). It may also describe a *cause and effect* (the effects of living with secondary smoke), or it may *compare or contrast* two ideas or events (Apple computers compared with PCs). In this chapter, we will explore the *basic expository* essay. We will also look at the type of expository essay which presents reasons or results of an action or idea (the cause/effect essay).

The purpose of the **persuasive composition** is to *persuade* or *convince* readers about a point of view. In a persuasive composition, you present an opinion and support that opinion with facts and ideas. So persuasive compositions also contain factual information. A well supported opinion can persuade a reader to think a certain way, or even to take a certain action.

EXPOSITORY COMPOSITIONS

The basic structure of an extended response essay consists of three main parts: an introduction, a body, and a conclusion. A **basic expository extended response** also contains these three parts. Its purpose is to inform or to explain a particular topic.

Let's say that a student named Emmi has a writing assignment. She must write an extended response about a particular animal. Since she is being asked to explain or inform her audience about this animal, she would be writing a basic expository response.

The **first step for writing** her extended response would be to **brainstorm** about the topic. Emmi's brainstorming list looks like this:

Expository and Persuasive Composition

Animals I Could Write About

dog	squirrel
cat	parrot
hamster	lizard
rabbit	monkey

The **second step for her extended response** is to **choose the animal** that she will discuss. Emmi chose her dog, a purebred Labrador retriever. Once she chose to write about her dog, Emmi moved to **step three, developing the thesis or controlling statement** for her extended response. Here is what she wrote for her thesis: **The Labrador retriever is an interesting breed of dog. Learning about this dog can help anyone who wants a Lab for a pet**.

Emmi's Outline

Creating a rough outline, Emmi used the **five Ws and H** to develop the body of her basic expository extended response. Here is what she wrote for the outline:

The Labrador Retriever

Who?	Labrador retriever, a type of dog
What?	Size, weight, colors, personality, life span
When?	Feeding times, play time
Where?	Origins
Why?	Benefits of owning a Lab
How?	Treating diseases, puppy care

Emmi's Rough Draft

Now that Emmi has decided on a specific topic, a thesis, and a rough outline, she is ready to write a rough draft of her basic expository extended response. As she writes, she will incorporate information from her knowledge and experience. Read her draft for content, organization, and English language conventions:

The Labrador Retriever

There are many kinds of dogs. Some are big. Some small. They come in many colors too. The Labrador retriever I know best because I own one. The Labrador retriever is an interesting breed of dog. Learning about this dog can help anyone who wants a Lab for a pet.

My veternarian, Dorothy Howe, says these dogs came from Newfoundland in Canada. The Labrador retriever stands about 2 feet tall. It weighs 60 pounds sometimes 75. Puppies weigh less of course. Howe says a dog should match your personality. So observe a dog before picking one out. So both of you get along. You can also expect Labs to live 8–12 years or longer. depending on keeping up with shots and illnesses.

116

Care of the Labrador retriever involves regualr feeding. Usually 2 cups of food each day with plenty of fresh water. A high qwuality dog food should be bought. Snacks are ok, but not too many. Labs will overeat if allowed. So don't overfeed them. labs also love to play fetch. So keep a frisbee or rubber bone handy. A Lab are also a very strong. They'll pull you, train it to walk with you and not chase other dogs.

I also know that these dogs can get diseases like dihrea, blindess, worms, especially heartworm, distempr, and hip disease so they deed regulr checkups. A Lab can also get skin infecsin. So be careful. Puppies can die quick if its too cold. So keep it warm. Pups are nice too because they play a lot. He knows you right from birth.

Lab retrievers are an animal that eevery one likes. They're playful, loyal, and good hunting dogs too. I look into my dog's eyes and see smart and lovable eyes. That's what I know about Labs.

look into my dog's eyes and see smart and lovable eyes. That's what I know about Labs.

Practice 1: Evaluating a Draft of a Basic Expository Extended Response

Reread Emmi's rough draft on the Labrador retriever. Then, answer the following questions.

1. What makes Emmi's extended response expository? Cite examples from her rough draft.

2. On your own or in a group, evaluate the content and organization of Emmi's extended response on the Labrador retriever. List the strengths of this extended response. Suggest ways that Emmi could improve the content and organization of her extended response.

3. Review Emmi's extended response for sentence variety. Does she vary the types of sentences she uses in her extended response? Or are the sentences similar? Would you change her sentences? How?

4. Read Emmi's extended response for correct use of English language conventions. What changes would you make in grammar, spelling, and punctuation?

Emmi's Revision

After feedback from other students and her teacher, Emmi wrote the following revision of her basic expository extended response on the Labrador retriever:

The Labrador Retriever

Dogs come in many sizes, shapes, and colors. Some dogs are large while others are small. I own a Labrador retriever which is an interesting breed of dog. Learning about this dog can help anyone who wants a Lab for a pet.

My veterinarian, Dorothy Howe, says Labrador retrievers originally came from Canada. These dogs stand about 2 feet tall and weigh between 60 and 75 pounds. They come in either black, yellow, or chocolate, and they are sometimes used for bird hunting. Howe says the personality of a Lab should match that of the dog's owner, so, before choosing a Lab, a person should observe its personality and behavior. Labrador retrievers can live 8–12 years or longer depending on the owner's attention to their health.

Expository and Persuasive Composition

Care of the Labrador retriever involves regular feeding, usually two cups of food each day with plenty of fresh water. Dog experts recommend a high quality dog food with a few nutritious snacks now and then. Labs should never be allowed to overeat. Labrador retrievers love to play fetch, so always keep a frisbee or rubber bone handy. Labs are also very strong dogs who will drag you along on their leash unless they are trained to walk with you. They also must learn not to chase other dogs or cars.

I learned that Labrador retrievers can get diarrhea, worms, especially heartworm, and distemper. They also can become blind, get hip disease or a skin infection. They need checkups and shots on a regular basis. As puppies, Labs can die quickly if they become too cold. Both puppies and adult Labs are fun-loving, affectionate, and protective of their owners.

Most people enjoy Labrador retrievers. They're playful, loyal, and good hunting dogs too. When I look into my Lab's eyes, I see a smart and lovable dog. That's what makes him interesting to me.

Practice 2: Evaluating a Revision of a Basic Expository Extended Response

Reread Emmi's revision of her expository extended response on the Labrador retriever. Then answer the following questions.

1. Based on your answers to Practice 1, did Emmi make changes in content, sentences, and English language conventions? Explain.

> **When writing a basic expository extended response, you can use the five W's and H to guide you in explaining a particular topic.**

Practice 3: Writing Basic Expository Extended Responses

To build your writing proficiency, write 2–3 basic expository extended responses. Organize each response into 4–5 paragraphs. Use Emmi's revised extended response on the Labrador retriever as a model. Follow the writing steps of choosing your topic, brainstorming, developing your thesis, creating a rough outline, writing a rough draft, making corrections, and revising your extended response. Decide on your own topics, or select some of the following topics:

an animal	a sport
an athlete	an entertainer
a book	a movie
a restaurant	a car
a hobby	a store
a place	a fad
a food	a planet

If you wish, use the following questions based on the five Ws and H as a guide for writing your basic expository extended response.

What is the title of your extended response?
State your thesis.

What will you explain about your topic?
When or where did you learn about your topic?
Why are you writing about this particular topic?
How will you explain your topic?
Express your concluding statement.

After you complete each extended response, share it with your teacher or with other students for feedback. Then revise each extended response as needed.

CAUSE-EFFECT EXTENDED RESPONSE

Using **cause and effect** is another way to explain a topic. Both cause and effect involve ways of showing relationships between one event or idea and another event or idea. Let's say that one morning you notice that a classmate is extremely cheerful, singing and telling jokes on the way to school or work. You are curious about this unusual behavior. You wonder why this person is acting so cheerfully. As a result of this experience, you soon find that you are feeling happy too. Later that morning, you learn that your classmate entered a contest and won a free computer. In this example, you can see how cause and effect work. You were curious about why your classmate was acting so cheerfully. You were trying to determine the cause of her happiness. Later, you found out the cause—winning a free computer. The effect or result of this good news was that you felt happy too.

> **The cause is the reason for an event, and the effect is the result of the event.**

The purpose for writing a cause-effect extended response is to explain relationships between issues, ideas, or events. These cause-effect relationships impact us, our friends, our community, and our world. For example, forgetting to put out the trash on time (cause) can affect you and others. The importance of graduating from high school requires that you understand the reasons and advantages (causes) of completing high school and the negative effects (results) of dropping out of high school. To reduce drug addiction, researchers must study the causes and effects of this social problem. To stop world terrorism, countries must investigate why terrorism occurs (causes) and its impact (effects) on humanity.

In the following diagram, notice how one cause can lead to an effect, which itself becomes the cause for another effect, and so on.

cause ⟶ effect (cause) ⟶ effect (cause) ⟶ effect

Expository and Persuasive Composition

Now, study the following diagram that Kurt created to show the causes and effects of his not putting out the trash on time. Notice how the main event (forgetting to put out the trash) has both causes and effects. As you read Kurt's diagram, think of other reasons (causes) and results (effects) of his action. See an example of this below.

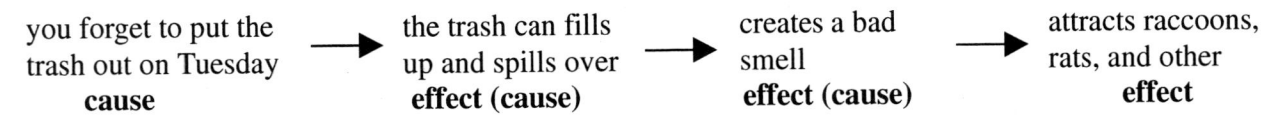

you forget to put the trash out on Tuesday → the trash can fills up and spills over → creates a bad smell → attracts raccoons, rats, and other
cause   **effect (cause)**   **effect (cause)**   **effect**

As an aid for his brainstorming about causes and effects, Kurt created the following **Cause-Effect Map** on forgetting to put out the trash on time.

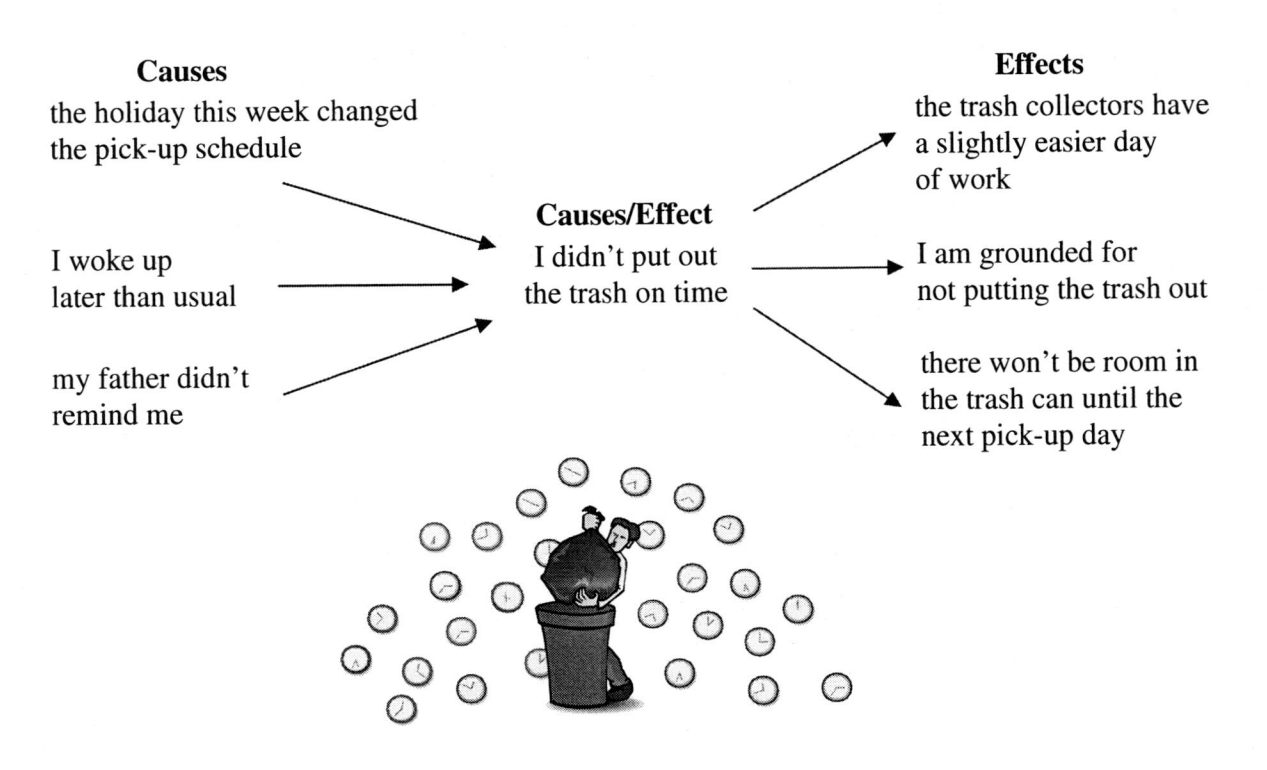

Causes
- the holiday this week changed the pick-up schedule
- I woke up later than usual
- my father didn't remind me

Causes/Effect
I didn't put out the trash on time

Effects
- the trash collectors have a slightly easier day of work
- I am grounded for not putting the trash out
- there won't be room in the trash can until the next pick-up day

Practice 4: Brainstorming Causes and Effects

A. Using Kurt's cause-effect map as a model, brainstorm about causes and effects for three or more of these topics. Or choose some of your own topics. Next, discuss your diagrams with a partner or with a group of other students. See if they can add any more causes or effects to your diagram. Then, share your findings with the class or your teacher.

exercise	dirty laundry
surfing	poverty
earthquakes	volunteering
overspending	stress
family harmony	family conflict
new hairstyles	tattoos
messy room	good grades
success	gossip

In the beginning of this chapter, you learned that expository extended responses present or explain information about a particular topic. When you write a cause-effect extended response, you can explain just causes, just effects, or a combination of both causes and effects. The audience and purpose of your extended response determine what your focus will be. For example, if your purpose is to explain the dangers of smoking, and your audience is composed of teenagers, you will probably focus on the unhealthy effects of smoking. If your purpose is to explain the reasons why teenagers smoke, and your audience is a group of parents, you might stress the causes of smoking. If your purpose is to explain the reasons and dangers of smoking, and your audience is made up of both teenagers and adults, you can discuss both causes and effects of smoking.

In the following sample extended response, notice how the writer focuses on the reasons (causes) for tardiness. After you read this extended response about causes, complete the activity that follows it. **This extended response also contains some key words that signal that the author intends to explain the causes of being late. Underline these words as you read this response.**

Why Are Some People Late?

There are many different reasons why people are late getting somewhere. The first thing that makes people late is incorrectly estimating how long it takes to do something. For example, if you think it will only take you 15 minutes to ride your bike to school, and it really takes you 30 minutes, then you will be late to school. Another thing that prevents people from being on time is getting distracted from the task at hand. If you stop to talk to someone while you are riding your bike to school, you may lose track of time and end up being late for school. Getting distracted happens much more easily if you don't have a watch on. Not having a watch or a clock nearby prevents people from knowing what time it is, and can lead to tardiness.

The last thing that can make people late is something called "unforeseen circumstances." An example of "unforeseen circumstances" is a flat tire. If you get a flat tire on your way to school, you probably won't have a repair kit with you which means you will have to walk to school. Walking takes a lot longer than riding a bike, so guess what? You're going to be late.

As you can see, even if you make every attempt to be on time, including planning enough time for travel, not getting distracted, and keeping an eye on your watch, your plans for being on time can still be undermined by the dreaded "unforeseen circumstances." Even if you do everything right to be on time, there are events that you just can't plan on. Everyone is late once in a while, so estimate time correctly, don't get distracted, and keep an eye on the clock. With this plan, your chances for being on time will improve.

B. The paragraph describes four general causes for one specific effect. Write these on the lines below.

Effect _____

Cause _____

Cause _____

Cause _____

Cause _____

Expository and Persuasive Composition

Which words in this extended response show that the writer is focusing on the reasons (causes) for being late? Here are some words you should have found: **why, reasons, then**. The writer uses these key words to focus on the causes of tardiness. Look below for a list of key words that writers use when they are explaining causes or effects in an expository extended response.

Causes	**Effects**
reason	result
why	consequence
because	outcome
source	product
basis	impact
due to	affect
therefore, thus	therefore, thus

Practice 5: Writing Cause and Effect Extended Responses

For practice, write 2–3 cause-effect extended responses. Each extended response can focus on causes or on effects. Organize each response into 4–5 paragraphs.

For a model extended response that presents causes, review the extended response "Why Are Some People Late?" Use the topics you developed in Practice 6, or create some new topics.

Brainstorm, develop a thesis, create a rough outline, write a rough draft, make corrections, and then revise each extended response. Whenever possible, use key words to signal the purpose of your discussion. If you wish, use the following outlines as a guide for writing your cause or your effect extended response.

Extended Response About Causes	**Extended Response About Effects**
Title	Title
Thesis	Thesis
First Cause	First Effect
Second Cause	Second Effect
Third Cause	Third Effect
Concluding Statement	Concluding Statement

After you complete each cause or effect extended response, seek feedback from your teacher or from other students. Revise each extended response as needed.

PERSUASIVE WRITING

In persuasive writing, you try to convince readers to agree with your point of view. Persuasive writing involves four important steps, which will be discussed in this chapter. These steps are listed below.

— Deciding on Purpose and Audience

— Using Persuasive Language

— Building an Argument

— Presenting a Strong Conclusion

PURPOSE AND AUDIENCE

Being aware of purpose and audience is particularly important with persuasive writing. Your purpose is fairly clear: you want to convince readers to agree with you. However, the amount of convincing you need to do may depend on your topic. For example, convincing your parents to take you on a ski vacation will be more difficult than convincing them to take you fishing.

Knowing your audience is especially helpful in persuasive writing. When you know your audience, you know what points of agreement or disagreement you may have with them. You also know which reasons your readers may accept and which they may not. Before you write, carefully consider who your audience is and what you know about your audience.

Practice 6: Purpose and Audience

In the following practice exercise, decide on the audience and purpose for each topic given. Keep in mind that you are trying to persuade your audience to agree with you in support of or against the topic. Then, compare your choices with those of other students. Use your own paper for responses.

Cloning Pets	**Body Piercings**
Audience	Audience
Purpose	Purpose
Homework	**Clothing Fads**
Audience	Audience
Purpose	Purpose

USING PERSUASIVE LANGUAGE

When you are trying to persuade, you need to present information in a particular way in order to make the reader agree with your position. You must emphasize points of interest to the reader and describe them in language that is attractive to your audience. For example, let's say you are applying for a special summer wilderness camp with a local university which teaches you wildlife management. When the course director asks what your experience is with animals, you could answer with either of the explanations below.

Example 1: I volunteered with my vet doing odd jobs.

Example 2: I helped feed and walk dogs. Once the vet ensured that they were safe, I assisted in the bathing of cats and ferrets. I observed surgeries and treatments of various animals and learned something about reading cat x-rays. I helped out with keeping files and paperwork in order, and sometimes answered the phones. Whatever job I was assigned I used as a chance to learn more about animals.

Both explanations provide the same truthful information. However, the second makes you sound like a responsible and hardworking student, while the first is vague and not very convincing. In the second example, the writer also uses vivid description, concrete words, and figurative language.

Expository and Persuasive Composition

NOTE: Paying attention to your audience does not mean telling people what you think they want to hear or giving false information. Make up your own mind, stay firm, and tell the truth. However, you want your audience to be able to understand and appreciate what you are saying. So, use language that will persuade your particular audience.

Practice 7: Persuasive Language

For each of the following situations, write two or three sentences that will influence or persuade the intended reader. The examples provided are NOT persuasive.

1. Convince your mother to let your friend sleep over.
    Example: Mom, can Chris please stay tonight?

2. Motivate your team to win.
    Example: It's halftime, and we're down by five points. We can win.

3. You took care of your sick brother last night, so you couldn't finish your homework. Persuade your teacher to give you an extension.
    Example: Is it OK if I turn in my homework tomorrow?

4. While mowing your neighbors' lawn, you ran over their flower bed. Convince them to give you another chance.
    Example: I think your flowers will grow back before I mow the lawn next time.

BUILDING AN ARGUMENT

Your ability to persuade depends not just on what you have to say and how you say it. You must be able to build a strong **argument**. In everyday speaking, an "argument" is a disagreement between family members, friends, or enemies who exchange heated words. However, in the context of persuasive writing, an argument is a carefully reasoned way of presenting a point of view. The three steps to building an argument are make a claim, support the claim, and answer objections. This process may be compared to building a pyramid.

MAKING A CLAIM

The first step in building a good argument is to make a claim. A claim is the position you take on a particular issue. It can't be just a statement of fact. A fact stands alone, cannot be argued, and requires no support. A claim, however, argues for one side of a controversy. Someone may disagree with your claim, so you must support it, just like the pyramid builder needs to support the top of the pyramid. The claim is the "point" you are trying to make, so keep it focused, like the pointed top of a pyramid.

The following statements provide good starting points for an argument.

1. Since increased oxygen in the brain improves thinking, middle school students should have at least minutes of outside physical exercise and every day.

2. We ought to be increasing programs that help stop pollution rather than giving more money to industries which cause the pollution.

3. The best way to teach people is by helping them develop a love of learning.

These three statements urge the reader to take a certain action or have a certain belief. In other words, they make a claim. They use words like should, ought, and best. These key words often indicate that the author is taking a position and encouraging the reader to do the same. You may also notice that the persuasive statements sometimes use the subject we in an attempt to involve the reader in the position or idea.

Practice 8: Making A Claim

For each topic, write a statement of fact and a claim statement. Make it clear that they are different types of statements. Number 1 is an example; use your own paper if you need more space for responses.

1. **Topic: placing parental advisory stickers on music CDs**

    Fact: There's a great deal of controversy over placing parental advisory stickers on music CDs.

    Claim: Record companies should not place Parental Advisory stickers on music CDs.

2. **Topic: a year-round school calendar**

    Fact:_____

    Claim:_____

3. **Topic: high salaries of professional athletes**

    Fact:_____

    Claim:_____

4. **Topic: using cell phones while driving**

    Fact:_____

    Claim:_____

SUPPORTING THE CLAIM

Look at the picture of the pyramid. The entire structure of a pyramid comes to a focused point at the top. Each and every block of the pyramid supports this point. In a similar way, each and every sentence of your argument should support your claim. And these sentences should be "solid blocks." A strong argument is supported by good logic, solid evidence, and reasons or examples. A weak argument suffers from poor logic, weak evidence, and faulty reasons or examples. Like a pyramid, a strong argument will stand the test of time.

Expository and Persuasive Composition

Read these two passages, and decide whether the arguments are strong or weak.

Burn Off Pounds And Inches
With SUPER DIET PILL!

You Can Lose 10, 20, 50, Even 100 Pounds!

This is it! This is the diet pill researchers around the world have hailed for its powerful, quick-working ingredients that help people shed stubborn fat fast!

Super Diet Pill Satisfies the Need for Fast Action Without Serious Dieting

So fast-working, you can see a dramatic difference in just two days, without calorie counting or suffering from hunger pains. Even people with longtime weight problems find they can burn off up to a pound of fat and fluid every five hours.

50% Fat Loss In 14 To 21 Days

The longer you use the super diet pill, the more weight you lose. You don't have to stop until you reach the weight that you want. Without making major sacrifices or drastic changes, you can shed as much as 50% of your fat in just 2 or 3 weeks.

Increased Metabolism Means Weight Loss

Half of the women and a quarter of the men in the United States are trying to lose weight and become fit. The truth is that most will regain their original weight in a year or less. What's the real secret for losing weight and keeping it off?

The answer is developing a healthy metabolism. Metabolism refers to how the body burns energy. A person with a high metabolism burns more calories than a person with a low metabolism. The person with a high metabolism has an easier time losing weight.

Here are some tips for improving your metabolism:

- Drink plenty of water. Filling up on water decreases the appetite. Drink at leas a quart of water each day.
- Don't skip meals, especially breakfast. Eat small meals every two to three hours. In this way, carbohydrates and protein will not be converted into fat.
- Eat fat-burning foods. Whole, natural foods are your best choices. Eat fruits between meals for extra energy. This healthy snack won't be converted to fat.
- Exercise regularly. Swimming, running, and walking are best. Also try lifting weights—a good muscle builder and fat burner. Exercise before you eat. It will decrease your appetite and increase your metabolism.

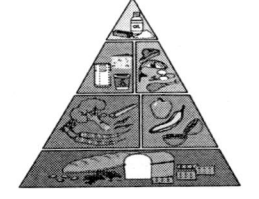

Each passage suggests a way to lose weight and provides reasons for its method Which one is based on valid reasons, and which is based on vague and unsupported statements?

There are two clues that the diet pill advertisement is based on false statements: 1) It sounds too good to be true, and 2) it's trying to sell you something. A good rule of thumb is that if it sounds too good to be true, it is, and if someone is trying to sell you something, beware. Beyond these initial clues, an examination of the ad shows that little proof is presented to support its dramatic claims. The ad never mentions the names of the diet pill researchers, the people who lost weight, nor where or when the testing was done.

The description of metabolism, however, bases its argument on biological principles that are common knowledge to most people who have taken a biology class. From this basis, it provides logical explanations of how to increase your body's metabolism. The author is not selling anything and is not offering an easy "quick fix." A decision to follow the suggestions for changes in diet would be based on much better information than a choice to try the diet pill.

FOUR WAYS TO BUILD A STRONG ARGUMENT

1. Show cause-effect connections between your position and the reasons you use to support it. Use clear logic and valid facts. Avoid fallacies and use commonly known, easily proven facts.

2. Illustrate your point of view with a personal story. Although each person's experience is different, your reader can understand or empathize with events from your life that illustrate your point of view.

3. Contrast your choice or position with another. One way to show the strength of your choice is to show the weakness of another choice.

4. Use credible sources to support your argument. Quoting one or more credible resources can validate (or prove the truth in) your argument.

Answer Objections

Knowing your audience not only helps you choose appropriate language and tone, but also helps you anticipate objections to your position. Answering these possible objections is like building a wall around your pyramid to protect it from anyone who may want to tear it down.

Let's say that you wanted to go out dancing on Saturday night until 1:00 AM. Your parents want you home by midnight. You would have to answer their objection to staying out until 1:00 AM. Since your audience is your parents, you would have to decide how you could convince them to let you dance for one more hour. Think of three ways you would respond to their objection. Would you use impassioned pleas, logical reasoning, or an objective third person's opinion? What type of language and tone works best with your audience? This is a good question to ask yourself before you begin any persuasive writing.

Read the following passage regarding capital punishment, and decide which objections the author is trying to answer.

No More Executions

I want to applaud the governor of Illinois for his recent decision to stop all executions in his state until further review of the capital punishment system. Contrary to popular belief, capital punishment is not a deterrent to crime. In fact, statistics show that states without capital punishment had a lower rate of violent crime in 1999: 3.6 murders per 100,000 persons. States with capital punishment had a higher rate of violent crime in 1999: 5.5 murders per 100,000 persons. Some people claim that the appeals process

Expository and Persuasive Composition

takes too long, and that's why the death penalty is not a deterrent. However, the Death Penalty Information Center reports that 21 condemned inmates have been released from death row since 1993. This includes seven from the state of Illinois. We cannot risk the execution of innocent people by speeding up the appeals process. The lengthy appeals process also makes capital punishment very expensive. Anyone who has been in a court case knows how much lawyers cost. Those who do not want tax money wasted on criminals should oppose capital punishment because it is actually more expensive to execute someone than to imprison him or her for life. Overall, the system is terribly flawed. The other 38 states with capital punishment laws should join Illinois in placing a moratorium on all executions.

The author of this passage opposes capital punishment and wants to convince others to oppose it as well. In doing so, the writer addresses three popular reasons that others use for supporting the death penalty:

1. capital punishment deters crime;
2. capital punishment would be a deterrent if the appeals process were shorter; and
3. execution is less expensive than life imprisonment.

The author answers these objections to her argument with statistics, authoritative information, and common sense.

Practice 9: Writing Persuasive Paragraphs

Write a persuasive paragraph for each of the three topics you worked with in Practice 7, making sure to support your claim and answer objections. Here's an example:

> Parents should not rely on record companies to decide what music their children should or should not buy. Each parent has different standards for what kind of music is appropriate for his or her children. Some people say that parental advisory stickers will "weed-out" the really rude music. However, couldn't this also lull parents into a false sense of security, tempting them to rely only on the record companies? When parents listen to what their children are hearing, they can then discuss the music with their children. They could forbid certain music in the home if they find it especially objectionable. If parents don't think they have time for this, then they should re-examine their priorities. Parents have the responsibility for raising their own children. They can't let the record companies do it.

Practice 10: Building an Argument

Write a persuasive paragraph for each of the topics below. Be sure to consider your audiene when supporting your claim.

1. Audience: city council members
   Claim: skateboards should be allowed on sidewalks downtown

2. Audience: other students
   Claim: the school mascot should be changed

3. Audience: principal

Claim: the class trip should be to the Grand Canyon

4. Audience: parents

   Claim: you can see your favorite musical group in concert

5. Audience: pet owners

   Claim: certain breeds of dogs should be banned from cities

6. Audience: high school students

   Claim: earning a high school diploma is important

7. Audience: shoppers

   Claim: shopping on the Internet is better than a trip to the mall

CHAPTER 6 REVIEW

A. To improve your understanding of expository writing, complete the following activities.

1. Find 3–4 examples of expository compositions in newspapers, magazines, textbooks, or on the Internet. Try to find compositions that are between 400–1000 words. Decide whether each of these compositions is primarily a basic expository composition, a process composition, a cause-effect composition, or a comparison-contrast composition. Form a group and make copies of these compositions for each member of the group. The group will exchange these compositions among the members, and each will respond to the following questions.

   A. Classify each composition as basic expository, process, cause-effect, or comparison-contrast. Offer 3–4 examples from the composition to support your answer.

   B. Evaluate each composition by responding to the following questions:

   1) Is the thesis clear and concise?

   2) Does the author support the thesis well? Cite 3–4 examples or reasons from the body paragraphs of the composition.

   3) What transitional words does the author use to connect the ideas together? List 3–4 examples.

   4) Is the composition organized around an introduction, body, and conclusion? Point out examples of each of these parts in the compositions.

   5) Are there any pictures, charts, or diagrams in the compositions? Do they help or hinder the understanding of key ideas and facts? Explain.

   6) Is the diction (use of words) vivid, concrete, and clear?

   7) Does the author include a variety of sentence lengths to maintain interest in the compositions?

   8) Who is the primary audience for the composition? Is there evidence in the composition to support your answer?

   9) Does the author use correct English language conventions such as grammar, punctuation, and spelling? What might account for any errors you find?

Expository and Persuasive Composition

2. Write a process composition consisting of directions to a particular place. Include specific turns, landmarks, and a map for a visual aid. Share your composition with the class, with a small group, or with your teacher. If the place is within walking distance, have members of your group follow your directions to see if they can find the place.

3. Lorrie wrote a cause-effect composition for her English class. Her topic was, if you could change some things in your life, what would they be? Why would you change them?

Read and evaluate her composition. Rate her composition based on the material in this chapter. Use a scale from 1 to 6 with 1 being the lowest score and 6 being the highest. Include reasons for your rating.

If corrections are needed, revise the composition. Then, share the revision with your teacher or with the class.

Oh, Grow Up!

I wish I were older so that I could drive and have money for things I want. But since I can't change time, I'll have to figure out how to get the government to change the driving age and the working age.

I want to change the driving age so that I can go places. I live far away from any kind of civilization. Any time I want to go to the mall with my friends, I have to ask my older brother or my parents. My parents are always busy working on something. My brother doesn't want to be seen anywhere with his little sister. He says it would kill his social life. If I could drive myself, I wouldn't have to bother any of them when I wanted to go somewhere. I could go where I want and do what I want. I could even get a job to buy a car and pay for the gas.

If the working age were changed, then I could work to earn money for the things I want. I could buy my own clothes and wouldn't have to wear the things my mom buys for me. I could even buy some things for my family. My dad needs a new briefcase. My mom could use a new cell phone. My brother could use a new attitude, but I can't buy that. He'll have to settle for a new CD burner.

If I were to try to change the ages for driving and working, I would start a campaign. First, I would talk to my friends and tell them my ideas. Then, I would ask them to tell their friends and have their friends tell their friends. Finally, I would get everyone to write letters to their congressman to lower the driving and working ages because kids shouldn't have to wait.

4. Work in pairs with another student, with each of you writing a comparison and/or contrast composition about yourself and another member of your family. Read and evaluate one another's compositions. Rate the composition you read based on the material in this chapter. Use a scale from 1 to 6 with 1 being the lowest score and 6 being the highest. Include reasons for your rating. When you get your own rated composition back, make any necessary changes. Then, share your results with the class or with your teacher.

B. To improve your skills in persuasive writing, complete these activities.

Read the following two reports. Then, answer the questions, using complete sentences.

Report 1

The county government meeting broke up after a long debate. Bill Smith's supporters claim that he is the duly elected representative of the people and should be allowed to take his seat on the council. His opponents disputed this, saying that his previous protests of council activities disqualify him from holding public office.

Report 2

We elected Bill Smith, and he's our man. His enemies are just jealous. They think they can throw some mud around and make it stick to Bill. No way! He's squeaky clean. There ain't nothin' they can do to make him look bad. He stood up for us before, makin' sure the council listened to us. Now those jokers say that's a bad thing. Stick by Bill. He stuck by us!

5. What is the author's purpose in each report?

6. Compare and contrast the persuasive language of these two reports. Which report appeals more to emotions? Explain your answer.

Read the following excerpt, and complete the writing exercise that follows.

> I stand as firm as the rock of Gibraltar on the right that women have to shape the thoughts, socially and politically, of the world. They can make our country better and purer, just as they appreciate their own rights. I am in favor of women's rights—in their rights to rise up in the majesty of the nature their Creator gave them and emancipate themselves from the foolish fashions and sentiments of the age. When they do rise, they will be more respected by all mankind than all the rulers of the Earth from Adam down to the present day.
>
> –Clarissa's speech in *Shams* by John S. Draper

7. Write one paragraph in which you evaluate the language and tone of this excerpt. What are some strengths of the author's choices in language and tone, and what are some weaknesses? How do these affect the persuasiveness of the writing?

Read the following excerpt, and complete the writing exercise after it.

> There is still a great deal of controversy about the future of the space program. While some people believe it is a waste of much needed funds, others point to the great scientific and technological advances that have resulted from the exploration of space. Supporters of the program most frequently cite the wide uses of microprocessors as one of the major contributions to space-related research. Opponents believe the billions of dollars dedicated to the space program would be better spent on the needs of education, health care, and job training for the poor and disadvantaged.

8. Pick one side of the controversy described in the above passage about the space program, and write a paragraph to persuade other students of your point of view. Share your paragraph with your classmates. Ask for feedback that would strengthen your argument, and incorporate it into your paragraph. Then, write a letter to the President of the United States expressing your opinion. Show the letter to your teacher. Then, mail the letter to President (Full Name), The White House, 1600 Pennsylvania Avenue, Washington, DC 20500.2635

Expository and Persuasive Composition

Chapter 7
Using the Writer's Checklist

LOUISIANA READING BENCHMARKS ADDRESSED IN THIS CHAPTER INCLUDE:	
ELA-3-M1	Writing fluidly and legibly in cursive or printed form (1, 4)
ELA-3-M2	Demonstrating use of punctuation (e.g., colon, semicolon, quotation marks, dashes, parenthesis), capitalization, and abbreviations (1, 4)
ELA-3-M3	Demonstrating standard English structure and usage by using correct and varied sentence types (e.g., compound-complex) and effective personal styles (1, 4)
ELA-3-M4	Demonstrating understanding of the parts of speech to make choices for writing (1, 4)
ELA-3-M5	Spelling accurately using strategies and resources (e.g., glossary, dictionary, thesaurus, spell check) when necessary (1, 3, 4)

When you take the LEAP 21 Grade 8 Writing test, you will be given a Writer's Checklist to help you with the 150–200 word essay you will be writing. The checklist is on one side of a card. The other side contains directions for writing your essay. The checklist is reprinted on the next page. In this chapter you will practice each step of the checklist.

Using the Writer's Checklist

ENGLISH LANGUAGE ARTS WRITER'S CHECKLIST

As you write your composition, remember these important points.

Composing:

☐ Write on the assigned topic.

☐ Present a clear main idea.

☐ Give enough details to support and elaborate your main idea.

☐ Present your ideas in a logical order.

Style/Audience Awareness

☐ Write with your audience (the person or group identified by the topic) in mind.

☐ Use vocabulary (words) that expresses your meaning well.

☐ Use sentences that make your main idea interesting to your audience.

Sentence Formation:

☐ Write in complete sentences and use a variety of sentence patterns.

Usage:

☐ Write using appropriate subject-verb agreement, verb tenses, word meaning, and word endings.

Mechanics:

☐ Write using correct punctuation.

☐ Write using correct capitalization.

☐ Write using appropriate formatting (e.g., indentations, margins).

Spelling:

☐ Write using correct spelling.

Remember to print or write neatly.

The checklist is used to make final corrections to your rough draft before you copy your essay to your final draft.

First look at the composing parts of the checklist:

Chapter 7

- Composing
- Write on the assigned topic.
- Present a clear main idea.
- Give enough details to support and elaborate your main idea.
- Present your ideas in a logical order.

Step 1: Look at the rough draft and make sure each paragraph didn't get **off the topic**.

Example 1: Topic: The fifth graders are nervous about coming to middle school next year. Write a composition answering the question: **What was it like for you starting middle school?**

Let me tell you about the first week of middle school. The classes were so different—we had to change classes and rooms every time the bell rang. The lockers were little cubicles, and unfortunately, mine was on the bottom by the floor. In high school we will get full length lockers. The books for the classes were heavy and ripped my backpack. School was exciting, though, because there were so many new kids to meet and make friends with. The seating was assigned in all my classes, which forced me to talk to kids that were not already my friends. Everyone seemed to laugh and talk the whole class. The lunch room was very loud. It was hard for the teachers to keep us under control in the beginning. But somehow, they always knew how to make us behave ourselves and start learning something important. Now I can't wait to get to high school. (153 total words.)

Practice 1: Topic

Going over the composing part of the checklist, the first thing we notice is that this is getting too long for a multi-paragraph composition. We need to write at least 2 more paragraphs to finish the composition and we already have 153 words. Let's fix this before we go on. If there can only be 200 words total, which means each paragraph can only average 66 words, where can we cut? Can some of these sentences go into another paragraph?

1. At least 2 sentences are off the topic. Which two are they?
2. The composition so far seems to be about school and friends. Friends are such an important part of middle school that we shouldn't cut them from the composition.   Take the sentences about friends and move them to the second paragraph. Be sure to cut the "off topic" sentences from question 1. You should be down to 135–40 total words for the 2 paragraphs.

Write a concluding paragraph of about 40–60 words.

Step 2 Look at the composition and make sure it presents a clear main idea.

Example 2: Present a clear main idea

David promised to protect us girls but at first scream he ran out. All of us hated brushing spider webs off our faces every time we turned a corner. It was so dark, I kept on tripping on things I couldn't see. Then this hand came out of nowhere and touched my shoulder and I began to feel a cold wind blow on my neck. I started to tremble all over and my stomach got sick. Why did we come here? When are we going home?

Using the Writer's Checklist

Practice 2: Clear Main Idea

1. In the composition above, the main idea is unclear. Are they inside or outside? It could be either. Are they in a haunted house or a cemetery? Rewrite the opening to this composition so the reader is clear about the main idea.

2. Write an opening sentence expressing the main idea for the second paragraph.

3. Write an opening sentence expressing the main idea for the third paragraph.

Step 3: Give enough details to support and elaborate your main idea.

Example 3: **Glacier Meltdown**

Glaciers are huge ice masses which slowly flow over land. They tend to form in high mountains and in the Polar Regions. Low temperatures year round allow snow to build up and become compacted into very dense ice.

Throughout many parts of the world, glaciers are shrinking in size. Researchers suspect this shrinkage is related to global warming. This glacial shrinkage should be the top priority in future global warming research.

Since the late nineteenth century, researchers from the United States and Russia have studied the world's smaller glaciers. The earth's climate is getting warmer.

Here we have a short 3 paragraph composition which makes a lot of general statements like "The earth's climate is getting warmer," but there are no facts to back up the statements. The author states that research has been done, but doesn't state what the researchers found out. The reader needs more details.

Read the following version of "Glacier Meltdown" with the details added. See how details make the difference. Then answer the questions that follow.

Glacier Meltdown – with details

Glaciers are huge ice masses which slowly flow over land. They tend to form in high mountains and in the Polar Regions. Low temperatures year round allow snow to build up and become compacted into very dense ice. The thickness of the ice varies between 300 and 10,000 feet.

Throughout many parts of the world, glaciers are shrinking in size. Researchers suspect this shrinkage is related to global warming. Since the late nineteenth century, researchers from the United States and Russia have recorded an eleven percent reduction in the total volume of ice in the world's smaller glaciers. In Central Europe, the mountain glaciers have been reduced to half their original size.

All is not lost, however. Greenland and Antarctica, which contain ninety percent of the world's ice, have not shown this shrinkage in glacier size. Nevertheless, the retreat occurring among the 500,000 smaller glaciers in the world does provide another convincing fact that the earth's climate is getting warmer.

Chapter 7

Practice 3: Details

1. Make a list of 5 sentences that added extra detail to "Glacier Meltdown."
2. Read the following paragraph noting the lack of interesting detail. Rewrite the paragraph adding at least 5 sentences of detail.

> This year I planted my first garden. It turned out okay. Some things grew and some things didn't. I learned some things and will do better next year.

Step 4: Put your ideas in a logical order.

Example 4: **What Happened?**

1. Mike climbed up the tower. **2.** He doubted his sanity. **3.** The wind rushing past his ears and face was deafening. **4.** He took one step and jumped off the tower. **5.** Mike got instructions on how to bungee jump from the instructor on the ground. **6.** Four times he bounced before the eternity was over. **7.** He never felt his heart throb so hard in his chest before. **8.** He fastened the bungee cord and harness to his legs before he went up. **9.** The ground came up fast and he was pulled back into the air.

1. Obviously the writer had an exciting time and got his thoughts down on paper, but the story is not easy to follow. What would be a logical order for the story? Just write the sentence numbers in the best order.

For questions 2–7, List the number of each sentence in the logical order that would make a good paragraph.

2.
  1. Do not leave the waiting room until your name is called.
  2. Make an appointment over the phone to see a doctor.
  3. Pay for services rendered.
  4. Sign in at the reception desk at the time of your appointment.

3.
  1. The guests paid their check and left a tip.
  2. The hostess found a table for the party of four.
  3. The server brought out the ordered meal.
  4. The server wrote down the guests' order.
  5. The server cleaned off their dirty dishes and brought the check.

4.
  1. When the drying cycle is finished, take out your clothes and fold them immediately.
  2. Turn on the washing machine for the appropriate water level and temperature setting.
  3. Place all clothes of similar color together into the empty washing machine.
  4. Take the clothes out of the washer, and place them in the dryer.
  5. Mom gave me directions for washing my own clothes.

5.
  1. The boy picked up his toothbrush.
  2. The boy swished water in his mouth and spit into the sink.
  3. Tad was four years old, and now he was a big boy.
  4. The boy brushed his teeth, gums, and tongue.
  5. Very carefully, he spread the toothpaste onto the toothbrush.
  6. His mom watched with pride from the doorway until he was through.

Using the Writer's Checklist

6.
1. Gather a large supply of dead branches in the forest.
2. Use a flint or match to light the kindling.
3. Add smaller twigs first, and then add larger branches.
4. Use pine straw and dead leaves as kindling.
5. The scout leader gave him directions on how to start a campfire.
6. Clear away a 4 foot circle down to the dirt and make a circle of rocks.

7.
1. Tape the wrapping paper together so that the paper will stay on the gift.
2. Tape a card or a bow to the top of the wrapped gift.
3. Buy wrapping paper, scissors, see-through tape, and a card or bow at the local drugstore.
4. Cover the gift with wrapping paper, and cut off the excess paper.
5. Cut the wrapping paper big enough to fit around the box.
6. Wrapping a present can take more time than finding the right present.

SENTENCE USAGE

Usage

Write using appropriate subject-verb agreement, verb tenses, word meaning, and word endings.

Step 1: Check your rough draft for subject-verb agreement

In the following composition, there are many subject-verb agreement problems. If you need to review, go back to Chapter 2.

1. The popularity of various baby names have really changed over the last century. **2.** Each decade seems to have its "top ten." **3.** Some names, however, was popular for many years. **4.** One example is the girl's name Mary: it was number one for many of the years between 1890 and 1969! **5.** The boy's name Michael has been first or second for most of the past 30 years!

6. Back in the 1970s and '80s, the number one girl's name was Jennifer. **7.** For boys Jason and David was favored, followed by Matthew and James. **8.** If you know anyone born in the '50s or '60s, you might run across women called Susan, Patricia,

9. Karen, Deborah, and Donna, and men named James, John, Robert, and William.

10. Over the last ten years, the most popular names for girls has been Emily, Madison, Hannah, Ashley, Jessica, and Sarah. **11.** Many of these are spelled in diverse ways. **12.** You may have met a Sara, an Emilie, or a Hana. **13.** Top names for boys includes Michael, Jacob, Christopher, Nicolas, Joshua, and Andrew. They do not seem to have the variety of feminine spellings, but they often have many nicknames. **14.** When one looks at the list above, it could says Mike, Jake, Chris, Nick, Josh, and Andy—or Drew!

15. What fun it is to look back at the names people chose for their babies during different eras. **16.** And we haven't even mentioned what influenced those choices, like the movie stars or sports celebrities of the day. **17.** For real fun, one can tries to predict which names will be hot next year!

For a a more detailed understanding of subject-verb agreement, see American Book Company's *Basics Made Easy: Grammar and Usage*.

COMMAS AND END PUNCTUATION

Mechanics:

- Write using correct punctuation.

Be sure to look over your rough draft for any punctuation errors.

Practice 4: Commas and End Punctuation

Each of the sentences below needs commas and end punctuation. Copy each sentence, adding end punctuation where needed. (Some sentences have comma hints.)

1. Jessie did not remember his name nor could he recognize his friends (compound)
2. After all Bryan didn't promise to come to the party (introductory phrase)
3. David as you know will not be with us next week (interrupter)
4. Mrs. Ringwald spoke read and wrote about astronomy (items in a series)
5. Tiffany's work nevertheless was displayed at the art show
6. Derek Johnson a talented quarterback ran to the right ran to the left and tripped over John's foot before being sacked.
7. Stephanie tore ripped and chewed her way through the ropes before her captors returned
8. My uncle a prisoner of war in Vietnam received an award from Congress
9. While the oven was hot Mom put in two more sheets of chocolate chip cookies
10. The cold dark cave had never been explored
11. Jennifer heard the joke and she laughed about it all day (compound sentence)
12. Michael lives at 431 Baker Street Baton Rouge Louisiana
13. The pilot full of fear landed the plane on the dark icy runway
14. Feeling tired Priscilla and Mary went straight to bed

CAPITALIZATION

Mechanics:

- Write using correct capitalization.

Be sure to look over your rough draft for any punctuation errors.

Using the Writer's Checklist

Practice 5: Capitalization

Each of the sentences below need capital letters. Copy each sentence, adding or taking out capitalization where needed.

1. pierre wrote, "i still haven't found what i'm looking for."
2. I heard that professor johnson headed south because he wanted to explore the southwest.
3. "The Summer," said steve, "Is my favorite time of year."
4. azaleas have been planted near the Martin Luther King center in atlanta, Georgia.
5. Mr. mccoy was eating steak at the dixie diner.
6. Here is the verdict: the jury finds the defendant to be not guilty on all charges.
7. Did you tell Mother that we can get mexican food delivered now?
8. Juan diaz said, "the Pacific ocean is about two miles West of here."
9. The renaissance was a time when great art and thinking flourished.
10. All jambalaya tastes better when it is made in the south.
11. President Bush gave the Senator a plaque last thursday, thanking him for his Help with the tsunami victims.
12. When amy and i go back to school in the Fall, mrs. Baker will be the Principal.

FORMATTING

Mechanics:

Write using appropriate formatting (e.g., indentations, margins).

Make sure when you write your final draft you indent the first line of each paragraph. Also, be sure not to write to the edges of the paper. There should be a margin of 1" to $1\frac{1}{2}$" on the right and left side of your essay.

SPELLING

Spelling:

always use appropriate spelling in your essay. For additional instructions and practice see **CHAPTER 1**.

PENMANSHIP

Make sure the handwriting on your final draft is clear and legible. Be sure to erase completely before correcting any mistakes in your work. If your cursive is difficult to read, print the final draft using both upper and lower case letters. Remember, an illegible essay will not be graded.

CHAPTER 7 REVIEW

A. Correct the spelling errors in the following passage. Use your dictionary to find words if you are not sure about them. The first sentence is done for you.

                     rinsing

    Brushing and ~~rinseing~~ are excellent ways to prevent cavities. Besides brushing, useing dental floss helps you clean between teeth. Flossing is important, but it may feel unatural at first. Be sure to wrap the floss securly around your fingers so it doesn't slip. Another vital step is seing a dentist regularly. Once a year is sufficient, unless you are experienceing problems. What you eat should support the effectivness of your cleaning routine. A healthy diet, includeing plenty of calcium, helps build strong teeth. Chewing hard candy or ice can crack teeth, and by the time cracks are noticable, the teeth need fillings. Avoid candy altogether; even when you let it disolve in your mouth, the sugar can attack tooth enamel. The more you take care of your pearly whites, the longer you can keep smiling!

B. Each of the sentences in the composition below needs commas and end punctuation and correct capitalization. Each paragraph needs to be indented. Copy the composition making all corrections needed. In addition, there are 3 extra capital letters that should be lower case and 3 extra commas. Be sure to remove them as well as add the missing capital letters, commas, and end punctuation. When you copy the composition, write so someone else besides you can read it. Remember, on the Leap test, if the reader can't read your composition then you will get a 0. If your handwriting is poor, then print.

    Bill Haast, an 85 year old Floridian, has developed a reputation as a man with an acquired immunity to snakes playing with a Cobra is an everyday activity with Mr. Haast, who has been bitten no less than 162 times by Venomous snakes. He began his experimentation, with snake venom, in 1948 by injecting himself with small amounts of Rattlesnake venom over the years, he has built up the dosage. He believes the snake venom has kept him healthy. He has not once been sick, since he began injecting himself with venom. He had his near death experiences, though in 1958, Haast was bitten by a blue krait, an asian snake which has venom many times more poisonous than a cobra's it has been known to kill elephants. In the late 1970s Haast produced a drug called Proven which mirrored the effects produced by his own immunity to snake, bites the drug has been used to treat rheumatoid arthritis and MS (multiple sclerosis).

Using the Writer's Checklist

Chapter 8
Word Meaning and Analysis

LOUISIANA READING BENCHMARKS ADDRESSED IN THIS CHAPTER INCLUDE:
ELA-1-M1   Using knowledge of word meaning and developing basic and technical vocabulary using various strategies (e.g., context clues, idioms, affixes, etymology, multiple-meaning words) (1,4)

WORD DERIVATION AND ANALYSIS

As children, we begin speaking by using simple words, such as cup, toy, and dog. This is the beginning of spoken vocabulary. Similarly, as we read, we learn simple words first, often by sight. Then we learn to sound out the syllables of longer words. As readers, we improve our level of reading by continuously building on our vocabulary.

You can build your vocabulary and discover new words by learning about the parts of words: **root words**, **prefixes**, and **suffixes**. This process of studying words is called **word analysis**. In word analysis, we study how the word is formed from its smaller parts. This is called the **derivation**, or make up, of the word. Studying word derivation will help you develop a deeper understanding of what you read. It involves learning about the **origin of English words,** or etymology, because most prefixes, suffixes, and root words in the English language came originally from foreign languages.

Analysis is an important part of learning new words. To **analyze** something means to look closely at it in order to examine its small parts. In word analysis, we detect the parts of a word—the prefix, the suffix, and the root—and their meanings. Then we analyze how these meanings go together to form the meaning of the complete word.

When we analyze a word, we also discover the **derivation** of that word. The term derivation refers to the fact that English words come from, or are *derived* from, words from foreign and ancient languages. The example on this page shows a word derivation. The word *photography* is derived from the Greek words *photo* and

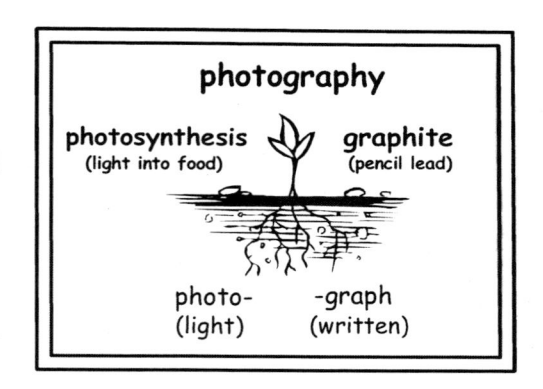

Word Meaning and Analysis

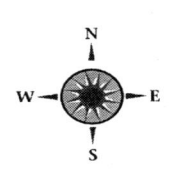

Since its beginning, the English language has borrowed and adopted words from many other languages. So, the origins of English words are found in foreign languages. The first three major languages that affected the English language were Latin, Norse, and French. Greek has also had a major influence. We will study many of the common root words, prefixes, and suffixes that English has gained from different sources.

Since many words are made up of smaller parts, breaking them down into these units is one way to determine word meanings. Different words can be formed from, or derived from, the same root word, or **etymology**. This is also called **word derivation**. Consider the root word *port*. From that Latin root, meaning *to carry*, English has formed many words, including transport, import, deport, and portable. Root words originate mostly from Latin or Greek, which were two of the first influences on the English language. **Word analysis** includes the process of determining the meaning of words based on the meanings of their smaller parts. These parts consist of the **root**, the main unit of a word; the **prefix**, a beginning word unit; and the **suffix**, an ending word unit. Note that not all words have prefixes and suffixes. However, a majority of English words are formed on this basis.

For example, in the word illumination, "-il" is a prefix which means, for this use, "in." The root, "lumin," comes from the Latin word *lumen* for "light." The letters "-tion" at the end of a word form a suffix which means an action or a state of being. By dividing illumination into its smallest units, you discover that it basically means "being in light." If you look in the dictionary for illumination, you will find there are several variations built on this meaning. You can use the same process for other words. The root "sol" found in desolate and solitaire comes from the Latin word for "one" or "alone." Desolate means lonely, as being abandoned, and solitaire refers to single items: for example, a game for one person, or a single gem.

Learning the word parts in the lists below will unlock the meanings of countless words in your reading. Mark the ones you do not know, and then learn their meanings.

Prefixes

Prefix	Meaning	Example	Prefix	Meaning	Example
ab	from	absurd	in	not, or into	inept inhabit
ad	to	advocate	inter	between	interstate
anti	against	antibody	intra	within	intranet
be	thoroughly	befuddle	post	after	postgraduate
com	with	community	pre	before	preheat
de	reverse	decompose	pro	onward	progress
dis	not	disinterested	re	back again	recapture
en	the state of	entangle	sub	under	subspecies
ex	out	exit	un	not	untold
il	not, or into	illegal, illuminate			

144

Chapter 8

Roots

Root	Meaning	Example	Root	Meaning	Example
ann	year	annual	multi	many	multifaceted
aqua	water	aquamarine	path	feeling	telepathy
aud	hear	audible	phon	sound	phonics
bio	life	biology	port	carry	portfolio
cent	hundred	century	rad	ray	radar
chron	time	chronicle	scope	see	telescope
dic	to speak	dictate	scrib	to write	scripture
gen	race, kind	genesis	tele	distance	telegraph
ject	throw	interject	ven	to come, go	convention
med	middle	mediator	viv, vit	life	vivacious

Suffixes

Suffix	Meaning	Examples	Suffix	Meaning	Examples
able	capable of being	capable, unbeatable	ly	in like manner	confidently, boisterously
age	related to	marriage, foliage	less	without	meaningless, thoughtless
al, ial	act of, or like	special, genial	logy	study of	geology, theology
ance	state or quality of	furtherance, performance	ment	condition of	contentment, entanglement
er, or	one who	buyer, actor	ness	quality, condition	kindness, likeness
ful	full of	wonderful, bountiful	ous	full of	clamorous, poisonous
hood	state of	fatherhood, parenthood	ship	position held	kinship, chairmanship
ish	having the quality of	clannish, sluggish	tion	action, or state of being	motion, education
itis	inflammation	bronchitis, gingivitis	ure	process of	overture, adventure
ive	having the nature of	positive, progressive	ward	in a specified direction	onward, afterward

Word Meaning and Analysis

Practice 1: Writing with Roots

People often have trouble using their time wisely in order to meet deadlines. In a paragraph of advice to younger students, tell about a situation in which you had trouble managing your time. Explain how you resolved this problem. Include five root words from the previous page along with prefixes or suffixes, and underline them.

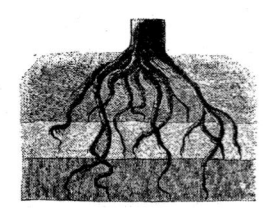

Practice 2: Word Meaning and Analysis

On your own paper, divide each of the following words into prefixes, suffixes, and roots (when possible), and explain how these parts make up the meaning of the word. If you need help, consult a dictionary.

Example: indelible

in (not) + del(ere) (to erase) + ible (capable of being) = not capable of being erased

1.	inscribe	2.	supplement	3.	restore
4.	subpar	5.	hullabaloo	6.	extraneous
7.	bronchitis	8.	bilingual	9.	prediction
10.	misadvise	11.	introvert	12.	pathology

Practice 3: Word Analysis

Match the prefix, suffix, or root with its meaning.

Matching Prefixes

___ 1.	de	A.	reverse
___ 2.	re	B.	again
___ 3.	inter	C.	out
___ 4.	com	D.	under
___ 5.	ab	E.	by
___ 6.	sub	F.	not
___ 7.	in	G.	to
___ 8.	pre	H.	with
___ 9.	be	I.	between
___ 10.	en	J.	before
___ 11.	ex	K.	from
___ 12.	ad	L.	In

Matching Roots

___ 13.	port	A.	year
___ 14.	ject	B.	kind
___ 15.	rad	C.	ray
___ 16.	path	D.	feeling
___ 17.	chron	E.	write
___ 18.	aud	F.	come
___ 19.	scrib	G.	throw
___ 20.	dic	H.	sound
___ 21.	phon	I.	hear
___ 22.	tele	J.	distance
___ 23.	gen	K.	time
___ 24.	ven	L.	to carry

Matching Suffixes

25. logy _____		A.	inflammation
26. itis _____		B.	capable of
27. ment _____		C.	one who
28. ward _____		D.	related to
29. ly _____		E.	study of
30. less _____		F.	condition of
31. age _____		G.	in a direction
32. tion _____		H.	state of being
33. ship _____		I.	full of
34. ful _____		J.	position of
35. er _____		K.	without
36. able _____		L.	in a like manner

Practice 4: Word Analysis Passage

Read the following article, and then answer the questions after it.

Pilgrim Life

When the Pilgrims landed in November of 1620 on the shore of what is now called Massachusetts, they needed to find food and build shelter if they were to **survive**. There were no stores for buying **provisions**, and no houses for the Pilgrims to move into. All their needs had to be met by themselves. Even the smallest hands **contributed** to that effort. They were a **resourceful** group though. They were able to overcome their hardships and establish an enduring colony which they named Plymouth.

The first winter was brutal and cold. Many of those who crossed the ocean to attain freedom never saw the next spring. Those who did survive **cooperated** to prepare for spring planting. Their hard work that first year was rewarded with a **abundant** harvest in the autumn of 1621. The Pilgrims celebrated the first Thanksgiving as a time of gratitude.

One of the **dictums** that the Pilgrims lived by was that hard work is one of life's greatest virtues. They believed that settling the wilderness of the New World was their destiny. so they were driven to survive despite chronic struggles. After that first Thanksgiving celebration, the Pilgrims realized that their **envisioned** destiny might come true.

Word Meaning and Analysis

Indeed it did! Over the next several years, Plymouth grew into a successful community of 180 colonists. By 1627, more than one-third of them were age sixteen or younger. There were no schools, but after working hard in the fields during the day the children enjoyed reading at home at night. Their work centered on providing **sustenance** for the family. The children performed **multifarious** chores, depending on their age and abilities. But by the time they were six years old, they provided **vital** help to their family. Most of them worked full days alongside their parents. These hard-working children became **committed** adults who passed on their determination and sense of destiny to their own children. This pattern **engendered** a new nation which became one of the strongest in history.

Take a moment to study the words (focus on their prefixes, roots, and suffixes) that are bolded and underlined in the passage. Then, for each of the following words from the passage, choose the response that is closest in meaning to the word's use in the passage.

1. **Survive:**
    A. live   B. grow   C. begin   D. move

2. **provisions:**
    A. cameras   B. ammunition   C. stocks   D. fuel

3. **contributed:**
    A. added to   B. cheered on   C. worked against   D. took away from

4. **resourceful:**
    A. happy   B. strong   C. weak   D. inventive

5. **cooperated:**
    A. understood   B.   C. planned   D. worked together

6. **abundant:**
    A. plentiful   B. sparce   C. tasty   D. beautiful

7. **dictums:**
    A. ambitions   B. fears   C. ideas   D. formal statements

8. **envisioned:**
    A. heard of   B. imagined   C. predicted   D. hoped for

9. **sustenance:**
    A. protection   B. work   C. care   D. support

10. **multifarious:**
    A. boring   B. varied   C. hard   D. easy

148

11. vital:

A. important B. minimal C. reluctant D. special

12. committed:

A. lonely B. dedicated C. happy D. educated

13. engendered:

A. created B. described C. governed D. affected

CONTEXT CLUES

One important method of finding the meaning of words is by using **context clues**. This means to look at the way words are used in combination with other words in their setting. Look at the words around an unknown word. Think about the meaning of these words or the idea of the whole sentence. Then, match the meaning of the unknown word to the meaning of the known text.

In the following statements, choose the word which best reflects the meaning of the bolded word.

1. Green algae remain **dormant** until rains revive them.

    A. dry B. dead C. small D. inactive

2. Exercise that increases your heart and breathing rates for a sustained period of time is called **aerobic**.

    A. of long duration C. requiring oxygen
    B. improving strength D. strenuous

If the bolded words above are unfamiliar to you, there are several ways in which you can still determine their meaning. Using context clues is the most common strategy. For example, in statement 1, the clause "until rains revive them" suggests that dormant is not a **dead** state but an **inactive** one, since the rains make the algae active again. In addition, the signal word "until" tells us that **dormant** is the opposite of **revive**. When two words are compared in this way, it is called a **contrast clue**.

For statement 2, you may use a **definition clue**. The signal word "is" indicates that the definition of aerobic is described in the first part of the sentence. Since heart and breathing rates are *increased* and all organisms need oxygen to live, aerobic must mean "requiring oxygen."

Context clues help us determine the meaning of words from the way they are used in a sentence. The idea or message of the whole text becomes clearer if we use the correct meaning. By looking at and analyzing the phrases and signal words that come before or after a particular word, you can often figure out its meaning. On the next page you will find a list of the main types of context clues with their signal words.

Word Meaning and Analysis

Context Clues	Signal Words
Comparison	*also, like, resembling, too, both, than* Look for clues that indicate an unfamiliar word is similar to a familiar word or phrase. **Example:** The accident felled the utility pole like a tree for timber.
Contrast	*but, however, while, instead of, yet, unlike* Look for clues that indicate an unfamiliar word is opposite in meaning to a familiar word or phrase. **Example:** Stephanie is usually in a state of *composure* while her sister is mostly boisterous.
Definition or Restatement	*is, or, that is, in other words, which* Look for words that define the term or restate it in other words. **Example:** The principle's idea is to *circuit*—or move around—the campus weekly to make sure everything is okay.
Example	*for example, for instance, such as* Look for examples used in context that reveal the meaning of an unfamiliar word. **Example:** People use all sorts of *vehicles* such as cars, bicycles, rickshaws, airplanes, boats, and motorcycles.

Practice 5: Using Context Clues

Above each bolded word, write its meaning. Use context clues to help you.

1. Those who cannot afford **bail** cannot be freed on pre-trial release.
2. Hank said the ocean was very **tranquil**; I also thought the ocean was peaceful.
3. Sometimes strong **herbicides** are needed to eliminate weeds from the garden.
4. **Residues** such as ammonia even show up in grain sprayed with **pesticides**.
5. Since Brian disliked working for others, he decided to become an **entrepreneur**.
6. This word is **ambiguous**; it can have two meanings.
7. Jennifer wanted no **remuneration** in money or gifts; her reward was saving the pet.

8. He was a **fastidious** dresser, always very neat and particular about what he wore.

9. After a **cursory** examination of only a minute or two, the doctor said he did not believe there was anything seriously wrong with the child.

10. Smoking too much is likely to have a **pernicious** effect on one's health; they're not called "cancer sticks" for nothing.

11. The bad odor from the leaking gas **permeated** the whole house.

Working with individual sentences is good practice. However, for a true practice of what you will be working with for classes and for any type of reading assessment, you will need to practice with longer passages of text.

Practice 6: Passage Practice

Read the following article. Then, answer the questions that follow.

What Is Ethics, Anyway?

Ethics is a concept we hear about, but few people today stop to think what it really means. However, philosophers and statesmen since the time of Plato have **contemplated** the definition and details of ethics, which is sometimes difficult to state. Clearly, ethics is not something invented by one person or even a society, but has some well-founded standards on which it is based.

Some people **equate** ethics with feelings. But being ethical is not simply following one's feelings. A criminal may "feel" robbing a person is okay, when really it is wrong and unethical to steal. Many people may identify ethics with religion, and it is true that most religions include high ethical standards and strong motivation for people to behave morally. But ethics cannot be confined only to religion, or only religious people could be ethical. There are even cases in which religious teaching and ethics clash: for example, some religions **inhibit** the rights of women, which opposes the ethical standard of basic justice.

Ethics also is not simply following laws or what is accepted by a society. The laws of civilized nations often **embody** ethical standards. However, unethical laws can exist. For example, laws have allowed slavery, which is unethical behavior as it takes the freedom of another human being. Therefor, laws and other conventions accepted by a society cannot be the measure for what is ethical. Doing "whatever society accepts" may be far outside the realm of ethics—Nazi Germany is an example of an ethically **debased** society.

What ethics really refers to is a system of people's moral standards and values. It's like a road map of qualities that people want to have to be "decent human beings." It is also the formal study of the standards of human behavior. Ethics relies on well-based standards of "right" (like honesty, compassion, and loyalty) and "wrong" (like stealing, murder, and fraud). Ethical standards **encompass** ideas such as respect for others, honesty, justice, doing good, and preventing harm.

1. In the context of this passage, what does the word **contemplated** mean?

    A. thought about   B. looked at   C. taken apart   D. peered into

2. In the context of this passage, which of the following is closest in meaning to **equate**?

    A. compare   B. multiply   C. balance   D. flatten

Word Meaning and Analysis

3. In this passage, which of the following is closest in meaning to the word **inhibit**?
   A. lie about   B. live in   C. give to   D. hold back

4. Which dictionary definition of the word **debased** best applies to its use in the passage?
   A. depraved   B. corrupt   C. impure   D. distorted

5. In this passage, which of the following is closest in meaning to the word **encompass**?
   A. steer   B. include   C. begin   D. mean

IDIOMS

Idoms are phrases or expressions in which the real meaning is different from the literal or stated meaning. For example, the literal meaning of "It's raining cats and dogs" indicates that cats and dogs are falling out of the sky with the rain. However, the real meaning is that the rain is falling heavily from the sky. Another example of an idiom is "The apple does not fall far from the tree." The stated meaning is clear, but the actual meaning is quite different. This expression really says that a child is very similar mentally or physically to a parent.

Practice 7: Idioms

Match the underlined idiom on the left with the actual meaning on the right.

_____ 1. Her life is an open book.　　　　　　　　　a. pay for expenses

_____ 2. You're driving me up the wall.　　　　　　　b. create a disturbance

_____ 3. Take up your complaint with Tito.　　　　　c. without thinking

_____ 4. You want your meal for here or to go.　　　d. stop doing something

_____ 5. Don't make waves when you're in this class.　e. turn off

_____ 6. Knock it off, or I'll tell Dad!　　　　　　　f. making crazy

_____ 7. Today we're going to have it out with Vinny.　g. eat here or take home

_____ 8. Mr. Sanchez picked up the tab for our class party.　h. got my attention

_____ 9. Bethany will catch cold near the window.　　i. confront

_____ 10. Off the top of my head, I'd like to go to El Paso.　j. get sick

_____ 11. Cut off the lights, please.　　　　　　　　k. not a secret

_____ 12. She caught my eye.　　　　　　　　　　　l. talk about

Chapter 8 Review:

A. Word Origins. Choose the best answer for each question.

1. What should you add to the word <u>legal</u> to make it mean "not legal"?
   - A. dis
   - B. il
   - C. un
   - D. pro

2. The "ness" in meekness means
   - A. condition
   - B. type
   - C. full of
   - D. capable of

3. What should you add to the word started to make it mean "started again"?
   - A. pre
   - B. post
   - C. re
   - D. de

4. The "able" in breakable means
   - A. opposite of
   - B. a way of life
   - C. similar to
   - D. capable of being

5. What root added to logy would mean the study of time?
   - A. chronos
   - B. viv
   - C. bio
   - D. post

6. The "cent" in centennial means
   - A. ten
   - B. hundred
   - C. thousand
   - D. ten thousand

C. Idioms. Choose the best answer.

7. She's a trip when she bowls.
   - A. funny
   - B. mean
   - C. happy
   - D. sad

8. In a nutshell, Fu got all Bs on his report card.
   - A. Sadly
   - B. In a short time
   - C. Finally
   - D. In summary

Chapter 9
Main Ideas, Summarizing, and Paraphrasing

LOUISIANA READING BENCHMARKS ADDRESSED IN THIS CHAPTER INCLUDE:	
ELA-7-M1	Using comprehension strategies (e.g., summarizing, recognizing literary devices, paraphrasing) to analyze oral, written, and visual texts

In informational writing, or non-fiction, authors write to communicate a message, some information, or a main idea. To help you understand what an author is saying, you need to study the **details** of the passage. These details go together to form and support the **main idea** of the passage. Details are made up of the answers to the *five Ws and an H*: Who, What, Where, When, Why, and How. These questions and their answers point to the main idea, or purpose of a passage and are essential to reading comprehension.

Knowing the details and the main idea of a passage will help you with the process of summarizing the information you have learned from it. **Summarizing** means condensing the information in a text to the most relevant points and ideas.

Summarizing informational resources helps you to understand what you read. If you can write a summary of an article, including in your summary the article's main idea as well as the most important details that support that idea, you will have a good understanding of the the text.

Paraphrasing is another way to improve your reading comprehension. Paraphrasing is actually rewriting what you have read, in your own words. Like summarizing, paraphrasing helps you understand what you are reading because in order to state the information in your own words, you must look closely at each sentence, each detail, and idea, and think about how you would say it. Paraphrasing is a powerful tool in both reading and research.

DETAILS

To present an idea or event clearly to a reader, an author will write may details to support and elaborate on it. These details usually, in some way, answer the 5 W's and H questions. What are these questions? They are

- **Who** is the story about, or, **Who** are the important people or characters mentioned in the text?
- **What** takes place in the story? **What** is the author mainly talking about?
- **Where** do the events of the story take place, or, **Where** does the information come from?
- **Why** do the events of the story take place, or, **Why** is the main idea important?

Main Ideas, Summarizing, and Paraphrasing

- **When** does the story take place, or, **When** was the passage written?
- **How** does the story resolve itself, or, **How** does the author present his or her conclusion or main idea?

The 5 Ws and H provide the details of a story or information article. These details give color and meaning to the writing. While the main idea is what *drives* the story, details are what *support* the main idea.

Think of an automobile. Without tires, an engine, and a steering wheel, the car would not work. In the same way, it would be impossible to understand what the author is saying without facts and details to support the main idea of a story or article.

Practice 1: Locating Details

Read the paragraph below, and answer the 5 Ws and H questions that follow it. Write in complete sentences.

Passing the Test

It was the day Claire had been waiting for all summer long. She would be tested for acceptance on her local competitive swim team. Claire had learned to swim by taking lessons at the beach near her home town of Gulf Shores. She had practiced her mechanics every day. She had learned the frog kick, the back stroke, the crawl, and even the butterfly. Today she was allowed to choose two strokes to complete the half-mile distance required for the test. When it came her turn, Claire decided upon the crawl and the back stroke. As Claire swam, a small boat, commandeered by her instructor, followed her. Claire forgot her nervousness after several minutes, as she concentrated on pacing herself and her breathing. This was one of the greatest tests of endurance she had ever faced.

1. Who is the main character in the story?
2. What events are taking place in this story?
3. Where did Claire learn to swim?
4. When (at what time of year) does the swim test take place?
5. Why is this test an important one to Claire?
6. How is the swim test given by the instructors?

MAIN IDEAS

Read the following sentence: "The main idea, or central point, of a passage can be found in two different ways." That sentence is a good example of a topic sentence. It says in a *broad statement* what the topic of this paragraph will be. **Main ideas** are broad statements about the topic, or subject, of a paragraph or passage. Details of a passage support this statement. Details alone cannot be main ideas. Read the paragraph below about the two ways a main idea can be presented in a passage.

The main idea, or central point, of a passage can be found in two different ways. Main ideas may be **directly stated** in a topic sentence. Topic sentences can be found in the title, the introduction, the beginning sentence or the ending sentence of a paragraph. They are almost never found in the middle of a passage. Another way an author expresses the main idea of a passage is by implying, hinting, or suggesting it through the details and facts in a passage. When a main idea is presented without being stated directly, it is called an **implied main idea**. When passages have implied main ideas, the reader must be observant and figure out the main idea from all the details and information given in the passage.

To review, there are two ways authors reveal the main idea:

- A directly stated main idea, and
- An implied main idea.

Now we will take a closer look at each of these types of main ideas and how to find them.

DIRECTLY STATED MAIN IDEAS

When you read information with a directly stated main idea, you will usually find some or all of the main idea in the title, in the beginning sentence, or in the ending sentences.

The example below shows a directly stated main idea in the first sentence.

Mockingbirds

Mockingbirds are common and popular birds in the eastern and southern regions of the United States. The Mockingbird is the state bird for Arkansas, Florida, Mississippi, Tennessee, and Texas. Residents of these states enjoy the surprising and musical range of sounds that these birds can produce. "Mockers," as they are affectionately called, can mimic other birds, mammals, and insects with song and sounds. Mockingbirds often live close to human homes, nesting in ornamental hedges. Mockingbirds have been frequently mentioned in literature, songs, and stories of the South.

After reading the *first sentence,* we know that the passage is about mockingbirds. The first sentence states the main idea. The rest of the sentences give details about how the mockingbird is common and why it is popular. Read the next two passages and their questions. An explanation for the correct answers is found after each set of questions.

Modern-Day Wonder

The title of modern-day wonder of the world should go to the Smithsonian Institution. It is the largest grouping of museums and art galleries in the world. You will find the Smithsonian in the heart of the nation's capital, Washington D.C. It is located near all the major federal government buildings such as the White House. The Smithsonian has more than 100 million objects and specimens in its collections. The objects range from the funny to the unique. You may see, for example, George Washington's false teeth, the Inauguration gowns of the presidential First Ladies, and the Apollo Lunar Landing Module. The Smithsonian is so large that it takes weeks to see all of its collections. The Smithsonian also contains a zoo which houses more than 2,500 animals. The National Zoological Park and the National Air and Space Museum are two of the favorite attractions in the Smithsonian Institution. This collection of human knowledge, experience, and accomplishment is truly a wonder.

Main Ideas, Summarizing, and Paraphrasing

1. What is the main idea of the paragraph?
   A. The zoo and the air and space museum are the most popular attractions in the Smithsonian.
   B. George Washington's false teeth are on display at the Smithsonian.
   C. The Smithsonian Institution is so massive, it could be called a wonder of the world.
   D. The Smithsonian Institution is located in the heart of downtown Washington D.C.

Choice C is correct: The main idea is directly stated near the beginning, and again at the end of the passage. Choices A, B, and D are all details that support the main idea. Remember the example of the car supported by its wheels.

Excerpt from The Prince and the Pauper by Mark Twain

In the ancient city of London, on a certain autumn day in the second quarter of the sixteenth century, a boy was born to a poor family of the name of Canty, who did not want him. On the same day, another English child was born to a rich family of the name of Tudor, who did want him. All England wanted him too. England had so longed for him, and hoped for him, and prayed God for him, that, now that he was really come, the people went nearly mad for joy.

2. What is the main idea of this paragraph?
   A. In London, a baby boy was born to the poor Canty family during the fall of the year.
   B. London is an ancient city in England.
   C. The Tudor family was wealthy and well liked.
   D. A prince and a pauper were born on the same day in very different circumstances.

The main idea is directly stated in the title. Choice D correctly describes what the passage is about. Choices **A**, **B**, and **C** describe only parts of the main idea.

Tips for Finding a Directly Stated Main Idea

1. **Read the title.** The main topic of the paragraph or passage is often mentioned in the title.

2. **Read the first and last sentence of each paragraph.** Most of the key words and ideas will be stated in these places.

3. **Choose the answer that is the best statement or restatement of the paragraph or passage.** Your choice should contain the key words mentioned in the title, the first sentence or the last sentence of each paragraph or passage.

4. **Always read the entire passage to get an overview of what the author is writing.**

Chapter 9

IMPLIED MAIN IDEAS

An author can give you important information without directly stating it, by giving clues or suggestions through the details of the passage. Be a detective and see what the clues in the following sentence tell you.

Sam's favorite part of the hike was watching the colorful leaves falling all around him.

What season of the year is it? The author does not say, but you can figure it out. You can conclude that the season is autumn because of the hints the author gives you. Because the season is described without using the word "autumn," it is **implied**.

Does Sam enjoy hiking? The author doesn't say it directly, but you can come to the conclusion that he does enjoy hiking since there is a "favorite part" to the hike. The author *implies* that Sam enjoys hiking.

An implied main idea in a passage can be found by reading more than one sentence and looking for clues. In a paragraph, you will be reading several sentences. If there is no directly stated main idea, you will need to think of the sentences as answers to the 5 Ws and H. The implied main idea will be a broad statement supported by these answers—like the car supported and steered by wheels. Read the following passage, and try to look for the implied main idea.

September Celebration

In Girard Parc, fiddles and accordions fill the air with lively music. People laugh, and dance on the grass, unable to keep still to the sounds of some of the world's greatest Cajun and Creole musicians. The fall evening breeze carries the aroma of simmering jambalaya and shrimp stew. After working up an appetite, the dancers will find no shortage of crustacean delicacies to enjoy before dancing again into the night. Crawfish pies, shrimp scampi, crab cakes, gator on a stick and countless other delectables await them. It seems a love of music is the force that brings all these people together each year for two days in Lafayette. The music is almost continuous, and workshops, great food, and folk crafts round out the extraordinary experience of Festivals Acadiens.

1. What is the implied main idea in this paragraph?
   A. There is a great variety of Cajun food to eat at Festivals Acadiens.
   B. The Festivals Acadiens is an enjoyable and unique yearly celebration in Lafayette.
   C. People are able have a good time and dance far into the night.
   D. Music and dance are central features of the Festivals Acadiens.

The title suggests the topic of the passage is about a celebration. But it does not give the reader enough information to conclude what the main idea of the paragraph is. It is only after we read the entire paragraph that we understand that the main idea is the fun and excitement taking part in a unique event. Choice **B** is the correct answer to the question. The other choices are details of the passage.

Main Ideas, Summarizing, and Paraphrasing

IMPLIED MAIN IDEAS IN PASSAGES OF SEVERAL PARAGRAPHS

Sometimes you need to determine an implied main idea in a passage of several paragraphs. In these passages, you will need to read more than one paragraph to determine the implied main idea. The implied main idea will be found in the combination of the details and facts found throughout the passage.

Read the passage below and answer the question that follows it. An explanation of the correct answer is provided.

The Other Side of Tourism

Have you ever traveled to another city or country? If you have, then you were a tourist. Tourism is popular everywhere, from small towns to large countries. It is one of the world's largest industries. In many regions it is the only source of money and jobs.

While tourism does not yet have a reputation as a polluter, it is not an environmentally friendly business. Tourism creates pollution and consumes natural resources. Tourists consume gas and produce garbage in natural areas.

The United States is a favorite destination for tourists from all over the world. It is a major part of the American economy. But it also presents a challenge. Beaches and cities must be kept clean to attract more tourists. At the same time, more tourists mean more pollution. Somewhere the balance between these two situations must be found.

1. What is the implied main idea of this passage?
   A. Being a tourist in another country can be fun and educational.
   B. The tourism industry can be a main source of money in some countries.
   C. Tourism is popular throughout the world.
   D. Tourism is an industry that has both negative and positive effects on a country.

The title, the first sentence, and last sentence in the passage do not state the main idea of the passage. They reveal only the topic. You have to read through all the paragraphs and note the details to understand completely what the author is saying.

Choice **A** is incorrect because the author is not concerned with how much fun a tourist has. Choices **B** and **C** are direct statements that are correct but do not state the main idea. Choice **D** is the implied main idea of the passage. The author does not directly state the sentence in answer **D**, but through examples and details, the reader can conclude that the tourism industry provides both advantages and disadvantages to a country

Tips for Determining an Implied Main Idea
1. **Read the title and first sentence.** Both will help you identify the topic of the selection.
2. **Read the entire paragraph or passage.** You'll get a general understanding of the selection.
3. **Note the facts and details in each paragraph.** Think of overall ideas they share in common.
4. **Choose the answer that summarizes all of the facts and ideas in the passage.** Confirm your choice by going back to the passage to check your evidence one more time.

Chapter 9

Practice 2: Main Idea in a Paragraph

Read each of the following paragraphs. Decide whether the main idea is stated or implied. If the main idea is stated, underline it. If the main idea is implied, write it in your own words in the space provided. Discuss your answers with your classmates and teacher.

A Golden Seal

In 1922, the American Library Association (ALA) adopted a way to reward outstanding works of children's literature. The award was called The Newbery Award, and it was the first children's book award in the world. The award was named after an eighteenth-century English bookseller, John Newbery. Newbery was considered to be the father of children's literature. As a publisher in England, he was the first to produce good quality illustrated children's books. Today, children's librarians from schools and public libraries nominate a winner every year for this very esteemed award. You can tell a Newbery Award winner by the bright golden seal printed on its cover. The Newbery Award is still one of the greatest honors a children's book author can receive.

1. Stated or Implied _____

Feeding the Fish

Last summer, the fishermen at Lake Chickasaw were puzzled. They weren't catching the bass and stripers as successfully as they had the summer before. They tried all sorts of lures and hooks, but nothing seemed to help. The fish they did catch were small and bony. Then a biologist studied the lake and found that the fish were starving. They had nothing to eat. The biologist told the fishermen to stock the lake with minnows, a small fish usually used as bait. The minnows would provide food for the starving fish. This year, the bass and stripers are healthy, and the fishermen are happy.

2. Stated or Implied _____

How to Make a Pizza

It is easy to order pizza. A telephone call, $15, and a parent's nod of approval can deliver a succulent pizza, complete with cheese sticks, to your door. But did you know that making your own pizza could be just as delicious and more fun? Pizza crusts are sold at most grocery stores. Once you have the crust, the sky is the limit. All you need after that is Italian tomato sauce or perhaps pesto sauce—or maybe a taco sauce, for something really different. Add to this some vegetables; perhaps fried mushrooms, green peppers and onions, or maybe broccoli, spinach, and cauliflower. You might even throw in artichoke hearts if you really get carried away. Then, top it all off with cheese: mozzarella, or perhaps cheddar—or maybe feta or gorgonzola, if you are feeling especially adventurous. So, instead of ordering that tired old pizza at your next party, try buying a pizza crust. Then just add some friends and a whole boatload of unbridled imagination!

3. Stated or Implied _____

Main Ideas, Summarizing, and Paraphrasing

How Important Is Oil?

There is a major debate taking place over a wildlife refuge in the United States. The Arctic National Wildlife Refuge is the second largest wildlife refuge in the United States. It is 19 million acres in size and is located in the northeast corner of Alaska. The refuge is home to hundreds of bird and animal species, including caribou, grizzly bears, polar bears, and snowy owls.

The refuge is also home to one of the largest oil reserves in the country. Some people think that our country needs the oil and that Alaskans would benefit from the jobs that drilling for oil would give them. Other people think of the refuge as a beautiful place that should be protected. Drilling for oil could cause harm to the animals, the coastal waters, and the natural habitat of the animals that live there.

4. Stated or Implied _____

Making a Comeback

It was in the 1960s when the Brown Pelican was named the official state bird of Louisiana. It was during the same decade that its population numbers took a dive as swift and steep as the plunge of the pelican itself, after prey. What was killing the Brown Pelican? The same assassin that put the Bald Eagle on the endangered species list: pesticides, especially DDT. This poison was present in coastal waters where fish would ingest it. Fish are the main course in the pelican diet.

The Brown Pelican is still on the Endangered Species list. However, due to the banning of many dangerous pesticides, it is recovering its numbers. It is the only pelican in the world that is not white. The Brown Pelican nests along rocky coastal areas and waterfronts. If you see a Brown Pelican on the beach, it may be nesting there, or it may have just flown in from Venezuela. Pelicans cover a lot of distance, flying in silent groups in single file between South America and the American Southeast. The Louisiana state bird is a strong and vigorous spirit who will survive forever if its habitat is not harmed.

5. Stated or Implied _____

School Safety is about more than Weapons

Today, police officers patrol school halls, and principals enforce backpack rules to prevent hidden weapons on campus. These measures are taken to make students feel safe at school. But many students—up to 80 percent in middle schools—never feel safe at school. They are students who experience bullying.

Bullying can involve physical abuse such as kicking or hitting a classmate. It can also be as simple as laughing at someone because that person dresses differently or eats different food at lunch. Bullying can leave a child with physical scars or with hurt feelings. Either way, it makes the whole school a sadder and more unsafe place for all students.

6. Stated or Implied _____

Practice 3: Media Search for Main Ideas

A. Idea Exchange. On your own or in a group, look for paragraphs and passages on different subjects in newspapers, magazines, books, or the Internet. Write out the stated or implied main ideas you find on a separate sheet of paper. Bring the articles to class. Exchange only the articles with another student or group members. See if they identify the same main ideas that you did. Then share the results of your efforts with your instructor.

B. Photo Titles. Share photos or pictures with a partner. Then think of titles or main ideas to go with them.

C. News Story Headlines. Bring news stories to class. Cut out the headlines, and keep them separate. Exchange only the articles, and write your own headlines. Compare your own headlines with the original headlines.

SUMMARIZING

Being able to determine main ideas and supporting details in an information source is useful in writing effective summaries. Writing a summary is a way to increase reading comprehension. In order to write a summary of a source, you must first read the source carefully and determine the main ideas and supporting details. Writing a summary is also a valuable research tool. A **summary** condenses the ideas in an article and allows you to use the ideas as a reference without having to reread the entire source repeatedly. Summaries are also a useful means of reviewing information that you need for tests. In this way, summaries are good study tools.

Here are the steps to take in creating a summary of an information source.

> **NOTE:** Remember that it is important that what you write in a summary is in your own words. If you use exact words or phrases copied directly from the passage itself, be sure to put quotation marks around those words.

- Read the entire passage or source.
- Make a list of brief notes on the details and main idea of the passage. These notes will serve as a framework for creating the summary.
- Write down the main idea of the article. It is a good idea to put the main idea in complete sentence form.
- List the major details. These do not have to be in complete sentences; phrases are sufficient.
- Now you are ready to write your summary. The first sentence of your summary should include the title of the source and the author. Write the summary in paragraph form, using the notes you just created.

How long should your summary be? A general rule for summary length is to try and keep it to about one-fourth to one-third of the length of the original source. If your original text is two pages long, your summary should be about one-half to about three-fourths of a page.

EXAMPLE OF A SUMMARY

Read the article below. Then read the notes that were written on the passage, and then the summary of the article.

Main Ideas, Summarizing, and Paraphrasing

Why You Need a Compost Pile in Your Backyard
by Ben Spiffel

The home compost pile is an efficient mulch factory, and mulch is very valuable in a garden. With the use of mulch, your garden will look more attractive and have fewer weeds. The mulch keeps moisture in the soil and also acts as an insulator. It keeps the soil temperature more consistent. Mulch can also be used to disguise bare dirt in the garden.

The process of decomposing plant matter into mulch takes time. That is why gardeners usually have several compost piles "cooking" at various stages of decomposition. Rather than putting grass clippings and leaves in the landfill, they can be composted and recycled back into your garden as mulch. Chemical fertilizers put on the lawn and absorbed by the grass then get recycled through the compost pile. A compost pile also benefits from some types of kitchen waste. These include potato and carrot peelings, coffee grounds, and egg shells. Putting those items in a compost pile is more ecologically friendly than sending them to the local landfill.

A healthy compost pile attracts worms, and the more worms the better. Some gardeners new to composting are unhappy to see earthworms in their compost pile. However, they soon come to realize that those worms are very beneficial to the health of the garden soil. They actually help in the decomposition of the vegetable material. Anything that is added to the compost pile becomes worm food.

A backyard compost pile takes some work and patience, but the rewards and benefits are well worth the time invested in getting it started and maintaining it.

Student Notes

Subject: backyard compost piles

Main idea: If you have a home garden, keeping a compost pile is easy, and the mulch it produces will help your garden in many ways.

Major details: may need more than one—garden plant waste is put to good use, not filling up the landfills—benefits of mulch: attractive, weed control, water holding, insulation for soil—worms attracted to the pile are "very beneficial to the health of your garden" and to the compost pile

Summary

The article "Why You Need a Compost Pile in Your Backyard" by Ben Spiffel discusses backyard compost piles. He says if you have a home garden, creating your own compost pile is easy, and the mulch produced is helpful. Having a compost pile allows grass cuttings and kitchen waste to be put to good use, not to fill up the landfills. Home gardeners may need more than one pile since the process takes time. Four benefits are listed: (1) mulch can improve the appearance of your garden; (2) mulch will help control weeds; (3) the mulch helps gardens retain moisture; and (4) it also helps insulate the soil from heat and cold weather. You need and want the worms that will appear in the pile since they help the composting process.

Chapter 9

Practice 4: Summarizing

Read the following passage. Write notes about the main idea and some of the details in the passage. Then write a summary of the information given in the passage.

Irreplaceable World Treasure Faces Destruction
by Terry Daley

The "land" is craggy, harsh, and remote. It is made up of the skeletons of still living communities. Creatures that live there are unknown in other parts of the world. And only they know how to survive there. They've learned over thousands of years. The water there is undrinkable. The ecosystem is delicately balanced. What can people do with such an ancient, fragile patch of earth and sea?

Consider this option: How about building a luxury hotel on it?

In the warm waters of the Indian Ocean, off the coast of East Africa, lies a rare and precious world treasure. It is called Aldabra, and it is the largest coral atoll in the world. It is home to 200 plant species and many rare and exotic water species. As an atoll, its harsh qualities make it unwelcome for human habitation. That is why it has survived for thousands of years. Until now.

What is an atoll, and why should we care? An atoll is a natural habitat. It is a very large coral reef that has grown above the surface of the water and formed a kind of island. Coral reefs are built by living organisms. They are, in fact, the exoskeletons of marine organisms, and they are home to other marine life. Most coral reefs across the globe have been destroyed by humans. They have been destroyed by pollution, by impacts of large ships, and by divers who break parts of them off to sell as jewelry or artifacts.

The Aldabra Atoll is part of the Seychelle Islands. The government of the Seychelles has maintained Aldabra as a nature reserve for many years. Giant tortoises, three-foot-long crabs, and rare flightless birds find what they need to survive on these islands and in these waters. Species that are nonexistent elsewhere in the world are increasing in numbers here. A slight alteration in the balance set up by these species could cause irreparable harm. The introduction of human habitation could be devastating.

The problem is money, according to the Seychelles Island Foundation (SIF), which manages Aldabra. It costs a half million dollars a year to maintain the sanctuary. The Foundation's solution is to build a luxury hotel on one of the islands. The hotel would cost $2,000 per night for tourists looking for exotic vacations. The government hopes to raise money in this way to continue maintaining the atoll. But along with tourism comes pollution and interference in the lives of the resident wildlife.

If money is the only obstacle to protecting this valuable ecosystem from being damaged and possibly destroyed, then there are other solutions. International environment organizations can produce the money necessary. World governments could contribute a small amount of money each year to help the SIF. Even individuals throughout the world could contribute enough to make a difference.

Main Ideas, Summarizing, and Paraphrasing

The world's largest coral atoll is a treasure and legacy of the whole world. A small amount of support by organizations and people throughout the world can keep this endangered ecosystem alive for many more generations.

Topic: _____

Main Idea: _____

Major Details: _____

_____

Summary: _____

_____

_____

_____

_____

_____

PARAPHRASING

Paraphrasing is different from summarizing. It deals with more exact information. You probably paraphrase people and sources every day. For instance, if at lunch today you talked to your friends about an argument you had with your mother before school, you may have paraphrased it something like this: "She said, like, she wasn't even going to drive me to the skating party because she didn't know any of the adults that were going to be there. I said, 'Mom, you're so annoying! Why do we have to be so different from everyone else on the planet?' I said, 'Jenna's mom *never* checks up on how many chaperones are going to be everywhere in the world before Jenna takes one step outside the house.' She said, well she's not raising Jenna, or something lame like that"

Paraphrasing must accurately present information, while *not using the exact words or phrases* of the original information source. Your description of the argument with your mother was probably very accurate, but it did not repeat **exactly** every word that was spoken by each person in the argument. For example, what your mother said might have gone more like this:

"Well, you're my daughter, and I'm concerned about you. Jenna is not my daughter, and I can't do anything about what she does."

She most likely did not say, as you described it,

"Well, I'm not raising Jenna or something lame like that."

However, your paraphrasing made the point well and accurately enough. That is what paraphrasing does.

An important aspect of paraphrasing which is sometimes forgotten, can also be seen in your retelling of your argument. That is, paraphrases, just like quotes, **must be cited**. Look at the description of the argument again. Most sentences start with "She said," or "I said." In other situations, you may find yourself saying, "you said," "he said," or even "the homework sheet said." Whenever you start a sentence in this way, and then go on to restate the information in that source in your words, you are **citing,** or giving credit to, the source of your paraphrase.

In paraphrasing information sources for research, for school papers, or as part of writing summaries, it is even more necessary to cite the source of your information, just as if it were a quote. You will learn more about citing sources in chapter 15. Here you will learn the difference between a good paraphrase and one that duplicates the original too closely.

Example: The article on the Aldabra Atoll on pages **–**, is being used as a resource for a report on dying wildernesses. The author of the report would like to paraphrase the information in a paragraph from the article.

Below is the source, or original, paragraph. Following that are two possible paraphrases of the paragraph. Read each one carefully and decide which one is a valid paraphrase, and which one quotes the material too closely without using quotation marks.

Source Paragraph

In the warm waters of the Indian Ocean, off the coast of East Africa, lies a rare and precious world treasure. It is called Aldabra, and it is the largest coral atoll in the world. It is home to 200 plant species and many rare and exotic water species. As an atoll, its harsh qualities make it unwelcome for human habitation. That is why it has survived for thousands of years. Until now.

Paraphrase 1

Aldabra is a coral atoll near East Africa. It is important to the world because many species of animal live there. These species are ancient, and would probably not survive anywhere else, because they would not be able to live where humans live. But on Aldabra, they thrive, because they are left alone. People cannot harm them because they cannot live in the environment of the atoll, and so they stay away. However, this may change.

Paraphrase 2

In the Indian Ocean, near East Africa, lies the coral atoll called Aldabra. Aldabra is a rare and precious world treasure. Two hundred plant species and many rare and exotic water species make their homes there. Humans cannot live there because of the harsh qualities of the environment there. That is why the atoll and its wild inhabitants have survived for thousands of years there. Until now.

The second one borrows many exact words and phrases from the original. Find all the exact quotes in the second paraphrase, and put quotation marks around them. As it is written, paraphrase 2 is not a valid paraphrase.

Paraphrasing is a valuable tool for presenting detailed information in a simple and clear way. You have to make sure, however, that you have understood the material enough to *put it into your own words*, without relying on the wording and phrasing of the original author. Also remember to cite paraphrases.

Practice 5: Paraphrasing

On a separate sheet of paper, write a paraphrase for each of the following short passages.

Main Ideas, Summarizing, and Paraphrasing

1. This world demands the qualities of youth; not a time of life but a state of mind, a temper of the will, a quality of the imagination, a predominance of courage over timidity, of the appetite for adventure over the love of ease. – Robert F. Kennedy, Day of Affirmation Address, 1966

2. The decision to get a family pet is usually surrounded by happy emotions. You see an animal in a shop window, fall in love, and bring it home. However, this kind of spur-of-the-moment decision may end up being a disaster. It is important to investigate different types of animals before making a decision. It's also a good idea to arrange visits with the pet to see how you interact. All animals need attention, some more than others, so you should also consider how much time you have to spend with your pet.

3. What's causing the increase in obesity in the United States? Health experts say junk foods and huge portion sizes are having a great effect. In a teenager's busy life of soccer practice and homework, this is the choice for dinner many nights of the week. The problem is that most fast foods are too high in calories, fat and artery-clogging cholesterol to eat them that often. The trend toward larger portions, or "super sizing," is also contributing to the problem. In 1957, the average fast-food burger weighed about one ounce. Today, the average burger weighs six ounces.

4. Few natural phenomena come close to the magnificent display of the Aurora Borealis. Folklore is filled with explanations about the origins of the spellbinding celestial lights. In reality, though, the aurora is a result of solar winds. Solar winds are particles that are ejected by the sun. These particles from the sun hit the earth's atmosphere. At the earth's two poles, they collide with gases. These gasses make them glow. The lights can best be seen from the far reaches of the Northern Hemisphere, around such places as Alaska, northern Canada, Scandinavia, and Iceland.

CHAPTER 9 REVIEW

A. Main Ideas. Read the following passages, and answer the questions that follow each passage. Compare your answers with your classmates.

Excerpt from <u>The Education of Henry Adams</u> by Henry Adams

Under the shadow of Boston State House, the little passage called Hancock Avenue runs, or ran, from Beacon Street, skirting the State House grounds, to Mount Vernon Street, on the summit of Beacon Hill; and there, in the third house below Mount Vernon Place, February 16, 1838, a child was born, and christened later by his uncle, as Henry Brooks Adams.

1. What is the main idea of the passage?
2. Is the main idea implied or directly stated?

Excerpt from the Essay "On Drawing," by A.P. Herbert

It is commonly said that everybody can sing in the bathroom; and this is true. Singing is very easy. Drawing, though, is much more difficult. I have devoted a good deal of time to Drawing, one way and another; I have to attend a great many committees and public meetings, and at such functions I find that Drawing is almost the only Art one can satisfactorily pursue during the speeches. One really cannot sing during the speeches; so as a rule I draw. I do not say that I am an expert yet, but after a few more meetings I calculate that I shall know Drawing as well as it can be known.

3. What is the main idea of the passage?
4. Is the main idea implied or directly stated?

B. Summarizing. Read the following passage carefully. Then use the space provided to write notes and then a summary of the passage.

Hidden Dragon?

American films today are filled with spectacular fight scenes that are mixtures of dance, gymnastics, martial arts, and pure fantasy. The American interest in martial arts was first sparked by legendary martial arts master and actor, Bruce Lee. Lee was born in San Francisco in 1940, in the year and the hour of the dragon. He practiced his art so devotedly, and had so much natural talent for it, that he developed the art further than it had ever been developed before. He made several martial arts movies during the 1970s. The most famous of these movies—and some say his best one—is titled *Enter the Dragon*. In his movies, there was little of the special effects you see today. Lee performed most of the amazing moves seen in these movies himself.

Lee dedicated his life to practicing and teaching martial arts. In his movies, he always included not only thrilling fight scenes, but also dialogue in which his philosophy of martial art is clarified. Lee's martial arts philosophy had little to do with unnecessary violence, and a lot to do with self discipline and art. Lee died at a young age. To this day, his brilliant demonstrations of martial arts have never been surpassed in film.

Topic: _____

Main Idea: _____

Major Details: _____

_____

Summary: _____

_____

_____

_____

_____

C. Paraphrasing. Read the following short passages and the paraphrases that follow them. Choose the paraphrase that is a valid one by placing a check mark in front of it.

Original: In 1905, a scientist named Albert Einstein published one of his famous theories. It is called the Special Theory of Relativity. The theory connects the speed of light with the passage of time. Part of Einstein's theory is that if someone were to travel the speed of light, time would slow down for that person.

5. **Paraphrase A.** _____ Albert Einstein, in 1905, published his famous theory called the Special Theory of Relativity. The theory connects the speed of light with time. Einstein said in his theory that if someone traveled at the same speed as light, time would slow down for that person.

Main Ideas, Summarizing, and Paraphrasing

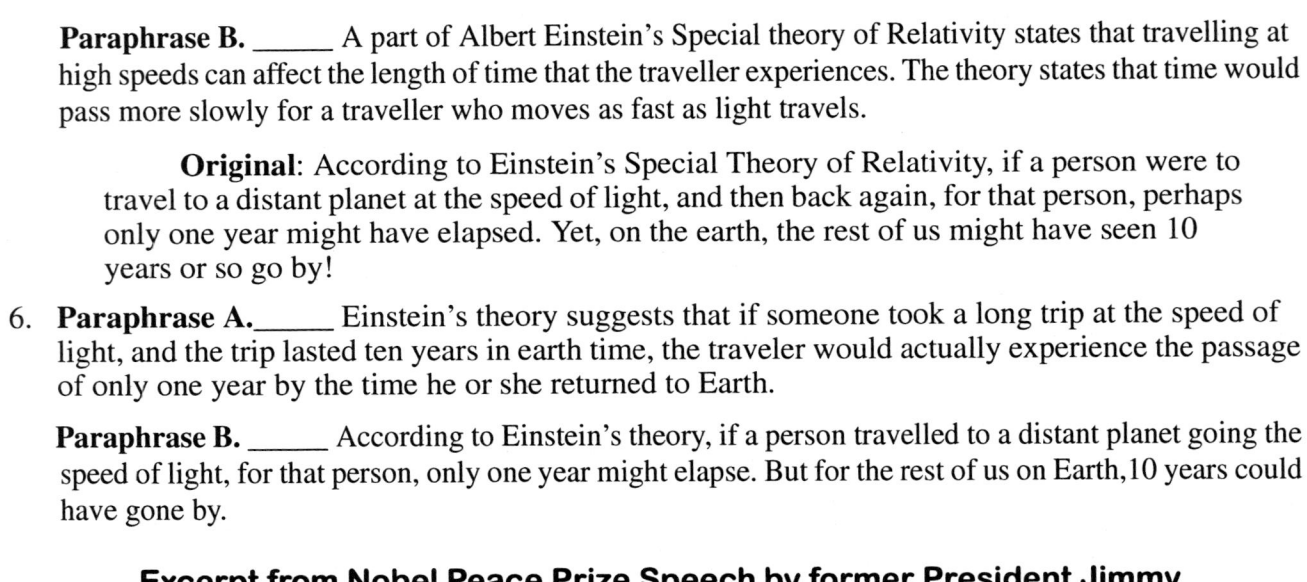

Paraphrase B. _____ A part of Albert Einstein's Special theory of Relativity states that travelling at high speeds can affect the length of time that the traveller experiences. The theory states that time would pass more slowly for a traveller who moves as fast as light travels.

Original: According to Einstein's Special Theory of Relativity, if a person were to travel to a distant planet at the speed of light, and then back again, for that person, perhaps only one year might have elapsed. Yet, on the earth, the rest of us might have seen 10 years or so go by!

6. **Paraphrase A.** _____ Einstein's theory suggests that if someone took a long trip at the speed of light, and the trip lasted ten years in earth time, the traveler would actually experience the passage of only one year by the time he or she returned to Earth.

   Paraphrase B. _____ According to Einstein's theory, if a person travelled to a distant planet going the speed of light, for that person, only one year might elapse. But for the rest of us on Earth, 10 years could have gone by.

Excerpt from Nobel Peace Prize Speech by former President Jimmy Carter, December 2002

Original: Within our country, ultimate decisions are made through democratic means, which tend to moderate radical or ill-advised proposals. Constrained and inspired by historic constitutional principles, our nation has endeavored for more than two hundred years to follow the now almost universal ideals of freedom, human rights, and justice for all.

7. **Paraphrase A.** _____ In his Nobel Peace Prize speech, Former President Jimmy Carter says that Americans make important decisions through democratic means. This tends to moderate the more extreme proposals. For more than two hundred years, our nation has tried to follow the ideals of freedom, human rights, and justice for all.

   Paraphrase B. _____ In his Nobel Peace Prize speech, Former President Jimmy Carter speaks about the importance of the democratic process in the United States. He states that when the democratic process is used to make important decisions, those decisions tend to be more balanced, and not extreme. He believes that the principles of the United States Constitution should influence our country in its decisions.

Chapter 10
INFERENCES, PREDICTIONS, AND CONCLUSIONS

LOUISIANA READING BENCHMARKS ADDRESSED IN THIS CHAPTER INCLUDE:	
ELA-7-M1	Using comprehension strategies (e.g., summarizing, recognizing literary devices, paraphrasing) to analyze oral, written, and visual texts

You have heard of interactive software. You may have played interactive computer games, used interactive Internet sites, and possibly even voted for a favorite television or music star on an interactive computer voting Web site. Have you ever thought that reading is an interactive activity? It is. Good readers are very active in the process of reading. When you read a text, you bring to that text a lot of knowledge and experience of your own. And people learn best by building on what they already know. So when you, as an active reader, know how to apply your knowledge and experience to a text, you will be able to learn new material in that text more effectively.

In this chapter, you will learn some of these skills. You will learn how to make **inferences**, **predictions**, **hypotheses**, and **conclusions** based on your reading. These skills use prior information and experience, and are important tools in improving your understanding of what you read. First, a brief explanation of these terms:

Inferences   Inferences are made when you read text and make an educated guess about what is happening in the story based on what is written, what is hinted at, and your past experience and knowledge. Inferences are made when you "read between the lines."

Predictions   Predictions are made when you predict what a story will be about or guess what will happen next. In predicting, you are using information already given in the text to make a statement about future events.

Hypotheses   Hypotheses are proposals. They are suggestions about future events in a text, based on first impressions. Hypotheses are formed at the beginning of reading a text, and checked and revised while reading further.

Conclusions   Conclusions are general statements that can be supported with details from a text. Readers use given information to determine a conclusive idea about the text.

Inferences, Predictions, and Conclusions

INFERENCES

An **inference** is an educated guess based on both information given in a text and previous experience and knowledge. You make inferences every day.

For example, you might walk into your classroom and see a notice on the board saying that today's Spanish test is postponed. Knowing that your Spanish teacher had mentioned feeling bad the day before, and knowing that substitute teachers do not administer tests, you can make an educated guess. You may infer that the Spanish teacher is ill and will not be in.

You also make inferences when you read. Authors do not always directly state what they want you to understand. When you make an inference, you are noticing relevant details, or clues, in the text and then combining those clues with what you already know. This allows you to figure out events in a story.

For an example, read the following excerpt from Richard Connell's "The Most Dangerous Game," and see if you can infer what has happened to the character at the end.

Excerpt from "The Most Dangerous Game"

Rainsford sprang up and moved quickly to the rail, mystified. He strained his eyes in the direction from which the reports had come, but it was like trying to see through a blanket. He leaped upon the rail and balanced himself there, to get greater elevation; his pipe, striking a rope, was knocked from his mouth. He lunged for it; a short, hoarse cry came from his lips as he realized he had reached too far and had lost his balance. The cry was pinched off short as the blood-warm waters of the Caribbean Sea closed over his head.

Did you guess that this character has fallen into the sea? You can correctly infer that he has fallen over the side of a ship because ropes and rails are common items on a ship and because the narrator describes the warm water closing over his head.

Making inferences is reading a passage carefully and then making connections among all the pieces of information. As a reader, you also have to notice what is implied or hinted at and use your prior knowledge to fill in any gaps. Being able to make inferences is one of the most important skills a reader can develop.

To infer information means to add your own understanding and feelings, based on your own experience, to the text. Inferring information from a text, while you read, deepens and enhances your experience of the story or text. It makes you more involved in the experience of reading.

Read the following passage. Then think about what information you inferred from the text. Also consider carefully how you inferred the information. What personal experience did you draw upon to make your inferences?

Chapter 10

Enough Adventure for One Day

"The next time you have any great ideas for raft engineering, keep them for the science fair," grumbled Anastasia LaPort, as she dipped the bucket lid into the murky river water, trying hopelessly to paddle. Beau, her 12-year-old brother, who came up with new schemes every week, fancied himself as Huck Finn today. But his raft pole had broken 10 minutes ago, and the swampy river seemed to have devised its own ideas about their destination.

Normally ready with a clever argument for his sister, Beau remained silent. A kind of pressure clutched at his chest and throat. He wasn't sure whether it was the shifting boards beneath his bare feet, or the slithering movement he had just noticed along the bank, about 50 feet ahead, that had caught his breath. But, for once he was speechless.

"Wait." He heard his sister's voice breaking the tension. "There's a tree trunk ahead. Let's try to grab onto it and walk it to shore." Beau looked up. She was right. Their one hope of escape lay ahead.

About 40 feet ahead.

Did you infer that the danger the two adventurers faced was an unsafe vessel and possibly a hungry alligator? How did you infer these facts? You might have inferred them from the following **statements in the text** and from **previous experience and knowledge**:

Statements in the text:

- Will comes up with "new schemes every week."
- Corrine was using a bucket lid as a paddle.
- Will was afraid of the "shifting boards beneath his bare feet."
- "The river seemed to have devised its own ideas about their destination."
- (and especially) "the slithering movement" Will had seen "along the bank, about 50 feet ahead."

Previous experience and knowledge:

- A 12-year-old boy who is full of ideas may not always have the skills to make those ideas real—and safe.
- A bucket lid is not an effective paddle.
- Shifting boards on a raft mean that the lashing is not as tight or strong as it should be—which can cause the raft to fall apart.
- If the river is deciding the destination of the children, then it means that they have lost control of their own destination.
- (and especially) if one notices a slithering motion along the bank of a river, there is a good chance that it means—alligator!

Inferences, Predictions, and Conclusions

One more inference can be made from the last phrase of the passage alone: "About 40 feet ahead." It requires some math, but it is clear to the reader that if a possible hungry 'gator was spotted 50 feet ahead, and possible rescue lies 40 feet ahead, it all equates to one very close call. What will happen? The reader cannot reach a definite conclusions here. One can only infer several possibilities. But these inferences bring the story alive for the reader and make it meaningful and engaging.

Practice 1: Inferences and Advertising

Advertisements are texts that almost always demand of the reader to make inferences. If the advertiser can guide a reader into making positive inferences from an ad, then the advertiser will probably sell more products.

Look at the magazine ad, and answer the questions that pertain to it.

1. What does the advertiser want the reader to infer about people who own camera phones?
   A. People with camera phones work hard to earn them.
   B. Teens with camera phones do not have many good uses for them.
   C. People with camera phones have many friends and plenty of fun.
   D. Most teenagers are uncomfortable having their pictures taken.

2. What does the advertiser seem to want the reader to infer about owning a cell phone?
   A. With a camera phone, you can go anywhere, anytime, even into the water at sunset.
   B. If you own a camera phone, you will need to earn money in order to pay for it.
   C. If you own a camera phone, you will not talk on the phone very much.
   D. With a camera phone, life is always like a vacation.

Don't Just Stand There Talking...

Capture Life!
Our new camera phone offer allows you to have the latest wireless technology in the palm of your hand without emptying your pockets.

Visit Neighborhood Wireless today to get in on this incredible deal!

Neighborhood Wireless

Practice 2: More Inferences

Newspapers and Magazines. Read 2 articles and 2 ads from newspapers or magazines. What inferences can you make from the information given? Support your inferences with facts or details from the articles. Share your findings with other students.

Chapter 10

PREDICTIONS

In homeroom one day, your friend Jeannine wants to tell you that her older brother is coming home from his tour of duty in Iraq that weekend. This is important news for Jeannine, and she wants to make sure she gets your full attention and your full appreciation of it. How do you think she will tell you? She might just mention, "My brother's coming home this weekend." That might get a polite reply from you before you turn to more pressing matters, such as the fact that your dog ate your homework. Or, Jeannine could walk up to you and say, "Guess what!" and wait with a big grin on her face. Most likely, you will forget all about your dog with bad manners and be all ears for what Jeannine has to say.

Why? Because people are curious and want to know what will happen in a future they cannot yet see. When you are an active reader, you also wonder about what is going to happen further on in the text. By doing this, you become more involved in the information. You begin to prepare yourself for what does come up in the reading by guessing what it will be and seeing if you were correct. The practice of **predicting** while reading is an important skill for improving understanding of what you read.

A **prediction** is a type of inference. It is useful in reading because it helps to focus your attention. When you make a prediction, you are looking closely at clues and details in a passage and applying them to possible future events. You combine what you already know about a subject with what you have just learned from the reading to guess what will occur next.

Like other types of inferences, we make predictions in our daily lives. One of the most common predictions we make is weather prediction. When predicting the weather, we look at the clues provided in nature. By examining the sky, seeing gray clouds, and feeling cold temperatures, we predict that it might snow. We can make similar predictions in our reading by examining the details an author writes.

Practice 3: Reading for Predictions

Read the following passages. Then put a check next to the valid prediction at the end of each passage. Support your answer with details from the passage.

Coyote Challenge

This year the winter has been rainy, and that has ranchers worried. There are more coyotes when there has been plenty of rain, and coyotes can be ranchers' biggest enemies. Coyotes' main diet consists of small rodents and rabbits. However, when they run out of rats and rabbits, they look for whatever they can find to eat, including cattle and sheep. Ranchers will do all that they can to protect their livestock. One of their options is the killing of coyotes through traps, bullets, and poison.

Some biologists see a problem with this option. Many believe that killing the coyotes actually leads to an increase in their numbers. According to scientific research, killing coyotes only reduces the number for a short time. Other coyotes soon expand the population by moving into new areas and by giving birth to more babies. The coyote population is increasing across the country, moving closer to where humans live. Coyotes now live in every North American habitat, including cities and suburban neighborhoods.

—excerpt from wildlife protection agency bulletin

Inferences, Predictions, and Conclusions

Based on the passage, which of the following is a valid prediction?

_____ 1. Hunting coyotes will continue to increase the population and hurt the ranching industry.

_____ 2. Coyotes will become extinct in the next few years because ranchers are killing them.

Evidence for your choice:

_____

_____

Science Goes For a Ride

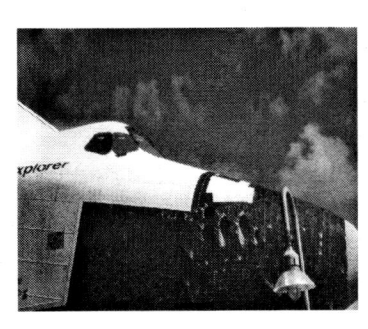

Sally Ride had a hard job as the first female astronaut. She now has a new challenge: keeping girls interested in math and science. She has started a company called Imaginary Lines Inc. to provide girls with a foundation in science, math, and engineering.

Why only girls? Eighty percent of the fastest-growing jobs today are in technical fields, but women comprise only 19 percent of the technical workforce. Ride says that too few women are seeking out these science-related careers because of changes that take place during middle school. In elementary school, girls enjoy math and science and perform just as well as boys. However, in middle school, girls begin to lose interest in these subjects even if they still have the ability.

By providing positive role models through her Community Science Festivals, Ride hopes to change all that. Her science festivals are science and math parties that make the subjects fun. Girls can attend workshops to learn how to sample their DNA, make rockets from Alka-Seltzer, and much more. The festivals also provide opportunities for young girls to meet female scientists and engineers. Ride says that one-on-one time can make a world of difference in how young girls view careers in science and math.

–excerpt from guidance office brochure

Based on the passage, which of the following is a valid prediction?

_____ 3. Achievement in science and math will continue to rise because of grammar school attendance.

_____ 4. Girls who attend Community Science Festivals will likely stay interested in math and science.

Evidence for your choice:

_____

_____

Practice 4: More Predictions

A. Short Stories. With your teacher, read a high-interest short story such as "The Utterly Perfect Murder" by Ray Bradbury," "A Rose for Emily" by William Faulkner, "The Tell-Tale Heart" by Edgar Allan Poe, or "The Secret Life of Walter Mitty" by James Thurber. Stop frequently to see if you can guess what will happen next. Stop just before the end, and write your own ending for the story. Finish reading the story, and then discuss how accurately you were able to predict the ending. Discuss what details led you to your predictions.

B. Story Titles. The titles of stories and articles often provide clues to predicting the content of the reading. As a class activity, look at some newspaper or short story titles and make predictions before you read. Then, after reading the article, compare your predictions to the actual topics in the readings. Discuss the details that helped you make accurate predictions.

C. DVDs. The next time you watch a DVD that you have not seen before, pay attention to the events and to the characters' personalities. Stop the DVD periodically, and see if you can predict what the characters will do next.

HYPOTHESIZING

Hypothesizing is a reading skill which makes use of both inference and prediction. **Hypothesizing** is a part of the science of logic, which uses given information, inference, and prediction to arrive at a possible explanation of events. In reading, we form hypotheses about what the text may be about, what may take place in the story, and even how it may finally end.

Hypothesizing makes you more involved in your reading. Instead of simply reading words and decoding their meanings into ideas, active readers think ahead of time about what the text may be about. They generate questions about what will happen, and then try to answer them. Their attempt to answer these questions is a hypothesis.

In order to form a hypothesis, first read the title of the text. Then quickly read the first line or two. These two steps should give you enough information to form a hypothesis. You may also skim through the text and read the last lines as well.

In forming a hypothesis, some guess work is involved. Therefore, a first hypothesis may turn out to be incorrect. Once you form a hypothesis, begin to read the passage again, this time carefully. As you read and learn more about the events in the passage, you may change your hypothesis—or you may discard it completely and form a new one. The value in hypothesizing is not guessing correctly the first time. It is in making reading a more engaged, enjoyable and productive activity.

> **NOTE:** Remember that forming a hypothesis while reading is only the beginning. As you read further, continue to check and revise your hypothesis as necessary

Read the title and the text of the following passage. It is the beginning of a longer passage which does not appear here. Then answer the questions that follow it. Remember that guesswork is involved in hypotheses. Compare your answers with the section "Possible Answers About Hypothesizing."

Inferences, Predictions, and Conclusions

The Day They Found Out

When Sandra walked into the room, she knew instantly that something was wrong. Things didn't sound right; it was too quiet. Robert and his crowd weren't horsing around as usual. In fact, nothing was as usual. Everyone was sitting quietly at the desks. Normally, it took at least five minutes for everyone to settle down. That was one of the great things about math class; she got a chance to catch up on all the latest gossip. Mr. Martin was always so cool about letting them relax into their assignments for the day. But today was different. Mr. Martin had that look on his face, the one that said today was not the day to mess with him. Sandra was familiar with that face. Her mother wore it often, especially on days when she had worked late.

1. Questions about what may be happening in the text and what will happen:

   _____

   _____

2. Possible answers to these questions (hypothesis):

   _____

   _____

3. What details are there in the passage to support your hypothesis?

   _____

   _____

POSSIBLE ANSWERS ABOUT HYPOTHESIZING

Answer 1: One question a reader might ask after reading the passage is, "Why is the class room so quiet?" Another possible question is, "What will the students find out today?" or "Why is the teacher so serious?"

Answer 2: From the title, a reader might hypothesize that the room is quiet because the students know something has happened, but they do not know what yet. And from the ominous and mysterious tone of the title, one could hypothesize that whatever is found out today may not be pleasant. It may be something scary or upsetting. The teacher may have bad news about having to leave his job because he is in the Army Reserve and has been called to duty.

Answer 3: There are several details that support the hypothesis about the students finding out that the teacher has to go away and serve in the army. (1) The title says they are going to find out something today. (2) The mood in the class room is somber, so what they find out will probably not be happy news. (3) The author says the teacher is "cool" and seems to hint that the students like this teacher. Therefore, if this teacher had to leave, it would be sad. (4) The teacher is very serious and probably tired (he has a look like the one the author's mother has after a long day at work). So what they find out probably affects him personally.

Practice 5: Forming a Hypothesis

Read the following excerpt and answer the question on hypothesis which follows it.

Excerpt from *The Errand Boy*
by Horatio Alger

Phil Brent was plodding through the snow in the direction of the house where he lived with his step-mother and her son, when a snow-ball, moist and hard, struck him just below his ear with stinging emphasis. The pain was considerable, and Phil's anger rose.

He turned suddenly, his eyes flashing fiercely, intent upon discovering who had committed this outrage, for he had no doubt that it was intentional.

He looked in all directions, but saw no one except a mild old gentleman in spectacles, who appeared to have some difficulty in making his way through the obstructed street.

Phil did not need to be told that it was not the old gentleman who had taken such an unwarrantable liberty with him. So he looked farther, but his ears gave him the first clew.

He heard a chuckling laugh, which seemed to proceed from behind the stone wall that ran along the roadside.

"I will see who it is," he decided, and plunging through the snow he surmounted the wall, in time to see a boy of about his own age running away across the fields as fast as the deep snow would allow.

"So it's you, Jonas!" he shouted wrathfully. "I thought it was some sneaking fellow like you."

Jonas Webb, his step-brother, his freckled face showing a degree of dismay, for he had not calculated on discovery, ran the faster, but while fear winged his steps, anger proved the more effectual spur, and Phil overtook him after a brief run, from the effects of which both boys panted.

1. What reasonable hypothesis about Phil Brent and his story can you make from the information given?

   _____

   _____

2. What can you hypothesize about what one of the conflicts in this novel will involve?

   _____

   _____

3. What other possible conflicts can you hypothesize might exist in this novel?

   _____

   _____

Inferences, Predictions, and Conclusions

CONCLUSIONS

Active readers are always drawing **conclusions**. Drawing conclusions is like making inferences. To draw a conclusion, you use information from the text as well as knowledge you already have. However, conclusions are also different from inferences. While inferences are informed guesses, conclusions are more definite. Conclusions follow more certainly from the information given. A conclusion is a statement that follows logically from the information in the reading. Drawing conclusions from what you read can help you to understand the ideas in what you are reading by generating a conclusive statement that connects or wraps up all those ideas. Conclusions from reading can also affect your own actions in life. For instance, if you were to read a passage about the benefits of learning a martial art, you might conclude that this kind of exercise can make a big difference to your health, both physical and mental. This conclusion may encourage you to consider taking lessons in Judo.

Read the following passage. Then check the most logical conclusion you can draw from this passage.

> Erin had been practicing for basketball tryouts. She had her older brother play with her every afternoon for weeks. She had dreams about playing basketball. On the morning of tryouts, her stomach began to ache. She could not eat breakfast, and could hardly keep still before leaving for the basketball court.

_____ 1. Erin will win a spot on the basketball team.

_____ 2. Erin is nervous about basketball tryouts.

_____ 3. Erin works hard for everything she wants.

If you chose statement 2, you are correct. Here is an explanation of the three answers:

Statement **1** is not a logical conclusion but is a prediction. Erin is not guaranteed to make the team. There could be a lot of competition for only a few spots, or Erin could not be very good at the game.

Statement **2** is a logical conclusion. We can conclude Erin is nervous about tryouts since she has practiced for long hours and has a stomach ache in the morning.

Statement **3** is a not a logical conclusion. The passage only mentions basketball. There is no evidence that shows she works hard at everything she wants.

When you read a passage with the purpose of drawing a conclusion, you need to read very carefully, paying special attention to the facts and details. Whatever conclusion you come to has to be supported by information from the paragraph.

To practice, read the following paragraph, and then answer the questions.

The Theory of Birth Order

According to some psychologists, the order in which you were born can help determine your personality. Where you are in the family plays a large role in determining the relationship between you and your parents and between you and your siblings. Those family relationships can also set the pattern for the way you will respond to people later in life. Psychologists have come to certain conclusions about behavior according to your birth order.

Oldest children tend to be responsible, productive, independent, and obedient. They are bolder and often take on leadership roles. Oldest children are typically well organized, precise, and prone to perfectionism. Middle children are negotiators. They can be very easy going. Middle children often make a place for themselves outside the family. Because they tend to go out on their own, middle children are often the most creative. Youngest children are usually affectionate, sensitive, dependent and charming. They are used to being taken care of and often become attention seeking or manipulative.

Of course, personality development is not completely explained by birth order, but thinking about birth order can give you insight into how the forces within families shape children.

1. According to the passage, if you visited a conference of civic leaders, you might conclude that most people there would likely be
   A. youngest children.
   B. middle children.
   C. oldest children.
   D. all the above

2. Which conclusion would you make about the career a middle child is most likely to choose?
   A. accountant
   B. nurse
   C. artist
   D. mathematician

3. How would you apply the information in this passage to your own life?

_____

_____

To answer **question 1**, you would look for any facts in the passage that would support your conclusion. Since the second paragraph says oldest children "take on leadership roles," the best answer would be **C**.

Question 2 asks you to remember the details about middle children before drawing your conclusion. After re-reading the sentences related to middle children, you then need to generalize about the careers listed and find the one that best matches those details. An artist is a career that requires a lot of creativity. That conclusion is supported by the sentence, "Middle children are often the most creative." Therefore, **C** would be the best answer.

Question 3 asks you to apply the information in the passage to your own life. Do you find the information to be true about yourself and your birth order? Do you think the theory about birth order is valid? Would it help you to choose a career for yourself?

Practice 6: Conclusions

Read the following passages. Check only the valid conclusions from the choices given after each passage. Then, support your answer with evidence.

What Kills Birds?

There are many ways birds can die, but countless die each year from human-related causes. Hunters kill 121 million birds each year. An estimated 50 to 100 million birds are killed each year by cars and trucks on America's highways. Agricultural pesticides poison 67 million birds per year. Dr. Daniel Klem conducted a 20-year study that looked at bird

Inferences, Predictions, and Conclusions

collisions with windows. He found that one billion birds are killed each year by flying into glass windows.

1. Which of the following is a valid conclusion?

_____ Birds are killed most often by cars and trucks.

_____ Glass windows are more dangerous to birds than any other human factor.

Evidence for your choice:

_____

_____

2. Using the information in this passage, what could you do to prevent birds from being killed near your house?

_____

_____

_____

Paying for the Win

Baseball teams spend a lot of money to recruit the best players. These teams hope spending top dollar for the best players will be the key to a winning season. The New York Yankees have high hopes for Alex Rodriguez. The club paid him $22 million in 2004, making him baseball's highest-paid player. In 2000, the L.A. Dodgers spent $15 million dollars for Kevin Brown but came in second place in their division. The Chicago White Sox spent $10 million for Albert Belle in 1997, a season in which they lost more games than they won. Several other teams over the past 13 years have had the highest-paid players in the league, but have failed to win a championship.

3. Which of the following is a valid conclusion?

_____ Having the highest-paid players does not guarantee success.

_____ Alex Rodriguez will guarantee the Yankees a successful season.

Evidence for your choice:

_____

_____

Practice 7: More Conclusions

Newspapers and Magazines. Read 2–3 articles from newspapers, magazines, or the Internet. What conclusions can you make from the information? Write down the facts or details that support your conclusions. Will any of the conclusions you reach make a difference in choices you make about your own life in the future? Share your findings with other students.

Chapter 10 Review

A. Inferences. Read the following passage. Choose the best inference or generalization for each question.

Excerpt from *The Adventures of Huckleberry Finn* by Mark Twain

1. At first I hated the school, but by-and-by I got so I could stand it. Whenever I got uncommon tired I played hookey, and the hiding [whipping] I got next day done me good and cheered me up. So the longer I went to school the easier it got to be. I was getting sort of used to the widow's ways, too, and they warn't so raspy on me. Living in a house, and sleeping in a bed, pulled on me pretty tight, mostly, but before the cold weather I used to slide out and sleep in the woods, sometimes, and so that was a rest to me. I like the old ways best, but I was getting so I liked the new ones, too, a little bit. The widow said I was coming along slow but sure, and doing very satisfactory. She said she warn't ashamed of me.

1. Based on the passage, we can infer that
    A. the narrator likes going to school.
    B. the narrator is struggling with his new life.
    C. the widow is wealthy.
    D. the narrator enjoys sleeping in a bed.

2. The passage suggests that the narrator is
    A. a good student.
    B. not used to living indoors.
    C. angry.
    D. trying to earn a living.

3. Which of the following inferences can be made based on the passage?
    A. The widow is strict but cares about the narrator.
    B. The narrator once lived in a tree house.
    C. The widow is a retired school teacher.
    D. The narrator will become a good student.

B. Predictions. Read the following passage. Then answer the questions that follow it.

The Dish Monster

Kenny came home one day and checked the job list to see what his daily chore was. Today, Kenny had to do the dishes. He went to the kitchen and rinsed the excess food off the dishes and silverware. He then loaded the dishwasher and made sure the plates did not touch each other. "Oh no!" Kenny said. "There is no dishwasher soap!" He kept looking on top of the sink and the counter. Finally, he found a bottle of soap for washing dishes by hand. "Oh great!" Kenny said. "I'll just use this soap instead." Kenny put the soap in the dishwasher, turned it on, and went into the living room to watch TV.

About thirty minutes later, Kenny's dad walked into the kitchen with two bags full of groceries. He slipped and slid, dropping the entire contents of both bags all over the floor. "Kenny!" his dad yelled when he regained his balance. "Come in here now!" Kenny ran into the kitchen and straight into a surprise. "Whoa!" Kenny yelled as he fell down and slid into the kitchen table.

Inferences, Predictions, and Conclusions

4. What can you predict will probably happen next in the story?

   _____

   _____

5. What can you predict that Kenny will do the next time he runs out of dishwasher soap?

   _____

   _____

C. Hypothesizing. Read the following passage. Then answer the questions that follow it.

Out of Luck, Out of Time

When Scott and Manuel started this whole scheme, they had no idea things would get so bad. It was due in part to poor planning, but bad luck had a lot to do with it. It seemed that the project was doomed from the beginning. Now they were in over their heads and didn't see any hope of things getting better. What were they going to do now? Confess was one option, but that choice didn't interest them much. They could always place the blame on someone else, maybe Louisa and her whole annoying group. That didn't really seem like the best choice either. They liked making mischief, but didn't necessarily want to be cruel. It seemed their choices were limited. Mom always said that honesty was the best policy. The problem is that honesty right now could really get them in trouble. They couldn't afford to spoil their records right now. It would make all their hard work a waste, not to mention the disappointment. Why didn't they listen all those times Mom told them to slow down and think about the consequences.

6. What hypothesis can you form about what Scott and Manuel have done?

   _____

   _____

7. What evidence from the passage supports your hypothesis?

   _____

   _____

8. Which part of your hypothesis is based on guessing?

   _____

   _____

D. Conclusions. Read the following passage. Then answer the questions that follow it.

They Keep Listening

Some scientists are listening to the stars. They belong to an organization called SETI, or Search for Extraterrestrial Intelligence, whose mission is to explore life in the universe. Most SETI enthusiasts believe it is just a matter of time before we make contact with aliens. Their belief is based on numbers. The Milky Way has an estimated 400 billion stars, including the Sun. SETI scientists believe that many of these stars have life-sustaining planets orbiting them.

The first SETI search began in the Allegheny Mountains of West Virginia. In 1960, Dr. Frank D. Drake, a young scientist at the National Radio Astronomy Observatory there, used an 85-foot antenna to listen for alien transmissions around a few stars. Since then, SETI's main strategy has been to use increasingly immense radio telescopes to keep listening. One such telescope is in Arecibo, Puerto Rico. The dish antenna at Arecibo is 1,000 feet wide, making it the world's largest radio telescope. The Arecibo Observatory recently celebrated its fortieth birthday and continues to be used by SETI scientists searching for alien life. The scientists focus their search on close stars, since signals from their inhabited planets would be strongest. They also look at stars similar to the Sun, the only star known to support life. Lastly, they search older stars, since they assume advanced life takes time to evolve.

SETI has found no extraterrestrials so far, but it has continued to probe the heavens regularly. Despite long hours and decades of failure, the scientists keep their ears open, waiting for their proof.

9. Which conclusion can the reader make about SETI scientists?

   A. They are dedicated to their mission.

   B. They get frustrated easily.

   C. They will locate alien life eventually.

   D. They believe aliens have visited us.

10. Which of the following sentences from the passage best supports the above conclusion?

    A. The dish antenna at Arecibo is 1,000 feet wide, making it the world's largest radio telescope.

    B. The scientists focus their search on close stars, since signals from their inhabited planets would be strongest.

    C. Most SETI enthusiasts believe it is just a matter of time before we make contact with aliens.

    D. Despite long hours and decades of failure, the scientists keep their ears open, waiting for their proof.

Inferences, Predictions, and Conclusions

Chapter 11
Organizational Patterns for Information

LOUISIANA READING BENCHMARKS ADDRESSED IN THIS CHAPTER INCLUDE:	
ELA-7-M1	Demonstrate understanding of information in grade-appropriate texts using a variety of strategies, including: • sequencing events to examine and evaluate information
ELA-7-M4	Analyze grade-appropriate print and non-print texts using various reasoning skills, including: • identifying cause-effect relationships • reasoning inductively and deductively

Day planners, calendars, and PDAs (personal digital assistants): What do these objects have in common? They are tools that help people organize their time and goals. Being organized lends a sense of order to daily life.

Writing also needs to be organized. If a piece of writing lacks organization, it will make no sense. A passage with no organization might look like this:

> As a result, we were late leaving the school. Backpacks and sleeping bags littered the walk outside the front of the school. Finally, we arrived at the adventure camp. The parents waved goodbye as the bus lumbered out of the parking lot. Early in February, Ms. Connor announced a field trip at an outdoor adventure camp. But one student was stuck in unusually heavy traffic. In the pre-dawn of the morning of the trip, the students looked sleepy but happy.

Pretty random, you might say—and you'd be right!

Authors avoid this lack of sense by organizing the ideas in their writing. They use **organizational patterns** to arrange details and connect ideas. Organizational patterns show how ideas are connected in order to communicate meaning effectively. Learning to identify these patterns helps you as a reader in two ways. First, it helps you understand a text better since you are able to follow the pattern in which information is given. Secondly, it makes you a more involved and critical reader. Since you are able to identify patterns of information, you will also be able to determine if a pattern is flawed.

Organizational Patterns for Information

There are many ways to organize passages. This chapter will discuss the organizational patterns of **chronological order**, or **sequencing**, and **directions**, which have to do with the *order* of events in writing. The chapter will also look at the organizational pattern of **cause/effect**, which presents *relationships* between events and ideas in a text. Finally, in this chapter you will learn about two patterns of logic for presenting ideas: **inductive reasoning** and **deductive reasoning**.

CHRONOLOGICAL ORDER

One of the more common patterns of organizing text is chronological (time) order. **Chronological order** is an arrangement of events in a time sequence. The sequence generally starts with the first event, followed by a second event, then a third event, and so on. This is called a *sequence of events*.

Chronological order is an effective organizational pattern for topics such as historical or news reports, stories, or directions for an activity. The following example shows a sequence of events.

First event:	All eighth grade students were invited to run for class president.
Second event:	Adele decided to run for the position.
Third event:	Adele made posters and hung them in the school halls.
Fourth event:	Before giving her campaign speech, Adele became very nervous.
Final event:	Adele gave a well received speech and won the election.

Chronological order usually uses *signal words* to make the order of events clear to the reader. Passages that are arranged in chronological order will usually contain some of these signal words. Some of these words are listed below:

Signal Words for Chronological Order					
first	next	when	later	now	While
once	second	until	finally	today / yesterday	begin / began
before	then	after	last	afterwards	continue

Practice 1: Chronological Order of Ideas

Read the following groups of sentences. For each group, decide the correct order of events or ideas. Then use the sentence numbers to write the correct order on the lines provided after each group.

1. We all piled out and ran for the beach.
2. As Janice went to sunbathe, I dove right into the refreshing water.
3. The van pulled into the parking lot.
4. Janice put her foot in the water, and then decided to sunbathe instead.

A. _____, _____, _____, _____.

1. Frank studied hard for the end-of-year exam.
2. After talking with his school counselor, Frank was able to take the test again.
3. Frank was nervous; he wrote right answers on the wrong parts of the form.
4. Frank was horrified to learn he had failed.

B. _____, _____, _____, _____.

1. In 1798, William Wordsworth wrote an essay about poetry.
2. Before 1798, poets wrote most commonly about royalty or religion.
3. Since Wordsworth's time, writers have found great poetry in everyday life.
4. From this essay, poets learned they could write about ordinary people.

C. _____, _____, _____, _____.

1. "Hold your horses," said Lana's father, pointing to Lana's messy room.
2. Finally, Lana's father allowed her to log on to Instant Messenger.
3. Lana cleaned up her room and made her bed.
4. Lana ran in from the school bus and headed for the computer.

D. _____, _____, _____, _____.

Practice 2: Chronological Order in a Passage

A. Read the following passage. Underline the signal words that indicate the sequence of events. Then answer the questions that follow the passage.

Terry Fox and the Marathon of Hope

"I'm gonna do my very best. I'll fight. I promise I won't give up." These words were spoken by Terry Fox, a young Canadian athlete, before he entered Royal Columbian hospital in September 1980. The cancer that had already taken his right leg had spread to his lungs. But all Terry could think of was that he had a job to do. He would continue his 5,300-mile run from one end of Canada to the other. He would raise money for cancer research because, as he said, "somewhere, the hurting must stop."

The tenacious fighting spirit that echoed in Terry's words had governed his whole life. He was born in Winnipeg, Manitoba, in 1958 and moved to Port Coquitlam, British Columbia, at the age of 10. As an athlete and basketball player, he was known more for his feisty, tough determination than for his natural talent. Still, through pure drive, grit, and daily drill, he began earning athletic awards by the time he was a junior in high school. More importantly, his tendency to never give up earned him great respect from his coaches, his team members, and even opposing team members.

After high school, Terry Fox entered Simon Fraser University, near Vancouver, where he continued to play basketball. But soon after that, tragedy struck, changing his life and Canada's history. Terry was diagnosed with a form of bone cancer. At the age of

Organizational Patterns for Information

18, he lost his right leg to the disease. But Terry was not defeated. The cancer patients he met in the hospital affected him so deeply that he decided he had to do something for them. As soon as he completed 18 months of cancer treatments, he began to train in cross-country running.

During this time, Terry wrote to the administrators of the Canadian Cancer Society. He told them of his plan and asked for their support. As he wrote, "I'm not saying that this will initiate any kind of definitive answer or cure to cancer, but I believe in miracles. I have to."

On April 12, 1980, Terry, with the backing of the Canadian Cancer Society and millions of Canadians from coast to coast, began his "Marathon of Hope." First he dipped his artificial leg in the Atlantic Ocean, off St. John's, Newfoundland, and then he started to run. Day after day, week after week, Terry ran westward, along the Trans-Canada Highway. Terry ran the equivalent of a marathon (26 miles) every day for 143 days in a row. Every night Canadian television reported his progress, showing both the pain and determination in his face and the smiles and laughter he shared with supporters along the route. Money began to pour in to the cancer research fund, as citizens across the country expressed in action the inspiration and hope Terry had given them.

Five months later, in September 1980, Terry's run was cut short. The cancer had spread to his lungs. He was flown to a hospital near Vancouver, where he vowed not to give up his quest.

While in the hospital, Terry was awarded many honors and awards. He became the youngest person to ever be granted membership in the Order of Canada, the highest honor in the country. He was honored by numerous sports, community, and health organizations. Terry continued to fight for his life and the opportunity to get back to his run. But ten months of treatment could not save him, and he died on June 28, 1981, one month away from his 23rd birthday.

Of all the honors bestowed on Terry, perhaps the one that would have meant the most to him was the one bestowed by the Canadian people. They organized a day once a year for people throughout the country to run for Terry and his dream. As one of the first organizers of the Terry Fox Run put it, "You started it. We will not rest until your dream to find a cure for cancer is realized." Today, people throughout Canada and in many other countries throughout the world take part in the Terry Fox Run to raise money for cancer. Several cities in the United States host a Terry Fox Run every year.

One determined young man who offered only what he had—his belief in miracles—set in motion an enduring succession of miracles that not even he could have imagined possible.

1. Was Terry Fox already an athlete while still in junior high school?
2. When did Terry find out that he had cancer?
3. What did Terry do after his leg was amputated?
4. What symbolic gesture did Terry make just before beginning his Marathon of Hope?
5. When did the cancer force Terry to abandon his cross-country run?
6. How is Terry Fox's influence still felt today?

B. Sequence Practice. Review some news stories or some short stories from this book. Underline the signal words that reveal the sequence of events. Retell or rewrite these stories in your words.

TIME ORDER

Time order is especially important when you are writing a narrative. A story doesn't make sense when the events are not presented in the proper sequence. Here is an example:

I arrived after the speaker had begun her presentation. As I was running down the hill, I remembered that I had left my car keys on the kitchen table. When I started the car, I saw the clock, and I knew I was going to be late. I had to go back and get my keys.

The lack of organization in this paragraph makes it very difficult to follow the story line. See below how organizing the passage in a time sequence makes it much easier to read and understand.

As I was running down the hill, I remembered that I had left my car keys on the kitchen table. I had to go back and get my keys. When I started the car, I saw the clock, and I knew I was going to be late. I arrived after the speaker had begun her presentation.

You can also use time order to organize other types of writing, including writing to explain why.

SPATIAL ORDER

When you describe a scene or a location, you can sometimes use **spatial order** to arrange your ideas in a paragraph. Imagine yourself holding a camcorder and moving it in every direction. You can order your observations from **top to bottom, left to right, clockwise, near to far, front to back, inside to outside, east to west, north to south,** etc., and all of these directions *reversed* (e.g., **bottom to top**). Read the following description which is organized in spatial order.

When I saw the horse, I knew I was looking at a creature of great athletic beauty and ability. The horse's head was finely shaped, as if sculpted by an artist. On either side of its head, the eyes were alert and far-seeing. The ears were pointed and moved attentively to the slightest sound. The horse's neck was crested in a proud arch, and its muscular shoulders tapered down to powerful legs. The spine of the horse was perfectly aligned, and the back legs were unblemished and moved freely. The hindquarters of the horse were well rounded, and the horse's tail flowed like silk in the wind. In short, this horse was a magnificent animal.

Organizational Patterns for Information

Look at the picture of the horse on the previous page. Does it make sense from the description you just read? If not, what additional details or observations would improve the description?

In the passage, the details of the horse are organized in a front to back order. First, the writer discusses the horse's head, along with the eyes and ears. Second, the writer provides details about the neck, shoulders, and front legs. Third, the writer describes the spine and the back legs. Finally, the author tells us about the horse's hindquarters and tail.

Spatial order can also be an effective way to organize other kinds of writing, as you can see in the following example of persuasive writing.

> *It's time for the city to clean up Jones Park. As visitors enter the park, they are greeted by a broken sign that is smeared with graffiti. Next, they pass the pond where they must hold their noses because of the smell of decaying trash. If visitors make it past all of this, they reach the playground in the middle of the park. Here they find swings with ripped seats hanging limp beside slides with broken steps. The park, in its current state, is a hazardous waste area that must be cleaned up.*

ORDER OF IMPORTANCE

The most common way to organize a paragraph is in **order of importance**. All of the details you include in your paragraph should be relevant to the topic and important to the reader. Some details, however, you will want to emphasize more than others. You can emphasize a certain idea by placing it either at the beginning or at the end of a paragraph. The following letter provides a good example.

Dear Aunt Jenny,

I would really like to spend the summer with you because I have never spent much time in Oregon. Also, I am interested in earning some extra money for my college savings, and many jobs are available in your area. Most importantly, I really enjoy our short visits when we get together over the holidays, and I want to spend more time with you so we can be closer.

Please write back soon, and let me know what you think.

Love,
Sandra

In this letter, Sandra begins with a simple wish that may be of some interest to her aunt. Aunt Jenny would be more likely to respect Sandra's second reason. However, Sandra's desire for a closer relationship will make the greatest impression upon her aunt's decision.

Of course, the letter could be arranged so that the most important idea comes first.

Dear Aunt Jenny,

I would like to spend the summer with you because I really enjoy our short visits when we get together over the holidays, and I want to spend more time with you so we can be closer. I am also interested in earning some extra money for my college savings, and many jobs are available in your area. Besides, I have never spent much time in Oregon.

Please write back soon, and let me know what you think.

Love,
Sandra

Sometimes you will want to start off with the most important idea. Other times you will want to "save the best for last." The decision is yours based upon your audience, topic, and personal preference.

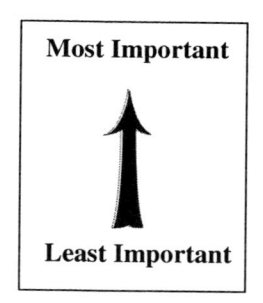

Practice 3: Time Order, Spatial Order, Order of Importance

Look at the pictures below. On a separate sheet of paper, write one paragraph for each picture. Make sure the sentences follow the order listed above the picture.

Time Order **Spatial Order**  **Order of Importance**

INDUCTIVE AND DEDUCTIVE REASONING

Authors use **inductive** and **deductive** reasoning in most writing, but especially in persuasive writing. Understanding these ways of reasoning can help a reader to determine if an author's arguments are valid or not. This prepares us to become *critical readers*.

Inductive and deductive reasoning are forms of **logic** that we use every day. For instance, let's say that you meet your friend Gussie every morning at the school bus stop. This morning, however, Gussie does not show up. You may come to a reasonable conclusion that your friend is sick. If you do come to this conclusion, then you have used **inductive** reasoning to do so.

Later, we will discuss the logical steps that you took to come to this inductive conclusion. Meanwhile, before you know it, and when you least expect it, you get a chance to practice the science of **deductive** reasoning as well! How? Well, you barely set foot inside your homeroom when you are greeted with grins and shouts of happiness. "The scores are in," marvels your teacher, "and ALL of the 8th grade students of True Blue County, Louisiana, have passed the LEAP 8 Reading test with OUTSTANDING marks!" Naturally, you think, "I am an 8th grade student of True Blue County, Louisiana." And then you correctly conclude that you, too, have passed the LEAP 8 Reading test with an outstanding mark! *You have just used deductive reasoning.*

Organizational Patterns for Information

It would be nice if all truth could be reasoned out as easily as were the two conclusions you came to this morning even before you were completely awake! It is, of course, not always that simple. In fact, the study of logic and reasoning is a very complex mathematical science. But for our purposes, we will examine some basic principles of inductive and deductive reasoning that will help us to follow the way an author organizes ideas. It will also help us to arrive at conclusions about the readings for ourselves.

INDUCTIVE REASONING

Inductive reasoning occurs when we make *observations* about life around us, then combine these observations with *what we already know*, and finally, reach a reasonable conclusion about what we have observed. In other words, we use small building blocks (observation and prior knowledge) to build a general conclusion. Another way of expressing the process of inductive reasoning is that it moves from the *specific* (observation and prior knowledge) to the *general* (general conclusion).

Specific (observation) + *Specific* (what you already know) = *General* (conclusion)

Example 1:
- Observation: Gussie is not at the bus stop this morning.
- What you already know: Gussie does not like to miss school.
- Conclusion: Gussie is sick.

Example 2:
- Observation: Eric failed his Spanish quiz in third period.
- What you already know: Eric is a good student who studies hard.
- Conclusion: Eric forgot to study for the quiz.

NOTE: While reading the examples above, you may have found yourself thinking: "How do I know that Gussie is sick, or that Eric did not study? There are other possible reasons for missing a bus or failing a test." Congratulations! That was very astute thinking on your part, because you have tapped into an important principle about inductive reasoning: ***Conclusions reached through inductive reasoning may not be the actual truth. They are more like reasonable guesses which can be supported by the information given.***

Consider the above examples again, this time with different conclusions:

Example 1:
- Observation: Gussie is not at the bus stop this morning.
- What you already know: Gussie does not like to miss school.
- Conclusion: Gussie now hates school.

Example 2:
- Observation: Eric failed his Spanish quiz in third period.
- What you already know: Eric is a good student who studies hard.
- Conclusion: Eric is not interested in Spanish anymore.

Given the same observations and prior knowledge, the conclusions reached in these last examples are not as reasonable as the ones reached in the first examples. None of the conclusions are certain, but some are more reasonable than others. Good inductive thinking simply chooses the more reasonable conclusions over the less reasonable ones.

When using inductive reasoning, you should be careful to reach conclusions that can be reasonably supported by the information given. You should also watch to see that the conclusions reached by authors in their writing are also reasonable, given the information provided. This is part of being a critical reader.

DEDUCTIVE REASONING

If inductive reasoning leads from the *specific* details to *general* conclusions, deductive reasoning does the opposite. In **deductive reasoning**, we go from *general ideas* to the *specific examples*. The general ideas in deductive reasoning are found in the *major premises*. Valid deductive reasoning needs at least two premises: a *major premise*, which states a general idea, and a *minor premise*, which states a more specific idea or fact. From these two premises, a conclusion about a specific example can be drawn.

Example 1: Major Premise: All clothes from the Habersham and Fritz store are expensive.
Minor Premise: My friend bought his shirt at Habersham and Fritz.
Conclusion: My friend's shirt is expensive.

Example 2: Major Premise: All human beings need sleep.
Minor Premise: I am a human being.
Conclusion: I need sleep.

NOTE: Deductive reasoning, unlike inductive reasoning, leads to an *automatic conclusion*. For instance, "All humans need sleep" + "I am human" = "I need sleep." This conclusion is not just a reasonable guess. It is an automatic conclusion which we must arrive at, given the premises.

Now, even though conclusions through deductive reasoning are *automatic*, it does not mean that they are always *true*. If the information in the premises is presented in different ways, then different—and sometimes *untrue*—conclusions can be reached. Consider the above examples again, this time written with a *slightly different minor premise*:

Example 1: Major Premise: All clothes from Habersham and Fritz are expensive.
Minor Premise: Julio's shirt is expensive.
Conclusion: Julio bought his shirt at Habersham and Fritz.

Example 2: Major Premise: All human beings need sleep.
Minor Premise: Our pet Catlet needs sleep.
Conclusion: Our pet Catlet is a human being.

Organizational Patterns for Information

In these examples, the premises are used to arrive at conclusions that appear reasonable but are not. It is up to readers to be aware of an author's use of logical premises and the conclusions that the author reaches through those premises. A critical reader can identify where premises and conclusions are weak or unreasonable. (For more information on false conclusions, consult the answer key to this book.)

Remember: Inductive Reasoning moves from specific observations to general conclusions.
Specific ⟶ General.

Deductive Reasoning moves from general statements to specific examples.
General ⟶ Specific

For a more detailed picture of inductive and deductive reasoning, study the following diagram.

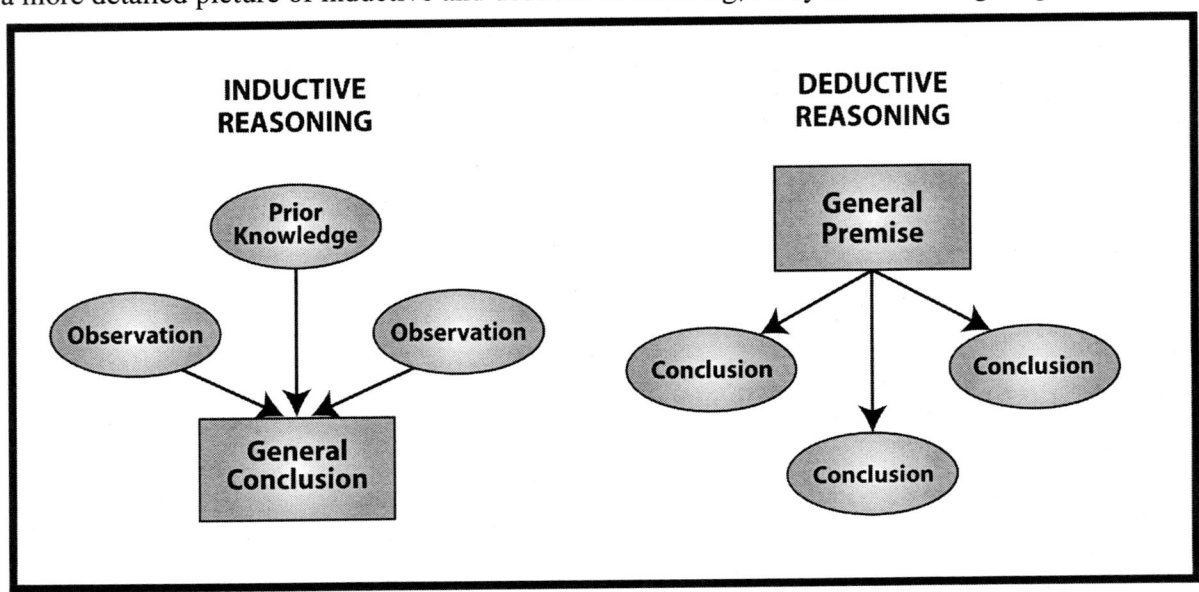

Practice 4: Inductive and Deductive Reasoning

Read the following examples of inductive and deductive reasoning. Then write on the lines provided whether each example is inductive or deductive reasoning and whether the conclusion reached is reasonable or unreasonable.

1. The Trees Forever Party supports protection of the environment. President A.J. McArthur supports protection of the environment. I guess President A.J. McArthur is a member of the Trees Forever Party.

   Inductive or deductive reasoning:_____

   Reasonable or unreasonable conclusion: _____

2. My final test in drivers' ed is scheduled for Friday. I've noticed I tend to feel ill before tests. Therefore, drivers' ed tests are bad for my health.

   Inductive or deductive reasoning: _____

   Reasonable or unreasonable conclusion: _____

3. Stars can be seen at night. The sun is a star. Therefore, the sun can be seen at night.

Inductive or deductive reasoning: _____

Reasonable or unreasonable conclusion: _____

4. Horses have manes, tails, and hooves. "We-Be-Jammun" is a horse. "We-Be-Jammun," therefore, has a mane, a tail, and hooves.

Inductive or deductive reasoning: _____

Reasonable or unreasonable conclusion: _____

5. The flag is at half-mast today. I know that when the flag is at half-mast, it is to mourn a death or a sad national event. I assume an important person has died.

Inductive or deductive reasoning: _____

Reasonable or unreasonable conclusion: _____

CHAPTER 11 REVIEW:

A. Read the passages in this review. On your own paper, write your responses to the questions that follow each passage. Use complete sentences.

Sponge Town

My family recently went camping near Tarpon Springs, Fla., the "Sponge Capital of the World." It was one of the coolest towns I've ever visited. Once we arrived, we set up camp. Then we went to the main attraction of Tarpon Springs—the Sponge Docks.

We first took a boat tour that showed us how sponges are harvested. Our guide put on an old-fashioned scuba diving suit and a round metal helmet with a long black hose attached to oxygen on the boat. Then he climbed into the water and showed us how difficult it was to move in the water with the heavy diver's suit—he had to bounce around the way astronauts do on the moon. After a few minutes, he submerged for a short time and speared a couple of sponges. Then he slowly climbed back into the boat to pass the gooey, wet sponge around for all of us to see.

After we left the boat, we went to the Sponge Museum where we watched a movie about the history of sponges and their many different uses. Later, we visited the gift shop where we got to see hundreds of different varieties of sponges. We stayed at the gift shop until we all started feeling hungry.

We decided to try one of the town's many Greek restaurants. We wanted to sample all different kinds of Greek dishes—cheeses, lamb, pasta, olives, and seafood. It all tasted

Organizational Patterns for Information

great, but finally we got to my favorite part—the baklava, a dessert made of flaky pastry dough coated with honey and nuts.

Next year I would like to go back to Tarpon Springs—perhaps for one of the many festivals held there each year. Trying something new makes me feel adventurous. Although we never left the country, I feel as if we were transported to another world!

1. Make a chronological list of the events in the story.
2. In a small group, scramble the story's events. Work in pairs to put them back in their proper sequence. Then compare your answers with the events in the original passage.

Chronicles of a Crazy Day

It all started when I helped someone in trouble. Believe me. There was so much crowding and hurrying in the hall that someone was bound to trip. That person was Anya, my friend from Peer Helpers Club. Well, what was I supposed to do? I dropped all my things and helped her up. Then, we had to collect the myriad and somewhat peculiar contents of her notebook, which had spilled out as a result of her fall. Anya is not terribly organized, but she's really smart—and interesting. She really is.

"Thanks," she said, smiling ruefully, as I helped her rescue the scattered collection of ginkgo-shaped erasers, now threatening to migrate to parts unknown under a parade of shuffling and stumbling feet headed for classes.

"No problem," I laughed. "But I have to rush. Science class." I grabbed my stuff off the floor and headed for Hall B.

Halfway through science, I realized my shoe bag was missing! It had my soccer cleats in it. I must have left it on the hall floor!

The bell rang. I had to find my cleats before catching the bus home. I had a test to study for and a game to play. I rushed to the office. No one had seen a shoe bag with cleats in it. I had to go from room to room looking for them. I finally found them, but not until after the buses had left!

I called home. My parents were at work, so there was no-one to pick me up. I had to walk the two miles home, but I made it. My feet were sore. My shins ached. I twas not inspired by the thought of playing soccer. But it was already time to go to the game.

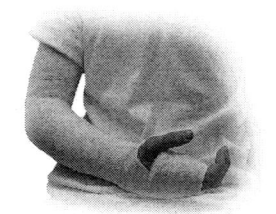

I got a ride to the field, but my legs were so tired, I tended to trip a lot. Once I fell on the ball just as another player was trying to kick it. Instead, his cleated foot found my upper left ribs.

I tried to tell Coach that it wasn't serious. But my inability to breathe made me unconvincing. Before I knew it, I was at the hospital.

Four hours later I returned home, arm in a cast and unable to write—even if I could think straight on all those pain killers. That is why, Ms. Sweeney, I was not able to study for today's social studies test. I hope you will grant me a two-day grace period before I am required to take it. And I promise to stay away from crowded hallways!

3. What was the effect of the author helping his friend Anya?

   A. He had to go to science class.
   B. He thought she was funny but smart.
   C. He lost his shoe bag.
   D. He missed his soccer game.

4. What caused the author to have to walk home?

   A. He had to find his cleats.
   B. His parents were not home.
   C. He had forgotten to take the bus.
   D. He had to train for soccer.

5. Why did the author collapse onto the ball?

   A. His legs and feet were tired.
   B. A player tripped him.
   C. He was slow and weak from hunger.
   D. His coach worked him too hard.

6. Open-ended response. Use your own paper to write your answer.

   Re-read the passage "Chronicles of a Crazy Day." List as many causes and their effects as you can find in the passage. Remember that *effects* can also be the *causes* of further effects! Compare your list with a classmate's for ideas.

7. Open-ended response. Use your own paper to write your answer.

   Think of a simple, common mishap in everyday life, such as forgetting your lunch, or going to class without your notebook. Begin a three-paragraph passage with that event, and write about all the consequences and further effects and causes that might come from that one mishap.

B. Inductive and Deductive Reasoning. Read the examples of inductive and deductive reasoning below. Then answer the questions that follow each of them.

> Toby met the new boy on the bus this morning. He was from the family that had just moved into the neighborhood. The boy was very quiet and did not talk with Toby after he had said "hi." Toby wondered about that. He remembered having passed the new family's house on his bike yesterday. He had thought that the decorations on their front lawn were different from anything else in the neighborhood. Toby concluded that the new family was strange and he did not want to be friends with them.

8. Is Toby using inductive or deductive reasoning? _____

9. Is Toby's reasoning sound or flawed? Why? _____

> Tabitha thinks that her school should require students to play video games as part of homework every night. She figures that video games are full of action and make you think fast. She also knows that you have to think fast when taking tests. She figures video games will help bring up her grades in school. Maybe they would do the same for everyone.

10. Is Tabitha using Inductive or deductive reasoning? _____

11. Is Tabitha's reasoning sound or flawed? Why? _____

Organizational Patterns for Information

Mrs. Bibeau wants to be able to spend more time with her children after work. She knows that families who spend time together are happier and healthier. She found that when she bought supper at a fast food restaurant one evening, she had more time to spend with her children helping them with homework. So she figures that if the family eats fast food every evening, they will be happier and healthier.

12. Is Mrs. Bibeau using Inductive or deductive reasoning? _____
13. Is Mrs. Bibeau's reasoning sound or flawed? Why_____

Chapter 12
Fact, Opinion, and Probability

LOUISIANA READING BENCHMARKS ADDRESSED IN THIS CHAPTER INCLUDE:	
ELA-7-M4	Using inductive and deductive reasoning skills across oral, written, and visual texts (1, 2, 4, 5)

While reading the sports section of the newspaper last Sunday, you might have come across a headline stating that skateboarding is one of the fastest growing sports among young people. You probably didn't argue with that headline. You probably accepted it as true. However, further on in the article, perhaps the reporter made a statement that skateboarding is the most exciting sport to watch in the Olympics. Here, you may have paused and thought, "Well, I don't think so. I would rather watch gymnastics."

As an active reader, in reading that one article, you have detected and responded to both fact and opinion. **Facts** are statements of information. Facts can be proven through observation or research. **Opinions** express a writer's personal viewpoint or belief about a person, place, event, or idea. Being able to distinguish a fact from an opinion is an important reading skill which will be explored in this chapter.

Some statements do not fall neatly into categories of fact or opinion. Therefore, another term that will be introduced in this chapter is **probability**. Probability is a measurement. It measures the likelihood of something happening or of something being true. It has to do with predicting events and outcomes. For instance, in the same article in Sunday's paper, you might have read that because of the growing interest in skateboarding, a need for an area to practice the sport has arisen. Skateboarders are being kicked out of regular parks, for safety reasons, and parents are writing letters to civic leaders asking for a place for skateboarders to enjoy their sport. So far, it looks as if civic leaders are open to the idea. Therefore, the community can probably expect to hear that a new skateboard park will be built in the area.

This would be a statement of probability. The writer of the article made a prediction that something was likely to happen, based on the information available. In this chapter, you will learn that probability is not as simple as fact or opinion. It involves some prediction, based on information available. We will, however, start with simple facts and opinions.

Fact, Opinion, and Probability

FINDING FACTS AND OPINIONS

Pick any topic, and you will find that both facts and opinions can be written on that topic. Good readers develop the ability to recognize the difference between the two. Knowing fact from opinion helps a reader avoid being misled by thinking that something is true, when it is only one writer's opinion. This skill helps a reader to develop his or her own opinions on topics and events, by responding to the views of others.

Below are some examples of facts and opinions about specific topics. Read each statement and identify which is fact and which is opinion. Then compare your answers with the explanation which follows. Remember that facts can be proven. Opinions are personal viewpoints.

A 1. American colleges often profit from football, both in money and in fame.
A 2. Watching college football is the best way to spend New Year's Day.

B 1. Texas Instruments made the first electronic hand-held calculator.
B 2. Texas Instruments calculators make math more fun for students.

C 1. Space exploration is expensive, but the knowledge gained is worth the price.
C 2. The U.S. space program has plans to send a human to the moon again by 2020.

Statement **A 1** is a **fact**. It can be proven by researching income earned by colleges through football games. It can also be shown that throughout history, football has made many colleges famous. Statement **A 2**, about the best way to spend New Year's Day, is an **opinion**. It may be true for many people, but not for everyone. Many people may not enjoy watching football at all.

Statement **B 1**, about Texas Instruments and the first hand-held calculator, is a **fact**. It can be proven through historical records that the first calculator was made by "TI." On the other hand, statement **B 2** is clearly an **opinion** since the phrase "more fun" describes one person's experience, but does not apply to everyone.

Statement **C 1** is an opinion. One writer may think that the cost of the space program is worth the price, and another writer may not. It is not a matter of who is right or who is wrong; it is *a matter of opinion*. Statement **C 2**, however, is not a matter of opinion. It can be proven to be true—or false—through research. (Even if a fact is proved false, it does not become an opinion. It is simply an incorrect or false statement.)

Key Phrases for Opinion. Often when an opinion is expressed, it is presented clearly as an opinion. A writer will do this by beginning the statement of opinion with a phrase such as "In my opinion." Key words and phrases like this one make it obvious that the statement is an opinion. Here is a list of some key phrases that signal an expression of opinion.

Key Phrases for Opinion			
I believe	I suggest	It seems to me	I feel
The way I see it	In my opinion	I figure	Apparently

202

Chapter 12

Practice 1: Fact or Opinion

For the following statements, write *F* next to facts and *O* next to opinions. Be able to support your responses.

1. _____ Bicycling is the best sport for building strong lungs!
2. _____ The use of instant messaging has affected the way teenagers write.
3. _____ Crab cakes are delicious and easy to prepare.
4. _____ The food pyramid advises eating five servings of vegetables every day.
5. _____ Nolan Ryan was the greatest pitcher in the history of baseball.
6. _____ Louis Armstrong had a significant impact on music in America.
7. _____ I think that middle school is more fun than elementary school.
8. _____ You should take part in at least 2 extra-curricular activities.
9. _____ Watching television is bad for your social life.
10. _____ Only one hundredth of one percent of people in Louisiana are bit by a snake each year.

Practice 2: Locating Facts and Opinions in Text

In the following passage, underline the sentences that express *opinions*.

The Old Turf

Today, the playing field at the New Orleans Superdome is covered with field turf. Field turf is a state-of-the-art version of artificial turf. It is much better than the turf which used to cover most sports stadiums. However, there might be no artificial turf today at all, if it had not been for the Houston Astros.

In the early 1960s, the city of Houston completed the first enclosed, air-conditioned sports arena ever built. The stadium originally had the rather dull name of Harris County Domed Stadium. The baseball team that played there was called the Colt 45s. But when the National Aeronautics and Space Administration (NASA) located its space center in Houston, all that changed. The name of the baseball team was changed to the Astros, and the stadium became the Astrodome.

At first, the stadium field was covered with normal grass. But the roof of the dome blocked out the sun, and so the grass died. Now, most self-respecting ball fans don't care what a field looks like, as long as they get to see good baseball. But on television, green grass looks a lot nicer than patches of dried up hay on top of dirt. So, one of the greatest inventions in the history of sport grew out of the dead grass of the Astrodome. Plastic, fake grass that never dies and needs no mowing was invented. This lush field carpet was named Astroturf, after the Astrodome. It has greatly improved the overall enjoyment of

Fact, Opinion, and Probability

ball games ever since. The new generation of artificial turf, Field Turf, has been enthusiastically received by fans and players alike..

Tips for Identifying Facts and Opinions
1. **Facts** state information based on observation, statistics, or research. Facts can be proved true or false based on information.
2. **Opinions** express a personal viewpoint or belief about a person, place, event, or idea. **Hint 1:** Opinions contain adjectives that evaluate, such as best, worst, dishonest, fun, boring, beautiful, and so on. **Hint 2:** Opinions sometimes include phrases such as "you should," "I think," "my view," "my opinion," and so on.

Practice 3: Creating Facts and Opinions

A. Think of two persons, places, things, or ideas on your own or with a partner. Then write a statement of fact and a statement of opinion about each one. Review your statements with a teacher or other students. Revise them based on the feedback you get.

B. Find five facts and five opinions in a newspaper article, magazine article, or Internet article. Underline them, and then share them with your instructor or classmates. Research the facts in one of the articles to make sure they are true. Present this research to the class.

PROBABILITY

Probability is a concept that we use in everyday life and in everyday language. If something is probable, it is not only possible, it is reasonably *likely*. "I'll probably pass my history test today, since I studied all week." "You'll probably make first string in basketball; you're one of the best players." "My parents probably won't let me go to the game because of my report card." All these statements guess at some future event which is likely to happen. Those guesses are based on knowledge you are certain of, and knowledge of possibilities. For instance, you are certain that you studied hard for your test. You know it is possible to pass history tests if you have learned at least 70% of the material. Therefore, you have a good idea of what is probable when facing your test.

Probability is part of the study of *statistics*. In a way, it measures the distance between two points—only, the points represent ideas. Look at the line in the diagram below. At one end of the line is a 0. This zero stands for the idea that an event is *impossible*. Think of it as something that has a 0% chance of happening. There is no chance of it happening at all. At the other end of the line is a 100. Think if this as the idea that something has a 100% chance of happening. An event with 100% chance of happen is actually *certain* to happen. Every point along that line, between 0 and 100, represents the probability of an event. If it is close to the 0, it would not be very likely, or probable. If it is close to the 100, it would be very likely.

Impossible   **Certain**

0 ■■100

Chapter 12

PROBABILITY AND READING

A few things in life are impossible, and a few things are certain to happen, given the right conditions. Everything else falls somewhere along the measuring line of probability.

The scientific study of statistics and probability has formulas to determine exact probability of certain events. However, in reading, probability is not an exact science.

As an active reader, you must develop a general idea of how probable events and ideas are, given the information in the texts, and given what you already know.

> **Example:** The headline in the school newspaper read, "Tornado Imminent." The story was about the fact that tornados hit this part of the country on average every 50 years. There has not been a tornado here for 50 years. Therefore, we will probably get a tornado this year.

What is the probability of the newspaper prediction being true? Probability depends on information, or data. The more and better the data, the greater will be your ability to assess probability. But this information must have certain qualities. It should be—

Reliable   The information must come from a reliable source. If you are reading an article about tornados which is written by an experienced meteorologist and published in a respected journal, then you know that the information is reliable.

Current   Information should be up-to-date. A report on the possibility of a tornado from three years ago would not be effective in this story. Today's story, or one from last week would be effective.

Thorough   There should be a sufficient amount of information given in the text. Information that is thorough includes a lot of evidence, research, statistics, and facts to back up any statements which are made. This makes an article thorough.

Inclusive   The information should include as many factors about the subject as possible. What factors influence a tornado, or influence the prevention of a tornado?

Practice 4: Probability and Reading

Read the following short paragraphs carefully. Underline the statements of probability in each one.

1. The seven spirited fillies, raised by the same owner, braced themselves in the starting gates of their first race. For two years since their births, their owner, Marika, had fed them on the finest grains and mixtures of hay. They all had sires who were national champions. Their mares were accomplished racers as well. They had been trained by the best trainers. As the crowd waited for the shot that begins the race, she was confident that her fillies were future champions. One of them would surely be Kentucky Derby material.

2. The frog population in Rory County has a dismal fate. Industrial pollution has been leaking for years into the swamplands as industry leaders ignore the problem. The few laws against pollution that the state has passed are not being enforced. There are not enough police to enforce them because the police department has been cut back. Scientists have already found many examples of mutation in the frog population. And worst of all, nothing is planned in the new congress to take care of the problem.

Fact, Opinion, and Probability

3. Eighth grade students today are being prepared to becoming critical readers and writers of tomorrow. Education departments are putting more emphasis on teaching students to be active, critical readers, not just passive believers of everything they read. School curriculums now include writing that involves analyzing topics and not just reporting facts about them. These are skills that are needed for success in college. After years of studying with the current curriculum, these students will be prepared to apply to some of the best universities in the country.

Practice 5: Reading for Facts, Opinions, and Probability

Read the following paragraph. Decide which numbered statements are facts, *F*, which are opinions, *O*, and which are statements of probability *P*. On the spaces that follow each passage, write *F*, *P*, or *O* next to each sentence number.

Walking for Fun and Health

1) Most school days involve too much sitting. 2) Many American children do not get the exercise they need for good health. 3) Exercise is fun. 4) You don't have to play a strenuous sport to get your exercise. 5) Expensive gyms and exercise clothing are not necessary either. 6) Research has shown that regular walking is as good for you as most other exercises. 7) Walking exercises the muscles and increases oxygen in the blood and lungs. 8) A brisk walk around the neighborhood every day will make you stronger in less than a month. 9) You can enjoy walking more if you walk with a friend. 10) In general, walking is an enjoyable way to end a long school day!

1. _____ 2. _____ 3. _____ 4. _____ 5. _____

6. _____ 7. _____ 8. _____ 9. _____ 10. _____

The Soul of Gospel

1) Mahalia Jackson was the greatest singer ever to come from the state of Louisiana. 2) Mahalia was born in 1911 in New Orleans. 3) From early childhood, she sang with a beautiful and powerful voice. 4) Mahalia learned her art almost completely from singing in church choirs. 5) She loved to sing Gospel music. 6) Her singing was brimming with love, joy, and hope. 7) If you could hear Mahalia sing "Precious Lord, Take My Hand," it would make you cry. 8) There are many extraordinary Gospel singers, but none can compare for shear inspiration with Mahalia Jackson. 9) Mahalia could have been a blues singer, but she refused to sing blues. 10) She thought Blues music was sad and hopeless. 11) Mahalia preferred the hope and promise of gospel music. 12) Mahalia's voice will always be known as one of the finest in Gospel music.

1. _____ 2. _____ 3. _____ 4. _____ 5. _____ 6. _____

7. _____ 8. _____ 9. _____ 10. _____ 11. _____ 12. _____

The Unexpected Gold

1) The 2004 Summer Olympics saw one of the most remarkable triumphs ever for a gold medal championship. **2)** During the final round of the men's gymnastics event, Paul Hamm, the leading American gymnast, almost wiped out his chance of winning any medal at all. **3)** Hamm had been very close to winning the gold medal. **4)** Then something happened that is every gymnast's worst nightmare. **5)** Paul Hamm fell so badly off his vault that his score plummeted him to 12th place. **6)** Afterwards, he had to face more competition on the parallel bars. **7)** He must have been deeply shaken emotionally by his fall. **8)** But you could not tell by the expression on his face; he remained focused and calm. **9)** He showed tremendous self control and positive attitude by focusing on the job ahead. **10)** His performance on the parallel bars was flawless. **11)** Even he was shocked when he was awarded the gold.

1. _____   2. _____   3. _____   4. _____   5. _____   6. _____

7. _____   8. _____   9. _____   10. _____   11. _____

Fact, Opinion, and Probability

CHAPTER 12 REVIEW

A. Fact and Opinion. Read the following paragraph about an American Sports hero. Next to each sentence number following the passage, write whether the sentence is a fact **(F)** or opinion **(O)**.

Lance Armstrong

(1) When Lance Armstrong was a teenager in Plano, Texas, he used to ride his bike on Saturdays. **(2)** But Lance's rides were not like normal bike rides. **(3)** He often cycled from Plano, near Dallas, to the border of Oklahoma. **(4)** Then, as if Texas were not big enough, after high school Lance took his bike overseas. **(5)** Soon, he was winning cycling races all over Europe. **(6)** Before Lance began to compete in Europe, cycling had always been a favorite sport for the Europeans. **(7)** American cycling teams could hardly compete with the talent of the Europeans. **(8)** But now, Americans are very proud of their winning cycling team. **(9)** As of 2004, Armstrong, the team's leader, has won a record six Tour de France races. **(10)** The Tour de France is an incredible sporting event to watch. **(11)** Cyclists race for almost 2,000 miles in all kinds of landscapes and weather. **(12)** Each day, the teams race one section of the whole race. **(13)** Whoever wins the section of the race gets to wear a yellow jersey (overshirt). **(14)** That jersey is starting to look like the uniform of the U.S. cycling team!

1. _____   2. _____   3. _____   4. _____   5. _____   6. _____   7. _____

8. _____   9. _____   10. _____   11. _____   12. _____   13. _____   14. _____

B. Fact, Opinion, and Probability. In the following passage, some sentences are underlined and numbered. Read the entire passage carefully. Then look at the underlined questions. Write in the spaces provided if the sentences represent a fact *(F)*, an opinion *(O)*, or a probability *(P)*.

Ukraine's Stolen Election is Taken Back

It took 36 days of camping out in freezing temperatures for thousands of citizens. It took one candidate almost being poisoned to death. It took international pressure by the United States and other countries. And it took a government act and a Supreme Court decision. But in the end, a non-violent revolution had taken place. The people of Ukraine had won back their country from the grip of Russian control. Another free country was born on December 27, 2004.

(1) Over a month earlier, Victor Yanuchovyk (pronounced Yah new KOH vitch), backed by Russia, declared himself the winner of the election and president of Ukraine. The Ukrainians didn't buy it. In fact, thousands of them were so angry that they left their homes that cold winter day and gathered in their town squares to protest. They were sure that their candidate, Victor Yushchenko (pronounced YOU shen koh) had won the election but that the election results had been rigged.

208

(2) The Ukrainian people had good reason to believe in the dishonesty of the Russian-backed candidate. **(3)** They had been oppressed by the Soviet Union for many years. Then, when the Soviet Union fell apart in 1989, they won their independence. But corrupt, Russian-backed politicians still controlled their government and economy.

(4) On November 21, 2004, many Ukrainians saw hope for breaking their ties with Russia. They voted for Yushchenko, who promised stronger ties with Europe and the rest of the world. But the election did not work out that way. So they camped in plastic tents on city streets. **(5)** They listened to speeches and waved the Ukrainian flag and sang the Ukrainian National Anthem. **(6)** They wore orange, their chosen color of protest, and that blazing color, against the wintery white and gray Ukrainian background, was the only warmth to be found.

On November 27th, the Ukrainian parliament itself took a vote and said that it did not support the new president. **(7)** The people grew more hopeful. Then, on December 3rd, the Supreme Court of Ukraine agreed that the election was a fraud and that another election must take place. Meanwhile, Yushchenko had become very ill, and doctors discovered he had been poisoned. **(8)** There was more than enough dioxin in his blood to kill him. **(9)** It is amazing that he somehow survived.

(10) On December 26th, a second election was held. Observers from around the world watched it closely to prevent fraud. Yushchenko won that election. That day he told his Ukrainian supporters that, while Ukraine has been independent since 1989, today they are truly free. **(11)** Ukraine faces a brighter future because of the courageous people of the "Orange Revolution."

1. _____   2. _____   3. _____   4. _____   5. _____   6. _____

7. _____   8. _____   9. _____   10. _____   11. _____

Jobs of Tomorrow

(1) In recent years, the level of education in the labor force has risen dramatically. (2) In the last 15 years, the number of workers in the labor force with a college degree has increased by 28 percent. (3) Jobs that require a college degree are increasing faster than jobs that do not.

(4) This need for higher education will continue to grow in the future. (5) The three fastest growing job types are executive, professional, and technical specialists. (6) These groups of jobs require at least a college education. (7) Therefore, it is very important to earn a degree.

Fact, Opinion, and Probability

(8) Jobs that do not require a college degree are decreasing. (9) Machines have replaced many factory workers. (10) Other jobs have been moved to other countries where labor is cheaper. (11) Opportunities for high school dropouts will become scarce. (12) The best thing students can do for their future is to stay in school!

1. _____   2. _____   3. _____   4. _____   5. _____   6. _____

7. _____   8. _____   9. _____   10. _____   11. _____   12. _____

Invasion of the Toads

(1) In June 1935, Australia's sugar industry imported 101 cane toads from Hawaii. (2) Farmers hoped the toad would eat the cane beetles threatening the sugar crop. (3) The toad is, as one person put it, is "ugly even by toad standards." (4) And it had no interest in cane beetles. (5) But it made itself at home. (6) Now it is a problem in many parts of Australia. (7) In fact, Australia's toad population is now in the millions. (8) Obviously, the idea to use foreign animals to solve problems is a bad one.

(9) The cane toad is also dangerous. (10) It can secrete a poison that can kill a dog in 15 minutes. (11) The best solution may be to import a parasite to wipe out the cane toad. (12) And this solution will most likely bring problems of its own!

1. _____   2. _____   3. _____   4. _____   5. _____   6. _____

7. _____   8. _____   9. _____   10. _____   11. _____   12. _____

Chapter 13
Author's Viewpoint

All four benchmarks may be measured by multiple-choice or short-answer questions. Items measuring M2 may involve steps in problem solving but do not require resolution. Items for Benchmark M3 **do not require identification of author's purpose, but instead focus on the author's point of view.**

LOUISIANA READING BENCHMARKS ADDRESSED IN THIS CHAPTER INCLUDE:	
ELA-7-M3	Interpreting the effects of an author's purpose (reason for writing) and viewpoint (perspective) (1, 2, 4)

The LEAP 21 Language Arts test for grade 8 will require you to show that you can analyze texts, including different types of literature. What does it mean to analyze a text? It means to look carefully at *why* and *how* the text was written.

In this chapter, you will learn to determine an author's **purpose** in creating a text. You will also learn skills for recognizing an author's **viewpoint** and how the author presents the viewpoint. An author's viewpoint is the author's feelings about or attitude towards a topic. A viewpoint can be *biased* (one-sided) or it can be *objective* (neutral). Knowing an author's viewpoint allows you as a reader to judge the text for its effectiveness. You can determine if a text is effective by looking at the amount and the quality of **evidence** (forms of proof, examples, or other facts) the author presents in order to support his or her viewpoint.

This chapter will also look at how authors use **persuasive techniques** in presenting their viewpoints. Persuasive techniques can be used in a positive way by authors to present good ideas supported by strong evidence. They can also be used to manipulate or even mislead the reader, when presented with little or no evidence.

With practice, these questions will become an automatic part of your reading process. They help you to become an active, involved reader, who can gain as much from a text as it has to offer.

AUTHOR'S VIEWPOINT

Authors have a viewpoint, or a perspective, on each topic they write about. An author's **viewpoint** is the author's perspective, or feeling, about a topic. This viewpoint may be *objective*, or based more on fact, or it can be *biased*, or based more on opinion.

Author's Viewpoint

Objective Viewpoint Authors often write mainly *facts* about a topic, in order to inform or teach readers. When an author writes only to inform, then the author has an objective viewpoint. This viewpoint is common in *expository* writing. Objective writing informs the reader of facts about a topic. It does not state an opinion about the topic.

Biased Viewpoint Authors also write to give their own *opinions* about a topic. When an author writes to express an opinion, the author has a biased viewpoint. A biased viewpoint is often used in *persuasive* writing. Persuasive writing urges the reader to agree with the author's opinion.

Following are two examples of objective writing and biased writing. Let's say your teacher has asked you to write about art and music in school. If you want to *inform* your reader about art and music in school, you would have an *objective* point of view. However, if you wanted to *give your opinion* about art and music in school, you would have a *biased* point of view.

Read the following two examples of different viewpoints on this topic.

Music in School: Objective Viewpoint

Art and music have been part of the American school system from its beginning. Today, the arts in public schools take many forms. American students may learn a lot about music. They may learn to sing, to play an instrument, and to read music. Students may also learn visual arts. These arts include painting, sculpting, and clay work. Some schools also offer classes in performing arts. The performing arts include acting and dancing. Music and visual art are the two most common taught in schools. They are usually part of the everyday class schedule for elementary and middle school students.

Music in School: Biased Viewpoint

The arts are an important and fun part of education. Nothing adds a fresh outlook to a school day like an hour in the art room smoothing wet terra cotta clay with your hands into any shape you can dream of!

And singing or playing your heart out in the choir or band room gets rid of any tension and worry you might have about that math test. Some studies even show that learning music helps improve your skills in math! Losing music and art from our schools would be a tragedy. We need to support these valuable programs.

The first paragraph gives facts and information about the arts in school. It does not express an opinion about the topic. This is **objective** writing.

The second paragraph voices an opinion about the arts in school. The author gives examples of how the arts make a student's day more enjoyable. The author also mentions studies that support the author's ideas. The author uses the pronoun "we" to draw the reader into action to support art and music programs. The author's perspective in this paragraph is **biased**. It is biased towards keeping the arts in public schools.

For further practice, look at the statements below and decide for each one of them if the author's perspective is *objective*, to inform, or *biased*, to persuade. Then read the explanation of each that follows.

1. According to the U.S. Fish and Wildlife Service, the California condor is an endangered species. In 2002, one condor chick was hatched in captivity for the first time in 18 years.
2. As responsible citizens, we must prevent the California condor, a national treasure, from disappearing from this earth.
3. Wolves are only trouble for ranchers. We should eliminate them through hunting and relocation.
4. The Louisiana Iris is celebrated in the spring of each year in Jean Lafitte, LA. Tours of swamps and gardens make it possible to get a good view of the flower in its habitats.

Statements **1** and **4** state information and facts. They do not encourage one belief over another. These statements have an *objective* perspective.

Statements **2** and **3** urge the reader to take a certain action or adopt a certain belief. These statements have a *biased* perspective. You will notice that these biased statements use words like *must* and *should*. These key words often show that the author has a biased viewpoint about the topic and is encouraging the reader to feel the same.

Practice 1: Biased Perspective

Read the following two passages. On your own piece of paper, write what you think the author's bias is. Cite phrases or sentences from the passage to support your ideas.

Space Camp

Space camp is a valuable educational experience for middle school students. At the U.S. Space and Rocket Center in Huntsville, Alabama, students can attend a space camp for one week. There, they can experience moon-like gravity and learn about mission control operations. While having fun, students may also be preparing themselves for a good education and an exciting career. Several students who attended space camp in the last five years have been accepted into the top technical colleges in the country. When they graduate from these colleges as aeronautics engineers, they will have some of the best career opportunities in their field. The price of space camp seems like a good investment in the future!

Cast Call for Drama Club!

Middle schools offer several extra curricular activities for students. You can play basketball, soccer, badminton, and even chess before and after school. But not all middle schools have an active drama club. Being involved in drama helps young people to develop self confidence. They learn public speaking skills, develop good memories, learn about hard work, and make many friends. Just learning to overcome stage fright can be a life-changing event for a child. Middle school can be a time of uncertainty and shyness. Drama club can offer students a place to belong and a way to discover their talents. If any teachers are interested in starting drama clubs, they are needed to make a difference in kids' lives!

Author's Viewpoint

BIASED VIEWPOINT: INDIRECT BIAS

In the last exercise, you could probably see that the author's bias was quite obvious and clearly stated. However, authors do not always express their viewpoints directly. Instead, they often present their bias **indirectly**. This means that the author writes in a way that persuades the reader to adopt the author's bias but does not clearly state the bias. Indirect bias can be expressed by:

- Emphasizing information on one side of an issue
- Minimizing the importance of information on the other side of an issue
- Carefully choosing words that influence the reader to feel a certain way
- Choosing what information to include and what to ignore

All the above techniques are effective in portraying an author's bias in an indirect way

Read the following two passages. What is the author's bias? Can you detect how the author feels about the subject from the information given? Write down your answers, and then check them against the discussion which follows the passages.

Spring Fling Shopping

By February, the malls are brimming with new spring and summer clothes. Teenagers flock to the stores on weekends to see what new fashions they can find to add to their wardrobes. Tank tops, tee-shirts, sandals, and shorts, all in bright spring colors, decorate the store windows like flags at an Easter parade. It's all so difficult to decide on which ones to buy! Teens shop for many reasons. The pressure to dress well is one of the strongest forces in their lives. Clothing styles change every year. Furthermore, teens often grow from one year to the next, and last year's clothes do not fit anymore. Therefore, many young people, with parents in tow, head to the mall at the beginning of each season. It is time for the expensive but enjoyable process of finding new clothes and shoes. The price of these clothes, may not always reflect their quality. Clothes often look old within weeks of purchase. This results in clothing being donated to charities or thrown away, as families replace them with new styles, colors, and sizes. All this spending, growing, and discarding add up to a lively economy and long days at the mall for teens.

Mall Shops and Sweatshops

High school is full of motivating clubs and activities to take part in. Some high school clubs promote awareness of injustices in our world. One club of this kind is the anti-sweatshop club. An anti-sweatshop club educates students about where much of their clothing comes from. Students are often surprised to learn that a large percentage of the cool clothes they buy in the mall are made in sweatshops—in America and around the world. What is a sweatshop? It is a place where people work from morning until night under poor conditions for extremely low pay. It is a place where women work so much that they hardly see their children. And even then, they earn too little money to buy enough food for their families. Yet the clothes they make will earn millions for large companies. Newspaper reports about sweatshops have caused some students to want to make a difference. Through anti-sweatshop clubs, students learn about sweatshops and the companies that use them. Then they can write to these companies. A letter from a high school student has a lot of influence on companies that depend on young Americans to buy their products. A student can also write to the major department stores and ask which of their products come from sweatshops. Large department stores do not want to be seen as supporting sweatshops. Students in anti-sweatshop clubs believe in the power of teenagers to make a difference in their world.

The first passage contains mainly facts and information, but the viewpoint tends to be biased towards the fun and benefits of shopping. Malls are described in colorful, vibrant language, and people are described as happy and active. The author makes the point that the money spent supports a strong economy. This supports the viewpoint that shopping has beneficial effects.

The second passage is also full of facts and information. That information brings out a different bias about the shopping situation. The author uses emotional images. The passage describes a mother too poor to feed her family while making clothes that make big companies rich. This idea will most likely influence a reader to feel that something is unjust in the clothing industry. The writer's opinion is not exactly stated in words, but it becomes clear to the reader through the choice of information given.

Tips for Recognizing an Author's Indirect Bias
Think carefully about the author's choice of words:
Objective: Students may study algebra when they are in 7th grade.
Indirect Bias: Students have the <u>opportunity</u> to study algebra as early as 7th grade.
Indirect Bias: Some students <u>have to</u> study algebra as early as 7th grade.
Study the supporting information the author chooses to include in the passage:
Objective: Many students enter medical school. Doctors earn large salaries. They also achieve a high level of education.
Indirect Bias: Many people enter medical school each year. A doctor's job is <u>very demanding</u>. Doctors can <u>suffer from</u> fatigue, anxiety, and depression.
Indirect Bias: Many people enter medical school each year. They are looking for the opportunity to <u>help people</u>. Doctors are able to make a <u>positive difference</u> in people's lives.
Look closely at how the author describes a situation or idea.
Objective: All the students in the class were busy with projects.
Indirect Bias: The business development classroom was a place of <u>activity</u>. The students worked cooperatively as <u>conversation</u> filled the air.
Indirect Bias: Students talked and moved around the <u>disordered</u> science lab while working on projects. The place seemed chaotic and <u>noisy</u>.

Practice 2: Recognizing Objective or Biased Perspective

Read each of the following selections on the same topic. Make a check mark next to the word at the end of each passage that describes the author's viewpoint as objective or biased. Then write 3–4 words or phrases from the passage which support your choice.

Author's Viewpoint

Animal Sacrifices

Every year, the U. S. military sends shoppers to Europe. These shoppers are looking for a very special product: well-bred, intelligent German shepherds or other dogs, suitable for use by U.S. armed forces. These government shoppers have a lot of money to spend: money that comes from the taxes each American citizen pays. They need a lot of money. They have to spend at least $3,000 for each dog. And they buy more than 300 dogs. These canine prizes are shipped back to the United States and trained in military camps for 100 days. After they graduate, they take on some of the most dangerous work any soldier can do. Often they are in the line of fire, along with their trainers. Many dogs suffer terribly and die on duty. In Vietnam alone, hundreds of dogs were killed in battle. Most military dogs brought to Vietnam never returned. Here at home, you would not want your pet to be put in harm's way on purpose. We have animal protection laws to prevent that. However, these laws don't seem to apply to all dogs.

1. Objective _____ Biased _____

Words from the passage: _____

_____

Uncommon Soldiers

Every year, hundreds of young Americans go into training for the U.S. military. And every year, over 300 of these "troops" are dogs: German shepherds and Dobermans. Dogs have been part of the U.S. military for decades. They have played a role in most American wars. The location for training these special soldiers is the Lackland Air Force Base in San Antonio, Texas. It takes about 100 days to train the dogs to work in the military. After graduation, the dogs serve in all areas of the military: Army, Navy, Marines, and Special Forces. They serve at home and at war. Some are scout dogs. They sniff out explosives, booby-traps, and dangerous chemicals. Others are sentry dogs. They walk the battle line with their handlers to watch for enemies. Dogs are a definite part of national security.

2. Objective _____ Biased _____

Words from the passage:_____

_____

Unsung Heroes

The cool, damp winds of November blow through the crowds along the Veterans' Day parade route. Flags fly and soldiers march, but all is not celebration. The skies are usually bleak. People's thoughts turn to lost heroes of past wars. They ponder the fact that they are safe and free today because of these fallen heroes. But how many Americans think, at this time, about dogs? Dogs have played a very important part in the safety of American troops in all wars. They are loyal, intelligent, courageous, and obedient. A dog is as good a soldier as anyone could hope to fight with. Many dogs have died bravely while saving the lives of other soldiers in their units. The United States War Dogs Association estimates that canine soldiers saved over 10,000 lives in Vietnam alone. Some soldiers who have worked with war dogs have created memorials to these outstanding war heroes. You may be sure they remember their lost companions very well on Veteran's day.

3. Objective _____ Biased _____

Explanation _____

_____

EVIDENCE: SUPPORTING A VIEWPOINT

Whether an author's perspective is biased or objective, it must be supported with evidence to be effective. Evidence can consist of examples, statistics, illustrations, or general facts. Evidence can also consist of good, sound logic. In any case, the more and better the evidence, the more an author's viewpoint will be considered valid.

Look at the following two paragraphs. The first one is not supported well with evidence. The second one includes evidence. As you read each paragraph, consider which one is more effective in influencing you to accept the writer's viewpoint.

The Marquis de Lafayette: Version 1

The French nobleman and soldier, whose name is about three feet long, but who is commonly known as the Marquis de Lafayette, is a model of revolutionary spirit. He was a great soldier who played an important role in the American Revolution. He had a noble and honest character, which won him the respect of his troops and of his countrymen. Lafayette hated the oppressive rule of kings and fought for the rights of people. He is one of the most important figures in American history. Louisiana can be proud of having this great man associated with its history. Lafayette brought about dramatic changes in the government of France as well. Both the Americans and the French deeply mourned his death in 1834. He was one of the greatest champions of liberty that ever lived.

The Marquis de Lafayette: Version 2

The French nobleman and soldier whose name is about three feet long, but who is commonly known as the Marquis de Lafayette, is a model of revolutionary spirit. A wealthy orphan, he was only 16 years old when he heard that the United States had declared independence from England. From the moment he heard that news, he determined to be part of the American fight for independence. Though very young, he disobeyed orders and sailed to America to join the Continental Army. He was a great soldier who played an important role in the American Revolution. He fought with General George Washington, who also became his friend.

Lafayette returned to France to convince the French to support the Americans in their fight. Because of his efforts, many French officers and troops sailed to America and fought with the Americans against England. One of these officers was Admiral Rocham-

Author's Viewpoint

beau, who, along with Lafayette and another French officer, brought about the defeat of the British in Yorktown, one of the most important victories in the war. For this reason alone, Lafayette is an important figure in American history.

Lafayette had a noble and honest character, which won him the respect of his troops and of his countrymen. When he returned to France after the American Revolution, the French gave him a hero's welcome, calling him a "hero of two worlds." Lafayette hated the oppressive rule of kings and fought for the rights of people. While in France, he fought successfully for a more democratic form of government called the National Assembly. Lafayette brought about dramatic changes in the government of France. He wrote the "Declaration of the Rights of Man and of the citizen" with some help from his friend, Thomas Jefferson. He then introduced this document to the General Assembly. The French Revolution against royalty followed soon after, leading to France's freedom from tyranny.

Louisiana can be proud of having this great man associated with its history. In 1803, Louisiana made a gift to Lafayette of a large portion of land. Lafayette also became an honorary citizen of the United States. Both the Americans and the French deeply mourned his death in 1834. He was one of the greatest champions of liberty that ever lived.

Authors may bring any point of view to their writing. Every writer has something to offer to the "conversation" which readers and authors take part in. However, the presentation of a viewpoint can be strong and convincing, or it can be weak and superficial. The difference lies in the evidence the author provides to support all points made in the writing.

PERSUASIVE TECHNIQUES

Many of the written—and non-written—messages that we come across every day have something to convince us about. An author may want to convince a reader of the author's viewpoint. A business may want to convince a viewer or reader to buy a product. They both use **persuasive techniques** to do so.

Persuasive techniques in writing can be powerful tools for thoughtful writers to introduce readers to great ideas or new knowledge. They can also be powerful tools for manipulating readers and viewers. Persuasive techniques are used in both good persuasive writing and in advertising and propaganda. Learning to recognize persuasive techniques wherever they are used can help you analyze text.

With some exceptions, the same persuasive techniques are used both in persuasive writing (editorials, articles about social or political issues) and in advertising. They are just used differently in the two areas. Below are two lists of persuasive techniques and how they are applied to these two areas of writing. The first list applies to advertising. The second list applies to other persuasive writing, such as editorials or essays. Study these lists, and try to see which techniques apply to the ads and passages in the rest of the chapter.

PERSUASIVE TECHNIQUES IN ADVERTISING AND NONFICTION

APPEAL TO AUTHORITY

In advertising, the use of **"experts in the field"** is a common persuasive technique. Experts add authority and believability to the claims of advertisers.

Example: A foot doctor, dressed in medical uniform, talks to a group of teens about the importance of supportive footwear. She says it will prevent serious pain from falling arches in the future. The purpose of this appeal to authority is to sell running shoes that claim to be supportive of feet.

In persuasive writing, the **appeal to authority** does not usually involve a professional in a uniform. But it may use the authority of a more experienced person or institution as an example of success. Referring to scientific studies is also a way of appealing to authority.

Example: George Jones Middle School in Washington state began a tutoring program in reading, using middle school students as tutors for younger students. Since the beginning of the program, the reading scores of the students doing the tutoring have increased by 25%. It would not be difficult to try such a program in our school.

IN-CROWD APPEAL

In advertising, **in-crowd appeal** creates a to a kind of fantasy which encourages viewers to identify with an admired, envied group. The idea behind in-crowd appeal is that if the viewer buys the advertised product, he or she will be part of this "in crowd."

Example: Young teens are shown at a festive party, very colorful, and full of balloons and decorations. They are all wearing the latest fashions from an expensive teens' clothing store. They all look happy and as if they are having a fantastically wonderful time. The idea is that most teens would like to be part of that crowd, and it seems that if you buy those clothes, you will be.

BANDWAGON

No one likes to be left behind. In advertising, **bandwagon** is a technique in which the reader is made to feel that a great movement is beginning. When it is used in advertising, readers are made to believe they will be seen as idiots or outcasts if they do not join the movement.

Example: "This is the age of the Internet. Which age do you belong to? Call our Internet service provider and get online...or get nowhere." The point of this slogan is that the reader should do what millions of people are doing or they will "get nowhere." It does not give specific reasons why this is a good idea.

Non-fiction text does not usually try to cause anxiety in its readers about being left behind, the way advertising might. However, it may very effectively draw upon facts and statistics to show where trends are going and what the benefits of being part of those trends could be.

Example: Employers today report that they are looking for workers who can think for themselves and who are creative in problem solving. Many high schools are encouraging creativity and "thinking outside the box," in order to prepare students for the better jobs the 21st century has to offer. Our school should consider being part of this way of thinking.

Author's Viewpoint

EMOTIONAL APPEAL

Words are effective when they evoke feelings. Emotional words and images are used to create a strong reaction in readers or viewers of ads and speeches.

Example: A television scene of a large family gathered around the Thanksgiving dinner table. Uncles, aunts, cousins, and grandparents all talk and smile happily. They pause and clap as Mom places a huge baked turkey on the table. A voice-over says, "When the best of the season calls for the best in cooking, don't settle for anything but Bestturkeys by Eiderdown Farms."

In nonfiction writing, an author will use powerful, descriptive words and images to affect a reader emotionally. This can be an appeal with positive emotions or with negative emotions.

Example: The mother dolphin glided like a spent arrow alongside our boat. Leaning to one side, her bright round eye looked up at us with a twinkle of pride, mischief and humor, all in one. She seemed to be sharing with us her delight in her baby, who glided next to her with the perfect harmony and grace of a Blue Angel. That magical experience on a dolphin cruise was the beginning of my commitment to preserving and protecting the oceans.

RHETORICAL QUESTION

Rhetorical questions do not expect an answer; they just set up the listener up to think about the answer. And that answer usually reminds the listener of a need or a want. Advertising is based on needs and wants. Once the listener has thought of the need, the advertiser can respond with a solution to that need.

Example: "Do you have blemishes that threaten to destroy your social life?" (Answer: "Well, I guess. Maybe. Sometimes...") "Then you need BeeTee, the Blemish Terminator made from bee pollen..."

In nonfiction, an author may use a **rhetorical question** to make the reader think about a situation or idea. If the question is asked in the right way, it prepares the reader to be willing to hear more about what the author has to say.

Example: The growing number of power cars on our roads are choking our atmosphere and clogging our lungs. What can we do to save the air, breathe more freely, and still enjoy driving good cars? Your federal representative will be debating that and other questions of energy use this week in Congress. Your voice can be part of that debate if you write today to your congressional representative.

REPETITION

Have you ever had a song stuck in your head? If you listen to a song enough times, it can sometimes refuse to leave your memory, and you must hum it to yourself in spite of your best efforts. Advertisers rely on this phenomenon. They would love to have their slogans playing like a broken record in your mind. At the very least, they would like you to remember the elements of their messages. So, they use repetition.

Example: "Call 806-900-0098 for your free in-home demonstration of this incredible product. That's 806-900-0098 for the product of a lifetime. Remember, that's 806-900-0098. Call now. 806-900-0098...!!"

In nonfiction and in public speaking, authors and speakers often use repetition of an idea. This technique adds to the author's or speaker's effectiveness in persuading a reader or audience.

Example: "As we graduate, we cannot just coast. We must go all-out to use the knowledge we've gained. We must go all-out to enter programs of higher learning that will take us to the next level. We must go all-out to find the work that will fulfill us and benefit our communities."

GLITTERING GENERALITIES

Glittering generalities are descriptions that sound great but are vague and unprovable praises of a product, an issue, or a person.

Example: "Our candidate is a true American and has the strong family values this country needs." The label "true American" has no definition. It just sounds like a good thing to be. The same holds true for "family values." Values are different in different cultures and age groups, so who can define them?

Practice 3: Recognizing Persuasive Techniques

Read the following passages. After each passage, write which persuasive technique is being used in that passage. Then briefly explain your choice based on the types of propaganda presented in this chapter's previous pages.

1. Do you want the state government to tax even more of your income? Don't let greedy Uncle Sam pocket more of your money. Write to your representative today, and send a "no more taxes" message to the leaders of our state.

2. The future of space exploration and safety rests with the continued orbit of the space stations. All people realize that life must continue to grow outward, to reach for the stars, and not be content to stay safely on the ground while the entire universe waits, unexplored. Threats to Earth's security continue to fill the outer regions of our stratosphere. There are exploding meteors, falling space junk, and sun spot rays, to name only a few. Don't fall behind in the efforts to understand and protect ourselves from our universal environment. Space station programs need your support. Join the millions of citizens who care about Earth security. Be among the first to invest in the inevitable space travel opportunities that are just around the corner for all who are willing to support it. Send letters of support and donations to your congressional leadership today!

Author's Viewpoint

3. This is how we are exploiting animals on this earth. Millions of animals undergo cruel treatment in unsanitary research laboratories. They are caged, addicted to drugs, and sometimes killed and dissected in these laboratories. Animals that perform in circuses, television, movies, and even zoos often suffer neglect, boredom, and harsh abuse at the hands of their trainers. Foxes, beaver, and mink caught in traps for their fur suffer a slow, painful death. Racing greyhounds are often killed once they can no longer compete, and only a few find homes through greyhound rescue organizations. - Excerpt from Animal Rights pamphlet

___

4. Many of the most famous names in the music industry are going public in their support of the newest CD technology. Storing capacity on the new CDs is greater than ever, and the clarity of sound will never be beat. Giants of the music industry are clamoring to be the first to take advantage of the new Super-CD technology. "I've never heard such trueness of timber," marvels conductor Victor von Caranova of the Kiev String Ensemble. "It rocks!" enthuses rock star Ashlee Thompson. Now the same technology used by the great recording studios of the world is available to you to use on your own home computer. Hear your favorite artists as you've never heard them before—and how they want to be heard!

___

5. What we need in the United States is not division; what we need in the United States is not hatred; what we need in the United States is not violence or lawlessness; but love and wisdom, and compassion toward one another, and a feeling of justice toward those who still suffer within our country, whether they be white or they be black. – Robert F. Kennedy

___

Practice 4: Activities for Recognizing Persuasive Techniques

A. Cut 'n' Paste. Collect a week's worth of newspapers, magazine ads, and editorials. See how many different types of persuasive techniques you can find and name. Cut out five ads/letters, tape each to a piece of paper, and write what type of persuasive technique it is on the paper by the example. Under the type, briefly explain the author's viewpoint and any evidence the author uses to help persuade. Bring your examples to class and discuss you findings.

B. Be the Persuasive Writer. Write two of your own examples of persuasive writing, using a different technique for each of the two. Think about what the purpose of each will be. Then decide which technique you will use to fulfill that purpose. Write your passages at least seven sentences in length. Remember to include evidence to support your points. Bring your passages to class. The class will discuss how successful each persuasive technique is and may vote on the most convincing persuasive passage.

Chapter 13 Review

A. **Author's Viewpoint.** Read the following three passages on the same topic. Then, on your own paper, write whether each passage is objective or biased. If it is biased, what is the author's bias toward the subject in each passage? Give two examples from each of the passages to support your responses.

Mangy Wolves and Little Lambs

Ranchers in Montana, Idaho, and Wyoming have lived as farmers for generations. Americans are fond of images of these cowboys and cowgirls rustling cattle and sheep through vast tracts of ranch land. Many Americans rely on the meat, produced by these ranchers, for nutritious and delicious meals. Yet, these symbols of the American West and providers of food for the country are facing a threat. For decades, there were no wolves in these states. But some people missed having wolves in the wild. In the 1990s, they transported sixty-six grey wolves from Alberta, Canada. These wolves were released in Idaho. They have now grown to over three hundred in population. Wolves live by hunting. A pasture full of sheep or grasslands full of cattle are attractive to them. When farmers lose livestock, they lose money. When farmers lose livestock, the price of those steak dinners that Americans enjoy goes up.

Princes of the Wilderness

Thousands of people from around the world come to Yellowstone National Park every year. They want to see a wilderness untouched by human hands. One of the favorite sights in the park is the noble wild beast, the gray wolf. Gray wolves are family animals. They are loyal to their pack. They support each other in survival. And all the members of a pack look after and play with the pups. The western United States was once home for hundreds of wolf packs. When ranchers arrived in the 1800s, they cruelly wiped out the whole population of wolves. Wolves became an endangered species. Then, in the 1990s, supporters of wildlife started a plan to bring the wolves back. The project was one of the most successful ever tried on an endangered species. Today this magnificent animal freely roams its former homeland. A species almost destroyed by humans has been restored by human care.

Superstition, Fear, and Admiration: A Story of Humans and Wolves

When settlers moved to the western American states in the 1800s, they faced many obstacles. Wolves were one of them. Many of the settlers came from a European background. For centuries, Europeans had thought of wolves as evil and dangerous. Most of the settlers kept these beliefs about wolves. Wolves roamed all of the western states at the time of settlement. They attacked livestock, making relations with farmers even more unfriendly. Finally, the federal government helped the farmers. It began a program to get rid of the wolves. That program was successful. By the 1930s, the gray wolf was extinct in America. Then, in 1995, steps were taken to bring the gray wolf back to the West. Wolves were brought from Canada, and the population began to grow. The project was so

Author's Viewpoint

successful that in 2000, the ranches again began to feel threatened by the presence of this predator in their midst.

B. Persuasive Techniques. Read the following ad. Then answer the questions that follow.

[Advertisement: Lance Handsome, star of the new spy movie, The World is Not Yours for the Taking, carries his state of the art JK47-16 laptop from Techwerks with him at all times. "It's the best laptop on Earth -- and in space. You can take my word for it." TECHWERKS defying convention. Be sure to catch Lance Handsome in The World is Not Yours for the Taking this summer.]

The ad makes the following statement:

"Lance Handsome, star of the new spy movie... carries his state of the art JK47-16 laptop with him at all times."

4. This statement is an example of which persuasive technique?

   A. Rhetorical Question   C. appeal to authority

   B. Band wagon   D. repetition

5. Short answer. Does Lance Handsome's endorsement of this product convince a reader of the quality of the product? Why or why not?

_____

_____

_____

Chapter 14
Using Information Resources

Louisiana Reading Benchmarks addressed in this chapter include:	
ELA-1-M4	Interpreting (e.g., paraphrasing, comparing, contrasting) texts with supportive explanations to generate connections to real-life situations and other texts (e.g., business, technical, scientific) (1, 2, 4, 5)
ELA-3-M5	Spelling accurately using strategies and resources (e.g., glossary, dictionary, thesaurus, spell check) when necessary (1, 3, 4)
ELA-5-M1	Identifying and using organizational features of printed text, other media, and electronic information (e.g., microprint, CD-ROM, e-mail) (1, 3, 4)
ELA-5-M2	Integrating information sources (1, 3, 4, 5)

Writing a report for school, seeing a movie, buying a new computer or video game, taking a vacation: What do all of these events have in common? They all benefit from a little research. Most research requires some type of resource materials.

What are **information resources**? Information resources are texts and electronic media which supply information. In this chapter, we will discuss the following common information resources:

Dictionaries	Scientific reports	Newspapers	Magazines
Atlases	Business memos	Encyclopedia	Technical Guidelines

Think about all the ways you use resource materials: Which resource would you look in to find descriptions of movies and time listings? Which resource would you use to find information on vacationing in Disney World? What kind of research would you do before buying a new video game? Where would you find information for an article on the dangers of smoking?

We live in an **information society**. There is an almost endless amount of information waiting for you to find it. Being able to find, read, and understand the exact information you are looking for is an important skill. Knowing what resource materials to choose and how to use them can help you find answers to your questions. This chapter will provide skill practice in using resource materials.

225

Organization of Information Resources

Resource materials are organized or arranged in similar ways. For example, encyclopedias, thesauruses, and dictionaries arrange information by using the alphabet. Books are organized by chapter and other book parts. Newspapers are organized by topic areas of their stories. Other resources, such as brochures, organize material by priority of information. They present the most appealing, or the most important information first. More specific details can be found as you read further into the brochure.

The Internet organizes information in "levels." You get to different levels by clicking on links. For instance, the home page of a Web site like NASA's site, is the first level. If you click on a link on the home page, it brings you one level deeper into the information. If you click on a link there, it brings you the third level, and so on. The deeper levels of an Internet site usually contain more specific information. Front pages contain general information.

Once you learn about organizing methods, reading these materials becomes easy. This section will explain how different materials are organized and how to find what you are looking for.

Alphabetizing

Alphabetical order is a common method of organizing information. When alphabetized, words and topics are arranged in order from A to Z.

When words in alphabetical order begin with the same letter, the second letter is used to put the word in order. If the second letter is also the same letter, such as *late* and *lazy,* the third letter is used, and so on.

> **Example:** <u>con</u>tact, <u>con</u>fident
> <u>cond</u>ense, <u>cond</u>uct
> <u>compa</u>nion, <u>compa</u>ssion

The **dictionary, thesaurus**, and **encyclopedia** list their topics in alphabetical order. These materials print two **guidewords** at the top of each page to help guide readers to the information they are looking for. Guidewords are the first and the last words that are found on that page. If the word you are looking for falls alphabetically between these two words, then it will be on that page.

> **Example:** The words *commuter* and *compass* are guidewords on a dictionary page. *Company* is a word you could find on that page because it comes between *commuter* and *compass* in alphabetical order.

In addition, encyclopedias, and even some dictionaries, have several volumes in a set. These volumes are also arranged in alphabetical order. For example, Volume 1 may have all entries which begin with the letter *A*, Volume 2 may have entries with all of the *B* entries and part of *C* also, and so on. Within each individual volume, the articles are arranged alphabetically.

Chapter 14

Practice 1: Alphabetizing

Circle the correct answers to the following questions.

1. If you are looking for the word *negative* in the dictionary, which words could you find at the top of the page?
    A. nectar–negotiable
    B. natural–naval
    C. near–needle
    D. nobody–noise

2. If you were looking for the word *permit* in the dictionary, which words would you find at the top of the page?
    A. personal–perturb
    B. perky–perpetuate
    C. philosophy–phony
    D. penalty– pensive

3. If you are looking in the *B* volume of the encyclopedia, which of the following articles will you find?
    A. Czechoslovakia
    B. penalty– pensive
    C. abacus
    D. Bosnia

4. If the guidewords *link* and *loathe* were at the top of a page in the thesaurus, which entry would be included on that page?
    A. linger
    B. lonely
    C. literal
    D. lobe

5. If the guidewords *significant* and *sincerity* were at the top of a page in the thesaurus, which entry would be included on that page?
    A. silent
    B. sign
    C. single
    D. skill

TYPES OF RESOURCE MATERIALS

There are resources to be found for almost any kind of topic of information you may hope to research. We will discuss some of the most common, starting with the dictionary.

DICTIONARY

A **dictionary** provides more than the meaning or meanings of a word. It also provides information about the word itself—its origin, its proper spelling, it pronunciation, its part of speech, its various forms, and other information. All the information on any one word in a dictionary is called a **dictionary entry**.

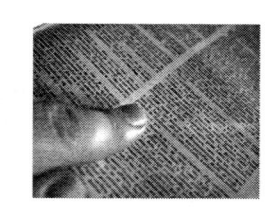

Dictionary entries include some or all of the following items of information.

1. The word, showing the correct spelling (Example: magnify)

2. The pronunciation, shown by syllable; accent marks; and sometimes an alternate spelling (mag´ ne fi)

3. The part of speech label (such as *n* for "noun," *v* for "verb," and *adj.* for "adjective")

Using Information Resources

4. Related word forms (magnified, magnifying)
5. The etymology, or origin, of the word (magni - Latin: *magnus*, meaning "great" or "large")
6. The meaning(s) of the word (magnify)
   a. to increase the apparent size of, as a lens does.
   b. to make greater in actual size; enlarge.
   c. to cause to seem greater or more important; attribute too much importance to; exaggerate.
   d. to make more exciting; intensify; dramatize; heighten.
   e. to extol; praise
7. Examples of the word in context (Deborah used a microscope to *magnify* the bacteria.)
8. Synonyms (word of similar meaning) *enlarge*, antonyms (words of opposite meaning) *shrink*; and sometimes idioms (figures of speech)

Practice 2: Dictionary

A.

Look up four new words in a dictionary. Notice the types of information provided for each word in the dictionary entry. For each word, list the spelling, pronunciation, part of speech, related words, etymology, or origin of the word, and the meaning or meanings. Note the sample sentences in which the word is used and any synonyms or antonyms. Then write a sentence using this new word. Share your assignment with the class or your teacher.

B.

Use this sample dictionary entry to answer the questions that follow.

> **habit** (hab't) n. **1.** A recurring pattern of behavior acquired through frequent repetition. **2.** Customary manner or practice. **3.** An addiction, especially to a narcotic drug. **4.** Characteristic appearance, form, or manner of growth, especially of a plant or crystal. **5.** A distinctive dress or costume worn by a nun. **6.** The outfit typically worn by a horseback rider. **habited, habiting, habits** Latin *habitus*, principal part of *habere*, to have. Synonyms: practice, custom It is my habit to begin my day with exercise.

For sentences 1–4, write the correct definition number for the italicized word.

1. Her *habit* had become dirty from all the riding._____
2. He was not in the *habit* of cleaning up after himself. _____
3. Because his parents were worried about his *habit*, they sought help._____
4. Nail biting is a bad *habit*. _____
5. What language does the word *habit* come from? _____
6. What part of speech is the word *habit*? _____

THESAURUS

A **thesaurus** is a book containing lists of synonyms and antonyms in alphabetical order. A thesaurus improves writing and one's knowledge of words. Beware that not all words have the same exact meaning. Some words may be similar in meaning but have different connotations.

Thesaurus Entry

88. HEIGHT

NOUNS:
1. height, tip, stature, elevation
2. top, highest point, ceiling, zenith
3. hill, knoll, volcano, mountain

VERBS:
4. heighten, elevate, raise, rear, erect
5. intensify, strengthen, increase, advance
6. command, rise above, crown, surmount

ADJECTIVES:
7. high, towering, exalted, supreme

Antonyms: depth, descent

Practice 3: Thesaurus

For Questions 1–3, circle the word that would best provide a synonym for the bolded word in each sentence below.

1. With a **height** of 20,320 feet, Mt. McKinley is an impressive sight.

    stature   top   elevation

2. The **high** skyscraper stood in the center of the city.

    exalted   supreme   towering

3. The frequent thunder **heightened** our fears.

    intensified   erected   crowned

4. **True or False: Increase** is the same part of speech as **heighten**.
5. **True or False:** A mountain is lower than a hill.
6. What part of speech is **height**?
7. What are the antonyms for **height**?
8. List the synonyms for **high**.

Using Information Resources

ENCYCLOPEDIAS

Encyclopedias are sets of books that contain articles in alphabetical order. Encyclopedias provide reliable information in articles which are thorough and accurate, yet relatively easy to read. They contain many pictures, photographs, diagrams, and other illustrations to make the information as clear and complete as possible. Encyclopedias come in sets of up to about 30 volumes or more. Each article in an encyclopedia is called an encyclopedia **entry** (for instance, "Lafitte, Jean" or "Angola"). The articles are organized in alphabetical order by topic. Each volume is labeled on the outside as to which part of the alphabet it covers.

The book versions of encyclopedias have provided important sources of reliable information for hundreds of years. Some of the most well known of these include *Encyclopedia Britannica*, the *World Book Encyclopedia*, and the *Funk and Wagnalls New World Encyclopedia*. Every several years, encyclopedia companies must publish new editions of their volume sets. This is necessary because not only does knowledge change continually, but new knowledge—new discoveries, people, events—must be added to each edition. Full sets of various encyclopedias, in their latest edition, can be found at public and school libraries.

ENCYCLOPEDIAS TODAY

As mentioned previously, the scope of available information today is far greater than it has ever been. The availability of information through the Internet and other electronic sources has also developed to a high standard. These two factors have affected the way encyclopedias are produced and read. The following is a description of the relatively new developments in encyclopedias. Electronic and specialized encyclopedias are now available on CDs, DVDs, and the Internet.

Practice 4: Encyclopedias

Find at least two electronic encyclopedias on the Internet. Is one better than the other? Or are they about the same? Explain.

PARTS OF A BOOK

Most books, including textbooks and literature collections, are organized into different **parts** to help the reader locate information. The three main parts of a book are the **front matter**, the **main text**, and the **back matter**. Within each of these sections, however, are several other sections. Not all books have all of these sections. Below is a partial list of the parts of a book that are common to many books. Almanacs and Atlases

Here is a partial list of the parts of a book that are common to many books: **Front matter** (title page, copyright information, contents page, and preface). **Main Text, or Body. Back Matter** (appendix, glossary, index, bibliography).

Practice 5: Parts of a Book

Examine one of your textbooks. Consult a dictionary or ask your teacher to define the parts of a book in the previous section. Then locate these parts in your textbook. How would these parts further your understanding of the book's subject matter?

ALMANACS

Almanacs are yearly publications. They appear at the beginning of each year and have articles about events of the previous year as well as expectations for the upcoming year. Almanacs are often organized by day or month of the year. Since almanacs are published every year, the information in them is current and timely.

One of the most well known almanacs is the Farmer's Almanac. The information in a farmer's almanac looks at current weather patterns, the best planting time, the kind of winter to expect, and other topics for people who are interested in nature and farming. Other almanacs focus on different areas of interest. For instance, the *Time Almanac,* from *Time Magazine,* covers various social and political topics, such as the World Series of Baseball, federal elections, holidays, and developments on the Internet. *The World Almanac for Kids* features articles on current news events, movies, science, sports and other subjects of interest to young people.

An **atlas** is a book of maps and other information about countries and regions of the world. Atlases also contain information about the countries, including charts, tables and text about population, climate, resources, history, and other topics. Atlases are usually much wider and taller than most other books. This is because they contain detailed maps, which cannot fit on regular sized pages. *The Hammond Atlas of the World* is one example of a world atlas.

Books of maps are similar to atlases, and some map Web sites such as mapquest.com are helpful for traveling to various locations.

MAGAZINES

Magazines are good resources for current information. They are published weekly, semimonthly (twice per month), monthly, or quarterly (four times per year). They are also good for a variety of information because they contain articles from many different writers. Libraries classify magazines and journals as **periodicals** (published *periodically*—weekly, monthly, and so on).

Magazines usually offer articles in a specific area of interest. They are written both to inform and to entertain. Magazine articles inform readers but can also express the writer's opinion. *People* is a popular magazine that features articles about celebrities and entertainers. *Time* is a news magazine which contains articles on current events and politics. Articles in magazines like *Time* are usually detailed and well researched.

Journals are academic magazines that have information about specific areas of study. Since experts in each field write the articles, journals are considered unbiased, reliable sources of information. For example, the journal *Nature* features science articles and has the latest research in areas such as biology and geology. Journals can be found in bookstores and in libraries. *Discover* is an example of a journal which is available online for free.

Practice 6: Magazines and Journals

Gathering information from magazines and journals. List three sources for research on the following topics: Calgary, Alberta; the effect of *El Niño* on butterfly populations; and the popularity of lacrosse. After listing the sources, write a brief summary of the information you found in your best source.

Using Information Resources

NEWSPAPERS

Newspapers provide current information on local and world events. Most newspaper articles are written to be brief and purely informative, and so they do not go into as much detail as magazine articles. Newspapers have both fact-based and opinion-based writing. **News reports** present information—facts, statistics, and statements by people in the news. They tell the *who, what, when, where, why,* and *how* of a specific event. **News features** also present information but reflect a reporter's opinion and personal style. Most newspapers now have Web sites on the Internet with current articles as well as archived copies of past articles. Many of these sites must be paid for in order to look at the articles. However, some newspapers and news services are available free. One example of an online daily news source that is available for free is MSNBC News at <msnbc.msn.com>. Search online for your local major newspaper to see if you can read all its articles for free.

Newspapers are organized into sections which help make it easy to locate articles on specific topics. Here is a list of typical sections of a newspaper:

Front Section	This section contains the most important news stories of the day. It is often divided into local, national, and world events. The front section usually includes several pages of news.
Editorial	This section prints the opinions and commentaries of the paper's editorial writers. They provide analysis and opinion of various current events. This is where you will also find letters sent to the editor by readers.
Travel	This section prints feature articles about various areas of the world. It also provides travel information such as airline prices.
Sports	This section contains the latest sports scores and articles about the day's games and events, and about famous athletes.
Entertainment	This section prints show times for movies, theater performances, dance, and musical concerts. It also contains reviews and articles about entertainment.
Obituaries	This section lists funeral notices and brief biographies of those who have died.
Advertisements	This section prints public notices or announcements recommending certain products or services.
Classified	This section lists job opportunities, homes and apartments for sale or rent, lost and found, items for sale, and garage sales.
Local and Community News	This section often contains several pages of information about local schools, industry, business, religion, crime, society, and other topics of interest to local residents.

Chapter 14

Practice 7: Newspapers

Answer the following questions concerning the sections of a newspaper.

1. Where would you find an article about a hurricane that hit Mexico? _____
2. Where would you find news about the NFL draft? _____
3. Where would you find a review of the latest movie? _____
4. Where would you find the details on the time for a funeral? _____
5. Where would you find an article about visiting Florida? _____
6. Where would you find a letter from an angry citizen? _____
7. Where would you find a notice for a boat for sale? _____

SCIENTIFIC REPORTS

While doing research for a school project or simply as a homework assignment, you may need to read scientific reports. The purpose of **scientific reports** is to present information and data that has been tested and accepted by scientists as the best explanation currently available of a scientific topic. Scientific institutions and publications, such as the federal Centers for Disease Control or *The Journal of the American Medical Association* regularly produce scientific reports which reflect new information in their fields. However, these reports are written for readers who are highly educated in science. For students, scientific reports can be found in online journals such as *Discover*, or in hard copy periodicals in the library.

Scientific reports contain scientific terms. They also often contain diagrams or graphs. They usually have subheadings throughout the text. Subheadings help a reader to follow the information and to locate information in the text. Before reading a scientific report, read through the introduction and the subheadings, and glance at the diagrams. This will prepare you to understand the full text of the article. Then read the article through carefully.

The following is an example of a short scientific report on tsunamis. It explains what causes tsunamis and why they are so devastating. As you read, try to find 5 facts about tsunamis and write them on the space provided. When you are finished, use your notes to explain to a partner what you learned from the report.

Shifts and Waves: How Tsunamis are Formed

Tsunamis are one of nature's most devastating events. Waves of ocean water taller than a school building and faster than a jet plane can crash into a coastal city, drag homes, people, and animals back out to sea, and then return in second and third waves. On December 27, 2004, in Southeast Asia, almost 200,000 people died within short, sudden minutes, from one of the largest tsunamis in history. That tsunami was caused by an earthquake in the Indian Ocean.

Can tsunamis be prevented? Can people be warned of them in time to save their lives? **Seismologists** have been working on these questions for years. In order to understand what these scientists are working with, it is necessary to know how tsunamis are formed.

Using Information Resources

Plate Tectonics

The earth consists of three main layers: the core, the mantle, and the crust. The **core** is the very center of the earth. It is surrounded by the mantle. The **mantle** is made of molten rock. The **crust** is the surface of the earth. It covers the mantle. The crust of the earth that is under the ocean is called the **oceanic crust**. The entire crust of the earth is made up of sections called **plates**. These plates fit together like a suit of armor. The study of these plates and how they move is called **plate tectonics**. The plates of the earth's crust move slowly, but when they do, they run into each other, scrape across each other, and even move over each other. Whenever you move an object under water, it affects the surface of the water. It causes ripples or waves.

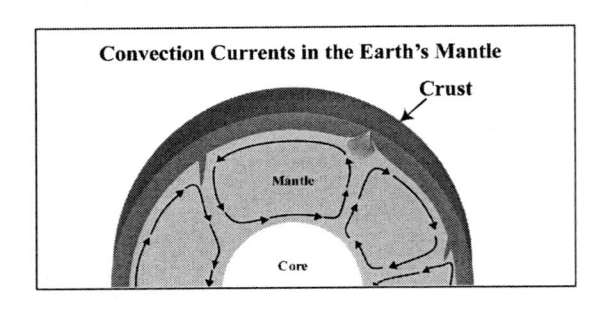

How do plates move?

First of all, remember that heat rises upwards. The molten mantle section of the earth is hot. (Molten means melted, so it would have to be hot to melt rock.) Therefore, hot currents of molten rock "rise" from the core of the earth towards the crust of the earth. When they meet the crust, they cannot go any further upwards. But their extreme heat forces them to keep moving. So they move along the underside of the crust. And as they do so, they carry the crust along with them, at least a few centimeters at a time. That is why the plates of the crust shift slowly towards, away from, over, and under each other.

The underwater earthquake

Sometimes, two plates of the earth's crust get snagged on each other's rough surfaces. They may stay that way for hundreds of years, grinding away at each other but not able to break free or to move each other. They build up a huge amount of strain. Then suddenly, they may break free and move. This causes violent shaking throughout the area. This becomes an earthquake. If the earthquake occurs under the ocean, it can cause drastic disturbance in the water. This may result in a tsunami.

Why are tsunamis so large?

When you move your hand under water, you can cause waves on the surface of the water. When a plate of the earth's crust suddenly jolts, sinks, or rises, it causes more than a surface wave; it moves the whole body of water, from ocean floor to ocean surface. That is why tsunami waves travel so far. If you have ever played in the waves at a seashore, you know that waves rise, **crest** (or break), then sink back into the water. They are normal waves with normal wavelengths. A **wavelength** is how far a wave travels before it collapses back into the ocean. Small waves have small wavelengths. A tsunami is a massive, mountain-sized quantity of water being pushed with such force that it travels up to 500 miles per hour. It maintains its height and speed over great distances, usually hundreds of miles. And when it reaches shore, it moves up over the land until it finally loses its force. Then its massive **undercurrent** carries it back to sea.

Can we prevent future tsunami disasters?

Seismologists believe that the only way to prevent the loss of life suffered in Southeast Asia in 2004 is by improving two crucial systems: an early warning system and an effective communication system. The science of plate tectonics has led to breakthroughs in the prediction of earthquakes, but it may never be exact. Geoscientists can be prompt and accurate in detecting and analyzing earthquakes that have already occurred. And there are systems for warning coastline communities of potential tsunamis. What is not as possible, according to scientists of the United Nations International Tsunamis Information Center in Hawaii, is the ability to warn people of how destructive the tsunamis will be. Geoscientists from around the world are working on this challenge with the hope that the world may never see another disaster like the 2004 tsunami in the Indian Ocean.

Practice 8: Scientific Reports

NOTES ON THE SCIENTIFIC REPORT ABOUT TSUNAMIS

1. _____
2. _____
3. _____
4. _____
5. _____

TECHNICAL GUIDELINES

Have you ever heard your parents say that these days you need a degree in engineering to operate a DVD player? The tools we use every day are becoming more and more sophisticated and complex. A new computer comes with volumes of technical guidelines. Electronic organizers, cell phones, and even telephones come with books of instructions on their use. Reading technical guidelines is an everyday activity. Being able to read them allows us to have access to the conveniences of all these necessary tools in our lives.

Technical guidelines must be read carefully. They are concise and dry. They are designed to convey information precisely, accurately, and clearly. Therefore, they cannot usually be skimmed. They must be read word for word. And all accompanying diagrams must be studied.

Study the following guidelines on fire extinguishers. Then answer the questions that follow them.

Using Information Resources

Fire Extinguishers and How to Use Them

Fire extinguishers are not all alike. That is because fires are not all alike. Fires burn differently from different types of materials. Each type of fire must be treated with a specific substance to extinguish it.

Classification Labels

Fire extinguishers are labeled for which kind(s) of fire they can extinguish. These labels consist of symbols and words and are found on the side of the fire extinguisher. Common fire extinguishers for household use often display multiple labels and are capable of fighting a variety of fires.

The 4 classifications of fire are as follows:

- A. Ordinary combustible fire (wood, paper)
- B. Flammable liquids fire (oil, gasoline, grease)
- C. Electrically energized fire (from electrical cords and outlets)
- D. Flammable metals (magnesium)

Storage

Store fire extinguishers near a building exit. Mount on the wall if possible, to avoid tripping. Fire extinguishers are used to protect people and to make escape possible—not necessarily to save a burning building.

Maintenance

A cardboard tag is tied to the top of every fire extinguisher. It is for recording maintenance work done. Extinguishers should be professionally serviced every year. Fire extinguisher specialists can be found in the telephone book. The service provider will write the date of service on the tag.

If the extinguisher is dropped or damaged in any way, bring it in for servicing.

Check the pressure on the pressure gage. If the needle is not in the green area, bring the extinguisher in for servicing.

Use

In the case of a fire, first of all, ensure your own safety. Secondly, call 9-1-1. Then, if you have time to use a fire extinguisher without endangering yourself, remember 4 letters:

P*A*S*S: Pull, Aim, Squeeze, and Sweep.

- **Pull**: Pull out the wire pin at the top of the fire extinguisher. This pin is there to prevent any accidental squeezing of the handle.
- **Aim**: Hold the nozzle of the fire extinguisher and aim it **at the base of the fire**.
- **Squeeze**: Stand about 8 feet away from the fire. Squeeze the handle of the fire extinguisher. This discharges the material which distinguishes the fire.
- **Sweep**: Move the nozzle back and forth so that the discharged material sweeps back and forth across the base of the fire. As long as you remain safe from the fire, continue to sweep back and forth, aiming at the base of the fire.

Practice 9: Technical Guidelines

1. You are examining your fire extinguisher at home, and you notice a symbol on it which portrays a garbage can and a pile of wood. What kind of fire would your fire extinguisher be useful for?
   _____

2. You are examining a fire extinguisher in a chemistry lab during your visit to your new high school. Which fire type symbols would you hope to find on that extinguisher?
   _____

3. When you need to use a fire extinguisher, what do you do with it after you pull the pin out of the handle?
   _____

BUSINESS LETTERS

Business letters are usually written in a formal tone and discuss various business matters. The names and addresses of both the sender and receiver are at the top of a business letter. The letter is usually addressed "To whom it may concern" or "Dear Sir or Madam." The closing of the letter is usually "Sincerely" or "Respectfully." The main body of the letter should be brief and clear but also thorough in expressing the purpose of the letter. See the example below. **Business letters** are usually written in a formal tone and discuss various business matters. The names and addresses of both the sender and receiver are at the top of a business letter. The letter is usually addressed "To whom it may concern" or "Dear Sir or Madam." The closing of the letter is usually "Sincerely" or "Respectfully." The main body of the letter should be brief and clear but also thorough in expressing the purpose of the letter. See the example on the next page.

Using Information Resources

Diagram of a business letter:

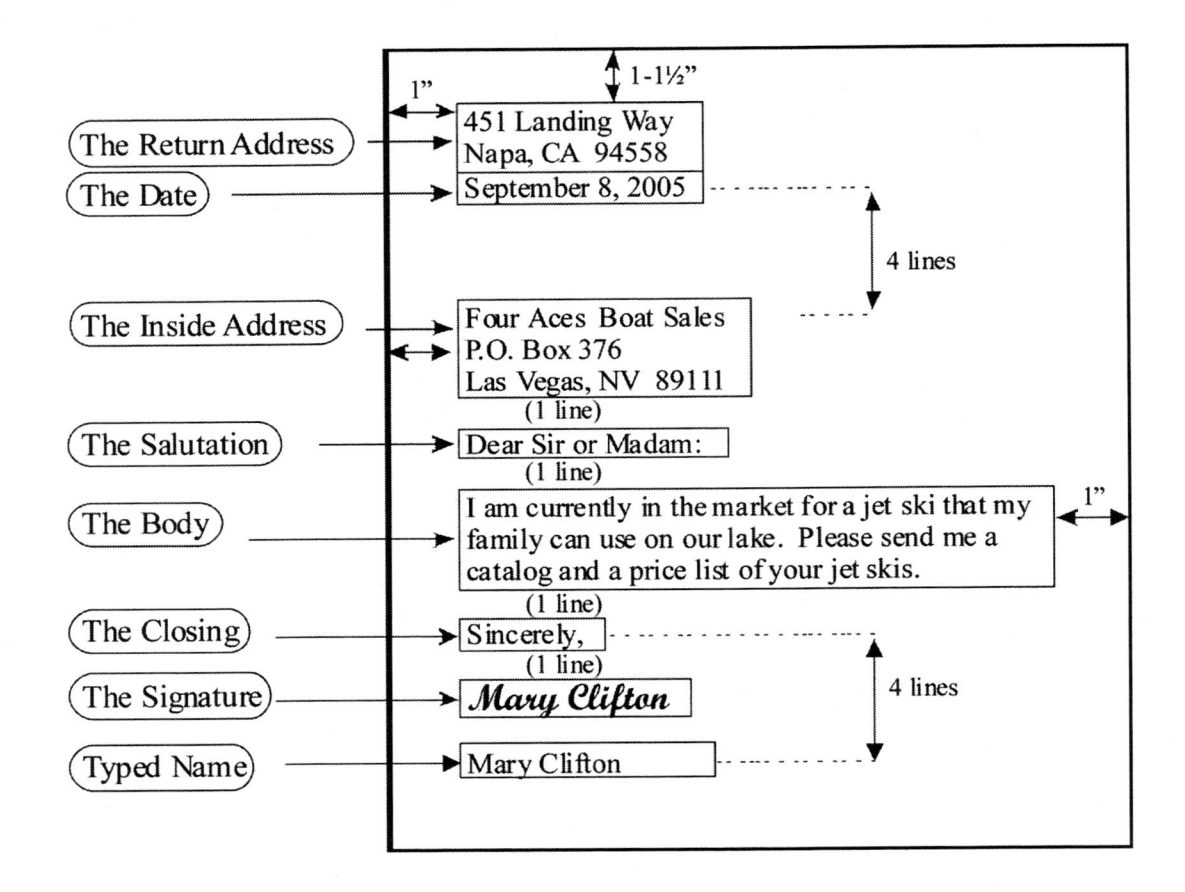

- **The Return Address**: 451 Landing Way, Napa, CA 94558
- **The Date**: September 8, 2005
- (4 lines between date and inside address)
- **The Inside Address**: Four Aces Boat Sales, P.O. Box 376, Las Vegas, NV 89111
- (1 line)
- **The Salutation**: Dear Sir or Madam:
- (1 line)
- **The Body**: I am currently in the market for a jet ski that my family can use on our lake. Please send me a catalog and a price list of your jet skis.
- (1 line)
- **The Closing**: Sincerely,
- (1 line)
- **The Signature**: *Mary Clifton*
- (4 lines between closing and typed name)
- **Typed Name**: Mary Clifton

Margins: 1" left, 1" right, 1–1½" top.

E-MAIL

E-mail letters have become very common because they are instant, and the sender does not have to pay for stamps to send them. Some people claim e-mails are replacing the personal letter. Howevr, the business letter is still commonly used for practical purposes such as applying for a job or requesting information about a product.

> **NOTE:** Personal letters will always have historical value to researchers and authors. Whether writing a book about the friendship between George Washington and the Marquis de Lafyatte or researching the American role in World War II, personal letters are a valuable source of information. In the future, it will be the same. A letter you might receive from a relative or friend may one day provide valuable information on culture and history to a historian.

MEMOS

As a student you occasionally receive memos from your school or your county school board. Although these memos are usually intended for your parents, the information in them is relevant to you, and it is important that you learn to read them too.

A **memo** is not a personal letter written to acquaintances. It is not a business letter written to a corporation either. It is more like a formal announcement or reminder on a topic of interest to you. It gives information and often direction on current activities in your life. A **business memo** informs office workers of current topics of interest to them. A memo to students relays information regarding the students' education. That is why it is important for students as well as parents to read them carefully.

The main characteristics of memos are the following:

- They are usually no more than one page in length.
- They should be clear and brief but thorough in presenting information.
- They are always dated.
- They address their audience clearly.
- They are written on letterhead or have a clear heading which indicates who the sender is.
- They usually have contact information for further information on the topic.
- If possible, they are signed by the person who sends them (even if it is an electronic signature).
- As with all computer generated documents, spell check and grammar check should be done before printing.

Using Information Resources

Below is an example of a memo an 8th grade student might receive.

Beauport Parish School Board
3845 Coushatta Drive, Beauport, LA 70321

February 15, 2005

Dear Rising Freshmen and Parents,

At this time of year, Beauport Parish teachers and counselors have begun a schedule of activities to focus on preparing you for beginning high school. We encourage you to participate in these activities, read all communications sent to you, and ask questions as you need to. We are confident that your involvement in these preparations will ensure an easy transition into high school.

At this time, our schedule of activities include the following:

February 24, 2005: Information meeting for parents and students. Time: 7:00 p.m. Topic: Registering and choosing electives for freshman year. At this meeting, counselors will explain how to fill out registration and elective course selection forms. They will explain the system of teacher assignment to honors core courses. Parents will take home registration forms.

March 10, 2005: Deadline for returning completed registration and elective selection forms.

March 15, 2005: Meeting with 8th grade advisors. Time 7:00 p.m. March 24, 2005: Deadline for submitting completed registration and elective course selection forms.

March 29, 2005: Shadow day. On this day, 10 students will be chosen to "shadow" a high school student for a day. If your student is chosen for this activity, please be available to drive your student to the high school, and sign him or her in by 8 a.m..

March 30, 2005: 10 a.m. Eighth grade assembly in the cafeteria. Students who participated in Shadow Day at the high school will share their experiences with the rest of the 8th grade. Breakfast foods and snacks will be provided by parent donation.

April 4, 2005: Open House at high school. Time: 7:30. There will be a presentation by high school students for middle school students and their families. This presentation is followed by a tour of the school and an opportunity to meet the teachers and become familiar with all the high school facilities.

Please feel free to contact your 8th grade advisor for any further information on these events. The Beauport Parish School Board will continue to keep you informed at this exciting time of opportunity for your student.

Sincerely,

Dr. Jena Thibodaux

Dr. Jena Thibodaux
Superintendent

Chapter 14 Review

A. Choose the appropriate resource for finding the information required in each sentence.

1. Margaret is reading a new book and needs the definition for the word *assuredly*.
   - A. dictionary
   - B. thesaurus
   - C. Internet
   - D. index

2. Sam wants to buy a used bicycle.
   - A. newspaper
   - B. encyclopedia
   - C. dictionary
   - D. computer software

3. Kim is writing a paper about the recent discovery of a possible 10th planet.
   - A. index
   - B. Internet
   - C. thesaurus
   - D. encyclopedia

4. Marco is researching the Nile River.
   - A. magazine
   - B. newspaper
   - C. encyclopedia
   - D. dictionary

5. Amanda wants to know about the next Jennifer Lopez movie.
   - A. encyclopedia
   - B. magazine
   - C. journal
   - D. dictionary

B. Directions: Choose the appropriate section of a book for finding the information in each sentence.

6. Rico needs to see a map of colonial America.
   - A. bibliography
   - B. appendix
   - C. index
   - D. title page

7. Tanya needs the definition of the word *allusion*.
   - A. index
   - B. table of contents
   - C. bibliography
   - D. glossary

8. Billy needs to know where and by whom his book was published.
   - A. table of contents
   - B. index
   - C. title page
   - D. glossary

9. Erin would like to find which pages in her literature book have poems by Robert Frost.
   - A. bibliography
   - B. index
   - C. title page
   - D. glossary

10. Joel would like to know where the articles in his book originally came from.
    - A. bibliography
    - B. index
    - C. title page
    - D. glossary

C. List three strategies for reading scientific reports.

1. _____

2. _____

3. _____

Using Information Resources

D. Directions: Use this sample index to answer the questions that follow.

Index	
Satellite Systems 509, 983	Sun 309, 404, 412
Saturn	Sun synchronous orbit 393, 407
Size and Matter 545	Superior planet 92
Moons 548	Terrestrial planet 395
Simulations 1105, 1107, 1109	Transducer 760
Space flights 407, 408, 1130	Transponder 1152, 1158
Statistical Analysis 1278	

4. On what page(s) would you find information about the moons of Saturn?
   A. 1109   B. 760   C. 548   D. 393

5. This index is found in a book on what subject?
   A. ocean life   C. planets in our solar system
   B. space   D. geography

6. How many pages in the book have information about space flight?
   A. one   B. three   C. two   D. four

E. List five characteristics of a business memo.

1. _____
2. _____
3. _____
4. _____
5. _____

Chapter 15
Electronic Information Sources

Louisiana Reading Benchmarks addressed in this chapter include:	
ELA-5-M1	Identifying and using organizational features of printed text, other media, and electronic information (e.g., microprint CD-ROM, e-mail) (1, 3, 4)
ELA-5-M2	Integrating information sources (1, 3, 4, 5)

A significant amount of the information you may ever need for research can be found through the use of the **computer**. You can access information on most subjects through a Web search, through on-line databases, and through information programs, such as Your First Ten Lessons in French, which you can purchase. Knowing how to find information through electronic sources is a necessary research skill today. Even if you do not have Internet access at home, public libraries offer that service for free. And since the electronic information system at your public library has more resources available to you than your home computer would, it is a good place to start learning.

FINDING RESOURCES WITH THE ELECTRONIC LIBRARY INFORMATION SYSTEM

One of the first objects you see when walking into a library today is a computer. In fact, you will likely see rows of computers. These computers give you access to countless resources both inside and outside the library. We can call this service the **Electronic Library Information Service**. This service is located on your library's home page. It provides links to all the information available through that library. Even if you do not have a library card, most libraries will give you a guest pass so that you can use the information system to locate resources.

The resources offered through library information systems may vary from one library to the next, but there are many features that almost every library will offer:

- **The electronic book catalog**. Also called the electronic card catalog, this feature allows you to find all cataloged resources in the library, including books, tapes, magazines and journals, and reference books.
- **Local major newspaper**. You can read complete articles from today's paper, or access archived. older articles through a search engine.

Electronic Information Sources

- **Access to the Internet.** You may search the Internet for information not available in the library.
- **Links to specific Web sites.** The library offers a list of links to Web sites they think will be especially useful or helpful for library patrons.
- **Youth and kids' pages.** These feature links and information on books and other resources of interest to young people.

Online Databases. This is where you will find information that you cannot access from home. It is where you will find databases like Nutrias, which is discussed on page... of this book. These databases are available by subscription alone, which most individuals cannot afford. They include complete sets of encyclopedias, dictionaries, and current events resources. They also include periodical resources such as articles from journals, yearbooks, almanacs, magazines, and a variety of word dictionaries and specialized dictionaries. Databases on every subject area can be found through your library online information system. (For information on the **Nutrias** database system of Louisiana Public Libraries, please see page...)

THE ELECTRONIC BOOK CATALOG

The part of the library electronic information system that you may be most familiar with so far is the **electronic book catalog**. This program lets you search for books by *subject, author, title*, or *keyword*. Once you have entered your search words, the catalog comes back with a list of books that match your search. From that list, you may choose a book to find out more information about it.

Each listing of a book on the electronic book catalog will include the following information:

Author's full name	Place of publication	Brief facts about the book
Title of the book	Publication date	The number of pages
Publisher's name	A call number for the book. This number tells you where you can find the book in the library.	An **ISBN**—or **International Standard Book Number**. This is assigned to every published book by the Library of Congress to uniquely identify the book.

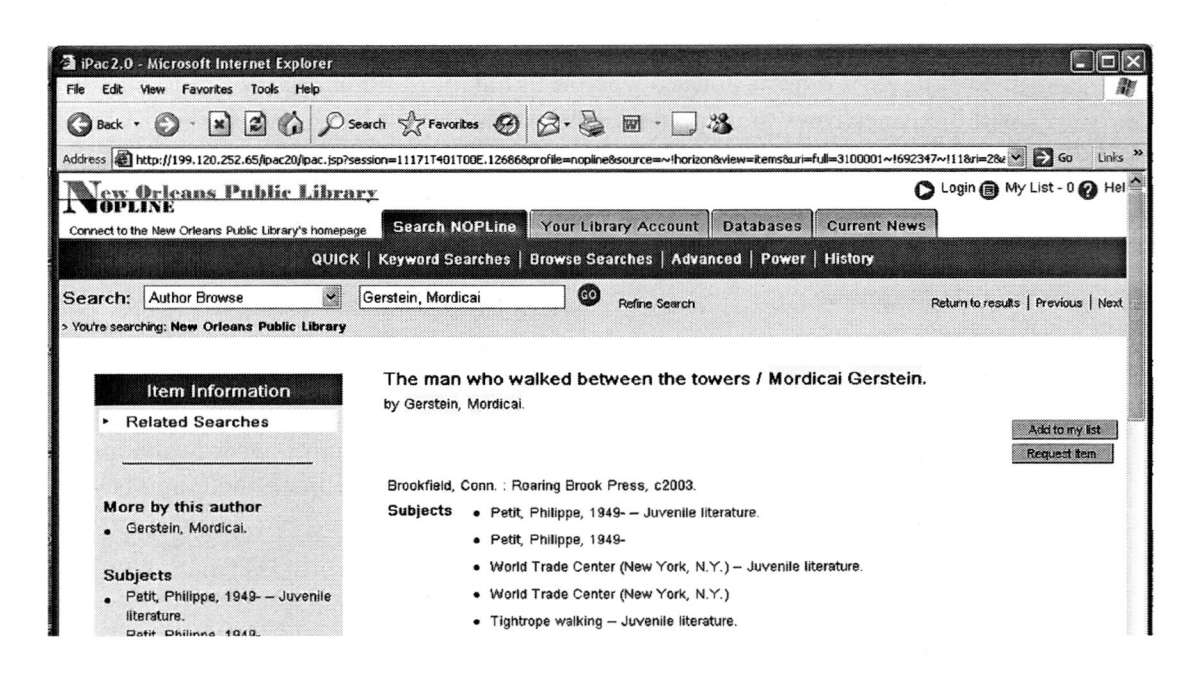

244

Chapter 15

COMPUTER RESEARCH

News, **features**, **scientific research material**, **literature**, and many other forms of information are all available through the computer. A touch of a button can enable you to search any topic from a search engine. The computer and the Internet have become important research tools. Like all tools, the computer needs to be used correctly in order to get the results you want.

The process of using computers for research is similar and yet different from other means of research. There are two main ways of researching on a computer. The first way is with **research software** programs, and the second is the **Internet**. Both sources can be reliable and provide useful information. However, they also offer challenges to researchers, who must be careful to evaluate them closely before accepting the material. Ways of evaluating computer resources are discussed in this section.

RESEARCH SOFTWARE

Research software comes in the form of **databases** for storing information. Databases can be installed on your computer's hard drive, or they can be inserted into the CD or DVD drives. Some examples of information database software include **dictionaries** and **encyclopedias**. They can also contain any one of hundreds of specialized subjects. An **astronomy database** might map out the sky above your home every night of the year. A **wildlife database** might provide information on hundreds of species of animals. Or a **language database** might help you through the first year of studying French or Spanish.

Some computer software programs are arranged like encyclopedias, while some are formatted like arcade games. For almost any type of educational software, there are instructions written into the program. Usually these instructions can be accessed through clicking on a "HELP" button found on the screen.

When choosing software for research, you will need to evaluate them for value and quality. To help in this evaluation, here are some questions you can ask yourself.

- Is the program written by a well respected company?
- Has the program been updated recently?
- Can you move easily through the program?
- Is the material in the program appropriate for your grade level: not too advanced or too basic?
- Can the information found on the software program be verified in another source?

If you can answer "yes" to all of these questions, then you have a good source of reliable information on your computer.

Practice 1: Using Electronic Resources

1. Find two Web sites that are geared to middle school math students. In 2–3 sentences, describe each site.

2. Locate two books in an electronic catalog at school or in your local library. Search by subject, author, or keywords based on a topic of interest. Print out your list. Find the books, and briefly describe them in writing.

Electronic Information Sources

NUTRIAS

Nutrias is the name of the huge database of information that is available through the public library system of Louisiana. Every state library system has a similar database, and each state has a different name for it. Nutrias was named after a small animal which lives in the swamps of Louisiana. The Nutrias database links you to informational Web sites through word searches. You may access the Nutrias from home. However, unless you have a public library card, you cannot access all the sites available on Nutrias.

If you do have a Louisiana public library card, go to <http://nutrias.org/>. You will see the home page for the New Orleans Public Library. Near the top of the page, you will see the words "Subscription Databases." Click on those words. Another window will come up, which asks you if you are using a computer in a public library, or if you are using a computer anywhere else. Click on whichever one applies to you, and follow the instructions that come up.

Note: At some point, you will be asked for your user ID and password, or your library card number. For this reason, it may be necessary for you to go to a local library the first time you access Nutrias, and get the help of the librarians in going through the process.

Learning how to use a library database may take some effort at first, but it is a resource that is worth the effort. Libraries pay thousands of dollars every year in subscriptions to databases. Most people would not be able to afford subscriptions to the large number of databases that libraries have. Therefore, your library card is a ticket to a world of information that you may not otherwise have access to.

THE INTERNET

The **Internet** can be a student's greatest resource for information or the biggest waste of time. There are so many sites to explore that you can easily lose track of your original topic. You have to know how to find the right information and how to evaluate it for accuracy and value.

Using the Internet requires some specific skills:

- You must use a **search engine** to find the best Web sites for your topic.
- You must know how to effectively use **keywords** in using the search engines.
- And perhaps most important is the skill of **safe research** on the information highway.

The ability to choose and use Web sites and search engines for locating information is a vital skill in this rapidly growing world of Internet access. Whether you are looking for the best price for your SCUBA gear, finding out the details of a volunteer opportunity you are interested in, or writing a paper for class, the Internet is a valuable resource if used wisely and efficiently.

SEARCH ENGINES AND KEYWORDS

Search engines can help you find the sites you need for information. Many search engines organize their listings by headings and subheadings. This allows you to browse through them to find the perfect resource. The Internet has many different search engines to aid you in your research. Some of the most common ones are **Google**, **Ask Jeeves**, **Alta Vista**, and **Yahoo**.

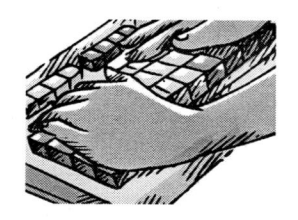

Keywords are like the bait on a fishing pole. They are entered into a search engine the way bait is cast into the water. And they cause a long list of information links to appear on your computer screen in a split second (a little more quickly than fish). The results of your search depend entirely on what keywords you enter.

This is how to run a search using keywords:

1. Type the URL (Web address) of the search engine you wish to use into the URL window: for instance, "www.google.com."
2. When the search engine appears on your computer screen, type in one or two keywords for the specific subject you want information about. For more information on keywords, see below.
3. Press "enter." The engine scans its listings for sites that match the keyword(s) you have entered, and then lists all the results.

Searching by a single keyword will usually produce more results than you need, so it is important to limit your search by carefully choosing your keywords. See the following list for tips on using keywords.

Tips for Using Keywords

1. Create a list of words describing the type of information you are looking for in a site.
2. Use more than one keyword to limit your search. For example, instead of searching *tigers*, you could search *Siberian tigers*.
3. To narrow your search even more, put your keywords inside quotation marks. This type of search will show only sites that have that exact phrase.
4. Try using both the singular and plural forms of the search words for your topic.
5. Check the spelling, hyphens, and spacing of your keywords before you click on the search button.
6. For some search engines, you will need to use the words AND and OR to limit your search to result entries that have either both words or one of them. For example, *Siberian tigers AND habitats* will yield listings containing both topics. Entering the keywords *Siberian tigers OR habitats* will yield listings that contain each topic.

On the following pages, you will find two examples of Web pages, each showing a different structure and focus for a Web search for "fossils." Notice the focus of the pages, and decide which would be the most appropriate source of information in a Web search for fossils.

VALIDATING INTERNET SOURCES

Why should you bother with validating sources? After all, if you can find material on a Web site, it must be OK, right? No, not always. Many Web sites are created by students and ordinary citizens who may believe what they have posted is true but are mistaken in that belief. "Let the searcher beware!" Researchers protect their work by screening the material they find for quality and accuracy.

Electronic Information Sources

Here are some steps you can take to validate your material:

1. Find two or more sources that agree with the information that you wish to use.
2. Read the material carefully, watching for any bias or particularly strong opinion expressed in it.
3. Look at the URL for the source of the material. It should name an organization or individual. If the organization is an educational, government, or professional center, the material is probably valid.
4. Look for "links" within the text of a Web site; these are an indication of a serious, validated work (they're like footnotes in a book). Go to some of the linked sites to check the accuracy of the source, as well as to find additional material.
5. Look at the home page of the source for other related works by the author of the site. The more the author has published on a topic, the more trustworthy the material probably is.
6. Check the date on the material. Obviously if your topic is on a current event, the more recent the date, the better the information.
7. If you are using informal sources like chat rooms for sharing ideas, again, the information needs to be confirmed by two or more other sources before it is validated.

Look at the following two Web pages. They were found through a word search for "fossils." Compare the two Web sites and decide which one would be useful for your research on fossils. Name the qualities that make that Web site one that you would trust for accurate information. Then compare your responses with the notes which follow the two Web pages.

Web Site A:

FOSSILS stone and rock

about | materials | tools | locations | quotes

quality stone and rock supplies

for all masonry projects

© 2003 Fossils Stone and Rock ← **Organization Name**
All Rights Reserved

Web Site B:.

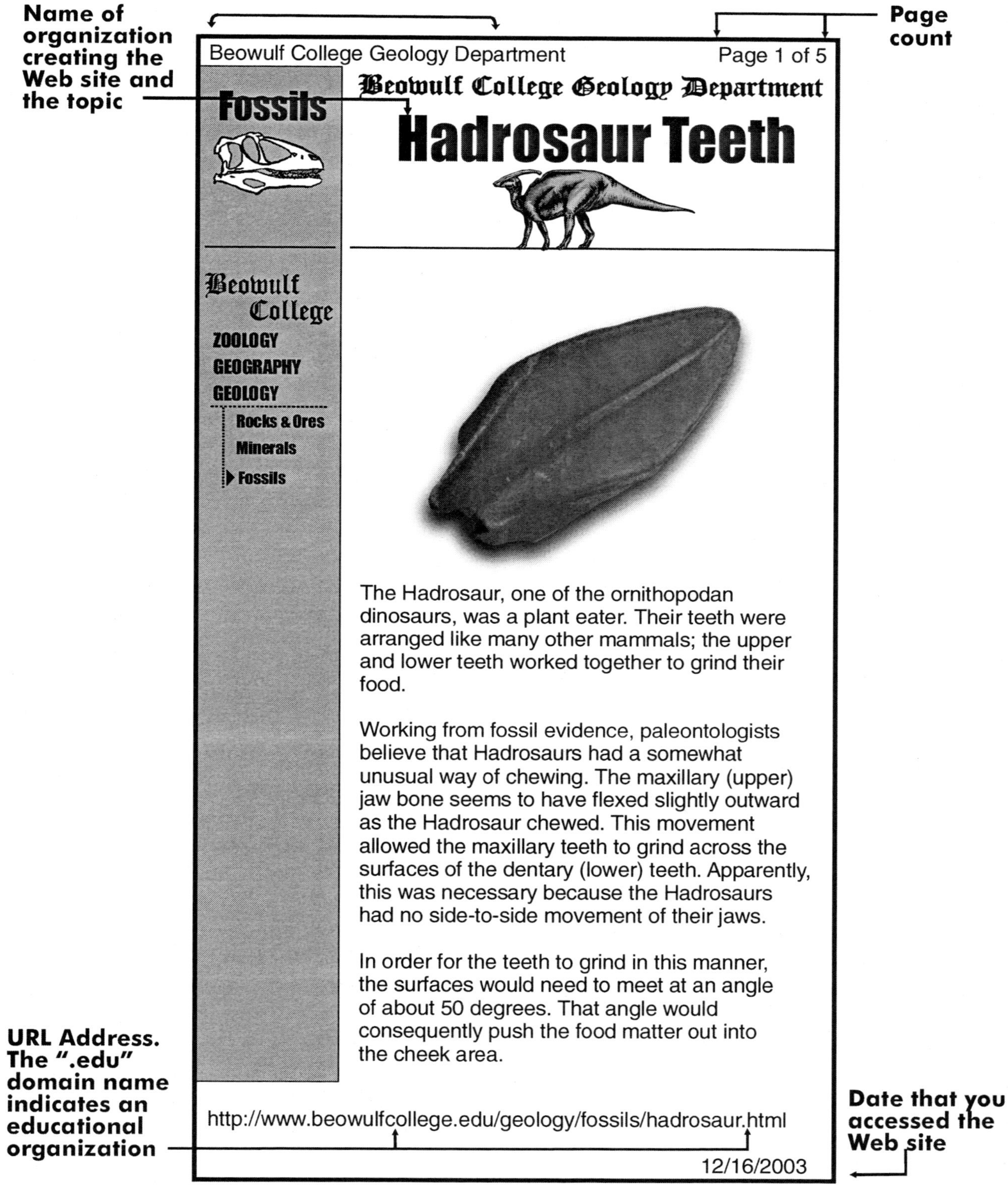

Name of organization creating the Web site and the topic

Beowulf College Geology Department — Page 1 of 5

Page count

Beowulf College Geology Department
Hadrosaur Teeth

Fossils

Beowulf College
ZOOLOGY
GEOGRAPHY
GEOLOGY
- Rocks & Ores
- Minerals
- ▶ Fossils

The Hadrosaur, one of the ornithopodan dinosaurs, was a plant eater. Their teeth were arranged like many other mammals; the upper and lower teeth worked together to grind their food.

Working from fossil evidence, paleontologists believe that Hadrosaurs had a somewhat unusual way of chewing. The maxillary (upper) jaw bone seems to have flexed slightly outward as the Hadrosaur chewed. This movement allowed the maxillary teeth to grind across the surfaces of the dentary (lower) teeth. Apparently, this was necessary because the Hadrosaurs had no side-to-side movement of their jaws.

In order for the teeth to grind in this manner, the surfaces would need to meet at an angle of about 50 degrees. That angle would consequently push the food matter out into the cheek area.

URL Address. The ".edu" domain name indicates an educational organization

http://www.beowulfcollege.edu/geology/fossils/hadrosaur.html

12/16/2003

Date that you accessed the Web site

Electronic Information Sources

In **Web Site A,** notice the name of the organization that has established this Web site. If you scan the page, you see that this is an advertisement. While it is an attractive and well designed site, you can see there is no educational material here. That is part of the drawback of using the Internet. It serves many purposes, and they are not always clear at first glance. This is not an appropriate or relevant source for scholarly research.

Web Site B is an example of a site that has relevant information. The facts may be accurate, but they should be double-checked against other sources before being used. Also, the information that is needed to validate the material is labeled.

DATABASE SITES

Information is generally found quickly in a **database**. Many databases are offered through schools and are free for the students of those schools. One example of a database available to all is EBSCO HOST. Using databases is not only a quick way to find information, but it's also a way to make sure the material you find is appropriate and credible. (For more information on databases, see page... Finding Information on the Library Information System.)

ELECTRONIC STORAGE

While doing research on the Internet, you may want to keep track of the most useful Web sites that you find. You may want to go back to them in the future to read them more carefully. Or, you may want to quote from one of them in a research report, and you want them to be easy to find again. To do this, you would store these Web sites in a folder called "**favorites**." Your Internet window has a menu on top called "favorites." When you find a Web site you want to save to use again, click on the "favorites" menu, and then choose "Add to favorites." A small window will come up which allows you to give a name to the Web site. You could call it "Information on hurricanes," for instance. Then click "OK." The name of your web site will be added to the list of favorites. When you want to go to that site again, click on the "favorites" menu and choose "Information on hurricanes."

Other ways to store electronic information include saving it to different storage sites. Say you are researching the Caribbean Island, Aruba. From you Internet search and from CDs, you find the perfect information which you would like to use in your report. You can copy and paste the information onto different storage areas on your computer. These storage areas are called "**drives**."

Practice 2: Search Engines and Databases

Choose one of the following topics for research:

Gulf of Mexico	levee	Louisiana Iris	pelican	Mardi Gras
port city	Cajun	riverboat	crayfish	New Orleans Saints

Write a 1–2 page typed report on your topic. Base your discussion on at least 3 databases or search engines such a Nutrias, Google, Yahoo, etc. Make sure you validate your sources. Use your own words for the report rather than coping directly from the Web site.

The C drive	The **C drive** is where most of the information you store goes on your computer. It is called the **main drive**, and it has a massive amount of space for storage.
The A drive	The **A drive** is a kind of computer drawer into which you place diskettes. The A drive is capable of storing information to those diskettes. When you save information to the A drive, you must first open the drawer and put the diskette into it. Then, when you select your material and press "save," you must choose "A drive" in the "Save to:" window. A diskette can hold a research project or two, but its space is limited. If you need more space, you have to use a CD, which goes into the **E drive**.

SAFETY

The use of the Internet, without special "safe" servers, is basically unregulated and unguarded. This situation brings up concerns over **credibility**, **safety**, and **privacy** issues. The following is an informal listing of ways to make your Internet use as safe and as productive as possible.

- Develop a "healthy distrust" of much of what you read on the Web. Databases are usually acceptable, but chat rooms and personal Web sites are open to all sorts of deceptions and suspect information.
- Do not share your name, address, phone number, or Social Security Number on Web sites without the approval of an adult.
- Always use a different name on the Internet, and understand that others are doing the same, either as a safeguard or as a false identity.
- Make sure that you understand and follow the guidelines that your school, library, or home have about the way the Internet is to be used.
- Understand that some sites have built-in roadblocks; there is no way for you to exit the site. Should you run into this trap, disconnect from your Internet server by clicking on the large X in the upper right corner. Then sign on again. You will also want to alert your teacher or the Webmaster to the problem.
- Watch out for anyone on-line who asks you personal questions. This is a flashing red stoplight. Do not respond to those questions and exit that site.

Practice 3: Safety on the Internet

Review the Internet safety tips listed in this chapter. Then find out how your school and local library protect students from unsafe Web sites, chat rooms, pop up ads, and dangerous viruses. Share your information with the class or your teacher.

Electronic Media Research

The printed page is only one of many sources of information. Today, information and data are easily available in various electronic forms. These include **television**, **radio**, **film**, **audio** and **video tapes**. However, a discussion about these media cannot take place without also including the CDs and the Internet. That is because information from all of these forms of media is available through internet sites.

Television and Radio

If you have access to cable television, there are several educational channels available to you. These include the *Arts and Entertainment* network, the *History Channel*, *The Nature Channel*, the *Biography Channel*, the *Discovery Channel*, and the *National Geographic* channel, to name only a few.

If you do not subscribe to cable television, you can find educational programming through the Public Broadcasting System. The PBS stations in Louisiana are WLAE and WYES out of New Orleans, and WLPB out of Baton Rouge. PBS stations often carry classroom series on topics in history, science or art. The level of teaching in PBS programs is often geared towards adults, but you can also find interesting feature programs aimed at young people as well. You can find the program schedule for your area by going to <www.http://pbs.org> and writing your zip code in the search box.

National Public Radio is available in all major cities in the United States. You can look for the station in your city by logging on to the NPR Web site at <www.http://npr.org> and clicking on "stations." NPR carries educational programming as well as news and classical music. They also broadcast short periodical features such as "National Geographic Expeditions," which lasts about five minutes and takes the listener to interesting places around the globe. Another short feature that is regular on some NPR stations is "A Moment of Science," which looks at ways that science is part of our everyday lives. This radio feature has its own Web site at <http://amos.indiana.edu/>.

Films and Documentaries

Films

Films can be useful research tools. Movies today cover many different subject areas. Biographical movies such as "Ray" (Ray Charles), "Ali" (Muhammad Ali) "The Aviator" (Howard Hughes), and others provide information about famous cultural and historic people. Historical movies such as "Gandhi," "Pearl Harbor," and "Gettysburg" bring historical eras and events to life. Literary movies such as Shakespeare's "Hamlet," "The Last of the Mohicans," and Jane Austen's "Emma" dramatize great works of literature. You can learn from watching well written movies.

The art of film making, however, has limitations in terms of accuracy. Events and information in movies are presented from a specific point of view of the directors and writers. The amount of information provided is limited by the movie length. Literature cannot be completely adapted to film without losing significantly in the translation. Therefore, careful researchers use films as a supplementary form of research. For instance, watching "The Aviator" will not give you a full view of the life of Howard Hughes. You would need to research that topic in encyclopedias, biographies, and other sources as well. Films can present useful information on topics, but they are made primarily to entertain.

DOCUMENTARIES

Documentaries are usually viewed on television. Public Television stations air documentaries on a large variety of subjects. Documentaries can also be seen on commercial television stations as well as on cable stations. One of the foremost documentary programs on television is PBS's *Frontline*. This program airs documentaries on issues such as government, biography, race, and religion. *Frontline* also has a Web site. If you access their Web site, you can view documentaries you may have missed. You can print out a transcript, a written version, of everything that was said on the program. Transcripts are valuable research tools. However, like all research material, transcripts must be cited if you use the information in them in a paper. In chapter 15, you will learn how to cite research materials.

Another well respected documentary program is *Nova*. This program is aired on PBS stations and deals with a wide range of topics, including history, nature, science, astronomy, and technology. Nova also has a Web site, on which you can find a wealth of research material on the topics covered in the Nova documentaries.

These are only two examples of the many documentary programs available to you on television or through the Internet. There are other programs and Web sites too numerous to list here. If you do not have access to the Internet in your home, it is available through your school library and through your public library. Librarians are very willing to help you to find the most useful documentary sites on the Internet. Some libraries also carry copies of documentary series on video tapes and DVDs. You may search for these by topic on your electronic library catalog.

VIDEO AND AUDIO TAPES AND CDS

Your school and public libraries are the best sources of information stored on video and audio tapes and CDs. Many libraries have an Audio-Visual Department, in which volumes of resources are available to borrow. The A-V department may hold a collection of film documentaries, feature films, and instructional and educational video tapes and CDs. You can also find educational audio tapes, as well as books on tape. Many classic and modern works of literature are now available on tapes and CDs. You can borrow and listen to these resources through your local library.

Electronic Information Sources

CHAPTER 15 REVIEW

A. Use this sample electronic catalog listing to answer the questions that follow.

> Entry search: Subject
>
> Biographies
>
> Susanna of the Alamo: a True Story
>
> | | |
> |---|---|
> | Author: | Jakes, John |
> | Title: | Susanna of the Alamo: a True Story |
> | Publication: | San Diego: Gulliver Books, c1986 |
> | Description: | 28 p. |
> | Summary: | Relates the experiences of the Texas woman who, along with her baby, survived the 1836 massacre at the Alamo |
>
> J BIOG JAK   1 Book   Juvenile Biography Collection
> ISBN: 0152005927

1. Where can you find this book in the library?
   - A. children's section
   - B. juvenile biography collection
   - C. biography collection
   - D. fiction section

2. This book was found by searching in what category?
   - A. subject
   - B. autobiography
   - C. periodical
   - D. author

3. When was this book published?
   - A. 1836
   - B. 1928
   - C. 1986
   - D. 2001

B. Choose the best keywords to search the Internet for the information in the following sentences.

4. Gavin is doing a science project on different types of mold.
   - A. mold
   - B. science projects
   - C. mold types
   - D. different mold

5. Marissa needs to write a paper about where alligators live
   - A. alligators
   - B. alligator habitats
   - C. where alligators live
   - D. alligator and lives

6. Rachel would like to see photographs of the moon.
   - A. moon
   - B. "photographs of the moon"
   - C. moons
   - D. moon photos

C. On your own paper, list 5 resources available through the public library electronic information system.

D. On your own paper list 4 practices you can do to ensure your personal safety while using the Internet.

Chapter 16
Evaluating and Citing Information Sources

Louisiana Reading Benchmarks addressed in this chapter include:	
ELA-7-M2	Using reasoning skills (e.g., categorizing, prioritizing), life experiences, accukmulated knowledge, and relevant available information resources to solve problems in oral, written, and visual texts (1, 2, 4)
ELA-5-M2	Integrating information sources (1, 3, 4, 5)
ELA-5-M3	Locating, gathering, and selecting information using formal outlining, paraphrasing, interviewing, and surveying to produce documented texts and graphics (1, 3, 4)
ELA-5-M5	Citing references using various formats (e.g., endnotes, bibliography)

USING INFORMATION IN RESEARCH

Through English Language Arts studies in Louisiana, you learn the skills necessary to be a critical and active reader. You also learn writing skills: grammar, spelling, paragraphs, and essays. In the previous chapter of this book you began to learn about the use of resource materials.

One of the most comprehensive ways to apply all your language arts skills is through producing a research project. A **research paper** involves accessing information sources, evaluating those sources, taking notes, generating a thesis and focus for your paper, writing about your topic by synthesizing all the information you have gathered from several sources, and finally, citing your sources. In this chapter, we will discuss the stages of producing a research report. We will concentrate on how to apply your research in your writing and how to properly give credit to the sources used in the research.

PRIMARY SOURCES OF INFORMATION

The resources discussed in Chapter 14, "Using Information Resources," are **secondary sources**. They have all been produced by someone other than yourself. Others—writers, scientists, researchers, and educators—have done the work of gathering the information and presenting it in a useful and clear way. They produce the articles, the encyclopedias, dictionaries, films, and the many other forms of published information. You, in turn, use their work for your own research. These sources of information are essential in research.

Evaluating and Citing Information Sources

However, a great deal of information has not yet been produced by others. You have the opportunity to seek it out yourself. This can be done by observation, by surveying, and by interviewing. This is called **primary research**. The source from which you obtain this type of information is called a **primary source**. The process of doing primary research can be as interesting as the information itself. In this chapter we will look at two forms of primary research: **surveying** and **interviewing**.

SURVEYING AND INTERVIEWING

Surveying and interviewing are a unique form of research because they involve you finding out information directly, instead of reading the information that other people have found. With surveying and interviewing, your research is original and unique.

Interviews can be used in research if you are not able to find the information you need already published. For instance, suppose one of your favorite teachers is retiring this year, and you want to write an article about what your school was like when she first started teaching there and how it has changed over the 20 years that she has been there. You cannot find that information in a book or on the Internet. You have to find it out yourself by asking questions.

Surveys are used in research to gather information that can be *quantified* or counted. The information you gather through conducting a survey is called **data**. Like information from interviewing, data is gathered through contact with people—through talking, e-mailing, or telephoning. However, unlike information from interviews, data collected from surveys has to interpreted. In other words, it should guide you towards drawing conclusions about the topic you are researching. An illustration of this will be made in the table which follows. First, let's look at some general steps which should be taken to conduct successful interviews and surveys.

Let's say that you will be conducting the interview, described above, of the retiring teacher. For a separate project, your friend is conducting a survey. It is a survey to find out how much soda pop your fellow 8th graders drink in a week. He has read articles about the national average of soda consumed by teenagers every week, and he plans to find out if the 8th graders at your school drink that much soda.

The four steps you will need to take, whether conducting an interview or a survey, are:

- **Prepare** your survey / interview. Questions for surveys must be carefully considered and written out before they are used.
- **Contact** your *subjects* (The people contacted for interviewing or surveying are called subjects.) (For school research, it is always recommended that you contact only fellow students at school or members of your family.)
- **Review** your data / information.
- **Present** your data / information

The following explanation shows how these four steps are put into practice in your friend's and your projects.

SURVEY: TEENS AND SODA-POP

1. Prepare your questions: Survey questions must **(a)** be carefully thought out and written ahead of time, **(b)** use unbiased, neutral language, and **(c)** be asked in the same way to everyone you speak with (read them out, if necessary).

For instance, instead of asking, "Do you drink a lot of soda every week?" you would ask, "How much soda do you drink each week?" You could add several other relevant questions to your survey. The more data you collect, the more accurate your analysis will be. However, surveys should be kept as short as possible so that people are willing to take the time to answer them.

You might also give them a multiple choice format so that they can choose their answers: 0-2 can, 3-4 cans, 5-6cans, or more than 7 cans.

2. Contact your subjects: You will have to arrange with your teacher how and when you will speak with fellow students at school. If you conduct a survey outside of school, it is important to use caution. The best way is to survey only your family, relatives, and close friends. Never conduct a survey of people you do not know. This should only be done by professional surveyors.

Have your question(s) ready and a pen for writing down their answers. Ask each question and write the answer. Do not react to the answer or question them further about the answer. This keeps the survey consistent from one subject to another.

3. Review your data: After you have finished collecting your data, review it carefully. Count how many of each response you get to each question. Then you must interpret the data. Think about what the information from your survey means about the soda-drinking habits of your classmates. Do they drink as much soda as the average American teens, or do they drink more—or less? Then think about what further questions your survey raises: If your classmates drink less soda than most Americans, then why? Good research often leads to further research.

4. Present your report: Data from surveys can be presented in many ways. It can be put in a table or used to make a pie chart or a graph. (Information on these and other visual aids can be found in chapter 17.) It can be used to compare with the results of other surveys: for instance, comparing your survey with the results of national surveys on the same subject.

The information gained from surveys can be used just because it presents interesting facts. However, normally, it is used as supporting evidence to back up a viewpoint or an argument. That is because professional surveys are very expensive to conduct. Therefore, they must have a practical use. Some of these uses include political research, marketing research, and scientific research.

INTERVIEW: A RETIRING TEACHER

1. Prepare your questions: The best way to prepare questions for an interview is by finding out as much as you can ahead of time about the topic of your interview (your school over the years) and about the person you will be interviewing.

Evaluating and Citing Information Sources

You might research these two areas by talking to other teachers or your school principal. Then you can start writing down your questions. Interview questions are open-ended questions. That means that a simple "yes" or "no" is not enough to answer them. For instance, instead of asking, "Have you enjoyed teaching 8th grade?" you might ask, "What have you enjoyed most about teaching 8th grade?" Ask "Why?" and "How?" and "In what way?" kinds of questions.

2. Talk with your Interviewee: Be prepared with your questions and a notebook to take notes in during your interview. Tape your interview, if you can. That way, when you quote what your subject says, you can do so accurately. Interviews are conversations. They are conducted to gather information, but they are also about simply talking to and learning about another person. And this cannot always be predictable. Therefore, a good interviewer will be well prepared with open-ended questions, and yet will also be very attentive to the interviewee's answers. That way, if something interesting is mentioned, you will be ready to pursue that topic.

For instance, your retiring teacher may mention the year in which she brought a group of students to Washington, D.C., and they all met President Jimmy Carter. Since that must have been important enough for her to mention, you might want to ask her for more details about that trip. An interviewer must be well prepared but flexible.

3. Review your information: Listen to your audio tape of the interview, or re-read your notes. If you taped the interview, take notes while you listen to it again. Highlight information that you want to be sure to use. If you want to quote your subject, copy her word exactly as she spoke them and put quotation marks around them. You may have to play that part of the tape several times to get the words exactly right. Then think of a way that you can present the information that will be engaging for the reader.

4. Present your report: Perhaps you could present the information as a story. Or, you may only need to use part of the interview for a research paper on the history of your school. Think of a way to organize your information into a story. (Information on organizational patterns for information can be found in chapter 11 of this book).

Practice 1: Surveying and Interviewing

A. **Surveying**. Prepare a survey of students in your class. You may use any topic you choose. Write at least 3 questions to ask each student. For example, you might conduct a survey on how many books a student has read in the last month. You might ask how many the student has read, what kinds of books they were (mystery, fantasy, biography), what the title of the books were, and if they would recommend one of the books to other students. Write the questions in complete sentences. Conduct the survey, asking 15–20 students. Present the data in a report or slide presentation for your class.

B. **Interviewing**. Decide on a relative that you would like to interview. Prepare 6–10 questions to ask during the interview. You might include questions about your relative's childhood, education, travel, any unusual adventures, and plans and hopes for the future. Have your teacher review you questions for feedback and suggestions. Then conduct your interview. Present the information you learn in the interview as an article for a newsletter.

VALIDATING INTERNET SOURCES

Anyone can create a Web site, and this means that there are many Web sites out there with false, limited, or biased information. It is your responsibility as the researcher to check the information you find. Answer these questions to validate the Web site:

- *Who created the site?* Look at the URL for the source of the material. The **URL** is the **u**niversal **r**esource **l**ocator, or the site's Internet address. Choose sites that are created by the government (.gov) or educational institutions (.edu). These sites are usually more accurate and factual than sites created by businesses or individuals. Sites created by organizations (.org) may or may not be dependable. Information from some organizations can be very biased, but others can be very accurate and balanced. The name of the person or group that is responsible for the web site can usually be found at the bottom of the home page.

- *When was the site created or updated?* If you are researching a current event, you want current information. Even with information that doesn't need to be current, you want a well-maintained site that is updated with new information when needed. The date when the site was updated can usually be found at the bottom of the home page.

- *Who else has this information?* If you find another site with the same information, then your information is probably correct.

- *Are there links within the site?* If a Web site has **links**, connections to other reliable Web sites, this shows careful planning and helps to validate the site. It also provides more information for your research. Be sure to check the accuracy of the other sites as well.

- *Does the site have a strong opinion?* Read the Web site carefully, and look for any bias or strong opinions. You want your information to be complete, and often material with strong opinions will leave out information that doesn't support that opinion.

SECONDARY SOURCES OF INFORMATION

Primary research such as interviewing and surveying are valuable and unique sources of information. However, students more commonly find their research information from **secondary sources**. Secondary sources like the ones discussed in Chapters 14 and 15 of this book are produced by people other than the researcher. Secondary sources are available in great quantity—especially through the Internet. But not all of them are trustworthy. Many, in fact, publish information that is incorrect or very biased. The Internet is the primary tool for research for most students today. It is important to know how to tell if you can trust the information on a Web site or not. This is called **validating**. Below are some tips for determining if a Web site is probably trustworthy or not.

Evaluating All Secondary Sources

Besides determining the trustworthiness of a source, as discussed above, you should evaluate all sources of information for accuracy and usefulness. You may evaluate secondary sources by using four categories of measurement: the **reliability of the source**, the **audience appeal** of the information, the **bias** or lack of bias of the information, and the **timeliness** of the information.

Reliability: Reliable secondary sources of information clearly show their authorship. The author may be an individual, in which case that individual's name will be clearly displayed. Alternatively, the source of the material may be an organization. There, too, the name of the organization and often its contact information will be clearly displayed. Encyclopedias, textbooks, and public or government` brochures and pamphlets all claim a level of objectivity and fact-based material. These are trusted information sources.

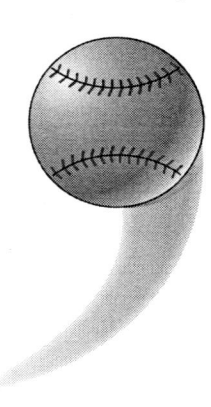

Appeal: The intended audience of information sources tells a lot about its authenticity. Look for sources that are written for people who are knowledgeable in the field. For instance, *Sports Illustrated* is a respected periodical which appeals to sports fans and sports professionals. It would be a reliable source of information on the greatest World Series upset in the history of baseball.

Bias is a second factor when considering the appeal of information. Biased information is written to appeal to a biased audience or to convince an audience of a specific point of view. A biased tone can be detected in an article if the author fills the article with judgments against one side or the other and does not consider opposing points of view. Bias can also be detected by knowing if the author is motivated by personal gain. For instance, a shareholder in the losing team who writes that the team lost because the players are overpaid and so are not motivated can be seen as biased.

Timeliness: For secondary research sources, current information is usually recommended. When researching political or scientific developments, for instance, you should try to find out about the latest research and events. For instance, for the research on the World Series upset, the most recent edition of the New York Times Sport Section would give you the most accurate picture of the players' statistics and history.

To summarize, trustworthy sources of secondary information have certain features in common, which you should look for:

- They are produced by respected publishers.
- They display all publication information, including date and place of publication.
- They show authorship and often include information about the author's credentials.
- If they are articles, they often include a bibliography or a list of references.
- They are written and reviewed by experts in the field of interest, and they often include quotes from leaders in the field, such as political, scientific, or academic leaders.
- They are written for an audience that is relatively knowledgeable in the subject area.
- They tend to be balanced in their point of view, and they support their information with well researched facts.

You may not always know at first glance if an information source is reliable and relevant. But with practice and experience, you will learn to assess the reliability of sources quite accurately. Even then, do not be discouraged if even reliable sources differ or even seem to contradict each other in their information. This is a common and a constructive element of research. It just means that further reading is necessary in order for you to resolve any questions and to come to your own understanding and conclusions.

QUOTING SOURCES IN TEXT

Once you have gathered the information you want to use, you will want to incorporate it into your research report. Quoting from sources is an effective way to convey an idea or to support one. There are three principles to keep in mind when using quotations in a research project:

- Quotations should not be overused. The majority of your writing should be your own ideas, written in your own words. Quotes are used to support those ideas.
- Quotations must be placed in quotation marks and be accurate. The words of others must be reproduced exactly as they were originally written or spoken.
- Quotations must always be cited. Citations are small notes in parentheses, usually at the end of the quote or at the end of the sentence that contains the quote. These notes are like a code which indicates where the quote came from. They refer the reader to the bibliography at the end of your paper. The bibliography contains the complete information on the origin of the quote.

We will look at the three most common ways to integrate a quote into your text.

Introductory Phrase or clause: When an *introductory phrase* is used (He said, she said) a **comma** always follows after the phrase.

> While in college, Rev. Martin Luther King once attended a lecture on Mahatma Gandhi, which affected him deeply. He said, "I left the meeting and bought a half dozen books on Gandhi's life and works" (Jaluobek 35).

When an *introductory clause* (a complete sentence) is used to introduce a quote, a colon is used after the clause.

> Mahatma Gandhi taught that oppression could be overturned by peaceful resistance in an attitude of love and tolerance. Rev. Martin Luther King Jr. preached this same ideal to his congregation: "We must meet the forces of hate with the power of love; we must meet physical force with soul force." (Jaluobek 51).

Making a quote part of your sentence: When making your own point about a topic, you can use some words from another source to make your ideas clearer.

> Just as Mahatma Gandhi used *satyagraha*, or nonviolent resistance, to end the oppression of British rule in India, Rev. Martin Luther King Jr. used protest with "dignity and Christian love" to end the oppression and discrimination against blacks in America. (Jaluobek 36, 48).

Evaluating and Citing Information Sources

Using an extended quote: An extended quote is one that is more than four lines long. Extended quotes are treated differently: They stand alone on their own lines of text. They are indented one inch from the left margin, and they do not require quotation marks. Extended quotes are usually introduced with a complete sentence followed by a colon.

In 2004, Senator Barack Obama spoke to the National Democratic Party about the American Dream that Martin Luther King had fought for:

> I stand here today, grateful for the diversity of my heritage, aware that my parents' dreams live on in my precious daughters... That is the true genius of America, a faith in the simple dreams of its people, the insistence on small miracles. That we can tuck in our children at night and know they are fed and clothed and safe from harm. That we can say what we think, write what we think, without hearing a sudden knock on the door. (Obama 1)

Citing your resource material is the correct way to present information. **Plagiarism** is not acceptable in any school. Plagiarism is using another author person's material in a way that makes it look like your own. Plagiarism can be done in two ways. The first is copying material directly into your own paper without using quotation marks around it and citing it. The second way to plagiarize is to *paraphrase,* or closely restate material without citing the source of the material. (For more information on summarizing, see Chapter 9 of this book.) Be sure to always cite your sources.

CITING SOURCES

There are two places in which you give credit to your sources for the information you use. The first place is in your text. After a quote, you place a short note in parentheses. You can see examples of this in the previous section on "Quoting Sources in Text."

The second place in which you cite information about your sources is called the **bibliography**. This section of your research paper is called by different names according to different styles. These names include **Bibliography**, **References**, or **Works Cited** pages.

The bibliography gives all the details about each source that you used in your research. This information allows readers to check the research sources that are named in your paper. A reader may also want to read more about your topic by looking up some of your works cited and reading them.

A bibliography is always separate from the rest of your research document. All information on this page must be written in a very specific way. The guidelines for writing a bibliography are explained in the MLA style guide, titled *MLA Handbook for Writers of Research Papers*. Here are some basic rules about the formatting of the page. All text in the bibliography is double spaced. The page's title, "Works Cited," is typed in the center of the top line. After skipping two line spaces, the first entry is made. The first line of the entry begins at the left margin of the page. Each following line of the entry is indented by 1/2 inch. This is called a "hanging indent." Entries are listed in alphabetical order by author's last name.

The following are the details on how to create specific Works Cited entries. They are written in MLA style, according to the 6th edition of the MLA handbook. A sample bibliography appears on **page ....**

BIBLIOGRAPHIC ENTRIES

Bibliographic entries are listed in alphabetical order by author's last name. When citing a book, first list the name(s) of the author(s). They are listed last name first and followed by a period. Leave two spaces after the period. Then write the entire title of the book; you must underline or *italicize* the title. Follow this with a period. Leave two spaces after the period. Now, write the city where the book was published and the name of the publishing company; these two elements are separated by a colon. A comma is placed after the publishing company. Only one space follows that comma. Then write the year the book was published. ***Follow every entry with a period***.

Treat a manual, handbook, or pamphlet the same as a book. If the document has no author, enter the title first, and list the entry by the title's first letter. The company or institution which had the text written goes next. Finish as a book entry.

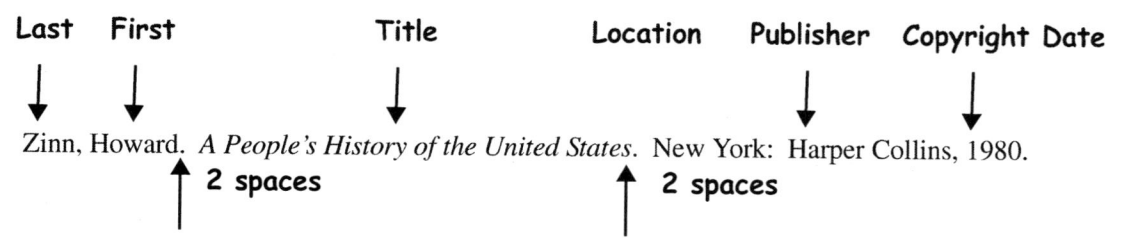

Last   First   Title   Location   Publisher   Copyright Date
  ↓   ↓   ↓   ↓   ↓   ↓
Zinn, Howard. *A People's History of the United States.* New York: Harper Collins, 1980.
              ↑ 2 spaces   ↑ 2 spaces

Zoo Managers' Guide to an Organic Zoo. Zoological Carousel Fund. Paris: La Raison, 2001.

CITING A MAGAZINE OR NEWSPAPER ARTICLE

When citing **articles**, begin by listing the author's name, last name first, followed by a period. Leave two spaces after the period. Next, list the title of the article in quotation marks. Follow that with two spaces. Third, you must underline or *italicize* the name of the periodical. Next, put the volume number, if there is one. Finally, write the date of publication, the month, and year. Follow this with colon and then the page number(s) on which the article appeared. The page numbers are followed by a period.

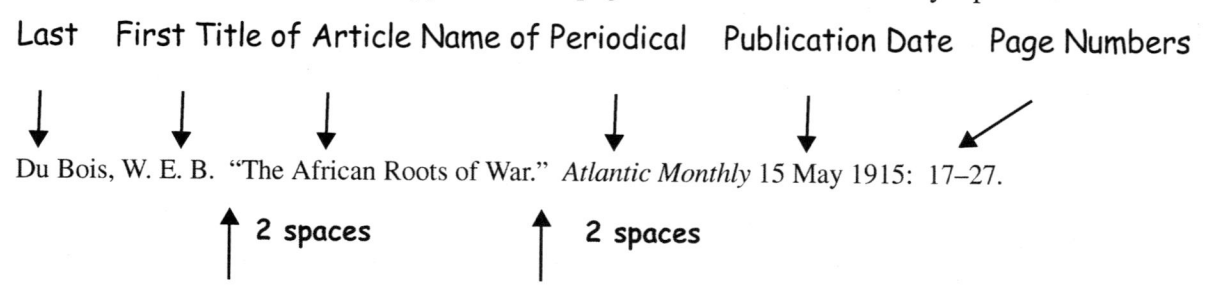

Last   First Title of Article   Name of Periodical   Publication Date   Page Numbers
  ↓   ↓   ↓   ↓   ↓   ↗
Du Bois, W. E. B. "The African Roots of War." *Atlantic Monthly* 15 May 1915: 17–27.
                  ↑ 2 spaces   ↑ 2 spaces

CITING A GOVERNMENT DOCUMENT

When citing a **government document**, list the author's name if there is one entered. If not, begin with the name of the government, then the government agency and any subgroup entered. You may use common abbreviations. Next, list the title (underline or *italicize*). Finally, list the publishing information as with a book. The publisher for these documents is often the Government Printing Office (GPO).

U.S. Dept. of the Treasury. IRS. *Circular E, Employer's Tax Guide.* Washington: GPO, 2001.

Evaluating and Citing Information Sources

CITING AN INTERNET WEB SITE

When citing an **Internet Web site**, give the author's name (if any), last name first, followed by a period. After two spaces, list the full title of the work, in quotation marks, followed by a period inside the quotation marks. Then list the title of the larger work, if any, in *italics* or underlined, followed by a period. Enter, next, the date of the document or last revision followed by a period. Finally, write the date of access (notice that the day comes before the month) and the full web address in angle brackets *followed by a period.* If it is necessary to break the Web address to fit on more than one line, only do so after slashes or other punctuation.

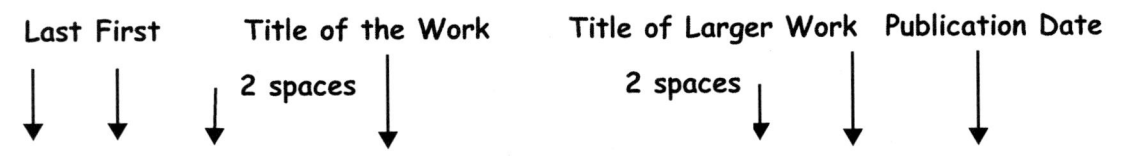

Last First Title of the Work Title of Larger Work Publication Date
              2 spaces   2 spaces

Burka, Lauren P. "A Hypertext History of Multi-User Dimensions." *MUD History.* 1993.
    5 August 1999. <http://www.utopia.com/talent/lpb/muddex/essay>.
    ↑ Access Date ↑ Web Address

CITING A PERSONAL INTERVIEW

If you spoke to or interviewed someone as part of your research, and used the information in your report, your interview must be cited. Citing a **personal interview** is quite simple. It consists of the name of the person you interviewed, the statement "personal interview," and the date of the interview, written as day-month-year.

Janaka, Kate. Personal Interview. 15 March, 2005.

CITING AN ENCYCLOPEDIA ARTICLE

When citing an encyclopedia article, give the author's name (if any), last name first, followed by a period. Next, place the title of article in quotation marks. Then write the name of the encyclopedia. This should be in italics or underlined. Follow this with the edition number (if any) followed by "ed." for "edition." Finally, write the year published with a period after it.

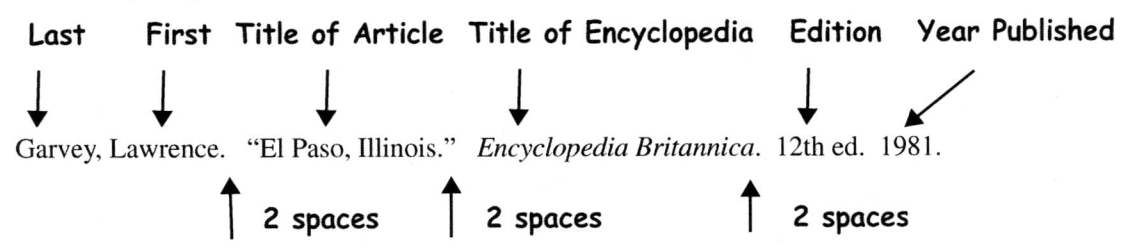

Last First Title of Article Title of Encyclopedia Edition Year Published

Garvey, Lawrence. "El Paso, Illinois." *Encyclopedia Britannica.* 12th ed. 1981.
                    ↑ 2 spaces   ↑ 2 spaces   ↑ 2 spaces

CITING ONLINE ENCYCLOPEDIA ARTICLES

Most online encyclopedias provide information on how to cite their articles. Some provide a link called "cite" or "cite this article" at the top or bottom of the article. If you click on that link, you will see how to cite the article. You may copy that information exactly. Other online encyclopedias or information sources simply write the citation at the bottom of the article. For example, in an article on Martin Luther King on the *MSN Encarta* site, an online encyclopedia, you will see at the bottom of the page the following explanation of how to cite that article in a research paper.

> **How to cite this article:**
>
> "King, Martin Luther, Jr.," Microsoft® Encarta® Online Encyclopedia 2005 http://encarta.msn.com © 1997-2005 Microsoft Corporation.

All you need to do with this information is to copy it exactly into your bibliography.

Sample Bibliography

> Bibliography
>
> Jakoubek, Robert. Martin Luther King Jr. Civil Rights Leader. New York. Chelsea House Publishers. 1989.
>
> "King, Martin Luther, Jr.," *Microsoft® Encarta® Online Encyclopedia 2005* http://encarta.msn.com © 1997-2005 Microsoft Corporation.
>
> Obama, Barack. "Speech from the 2004 National Democratic Convention, Boston, MA." residential Rhetoric.com. 1 August 2004. http://www.presidentialrhetoric.com/campaign/dncspeeches/obama.html

Practice 2: Documentation

Study each of the following groups of information. Then on a separate sheet of paper, correctly rewrite the information into a MLA style bibliography entry.

1. An article, titled "Exercise Your Visa," was published in the magazine *Family Circle*. This article was found in the October 2000 issue and was written by Leigh Anne Jasheway. It would be found on pages 31–43.

2. A Web site was accessed on September 24, 2000, at the following address: http://europe.cnn.com/2000/TECH/computing/07/11/g7.agree.idg/index.html. The article, written by Martyn Williams, was posted on July 11, 2000 and titled "G7 Finance Ministers Agree to Promote IT."

3. The United States government sends out tax forms yearly. Fred is writing an essay arguing that government is out of control and too big. One of the sources he will cite is the Department of the Treasury: IRS (Internal Revenue Service) form, *Alternative Ways to Get Employment Tax Forms and Instructions*. It was printed by the Government Printing Office in 2001.

4. *The Atlanta Journal-Constitution* published an article by Leslie Everton Brice. The newspaper was printed for September 10, 2000, and the article was titled "Brick Defines Atlanta in Choice of Home Style." The article can be found on page C12.

Evaluating and Citing Information Sources

5. Fabio Da Silva wrote an article called "Competitive Edge" inside his computer folder, <u>Fabio's Journal</u>. He posted the article on August 23, 2000 at http://extreme.lycos.com/ AthleteDirect/lycos/freestyle/athletes/fc_journal/jsp?statCategory=AWAY& ATH_ID=120015. This article was accessed on September 16, 2000.

CHAPTER 16 REVIEW: EVALUATING AND CITING RESOURCES

A. Validating Sources.

1. You are writing a paper on pollution in the Gulf of Mexico. You find several Web sites on the Internet on the subject. Write 5 questions you can ask yourself about each site to determine if you can trust the information on that site.

   _____
   _____
   _____
   _____
   _____

2. What 4 categories of measurement should you use to evaluate the usefulness and accuracy of secondary sources?

   _____
   _____

B. Citing Sources

3. You are preparing to write a paper on the Vietnam War. On April 23, 2005, you discussed with your Uncle Roderick Bacon his experience on the Landing Ship Tank boats which cruised the Mekong Delta during the war. How would you cite this source in your bibliography?

   _____
   _____

4. In researching careers with international organizations, you read a book titled *So, You Want to Join the Peace Corps: What to Know Before You Go*. It is written by Dillon Banerjee and published by Ten Speed Press of Berkeley in 2000. Write a bibliographic entry for this book.

   _____
   _____

5. While writing a paper on the Holocaust, you read a book by Nobel Prize-winning author Elie Wiesel called *Night*. The book was published in by Bantam books of New York in 1960. How would you cite this book in your bibliography?

_____

_____

6. In the same paper on the Holocaust, you did further research on the author Elie Wiesel because he is a living survivor of that time. You found an article in the online encyclopedia called *Britannica Encyclopedia Online*. At the bottom of the article, you found the following information:

>   MLA Style:
>
>   "Wiesel, Elie." Britannica Concise Encyclopedia. 2005. Encyclopedia Britannica Premium Service.
>
>   2 April 2005 <http://www.britannica.com/ebc/article?tocId=9382682>.

   How would your write a bibliographic entry for this article?

7. For a literary research paper about author Betsy Byars, you read three of her novels: *Pinball*, *The Summer of the Swans*, and *Tornado*. The edition of *The Summer of the Swans* that you read was published by Scholastic INC. of New York. Its copyright is 1970. How would you write a bibliographic entry for this book?

Evaluating and Citing Information Sources

Chapter 17
Graphic Aids and Organizers

LOUISIANA READING BENCHMARKS ADDRESSED IN THIS CHAPTER INCLUDE:	
ELA-5-M6	Identifying and interpreting graphic organizers (e.g., flowcharts, timelines, tree diagrams) (1, 2, 3, 4, 5)

Sometimes more than words are needed to present information. **Graphic aids or organizers** such as **tables, graphs, diagrams,** and **timelines** can provide information more clearly than words alone. Graphic aids are a visual representation of data. Because they present information visually, they are often used in magazines, newspapers, and advertisements. When reading material which uses graphic aids, you should take the time to examine these aids. They will help you understand what you are reading.

Knowing how to read graphic aids is an important skill because they help with research and decision-making. In order to figure out a graphic aid, you need to understand how the information presented is organized. This chapter will explain some common types of graphic aids.

TABLES

Tables show data in an organized way. Data is arranged into rows and columns, letting the reader compare the information. The **rows** of a table go across; the **columns** of a table go up and down. Tables are useful in summarizing information which would take many words to explain.

When reading tables, first look at the table headings. These are usually found at the top and/or the sides of the table. They describe what information is contained in the table. They also direct you to where you should look to find exactly the information you need. Besides a heading, some tables also include extra information to guide you in reading the table. For instance, in the following table, the heading, found on the top, tells you that the information in the table is a schedule of movie showings. Below the heading some extra information explains that you need to be sure and look at either the gray or the white areas, depending on which day of the week you want to go to the movie.

Carefully read the table on the next page, and answer the questions that follow

Graphic Aids and Organizers

Practice 1: Tables

Theater	AFTERNOON MOVIE SCHEDULE								
	Friday - Sunday gray and white				Monday - Thursday gray only			
	A	**B**	**C**	**D**	**E**	**F**	**G**	**H**
	12:00	12:10	12:20	12:30	12:00	12:10	12:20	12:30
	2:30	2:40	2:50	3:00	2:30	2:40	2:50	3:00
	5:00	5:10	5:20	5:30	5:00	5:10	5:20	5:30
	7:30	7:40	7:50	8:00	7:30	7:40	7:50	8:00
	10:00	10:10	10:20	11:00	10:00	10:10	10:20	11:00

1. How many individual theaters does this cinema complex have?_____
2. When is the earliest you can see a movie on Sunday?_____
3. How many total showings are there on a Friday?_____
4. How many total showings are there on a Monday?_____
5. If you wanted to see the movies in Theater C and Theater G on Wednesday, what showings could you attend? _____
6. What is the latest show you could see on Thursday night? _____

GRAPHS

Graphs are helpful for showing muchinformation in a small amount of space. For graphs, researchers use numbers to present data. Graphs let you compare information and figure out how items are related. The three following types of graphs—**line graphs, bar graphs**, and **symbol graphs**—all show how one factor or piece of information changes in relation to another.

Graphs almost always include keys. **Graph keys** show you the types of lines or colors or other symbols which are used in the graph and what they stand for. As with tables, reading graph titles and keys first is important in understanding the information in the graph.

How to Read a Graph
• Read the title to find out the subject and purpose of the graph.
• Read the headings, labels, and key to find out what information is shown.
• Study the information, looking for relationships, increases or decreases, order of events, etc.

LINE GRAPHS

Line graphs usually show how things change over time. They often compare trends or show how two or more events affect each other. Line graphs have information charted in the **horizontal** (side to side) direction, called the *x*-axis, and in the **vertical** (up and down) axis, called the *y*-axis. The horizontal, or *x*-axis, usually shows the time segments, and the vertical, or *y*-axis, shows what is being measured.

Practice 2: Line Graphs

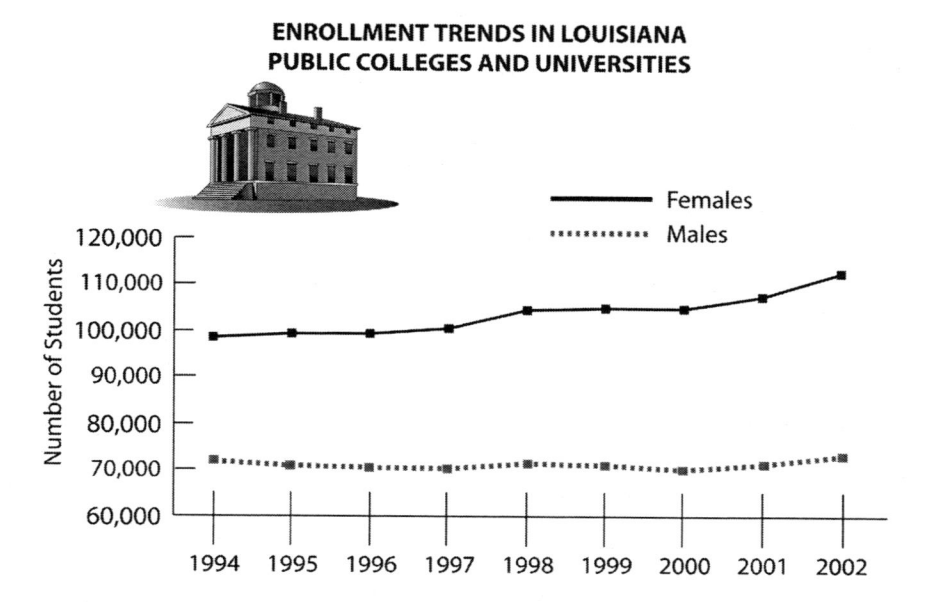

ENROLLMENT TRENDS IN LOUISIANA PUBLIC COLLEGES AND UNIVERSITIES

1. What is the title of this graph? _____
2. Which group of people does the solid line represent? _____
3. Which group of people does the dotted line represent? _____
4. How many years does the study period cover? _____
5. Which group of people increased enrollment more over the study period? _____
6. From this graph, what conclusion could you reach about college enrollment in Louisiana?

_____

_____

BAR GRAPHS

Bar graphs are made up of bars. The different lengths of the bars represent the different quantities or other measurement of two or more items. Seeing the different lengths of bars next to each other gives a very clear and immediate idea of the comparison between the two items. A bar graph can also show changes over time. Carefully study the line graph and bar graph below and answer the questions that follow.

Graphic Aids and Organizers

Practice 3: Bar Graphs

PIZZAS SOLD BY TWO COMPANIES IN ONE WEEK

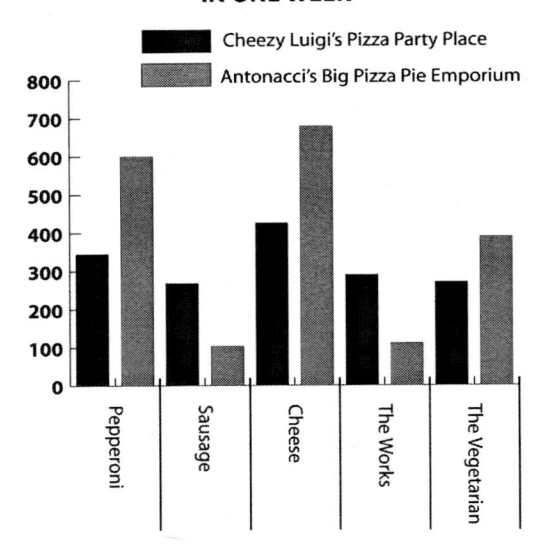

■ Cheezy Luigi's Pizza Party Place
▨ Antonacci's Big Pizza Pie Emporium

1. What is the title of this graph? _____
2. Which pizza place sells the most pizzas overall? _____
3. If you were to go into Antonacci's pizza today, what kind of pizza, according to the graph, are you most likely to order? _____
4. Which two pizzas are the least favorite with customers? _____
5. How many of the favorite kind of pizza does Luigi's sell in one week? _____
6. From this graph, what conclusion can you draw about peoples's taste in pizza?

PIE OR CIRCLE GRAPHS

As its name implies, a **pie graph** is a circle which is cut into wedges the way a pie is. The whole pie represents all the data together. Each "slice" of the pie represents one piece of that data. By looking at a pie graph, you can tell which piece of data is larger or smaller than the others.

Practice 4: Pie Graphs

The pie graph below gives us more information about the comparison between our two pizza places. This time we compare the different pizza crusts and how many of each are sold at each pizza place. Study the graph and answer the questions which follow it.

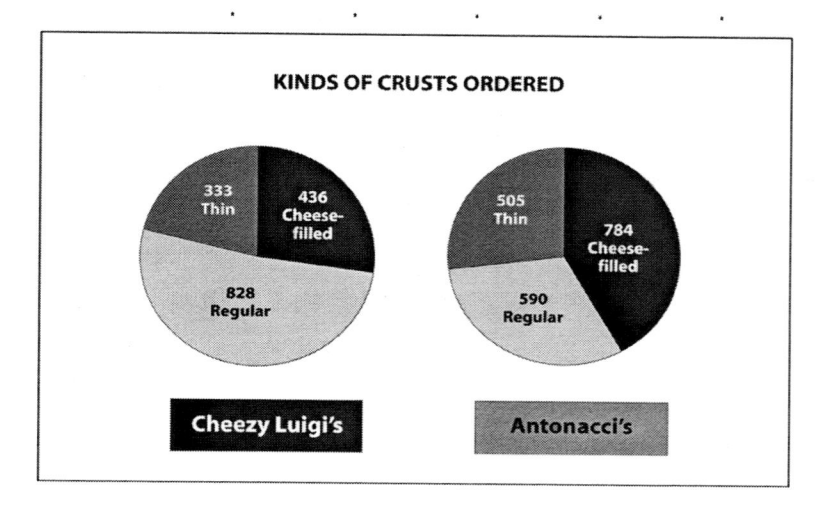

KINDS OF CRUSTS ORDERED

Cheezy Luigi's:
- 333 Thin
- 436 Cheese-filled
- 828 Regular

Antonacci's:
- 505 Thin
- 784 Cheese-filled
- 590 Regular

1. Which kind of pizza crust is ordered most often at Antonacci's?_____
2. How many regular pizza crusts are ordered at Luigi's? _____
3. Which pizza crust is the least favorite at Antonacci's?_____
4. Use your skills in hypothesis for this question: Speculate about why people order a lot of regular crusts at Luigi's, but far fewer at Antonnacci's.

_____

SYMBOL GRAPHS

Symbol graphs use symbols or pictures to represent data.

Carefully study the symbol graph on the following page, and answer the questions that follow

Graphic Aids and Organizers

Practice 5: Symbol Graphs

Length of School Year

● Each symbol represents ten days

Germany ●●●●●●●●●●●●●●●●●●●●●●
Japan ●●●●●●●●●●●●●●●●●●●●●●●
New Zealand ●●●●●●●●●●●●●●●●●●●
Sweden ●●●●●●●●●●●●●●●●
United Kingdom ●●●●●●●●●●●●●●●●●●●
United States ●●●●●●●●●●●●●●●●●●

1. What is the title of this graph? _____
2. Which country has the longest school year? _____
3. Which country has the shortest school year? _____
4. How many days per year do children in the United States attend school? _____
5. How many days per year do children in Germany attend school? _____
6. What is the purpose of this graph? _____

GRAPHIC ORGANIZERS

Graphic organizers help you put together your thoughts. They are useful for organizing or arranging what you know about a topic. Graphic organizers can help you prepare for a test by reviewing your knowledge. They can help you gather and organize your information for writing a paper. Like other graphic aids, graphic organizers show the relationship between pieces of information. This section will discuss three graphic organizers: **Venn diagrams**, **Spider maps**, and **H-maps**.

VENN DIAGRAMS

Venn diagrams are useful for comparing and contrasting objects or ideas. Venn diagrams compare and contrast characteristics of people, places, events, ideas, objects, and so on. They accomplish this by listing all the characteristics of each item being compared. Then they organize these characteristics into two categories: characteristics that are shared (common) between the two objects, and characteristics that are not shared (different) between the objects. These categories are placed in different sections of the diagram.

A basic Venn diagram is made of two overlapping circles. It is designed to compare two objects or ideas. An expanded Venn diagram has three (and sometimes more) overlapping circles. It compares and contrasts 3 or more objects or ideas. Each circle represents one object. The overlapping areas contain the similarities, or points you can compare between the objects. The areas that are separate and do not overlap are where the differences between the objects are listed. These are points you can contrast.

Models of Simple and Expanded Venn Diagrams

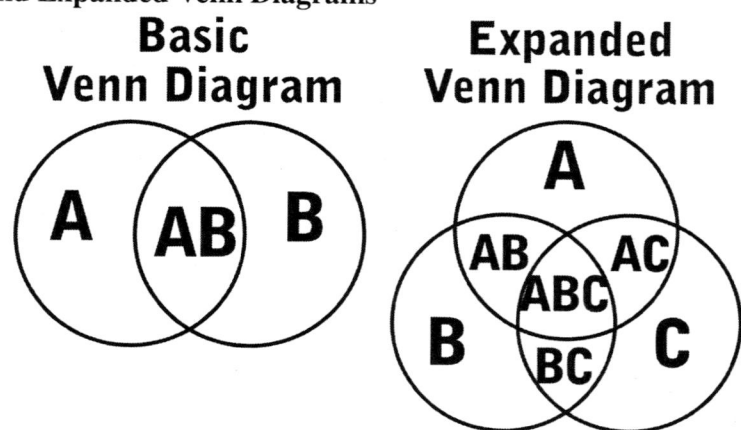

Basic Venn Diagram

Expanded Venn Diagram

In the model of the **basic Venn diagram** above, the area marked **AB** would contain all the characteristics common to both object **A** and object **B**. The area marked **A** would contain the characteristics of only object A; the area marked **B** would contain the characteristics of only object B. These same principles apply to the model of the expanded Venn diagram. Look at the model of the expanded Venn diagram. Knowing the basic principles described for the basic model, you should be able to identify what information would go in each section of that model.

To create or read a Venn diagram, ask the following questions:

- What items are being compared?
- What are all the characteristics of each item?
- Which characteristics do the items have in common (**AB**— intersecting portion of two circles or **ABC**—intersecting portion of three circles)?
- What are the differences between the items (**A & B**—non-intersecting portions of two circles or **A, AB, AC, B, BC, C**—non-intersecting portions of three circles)?

The following example of a Venn diagram compares two planets in our solar system. It would be a useful illustration in an article about the two planets. It would also be a good tool for organizing your information for writing an essay or as a study guide for a unit on the planets. Read the diagram below, and answer the questions that follow.

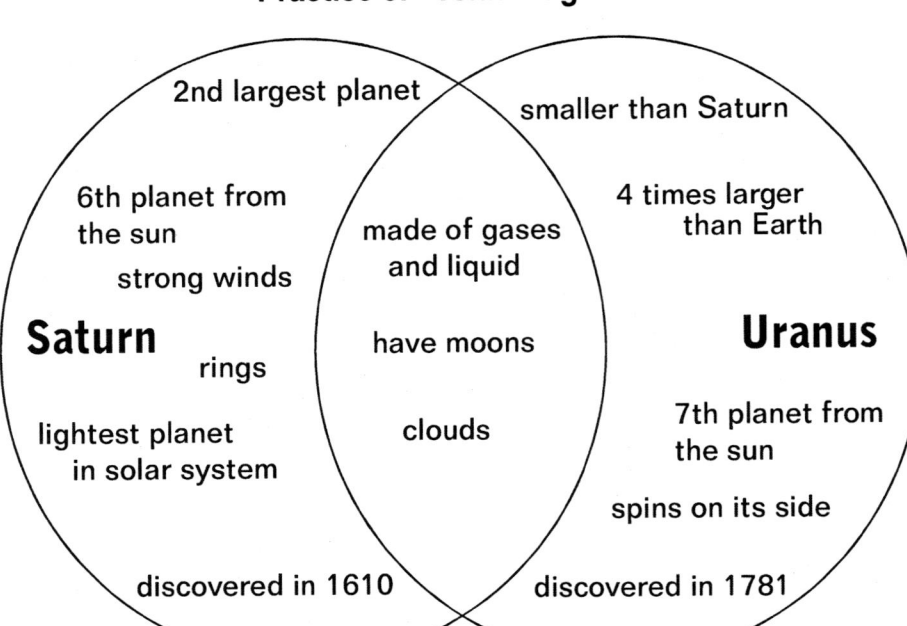

Practice 6: Venn Diagrams

Saturn
- 2nd largest planet
- 6th planet from the sun
- strong winds
- rings
- lightest planet in solar system
- discovered in 1610

Shared
- made of gases and liquid
- have moons
- clouds

Uranus
- smaller than Saturn
- 4 times larger than Earth
- 7th planet from the sun
- spins on its side
- discovered in 1781

1. What two planets are being compared in this Venn diagram? _____
2. What are two characteristics the planets share? _____
3. What are two differences between the planets? _____
4. Which planet is farthest from the Sun? _____
5. Which planet was discovered first? _____
6. **Open-ended response.** Use your own paper to answer the following question.

    How would this diagram help you organize and write an essay about the two planets?

H-Maps

H-Maps are another type of graphic organizer used to sort out your thoughts on a topic. Like Venn diagrams, they organize the similarities and differences between topics. Unlike Venn diagrams, H-maps cannot compare or contrast more than two items. An H-map is a simple diagram shaped like the letter H. In the middle of the H, the **similarities** between the two items are listed. Each column of the H is labeled with one of the items being compared. In each column are listed the characteristics of that item which are not shared with the other item.

Practice 7: H-Maps

Look at the following example of a completed H-map. The H-map compares and contrasts two sports. Answer the questions that follow.

Soccer (differences)	Similarities	Basketball (differences)
• use feet to move ball • score goals • goal protected by goalie • 11 players • played on a field	• team sport • "dribble" ball • penalty shots • constant aerobic activity • running • defensive play	• use hands to move ball • score baskets • 5 players • played on a court

1. What two sports are being compared in this H-map? _____
2. What are two characteristics the sports share? _____
3. What are two differences between the sports? _____
4. Are there more differences or similarities between the two sports? _____
5. **Open-ended response.** Use your own paper to answer the following question.

How might your answer to #4 affect a paper you would write about the two sports?

SPIDER OR WEB MAP

Spider maps are graphic organizers used to arrange your thoughts on a topic. They are useful as preparation tools for writing assignments and tests. They can also be used for organizing notes that you take while reading. Like all graphic aids, the spider map is a visual presentation, and, therefore, makes information and ideas available at a glance. Also like all graphic organizers spider maps have many uses. Here are a few of them:

- figuring out solutions to problems
- mapping out different meanings of words
- organizing main ideas and details
- creating descriptions of objects, people, or places
- organizing sub-topics related to a general topic

Graphic Aids and Organizers

To create a spider map, write the main topic in the center circle. The ideas that you want to develop are then written on the diagonal "legs" of the map. Then, you write the supporting details on the offshoot lines ("feelers") of each leg.

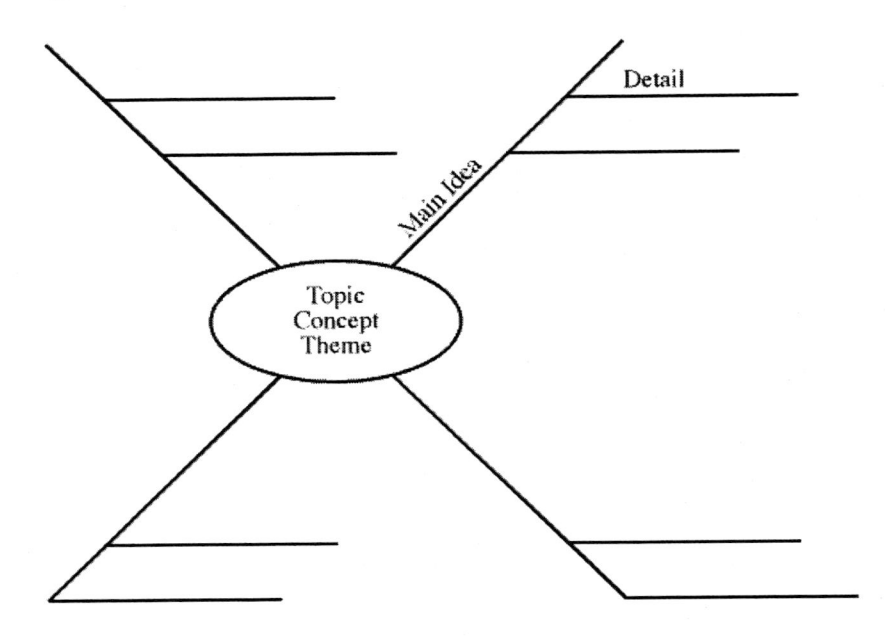

The following sample spider map was created as a pre-writing activity for a writing assignment. Look at the sample map, and answer the questions that follow.

Practice 8: Spider Maps

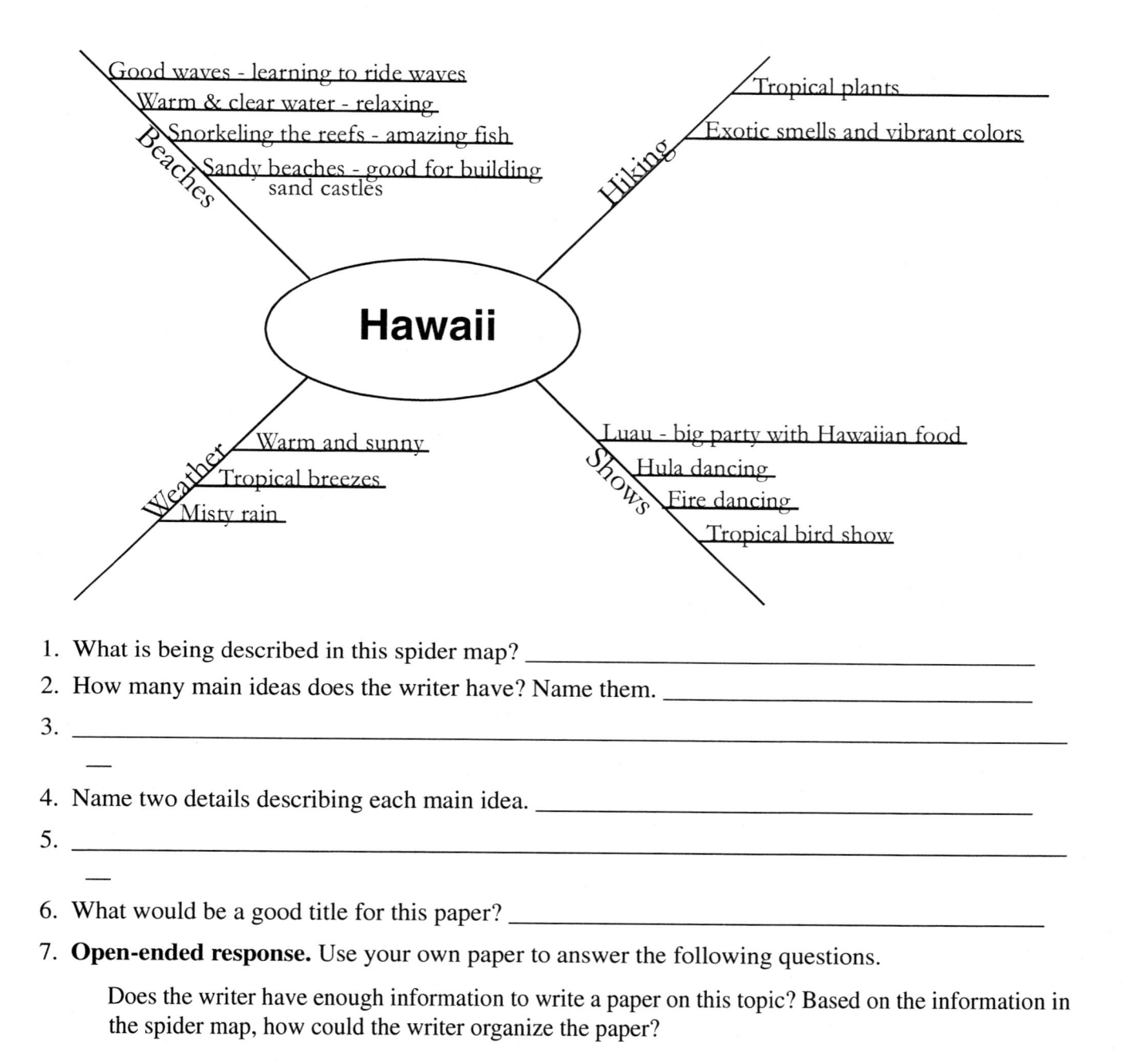

Hawaii

Beaches
- Good waves - learning to ride waves
- Warm & clear water - relaxing
- Snorkeling the reefs - amazing fish
- Sandy beaches - good for building sand castles

Hiking
- Tropical plants
- Exotic smells and vibrant colors

Weather
- Warm and sunny
- Tropical breezes
- Misty rain

Shows
- Luau - big party with Hawaiian food
- Hula dancing
- Fire dancing
- Tropical bird show

1. What is being described in this spider map? _____
2. How many main ideas does the writer have? Name them. _____
3. _____
   —
4. Name two details describing each main idea. _____
5. _____
   —
6. What would be a good title for this paper? _____
7. **Open-ended response.** Use your own paper to answer the following questions.

   Does the writer have enough information to write a paper on this topic? Based on the information in the spider map, how could the writer organize the paper?

Practice 9: Creating Graphic Organizers

Create a graphic organizer.

A. Choose a partner and create either a Venn diagram or an H-map comparing and contrasting each other. Be sure to list all your similarities and differences.

Graphic Aids and Organizers

B. Read an assigned chapter from one of you school text books. As you read, create a spider map on the topic of the chapter. Fill in the map with the main topic, sub-topics, and supporting details. Use the map as a study guide for the class.

TIMELINES

Timelines help organize events into chronological order, so that one event follows another in a time sequence. They are useful graphic aids for showing historical information or biographical information about people.

Timelines are good tools for taking notes on information that is given in chronological order. For example, while reading from a history book, you can write the main events from a historical period on a timeline. Timelines can also help a reader keep track of the main events in the plot of a story. Like other graphic organizers, timelines are useful study guides.

Practice 10: Timelines

Look at the following example of a timeline, and answer the questions that follow.

Important Inventions of the 20th Century
1976–1996

1976	1979	1981	1984	1986	1987	1988	1989	1990	1991	1995	1996
ink-jet printer		IBM Personal Computer		super-conductor disposable camera		digital cellular phones Doppler radar		World Wide Web		DVD	
	cellular phones Cray supercomputer Walkman roller blades		Apple Personal Computer		3-D video games		high definition TV		digital answering machine		gas-powered fuel cell

1. What is the title of this timeline? _____
2. What years does this timeline cover? _____
3. Which came first, the IBM or Apple computer? _____
4. When was the Walkman invented? _____
5. **Open-ended response.** Use your own paper to answer the following question.

    What could the information in this timeline be used for?

280

Practice 11: Creating Timelines

A. Draw a timeline of your life so far. Be sure to include the dates of important events that have happened to you. Use the format of the timeline at the top of this page.

B. Read a short story with your class. Create a timeline of the events that take place in the story. Use the timeline to answer questions about the plot of the story.

C. Create a timeline of an important historical period such as the Roman Empire, the discovery of America, events from 1990 to 2004, or another topic. Be sure to include the important dates and a brief description of the events connected to each of those dates.

OUTLINE

An **outline** is a common, easily used method of organizing material you have read, helping you to remember main ideas and important details. It is the road map you will follow when summarizing material or framing a research report from materials you have read. You will get to your destination—reading comprehension— more easily if your road map looks something like the following:

Basic Outline for a Paper or Article
I. Introduction: Brief general discussion, including statement of the main idea
II. Body A more specific discussion of the major ideas. Give each idea a separate paragraph or more. Discuss each idea separately.   **A.** Topic 1 (from statement of main idea) and supporting details   **B.** Topic 2 (from statement of main idea) and supporting details   **C.** Topic 3 (from statement of main idea) and supporting details
III. Conclusion: Summary of discussion, including any concluding ideas

Following is an example of the use of an outline. This outline is for an article or paper about the effects of television viewing on young children. The specific <u>key points</u> in each section are underlined.

Graphic Aids and Organizers

Outline of an Article on Children and Television

   I. Introduction: Television can have a bad effect on the <u>social development of children</u>.

  II. Body

      A. Television exposes children to <u>adult programs</u>.

         1. Crime

         2. Violence

         3. Obscenity

      B. <u>Commercials</u> increase children's wishes for needless products.

         1. Children find it difficult to tell reality from pretend

         2. Products bring happiness

      C. Television takes away from <u>children's playtime</u>.

         1. Lack of play with others

         2. No fresh air and movement

 III. Conclusion: Young children should watch <u>less television</u>

MAPS

A **map** is a flat drawing of all or part of the earth. A **globe** is a model of the earth shaped like a ball or sphere. North, south, east, and west are called **cardinal directions**. North is usually at the top of a map or globe, south is at the bottom, east is to the right, and west is to the left.

Maps and globes also contain a symbol to help you find directions. This symbol, called a **compass rose**, is shown on the following world map. A compass rose shows the four cardinal directions. It may also show the **intermediate directions** (in-between directions). These intermediate directions are northeast (NE), northwest (NW), southeast (SE), and southwest (SW).

Now practice finding directions on the world map shown below.

Practice 12: World Map

1. Which continent is south of Europe? _____
2. Which ocean is north of Europe? _____
3. Which continent is east of Europe? _____
4. Which continent is west of Europe? _____
5. What ocean is northwest of Australia? _____
6. What continent is southeast of Asia? _____
7. What direction is Africa from South America? _____
8. What direction is South America from Europe? _____
9. What island is northeast of North America? _____
10. Which ocean lies east of Asia? _____

Economic Maps

An **economic map** shows the resources and products of a country. These resources and products provide an income and standard of living for the people of that country.

Graphic Aids and Organizers

Study the following map of Australia, and then answer the questions.

MAJOR MINERAL DEPOSITS AND AGRICULTURAL PRODUCTS IN AUSTRALIA

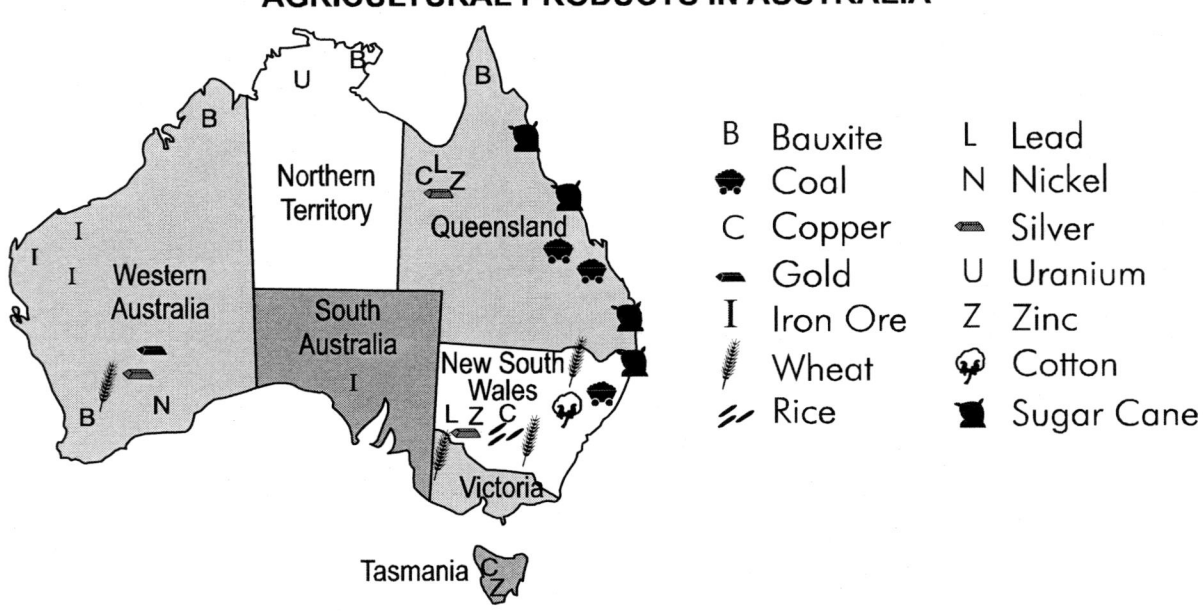

B	Bauxite	L	Lead
	Coal	N	Nickel
C	Copper		Silver
	Gold	U	Uranium
I	Iron Ore	Z	Zinc
	Wheat		Cotton
	Rice		Sugar Cane

1. Based on this map, which agricultural crop is most plentiful in New South Wales? _____
2. Based on this map, which mining industry is the largest in Western Australia? _____
3. Which region of Australia contains the most minerals? _____
4. Which three provinces in Australia show no agricultural development? _____
_____
5. Which provinces have mines for precious metals (gold or silver)? _____
_____

284

CHAPTER 17 REVIEW: GRAPHIC AIDS

Use the table, graphs, and timelines presented in the next pages to answer the questions that follow each.

GAME SCHEDULE								
Gray for away games				*White for home games*			
DATE	Team 1	Team 2	Team 3	Team 4	Team 5	Team 6	Team 7
May 7	12:00 n.	1:00 p.m.	2:00 p.m.	3:00 p.m.	10:00 a.m.	11:00 a.m.	4:00 p.m.
May 14	1:00 p.m.	12:00 n.	3:00 p.m.	10:00 a.m.	4:00 p.m.	11:00 a.m.	2:00 p.m.
May 21	3:00 p.m.	2:00 p.m.	12:00 n.	4:00 p.m.	1:00 p.m.	11:00 a.m.	10:00 a.m.
May 28	11:00 a.m.	4:00 p.m.	12:00 n.	3:00 p.m.	1:00 p.m.	10:00 a.m.	2:00 p.m.
June 4	10:00 a.m.	3:00 p.m.	11:00 a.m.	12:00 n.	4:00 p.m.	1:00 p.m	2:00 p.m.

1. How many teams does this chart schedule? _____
2. How many away games does each team play? _____
3. When is the first game of the season? _____
4. At what time does Team 4 play on May 28? _____
5. At what time is the last game played each day? _____
6. If you wanted to watch Team 3 play a game, and you were only available in the mornings, which day would you attend? _____

**Favorite After-School Activities
Ms. Smith's 8th Grade Class**

○ Represents Girls   ● Represents Boys

Watch TV	●●● ○
Play Sports	●●●●● ○○○○
Talk on the Phone	● ○○○○
Play Video Games	●●●● ○
Work on the Computer	●● ○○
Visit with Friends	● ○○○

7. What is the title of this graph? _____
8. What activities are the least popular with the boys? _____

285

Graphic Aids and Organizers

9. What activities are the least popular with the girls? _____
10. How many students are in the class? _____
11. Which activity is the most popular with boys and girls? _____
12. What conclusion can you come to about the types of activities boys and girls enjoy? _____

Study the graph below and answer the questions that follow it.

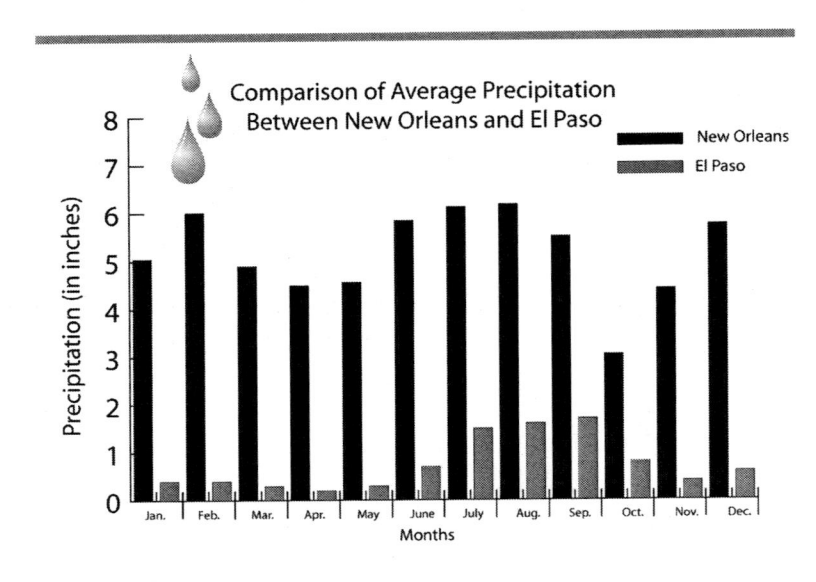

1. What is the title of this graph? _____
2. What information is this graph showing? _____
3. What is the average precipitation in El Paso for the month of June? _____
4. What is the average precipitation in New Orleans for the month of February? _____
5. What are the two wettest months in New Orleans? _____
6. How much precipitation falls during the driest month in New Orleans? _____
7. What unit of measurement is used in measuring the precipitation? _____
8. In which month is the average precipitation in El Paso 2 inches? _____
9. In which city would you have to regularly water your backyard garden? _____
10. Integrate your knowledge: What kind of precipitation is this graph probably referring to?
_____

Chapter 18
Literary Genres and Story Structure

LOUISIANA READING BENCHMARKS ADDRESSED IN THIS CHAPTER INCLUDE:	
ELA-1-M2	Interpreting story elements (e.g., mood, tone, style) and literary devices (e.g., flashback, metaphor, foreshadowing, symbolism) within a selection (1, 4)
ELA-6-M1	Comparing, contrasting, and responding to United States and world literature that represents the experiences and traditions of diverse ethnic groups
ELA-6-M2	Identifying, comparing, and responding to a variety of classic and contemporary literature from many genres (e.g., folktales, legends, myths, biography, autobiography, poetry, fiction, nonfiction, novels, drama
ELA-6-M3	• classifying various genres according to their unique characteristics

To analyze something means to break it down into small parts and study those small parts in order to better understand the whole. To understand how a bike works, you might look closely at all of its parts. You would examine the gears, chains, and wheels to see how each of them worked. Then you would see how they all fit and work together. By examining these elements of the bike, you would arrive at an understanding of how a bike functions the way it does.

The analysis of literature is very much like the study of machinery. The **elements,** or parts, of a literary work are studied and then put together to understand the whole work. The elements of literature include **literary genres, plot structure, characters,** and **setting**. These are the elements that you will study in this chapter.

LITERARY GENRES

A bike is classified by what it looks like and what it does—in other words, its structure and its function. For example, the all-terrain bike is heavy and rugged. It will ride well on mountain paths and in muddy fields. The racing bike, on the other hand, is built for roads. It is more streamlined and refined. It is made of lighter, stronger metals than the ATB. It performs well when speed is called for.

Literary Genres and Story Structure

Written works are also grouped into or categories called **genres**. And, like bikes, they are also grouped according to their structure and function. For instance, a short story does not look like a play or a novel or a letter. Nor does a short story function the way a play or letter does. Like the racing bike which would not take rocky mountain paths very well, a short story cannot relate the history of the state of Louisiana. Nor could a short story be produced on stage with actors, unless it is rewritten as another genre—a play.

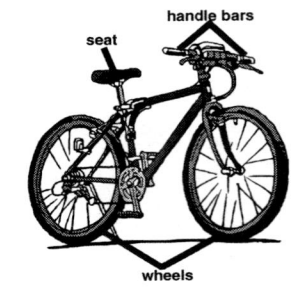

Once you learn to recognize the structure and function of literary genres, you will be able to easily identify anything you read according to which genre of literature it belongs to. The following is a list of some literary genres and their descriptions.

NONFICTION

Nonfiction is writing that is true or factual. It is written to teach or to inform the reader. Examples of nonfiction include historical accounts, scientific reports, instructional manuals, and articles in newspapers or magazines. Biographies and autobiographies are also part of this genre.

BIOGRAPHY

A **biography** is the story of a person's life, **written by someone else**. One example of a biography is *On the Court With... Michael Jordon*, by Matt Christopher. Another example is the book written about the author of the Harry Potter books. It is called *J.K. Rowling: A Biography*, and it is written by Sean Smith.

AUTO-BIOGRAPHY

An **autobiography** is the story of a person's life **written by that person**. An example of an autobiography is a book about Rosa Parks, "the Mother of Civil Rights," written by Rosa Parks. The book is titled *Rosa Parks: My Story*. Another example of an autobiography is *The Cage*, a book written by Ruth Minsky Sender. In this book, Minsky Sender tells the story of her childhood and adolescence as a Polish Jew during World War II. In the book, the author gives the main character a different name, but the story is of her own suffering which she experienced through the Nazi domination of her country.

FICTION

Fiction is *narrative writing*, which means writing that tells a story. Writers create fiction by using their imaginations rather than fact alone. This does not mean that there is nothing factual in fiction. Fiction often draws upon real situations, places, events, facts, and people. However, the main element in fiction is the author's use of imagination and creativity in shaping and presenting those real elements. In "Number the Stars" by Lois Lowry, the story is based on factual history and real events. However, it is fiction because the author creates the characters and situations within these historical truths. Fiction which is entirely based on imaginary elements is called **fantasy**, as you will read further on.

Fiction is most often used to describe novels and short stories but can also include myths and fairy tales. Fiction can be short but powerful, as in O Henry's "The Last Leaf," or it can be long and full of adventure, as in *Hatchet* by Gary Pulson.

NOVEL

A **novel** is any long, fictional story, written in **prose**, or writing that follows normal sentence structure and is not verse. Novels are long enough to be divided into chapters or sections. They are published as complete books. Novels can be based on fact and often are based on the experience of the author. Or, they can be purely fictional. Two examples of novels are *Island of the Blue Dolphins* by Scott O'Dell, and *Julie of the Wolves* by Jean Craighead George. George's novel is based on her experience as a naturalist and her study of wolves living in the frozen northern tundra.

SHORT STORY

Short stories are works that tell a complete story in just a few pages. They are too short to be divided into chapters. And they are usually not published as complete books but rather as part of a collection of short works. Short stories usually have a clear beginning, middle, and end. They often reveals the characters' personalities through actions and thoughts. Examples of a short story include "The Treasure of Lemon Brown" by Walter Dean Myers, O. Henry's "The Gift of the Magi," and Toni Cade Bambara's "Raymond's Run."

FANTASY

Fantasy is a popular genre of fiction writing. Fantasy consists of stories that are entirely made up through the imagination of the author. The genre of fantasy is marked by boundless possibilities. Characters may be endowed with magical powers. Animals and plants may speak and have powers of their own. The world and the characters created by the author of fantasy are limited only by the author's imagination. Fantasy is also often marked by a very clear distinction between good and evil in the plot. Examples of fantasy include the series of books by Brian Jacques called the Redwall series. These books are filled with very evil and very good and brave characters, high adventure, danger, and heroism. It involves characters like squirrels, badgers, mice, rats, hares, and other animals. J.R.R. Tolkien's trilogy, *The Lord of the Rings*, is another well loved series of fantasies. Of course, J. K. Rowling's Harry Potter series is also a good example of fantasy.

FOLK TALE

Folk tales are simple stories set in the past which have animal, human, or supernatural characters. These last characters use their special powers to solve problems. Often, events in folk tales happen in threes. Examples: *Grimm's Fairy Tales* and Asian folk tales from Laurence Yep's *The Rainbow People*.

TALL TALE

A **tall tale** is a funny tale common on the North American frontier. Tall tales use real details and an overstated manner to explain seemingly impossible deeds and events done by a superhuman character. Examples: the stories of Paul Bunyan and Pecos Bill.

LEGEND

Legends are stories connected with some period in the history of a people or nation. The story is written to glorify (sometimes exaggerate) a human hero or an object that is important to a people. Examples: England's King Arthur, Colonial America's Johnny Appleseed, and the Shawnee leader, the Prophet.

Literary Genres and Story Structure

MYTH

A **myth** is a story with supernatural characters and events, sometimes joined with religious beliefs or rituals. Myth tries to explain the natural order of the physical world or certain natural occurrences. For example, in Aztec mythology, the creation of the people on Earth is explained by the god Quetzalcoatl's trip to Mictlan, the underworld. Quetzalcoatl brought up bones and ashes from groups of people who had been destroyed before. He planted these bones, and they grew into people.

DRAMA

Drama is a story told in action and **dialogue** (conversation) between actors who perform as characters. Dramas, or plays, can be written in prose and poetry. They may be read as books, but they are intended to be acted out on the stage. Shakespeare's *Romeo and Juliet,* which is written in verse, and William Gibson's *The Miracle Worker,* which is written in prose, are well-known and admired dramas.

The symbol of drama is that of two masks: one is crying and represents tragedy, while the other is laughing and represents comedy. Tragedy and comedy are the two main subcategories of drama. **Tragedies** take a serious view of the world and display the hard times in life. The main character in a tragedy usually experiences a terrible fall from a positive position in society to one of a hopeless human being. A tragedy usually has a sad ending, often involving a death. **Comedies** portray the humor or the irony of the world and are usually funny, although many can have serious aspects to them. Shakespeare's *Hamlet* is a tragedy, while the movie *Shrek* is a comedy. Comedies always end happily. Problems are usually solved and characters resolve their arguments. In classical comedy, stories often end with a marriage.

POETRY

Poetry is literature written in lines and verses. Poetry often involves rhythm and rhyme, although neither are necessary for this genre. For many hundreds of years, poetry was almost always written in rhyming verse. The last century or so, however, has brought about a change in the rules for poetry. Rhyme is not necessary, nor is any set pattern of rhythm. Today, poetry is written in a wide variety of forms. Still, the genre of poetry is different from prose. It is unique because it conveys powerful images and feelings in fewer words than prose does. Often it uses only phrases or single words to evoke ideas. Well-known poets include Robert Frost, an American poet of the 20th century, John Keats, a British poet of the 19th century, and Dr. Seuss, an American children's poet of the 20th century.

EPIC

The **epic** is an ancient genre. In fact, the oldest literatures in Western civilization were epics. The Greek poet Homer's two great works, the *Iliad* and the *Odyssey* are epics. They were written around 800 BC. Other classical epics in Western literature include *Beowulf*, written in Great Britain around 750 AD and later, John Milton's *Paradise Lost*, written around 1650 AD. Milton's great narrative about the clash between angels and devils, however, is considered the last epic to be written in the English language. Since that time, there have been works that contain epic characteristics, such as **Star Wars** and **Lord of the Rings,** but no true epics have been written.

What are the characteristics of an epic? The following table lists some basic ones.

Characteristics of an Epic
• An epic is first of all a narrative, a story.   • An epic is quite lengthy and usually divided into "books," or parts.   • Epics are written in verse. They are long poems.   • Epics tell of the extraordinary stories of great heros, either legendary heros like Beowulf, or national heros like Odysseus. These heros are of exceptional stature and character. They often have supernatural powers. They may fight mythical monsters or have gods and goddesses as companions or adversaries.   • Epics are not set in everyday, mundane reality. They are usually set in mythical or magical places.   • Epics fulfill certain literary *requirements*, or *conventions*. One of these conventions is that they almost always begin with an **invocation**. An invocation is an **epic convention** which involves the author addressing a "higher power," usually the gods, or the poet's **muse**, to help him in the writing of the epic. A muse is regarded as the source of inspiration for a poet. Another epic convention is the **epithet**. When characters talk about each other without using a name but rather by describing them poetically, that is an epithet. An example of an epithet in the Odyssey is when Odysseus tells Cyclops of how his ship was destroyed by the god of the sea, Poseidon: "<u>Poseidon</u> Lord, <u>who sets the earth a-tremble</u>, broke it up on the rocks of your land's end."

Practice 1: Literary Genres

Read the following passages. Circle the genre of literature for each passage, and then explain why you chose your answer.

The First Woman

Once there was a beautiful woman who lived in a pleasant valley on the earth. The rest of the world was filled with rocks and mountains. In this valley, summer was the ruling season, and honey and fruit were always available. Her only companions were the dove and the doe. She was the reigning spirit of this world, and nothing ever grew old or died.

One morning the woman followed a scarlet butterfly to a remote waterfall where the butterfly disappeared. Realizing she was lost, the woman fell asleep from exhaustion. When she woke, a being like herself stooped down and lifted her off the ground. Clothed in a robe of clouds, the man being told her he saw her as he traveled across the sky.

Literary Genres and Story Structure

Because he rescued her, the man being had broken the command of the Great Spirit. He would remain on earth and share her companionship. For many moons, they lived happily in the valley. The woman bore a child. Sad because he broke the law, the man sought the guidance and forgiveness of the Great Spirit. The Great Spirit took pity on the man and the woman. He opened up many more valleys and plains for the future inhabitants, but because of the broken command, the Great Spirit caused the man and woman to labor for their food. They would also suffer from cold, grow old, and die when their heads became as white as the feathers of swans.

1. myth   nonfiction   autobiography

2. Why did you choose this answer?

Excerpt from an Old Folk Song

Work, work, my boy, be not afraid;
    Look labor boldly in the face;

Take up the hammer or the spade,
    And blush not for your humble place.

There's glory in the shuttle's song;
    There's triumph in the anvil's stroke;

There's merit in the brave and strong,
    Who dig the mine or fell the oak.

– Eliza Cook (1879)

3. poem   epic   fable

4. Why did you choose this answer?

"The First Confrontation"

After we had conversed, he stated to me that he was completely undone; he had not been able in a long time to take any Indians; he knew not which way to turn, and his men had well begun to experience hunger and fatigue. I told him of Castillo and Dorantes, who were behind, ten leagues off, with a multitude that conducted us. He thereupon sent three cavalry to them, with fifty of the Indians who accompanied him. The Negro returned to guide them, while I remained. I asked the Christians to give me a certificate of the year, month and day, I arrived there, and of the manner of my coming, which they accordingly did. From this river to the town of the Christians, named San Miguel, within the government of the province called New Galicia, are thirty leagues.

From the *Relation of Alvar Nunez Cabeza de Vaca*, March 1536

5. fable autobiography tall tale

6. Why did you choose this answer?

How Candlemas Became Groundhog's Day!

What do candles and groundhogs have in common? They share a holiday, or rather, a holy day. For Christians, this holy day began in the 4th century, but it has even older roots in Judaism. Ancient Jewish law said the new mother of a baby boy must be purified at the temple forty days after the birth. When December 25 was set as Jesus' birth, the feast of Mary's purification, the day she would have gone to the temple, was begun on February 2. The Catholic Church has always celebrated the day with processions and the blessing of candles for the year: Candlemas.

The connection with groundhogs comes from Europe. Long ago, Europeans came up with weather-predicting rhymes for February 2, Candlemas Day. All the rhymes predicted that if clear weather dawned on Candlemas Day, there would be more winter weather before spring. Historically, the Germans were the ones who predicted the weather based on whether or not they could see an animal's shadow. The Germans thought hedgehogs were wise enough to know if they needed to return to their dens for more winter. So, Germans watched those animals on February 2. Europeans immigrating to America saw the groundhog as the closest relative to the hedgehog. The new Americans wanted to keep their traditions and chose the groundhog as their new weather expert. On February 2, people still watch groundhogs to keep them enlightened about spring's arrival.

7. allegory biography nonfiction

8. Why did you choose this answer?

The Fox and the Grapes

A hungry fox came into a vineyard where there hung delicious clusters of ripe grapes. His mouth watered to be at them; but they were nailed up to a trellis so high, that with all his springing and leaping he could not reach a single bunch. At last, growing tired and disappointed, the fox said, "Let someone else take them! They are but green and sour; so I'll leave them alone."

– Aesop (ca. 6th century B.C.)

9. myth fable fantasy

10. Why did you choose this answer?

Literary Genres and Story Structure

Practice 2: Activities For Literary Genres

A. Folder Free-for-all With a partner or on your own, use your literature book and other books and periodicals your instructor suggests; look for one example of each type of literature listed in this section. or think of the literature that comes from your cultural background. Find an example of as many genres as you can from this chapter. Include the title, author, and a 2-3 sentence description of the literary work. Write down your results and save them in a brightly decorated folder for later reference.

B. Who am I? Two contestants (students) form a team with the moderator describing a particular literary genre without saying the name. For example: "I am an exaggerated story about the frontier days. What type of literature am I?" Answer: tall tale. The moderator could also provide four choices for the contestants such as: A. mystery; B. tall tale; C. advertisement; D. sonnet.

The format of the popular game show, *Who Wants to be a Millionaire?* could be used with lifelines, such as (1) ask the audience (class), (2) eliminate two answers from four choices, and (3) phone a friend (asking a classmate).

C. Drama Student groups select a fable, tall tale, or legend to rewrite as a play and perform for the rest of the class. Each member of the group will dress and play a character in the play.

D. Historical Letter Imagine you are a witness to a historical event, such as the assassination of JFK or the fall of the Berlin Wall. Look up factual information about the event. Write a letter to a friend and include facts from your research. You may create fictional scenes to fill in the gaps in your research, but make your letter as believable as possible.

PLOT STRUCTURE

A bicycle needs a frame to hold all the different parts together. If the frame is not strong, the bike will not hold its rider for long. In a similar way, authors use **plot structure** to organize and build stories. If a story's structure is not strong, the story will not keep the reader's interest.

A story can be told in many different ways. Good writers use the following structural tools to build a successful story. Knowing and understanding these tools will help you develop strategies for analyzing literature.

PLOT

Plot is an element of fictional writing. It is the pattern of events in a story, or what happens in the story. A classical plot has several parts. There is the **introduction** to the story. Then there is the **rising action**, the **conflict**, the **climax**, the **falling action**, and the **resolution**.

If we were to draw a picture of a typical plot, it would look like a mountain. Imagine climbing over a mountain. The **introduction** would represent the foot of the mountain, where you would start. The story's **rising action** would represent the rising slope of the mountain. It is where most of the story's **conflict** occurs. The **climax** of the story is the mountain peak. The **falling action** would be the other side of the mountain, as you travel the downward slope of the mountain. Finally, the **resolution** is the end of the journey, or the bottom of the downward slope of the mountain.

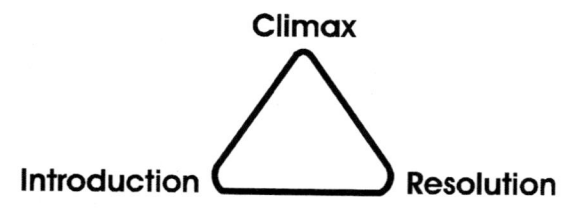

```
         Climax
          /\
         /  \
        /    \
       /      \
  Introduction  Resolution
```

As an example of this model of a story plot, think about the fairy tale "Cinderella" as you read further about plot elements

Introduction The **introduction** is the opening of a story. In the introduction, the author describes the setting of the story, introduces the characters, and reveals the conflict. Sometimes the author does not include all of these items in the introduction. Some authors choose to introduce a main character after revealing the conflict. The beginning of *Cinderella* introduces us to the main characters: Cinderella, her stepmother, and her stepsisters. We are also given background information in order to understand the rest of the story; for example, Cinderella is treated badly under the care of her wicked stepmother.

Conflict The **conflict** of the story usually makes up a lot of the **rising action**. It is the struggle between different forces in a story. Conflict consists of problems and difficulties faced by the characters. This struggle may be between a character and nature, between a character and himself or herself (inner conflict), a character and other characters, or between the character and society—its laws, or its expectations and pressures. The conflict in *Cinderella* is between characters. It is between Cinderella and her stepmother and stepsisters. This conflict causes Cinderella much hardship and suffering.

Climax The **climax** is the turning point in a story. It may occur when the conflict is at its worst, or when circumstances change for the character. On the night of Cinderella's ball, the fairy godmother shows up, changes Cinderella's rags to a beautiful dress, and sends her off to the ball. The night at the ball, including Cinderella's loss of her shoe, is the climax of the story, or the peak of the mountain.

Resolution In a story's **resolution**, the conflict is resolved in some way. The resolution takes place during the falling action of the plot, which is almost always shorter than the rising action. In the resolution, the mystery is solved, or the problems of the character are settled. In tragedy, the resolution is often a sad but final one. For instance, in MacBeth, most of the main characters of the play are killed in the final scene. However, in a comedy, the resolution is usually a happy solution to all problems. In *Cinderella*, the resolution occurs when the Prince searches for the woman who fits the glass slipper, finds Cinderella, and marries her so they live happily ever after.

Literary Genres and Story Structure

SETTING

Setting is the time and place of the action of a story. In some stories, the setting is not clearly described. In other stories, the setting is very important because it helps create a mood, contribute to the conflict, or reveal a character. In *The Secret of the Andes,* by Ann Nolan Clark, the setting plays an important role in the story. The story is about Cusi, a young Inca boy in Peru, who lives with his uncle and tends his beloved llamas. The story takes place in the Andes Mountains of Puru. It is an isolated and natural setting. As the author describes it, Cusi lives surrounded by "mountain peak upon mountain peak, sheer and hard and glistening in frozen mantles of ice and snow." The mountains are so high that few people ever visit Cusi's home. This is important, because it sets up Cusi's motivation to travel and to learn about people. He longs to know what a family is and what people are like. If the story had not been set in such a lonely place, Cusi would not need to set out on the journey which makes up much of the story. Therefore, the plot of the story would be completely different.

The setting of a story affects the mood, creates conflict, and influences the characters. Below are two aspects of setting.

Time   when the story takes place. It may be past, present, or future. The setting in *The Secret of the Andes* is the present. However, the story, through the thoughts and experiences of Cusi, the main character, brings the reader back in time to the ancient Incan culture and Cusi's ancestors.

Place   where the story happens, including such details as geographic place, scenery, or arrangement of a house or room. The place may be real or imaginary. *The Secret of the Andes* takes place on the beautiful peaks of some of the highest mountains in the world. Place may change throughout a plot. As Cusi travels, the setting changes to villages, mountain paths, and eventually a city.

Practice 3: Setting

1. Read the passage below carefully. Then answer the questions which follow it.

Excerpt from "Two Friends" by Guy de Maupassant

Paris was blockaded, starved, in its death agony. Sparrows were becoming scarcer and scarcer on the rooftops and the sewers were being depopulated. One ate whatever one could get.

As he was strolling sadly along the outer boulevard one bright January morning, his hands in his trousers pockets and his stomach empty, M. Morissot, watchmaker by trade but local militiaman for the time being, stopped short before a fellow militiaman whom he recognized as a friend. It was M. Sauvage, a riverside acquaintance.

1. **Short answer.** Use your own paper to respond. The story takes place during the war between the Germans and the French in 1870. Write a list of words and phrases in the description of the setting, which indicate that the story takes place during a war.

2. **Short answer.** Use your own paper for your response. Which details from the passage show what the mood of the characters and their world will be in the story?

3. **Short answer.** Use your own paper for your response. What details from the passage describe the characters and their lives?

LITERARY CHARACTERS

On a bicycle, the wheels, gears, and chain all work together to make the bike go. None of these parts would operate the same without the others. In fictional literary works, **characters**, the people, animals, or creatures that take part in the action of a work, tell each other and the reader about their ideas and feelings.

The interaction or relationship between characters in a story is an important part of the story. Through a character's words and actions, the story comes alive for readers.

There are different types of characters in a story. The **main characters** are the focus of a story. The story centers on their thoughts and actions. They are the most important characters. The **minor characters** may be friends, relatives, neighbors, etc. of the main character. They interact with the main characters and with one another, moving the plot along and providing background for the story.

CHARACTER TYPES

When talking about characters in literature, it is important to note whether they are **dynamic or static character,** and whether they are **round** or **flat** characters.

DYNAMIC CHARACTERS

Dynamic characters are changed in a significant way from the events in the plot. And that change is a major aspect of the plot. It is part of the conflict, the climax, the falling action, and the resolution. In fact, the resolution of a story plot often centers on the change which the dynamic characters have experienced, and how they come to terms with that change.

Therefore, if a character has merely grown older during the time frame of the plot, that character is not dynamic. If the character has grown in some personal way, for instance in emotional maturity, then he or she is a dynamic character. In the short story "The Treasure of Lemon Brown" by Walter Dean Myers, the main character, 14-year-old Greg Ridley, is an example of a dynamic character. He changes in many ways by the end of the story. At the beginning of the story, we meet him as an angry, frustrated boy. He is not doing as well as he could in school, and his father is unhappy with him because he would rather play basketball than study. We meet Eric walking the streets of his neighborhood, Harlem, looking for a way to avoid his father's lectures. But instead, he soon finds himself in trouble. By the end of the story, Greg has had his life threatened. He has also met an old man who teaches him a lesson about a father's love. Greg returns to his apartment as a different person. This is what makes a dynamic character.

STATIC CHARACTERS

You may have encountered the term *static*, meaning *not moving*, in a science class. The same definition applies to the personal growth or change in a literary character. **Static characters** are not changed by plot events in which they are involved. A static character is instrumental in moving the story forward, but does not change through the story. In "The Treasure of Lemon Brown," one of the static characters is Greg's father. It is important to note that *static* does not mean *shallow*. It means not changing. The character of Greg's father is a man of principle who cares about his son. We even know something of his past; he had to leave school at a young age to help support his family. So he knows the importance of education and hopes his son will realize it too. However, he remeains the same throughout the story. He plays an important role in the plot:. He establishes the conflict. The conflict is between Eric and his father, and between Eric and himself. Eric would like to please his father, but he wants very much to play basketball. But through it all, (though the father has a brief "presence" in the story) Greg's father remains the same caring man. He does not change. It is Eric who changes. Therefore, Greg's father is a static character.

ROUND CHARACTERS

Just as a well-rounded person has many different aspects to his or her life, a **round character** is one that is complex. The reader knows a great deal about a round character. Round characters are well developed. As readers, we may know the round character's thoughts, conflicts, and history. A round character is usually a main character in a story. In "The Secret of Lemon Brown," Greg, the main character, would, of course, be a round character. Another round character is Lemon Brown. We learn a lot about this old man through his dialog and through his actions. As a character, he is revealed as much more than simply an old, homeless man. We learn that he has an amazing past and many feelings. We learn that he has courage and that he is quick-witted and wise. This kind of multi-leveled person is what makes a round character.

FLAT CHARACTERS

In contrast, a **flat character** is almost one dimensional. Sometimes a flat character may be a stereotype, and the character's role is merely to represent that stereotype. Flat characters are usually minor characters, but not always. In "The Secret of Lemon Brown," the flat characters would be the street thugs. We learn nothing of their lives or backgrounds. They act in the way that one would expect street thugs to act. They move the plot along by making Eric face something that teaches him about priorities in life. But they themselves are flat characters.

Types of Characters	
dynamic	a character that undergoes a significant change or personal growth during the time frame of a literary work; usually round
static	a character that does not experience change or growth during the time frame of a literary work; at the end of a work, they are essentially the same as at the beginning of the work; often flat
round	a multi-dimensional character; reader knows many personality aspects of the character; usually a dynamic and/or a major character
flat	a one-dimensional character; reader has limited knowledge about the character; often a stereotype and/or a minor character and/or static

CHARACTERIZATION

The main trait of a dog is loyalty to its master. In literature, characters must also have clear traits. Authors must portray the characteristics of the characters in a story in order for the reader to know what to expect of their behavior

Chapter 18

Characterization consists of the statements an author makes about a character through description of or narration about that character. It also includes what can be observed about a character outside of direct descriptions, such as how the character speaks, other character(s)' observations, the character's actions, and how the character reacts to others. Following is a list of the main ways in which an author develops characters.

How Authors Develop Characters

Description   An author uses description to tell how characters look and dress, and what their ages are, just as you might describe a friend of yours to someone. In *The Secret of the Andes*, Ann Nolan Clark describes the minstrel who comes to visit Cusi as "as Indian, with shin-length cotton trousers and a woven cocoa bag." In further describing the minstrel as having a "fierce look of Inca kings," Clark depicts him in a way that not only shows his appearance, but also his history and heritage.

Narration   **Narration** is the telling of the story through a speaker. The speaker could be a character or could be an unknown observer. Narration can change from one to another, as happens in Cusi's story. At one moment, the author narrates how Cusi awakes to the sound of llama-humming. Immediately the author takes the reader inside the character's thoughts, as we hear Cusi thinking what a "beautiful sound" the llamas make. From this narration, we learn that Cusi sleeps outdoors, close to his llama, and that he loves his llamas and enjoys looking after them.

Dialogue   **Dialogue** is conversation between two or more people. Through dialog between characters, an author can reveal information about the characters. A sample of dialog between Cusi, the Incan boy in *The Secret of the Andes*, and the old man who looks after him illustrates this. In the conversation, Cusi expresses his happiness at seeing people in the valley. The old man remembers that Cusi had not seen people since coming to live with him as a small child. Then he tells Cusi it is time for them to go on a trip and meet other Indians. In this conversation, we learn the situation of a boy who has never really seen people, we learn how excited he is to finally see some. We also learn about the character of the old man, who cares about Cusi and who knows that it is time to let him learn about the world and other people.

Dialect   **Dialect** is used to portray a character's cultural and regional heritage by illustrating his manner of speaking. Dialect is not a unique language. It is the way a language is spoken in a particular region of the country or the world. "The Treasure of Lemon Brown" contains a good example of dialect in the character of Lemon Brown. Notice the way his language contains missing words and non-standard usage when he responds to Greg's doubt about his treasure: "What you mean, *if* I have one? Every man got a treasure. You don't know that, you must be a fool!"

Actions   Sometimes the **actions** of a character speak louder than words to show the character's true self. Saruman the White, the head wizard in J.R.R. Tolkien's The Lord of the Rings, is the protector of the inhabitants of Middle Earth and Gandalf the Grey's mentor. He should protect Gandalf, but he betrays him for the power that Sauron, the evil protagonist in the story, promises. On the other hand, the main characters in O. Henry's "The Gift of the Magi" show positive characteristics through actions. They show their love for each other by placing the happiness of the other before their own happiness.

Literary Genres and Story Structure

THEME

The **theme** of a literary work is the central idea or message that is communicated through the short story, novel, poem, or play. Literature is all about ideas. In most works of literature, there are many ideas, but there is usually a main idea which the story is based on. This is the theme. Themes are specific kinds of main ideas. They are ideas that apply to all humans, not just the characters in the particular story. For instance, in the novel *Shiloh*, by Phyllis Reynolds Naylor, the theme of loyalty is prominent. The main character, 11-year old Marty Preston, must chose between his loyalty to an abused dog, and his honesty to his parents.

Some themes are messages about major issues in life or human nature. Many themes have been used over and over in different literary works throughout time. They apply to people of all times and places. These are called **universal themes**. Here are some examples of universal themes:

- Love (unrequited love, selfless love, young love)
- Change (its inevitability, its challenges)
- Friendship (loyalty, problems between friends)
- Growing up (new discoveries, new accomplishments, loss of childhood).
- Family (ties, relationships, problems)

The theme is not usually stated in a literary work; the reader has to infer the theme by looking at all the details from the work. Figuring out the theme of a literary work is not always easy, but there are some ways to make it easier:

- **Look at the lessons the main character has learned.** How has the character changed throughout the work? Has the character learned anything new? Often the truth revealed to a character is the same truth the author wants to reveal to the reader. For example, in *Beauty and the Beast*, Beauty is at first afraid of Beast and finds his appearance repugnant. As she gets to know him, she is able to see the kindness inside him, and she falls in love with him. This change in the main character points us to the theme: Real beauty is often found within a person, not in their appearance.

- **Look at the conflicts and how they are resolved.** For example, in *A Wrinkle in Time*, by Madeleine L'Engle, the conflict is between the characters. Meg and her family, who are clearly described as good, must battle against the Man with the Red Eyes and It, which is clearly described as evil. In the end, the conflict is resolved when Meg overcomes both enemies. She rescues her family because her ability to love has defeated It. This resolution of the conflict points us to the theme: Good always triumphs over evil.

- **Look at the title of the work.** Sometimes titles have special meaning or give clues about the theme. For example, the title of a novel by S.E. Hinton, *The Outsiders*, makes the reader think about things that do not belong, things on the outside. The characters in this story are on the outside of society and yet have their own form of society, with rules of behavior and honor. The title points to one of the themes of the novel: Honor can exist among outsiders. Not law, but human beings create honor.

CHAPTER 18 REVIEW

Loveliest of Trees, the Cherry, Now
By A. E. Housman

Loveliest of trees, the cherry now
Is hung with bloom along the bough,
And stands about the woodland ride
Wearing white for Eastertide.

Now, of my threescore years and ten,*
Twenty will not come again,
And take from seventy springs a score
It only leaves me fifty more.

And since to look at things in bloom
Fifty springs are little room,
About the woodland I will go
To see the cherry hung with snow.

*A score of years is 20 years.

1. Which literary genre can the above work be classified as?
   A. fiction   B. drama   C. nonfiction   D. poetry

2. What is one of the main themes in this work?
   A. first love
   B. the passage of time
   C. war and peace
   D. loss and grief

A Letter Home

Platte River, June 3rd, 1836

Dear Sister Harriet and Brother Edward:

   Friday eve, six o'clock. We have just encamped for the night near the bluffs over against the river. The bottoms are a soft, wet plain, and we were obliged to leave the river yesterday for the bluffs. The face of the country yesterday afternoon and today has been rolling sand bluffs, mostly barren, quite unlike what our eyes have been satiated with for weeks past. No timber nearer than the Platte, and the water tonight is very bad — got from a small ravine. We have usually had good water previous to this..

Farewell to all,
Narcissa Prentiss

Literary Genres and Story Structure

3. Which literary genre can the above work be classified as?

    A. nonfiction   B. fiction   C. poetry   D. drama

Read each of the passages, and answer the questions that follow.

"Dread" Locks

Elizabeth sat on the stool in the center of the room, terrified of moving. The scissors seemed to be on all sides of her.

She must be patient, she kept telling herself. No moving. Be good. One small move and she might lose an ear, or an eye. How much longer was this going to take? She realized she had been holding her breath and let a sigh escape.

"Be still," the voice said.

"Are you almost done?" she dared to ask.

"Yes, we're almost done. Keep still, and it will go faster."

Time seemed to slow down. She saw the hair fall to the ground and began to worry. Elizabeth looked out the window and let her mind wander. She thought of sunshine, swings, slides, and sodas.

"Okay, you're all done Elizabeth. What do you think?" asked the woman handing her a mirror.

Elizabeth looked in the mirror and slowly a smile spread across her face. She looked okay. The same girl still looked back at her from the mirror.

"You look great, Lizzie. Now let's get your treat and head to the park. Thank you for being so good," said her mother, taking her hand and helping her off the stool.

4. Which literary genre can the above work be classified as?

    A. fiction   C. drama
    B. poetry   D. nonfiction

5. Which of the following is the best statement of the plot in this passage?

    A. Elizabeth is not comfortable sitting still for so long.
    B. Elizabeth is being forced to sit in a time out.
    C. Elizabeth is getting her haircut and is worried about the outcome.
    D. Elizabeth always complains when she has to get a haircut.

6. Which method of characterization is used *most* to reveal the character of Elizabeth?

    A. thought   B. action   C. dialog   D. observation

7. Which of the following is the best statement of theme for this passage?

    A. Fear can be overcome with patience.
    B. Things can turn out better than expected.
    C. Haircuts are painful.
    D. Good behavior is always rewarded.

8. The main conflict in this passage is between Elizabeth and

   A. society   B. herself   C. her mother   D. nature

9. **Short Answer.** Use your own paper to write your response. Explain the conflict from the passage. What is Elizabeth struggling against? Use details from the passage to support your answer.

Spring Training

The soothing notes of Pachelbel's Canon in D major drifted through the barn doors into dappled morning light. A muffled grunting could be heard over the music as Martin trudged out, burdened with a CD player about the size of a carpenter's toolbox. As the dark-haired, black-eyed boy made his way down the graveled lane, music trailed after him like threads spun from a spider's web.

Coming to a stop by the pasture gate, Martin waved a hurry-up wave to his friend Casey coming down the road. Casey often came to hang out with Martin on Saturdays. The two friends joined forces on the high school baseball team and liked to get some spring hitting practice in before the season's start. Since Martin was responsible for exercising his family's six horses on Saturdays, it was difficult for the boys to get their practice in till long after lunch. Martin had a new plan. For the past month, he'd slowly been getting the horses ready for this as he rode each of them through the pasture.

Pointing to the CD player, Martin asked Casey, "You ready to see the exercise gallop?" Casey grinned and signed a *Yes, and I'm glad I made it in time* emphatically with his hands.

"Here, hold this, then" Martin handed his friend the player, so Casey could feel the change in vibration when Martin switched the music. Six glossy geldings idly watched the two boys. The horses stood soaking in May sun and blinked their eyes lazily against the buzzing of early deer flies.

"I got some great music. Watch this," Martin said, forming the words carefully with his mouth so Casey could read them, as he switched the classical CD to alternative rock; it was a selection he'd burned from a friend's copy. One by one, the horses lifted their heads high, ears swiveling towards the new sound. They began shifting from hoof to hoof, jostling each other... Then, like a flock of birds taking flight; the horses took off galloping around the pasture—carefree, joyous, and together. The music? It was one of the earlier *Good Charlotte* CDs.

Casey lifted the player to the top rail of the fence. He and Martin watched manes and tails whipping in the wind, taunt muscles working under glistening hides, and noses stretched in an ageless contest of high spirits. Martin could also hear an occasional challenging whinny from the lead animal while Casey could see the change in stride and half-opened mouth of the horse making the trumpeting sound. After watching for a few songs, Martin knew the horses had run enough for the morning exercise, and he slowly turned the music down to a whisper. Now that the pounding beat no longer supported their race, the horses wheeled slowly towards the boys and strolled, huffing a little, over for carrots and praise.

Casey handed the player back to Martin and spent several minutes telling the horses how great they were by patting necks and rubbing foreheads. Turning to Martin, Casey signed with a flourish, *They have gotten faster since I saw them training for barrel races last spring. Now, let's go train hitting pop flies instead of dodging deer flies!*

Literary Genres and Story Structure

10. Which is the best description of the setting for this passage?

    A. Saturday morning in a horse pasture in May.

    B. Horses galloping outside on a sunny day

    C. Saturday afternoon at Martin's barn

    D. Casey and Martin outside before batting practice

11. Which of the following is the best statement of plot for this passage?

    A. The horses are being trained to perform to music.

    B. Two friends exercise the horses to music before going to play ball.

    C. Two friends are hanging out on a Saturday morning.

    D. The horses enjoy galloping to music.

12. Which is the best statement of theme for this passage?

    A. There's more than one way to exercise a horse.

    B. There's a long way and a short way to do everything.

    C. Doing chores should always precede sports.

    D. Caring for animals builds friendships.

13. The passage can be classified as

    A. short story.   B. biography.   C. drama.   D. nonfiction.

14. **Extended Response.** Use your own paper to write your response. Write a description of each of the characters from this passage. Explain how you learned about the characters. What methods of characterization are used to reveal the characters?

Chapter 19
Literary Elements and Devices

LOUISIANA READING BENCHMARKS ADDRESSED IN THIS CHAPTER INCLUDE:	
ELA-1-M2	Interpreting story elements (e.g, mood, tone, style) and literary devices (e.g., flashback, metaphor, foreshadowing, symbolism) within a selection (1, 4)
ELA-7-M1	Using comprehension strategies (e.g., summarizing, recognizing literary devices, paraphrasing) to analyze oral, written, and visual texts for summarizing and paraphrasing (1, 2, 4)

Two literary devices are discussed in this chapter.

The first literary device concerns time and sequence of events. Identifying periods of **time** in a literary work helps to set up background information. If you know when a story takes place in history, you already know something about the background and characters of that story. Most literary works also have a sequence of events. **Sequence** can be arranged in many ways to change the telling of the story. Understanding a story's time and sequence is important to understanding the story.

The second literary device discussed in this chapter is figurative language. **Figurative language** is a way of expressing an experience without having to use merely plain, dry facts. Figurative language is a creative and effective way of using language to express ideas. There are several common types of creative language, many of which you see in writing or use in speaking every day.

TIME AND SEQUENCE

You might recall the diagram of the typical story plot on **page ...** This diagram, which includes the introduction, rising action, climax, falling action, and conclusion, is a classical model, and it applies to most stories. However, within that structure, authors are free to experiment with the passage of time and the sequence of events. Many authors choose to mix up the normal flow of time if it suits their dramatic purpose.

Literary Elements and Devices

Time. In a literary work, time may move straight forward from the first event to the last event. An example of this can be found in J.K. Rowling's *Harry Potter and the Chamber of Secrets*. However, an author might feel that the story might have a greater impact and be more intriguing if time is mixed up. An example of this is Louis Sachar's *Holes*, in which 3 connected stories are told: one in the present, one 110 years earlier, and another even further in the past.

Sequence. Sequence is the order in which events happen in a story. The sequence may not go in a straight time order but may go back and forth with the use of **flashbacks** and **foreshadowing**.

FLASHBACK

A flashback is a scene or event that happened before the story began. It is often introduced in the story as a memory or a dream, or as dialogue between two of the characters. The purpose of a flashback is not just to add extra information to a story plot. Its main purpose is to help the reader to understand the present circumstances of the story better. For example, in the novel *Julie of the Wolves*, Julie, while living with the arctic wolves, thinks about her earlier life in a small village living unhappily with a cruel husband. That memory helps the reader to understand what brought Julie to choose such a challenging existence in the frozen wilderness.

You can also find a good example of flashback in the movie *Spiderman II*. In one scene, late in the movie, Peter Parker sits at the dining room table with his aunt and tells her finally the real story of her husband's death. The story implies that Peter may have been to blame for the death. But the scene of the flashback serves to illustrate Peter's character, in that he had the courage to tell the truth, even though it hurt his aunt and threatened their relationship.

FORESHADOWING

Foreshadowing is another way of affecting the flow of time in a story. Foreshadowing takes place when an author includes certain details in one part of the story which hint at events to come. These details are like clues which help readers to predict what might happen later in the story.

For example, in the movies or on television, a dark stormy night or a sudden windstorm often foreshadows a murder or the appearance of a monster or some kind of evil. A certain kind of music in a movie can accomplish the same purpose.

Sometimes foreshadowing is not that easy to recognize. It may take the form of symbolism or other hidden meaning. For instance, in Washington Irving's "The Specter Bridegroom," a mysterious knight arrives at a castle. At first it is not known at first who he is, but if you consider that a the black horse he was riding is a symbol of death, you would have recognized foreshadowing of future events!

Chapter 19

For an illustration of variations in time and sequence, look at the diagrams below. The first diagram shows the events of a story line that moves forward in a straight path. A baby boy is born. As a toddler he flies on an airplane for the first time. He later reads a book about the Wright brothers. Then, after becoming an Air Force pilot, he sets a new record for altitude.

Now, look below at this next diagram of the same story line events. Notice how a writer can use flashbacks and foreshadowing to move backward and forward in time.

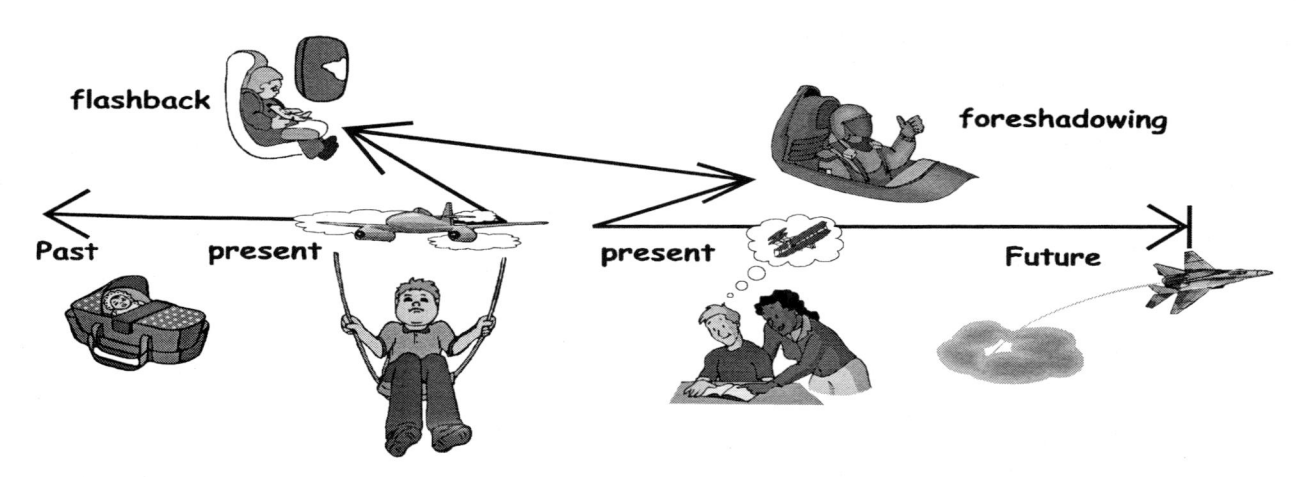

The second diagram shows the same plot, using flashback and foreshadowing. In this version, A boy is out swinging, in the present time. He sees an airplane overhead. He remembers (**flashback**) flying on a plane as a toddler. As he grows and attends school, he reads a book (**foreshadowing**) about two famous men who made the first successful flight in an airplane. The boy joins the Air Force. In the middle of a successful career, he sets a new record for altitude.

Practice 1: Flashback and Foreshadowing

Read the passage below, and answer the questions that follow.

The Mysterious Art Avenger

Lieutenant Richards stepped out of the squad car amidst the gawking onlookers in front of the dilapidated apartment house. Only hours before, he had received the errant artist's latest communication: He—or was it a she?—had sent this building's address to him on his pager. Last week, it had been an e-mail, and the first time, two weeks ago, it had been a phone call. Richards remembered that first call vividly.

Literary Elements and Devices

He walked in at quarter of ten, late as usual, and his telephone began ringing before he even took off his jacket.

"Richards here. Talk to me."

"The subway platform downtown is an eyesore," someone said in a horse whisper. "Something has to be done about it. I thought it was futile, but the mosaic worked out anyway."

"What? You must think you're talking to Public Works. Who is this?"

"I've taken it upon myself to beautify this town. People should have pleasant scenes to gaze at, and no one else will do anything about it. In fact, when I tried to offer my services to city officials, I was wrapped up in red tape!"

Before Richards could say anything else, the caller hung up. The lieutenant sent a patrol past the downtown subway station, just to check it out. Half an hour later, the officers reported that they couldn't believe their eyes. The previously graffiti-filled station had been transformed into a tropical paradise by someone with lots of paint, lots of tiles, and lots of talent. Richard thought back. Futile... Right. The guy had plenty of tiles!

Now, as Richards stood before the condemned apartment house, he thought the same thing—wow. He craned his neck to take in the patterns and textures of what was now painted as a giant wrapped-up gift, complete with an enormous red bow.

No one ever saw this vigilante—at least, no one was saying anything. Why should they? Their city was being decorated, thanks to this strange but talented eccentric, and if the police knew who it was, they'd only put a stop to it, fearing that one of these decaying "art projects" would fall down and hurt somebody—like maybe the artist. Little did Richards know that this is exactly how he would soon come to meet the mysterious art avenger.

1. Where is flashback used in this passage?

2. Is foreshadowing present in this passage? If so, where is it used?

3. How do flashback and/or foreshadowing help the author shape the plot of this story?

4. Identify the pun in the passage.

FIGURATIVE LANGUAGE

Figurative language is used in literature to convey information in a creative way. It is not literally true, but it produces effective descriptions and images. As an example, think about the phrase "He can't carry a tune in a bucket." No one can really carry a tune in a bucket. And if a tune could be carried in a bucket, that person might still have no clue as to how to do it. The phrase actually means that a person sings badly—off key and out of tune. The expression "can't carry a tune in a bucket" says the same thing as "sings badly and out of tune," but with more impact and with a vivid image. It also makes reading more enjoyable.

Figurative language is the opposite of literal language. Literal language makes plain, straightforward statements: "I don't understand what **irony** is." Figurative language expresses the same information with more of a creative impact: "I don't know **irony** from a load of coal!" Well, then, read on.

Below is a list of some of the common forms of figurative language.

Sound Devices	Some of the types of figurative language that authors can use are included in the category of **sound devices**. As the name implies, these are devices that have a particular sound to the ear, and they can create a mood or appeal to the senses. The types of figurative language included as sound devices include **alliteration**, **onomatopoeia**, **rhyme**, and **rhythm**.
Onomatopoeia	words whose sound suggests their meaning. Examples: (1) splash, buzz, hiss, boom (2) "The *moan* of doves in immemorial elms; / And *murmuring* of innumerable bees," – Alfred Lord Tennyson.
Alliteration	Alliteration is the repetition of the same consonant sounds in lines of poetry or prose. Examples: (1) "Droning a drowsy syncopated tune,"– Langston Hughes (repetition of "d" sounds). (2) "I like to see it lap the miles, / And lick the valleys up," – Emily Dickinson (repetition of "l" sounds).
Rhyme	when words have the same sounds. Examples: (1) "Tyger! Tyger! burning bright / In the forests of the night" – William Blake (**bright** and **night** rhyme.) (2) "Happy the man who, safe on shore, / Now trims, at home, his evening fire; / Unmov'd, he hears the tempests roar, / That on the tufted groves expire" – Philip Freneau (**shore/roar** and **fire/expire**).
Rhythm	the arrangement of stressed and unstressed syllables into a pattern. While rhythm is almost always found in poetry, quality prose writing also involves regular patterns that appeal to the reader. Read the following example out loud: "Vanishing, swerving, evermore curving again into sight, / Softly the sand beach wavers away to a dim gray looping of light." – Sidney Lanier
Analogy	An analogy is an explanation or description of something unfamiliar or difficult to explain by comparing it with something familiar. **Example:** Similes and Metaphors are forms of analogy.

Literary Elements and Devices

Metaphor   A simile is a direct comparison between two unlike things *without* using the words "like" or "as." Example: The sun is big ball of fire. The moon, a luminescent pearl, nestled in a cushion of stars.

An **extended metaphor** is when an item with several characteristics is compared with another item. The separate characteristics are compared with the characteristics of the second item. In her poem "The Fish," Elizabeth Bishop compares the skin of the fish she catches to old wallpaper. She compares several qualities of the two, including the colors, the patterns, and the general appearance.

Simile   comparison between two things *using* "**like**" or "**as**." Examples: (1) "Sometimes I feel **like** a motherless child" African-American spiritual (2) "My love is **like** a red, red rose" – Robert Burns. (3) Free **as** a bird.

Allusion   Allusion is a reference to a well-known place, literary or art work, famous person, or historical event. Today, these references are often related to current pop culture. In order for an allusion to work, the reader must be familiar with the work or item being referred to.

Many allusions are to Greek and Roman mythology. For example, you may hear the expression "Be careful, the gift may be a *Trojan horse*." This refers to the myth about the Greeks who hid inside a large wooden horse which was delivered to their enemy as a "gift."

Allusions also often refer to the Bible. In Katherine Mansfield's short story "The Apple Tree," the author tells of one summer when "the orchard had it Forbidden Tree. It was an apple tree." The story is about a father who did not want his children to eat from his prized apple tree until the apples were perfectly ripe. But the allusion is to the biblical story of Adam and Eve and the apple tree in the Garden of Eden.

Many allusions also refer to other works of literature. Pixar produced a popular movie called "Finding Nemo," about a father fish finding his son. The name Nemo is an allusion to Captain Nemo, the famous character in the novel *20,000 Leagues Under the Sea*.

Hyperbole   Hyperbole is the use of exaggeration to create an effect. Examples: (1) I was so surprised, you could have knocked me over with a feather. (2) I would rather die than eat brussels sprouts.

Understatement (Meiosis)	Meiosis is the opposite of hyperbole. It is a way of stressing the importance of an issue by minimizing the expression of it. For instance, if you were to describe a particularly chaotic evening you were facing tonight, you might list the 3 tests you have to study for, the soccer practice you have to attend, the projects you have due tomorrow, the band meeting that you are not supposed to miss, and the spanish tape you have to listen to. And then, instead of stating the obvious by saying how busy you are going to be, you would instead understate that fact by saying "I guess I'm not going to be bored tonight." This **understatement** actually gives more impact to the idea that you are going to be extremely busy.
Imagery	Imagery is the use of words or phrases that evoke the sensations of sight, hearing, touch, smell, or taste. For example, Edgar Allan Poe opens "The Fall of the House of Usher" with "During the whole of a dull, dark, and soundless day in the autumn of the year, when the clouds hung oppressively low in the heavens..." Poe's word choices help the reader picture the day and perceive the mood.
Personification	giving human qualities to something not human. For example, (1) "As she sang softly at the evil face of the full moon." – Jean Toomer (2) "The oak trees whispered softly in the night breeze." – John Steinbeck. And Stephen Crane writes an extensive personification of fire in *The Red Badge of Courage*: "The smoke from the fire at times neglected the clay chimney and wreathed into the room, and this flimsy chimney of clay and sticks made endless threats to set ablaze the whole establishment."
Symbol	any object, person, place, or action that has a meaning in itself and that also represents a meaning beyond itself, such as a quality, an attitude, a belief, or a value. For example, a skull and crossbones is often a symbol that warns of poison, and a dove is a symbol of peace. In Nathaniel Hawthorne's short story "The Minister's Black Veil," the black veil symbolizes secret sin.
Pun	A **pun** is a way of using words so that their meaning can be taken in different ways, which makes what is said humorous. William Shakespeare loved using puns. Sometimes he would use the humor of puns even in a tragic situation. One example of this takes place in *Romeo and Juliet,* when Mercutio, about to die of a stab wound says, "Ask for me tomorrow and you shall find me a grave man." The double meaning here is that a grave man is one who is serious, while Mercutio is implying he will be in his grave.

Practice 2:   Figurative Language

Read the following examples of figurative language. Then write on the answer line which type of figurative language each example represents.

1. Grey gorillas gather green grapes. _____

Literary Elements and Devices

2. I'm so hungry I could eat a horse._____
3. The aroma of freshly baked cookies filled the kitchen, making my mouth water. _____
4. Her voice was an angel's song. _____
5. click, hiss, pop, snap _____
6. The stubborn rock refused to be moved. _____
7. bore/snore, head/bed _____
8. We need to hear the sound of laughter_____
9. A dove is a symbol for peace _____

CREATING MOOD

When we discuss **mood** in a text, we mean the feeling a reader experiences while reading the text. To create this feeling, authors must use just the right images and words to cause the reader to feel happy, sad, anxious, or other emotions. Mood supports the plot as well. If unhappy events are part of the plot, the author will normally create a sad mood. If a daughter is seeing her father again for the first time since he went to war, the mood would be a happy one. Following is a list of some of the moods an author can create:

Sample of Moods				
dismal	peaceful	anxious	joyful	elated
melancholic	chaotic	mysterious	creepy	humorous

MOOD AND WORD CHOICE

Many words can imply specific feelings: for example, "bright" or "mournful." An author develops mood in writing through the choice of specific words that convey exactly the feeling the author wants to convey. One of the most famous examples of an author creating a mood for a story with word choice is taken from Thomas Gray's well-known poem "Elegy Written in a Country Churchyard":

The curfew tolls the knell of parting day,
 The lowing herd wind slowly o'er the lea,
  The plowman homeward plods his weary way,
  And leaves the world to darkness and to me.
(1746)

It is easy to see that the passage is full of somber words. Many of the words themselves even have a slow and sad tone to them. Read aloud and listen to the words *tolls, lowing, slowly,* and *homeward.* The mood of this first verse of Gray's poem is slow, depressed, and pensive. The words *plods* and *weary* describe a man walking with fatigue and possibly sadness. And the last line of the verse places the author in a world of isolation and darkness.

Chapter 19

All these solemn words together create an atmosphere of gloom and loneliness. There is nothing optimistic, cheerful, or exciting in the passage. Gray's intent in this passage was to make the reader feel the lonely, weary darkness that surrounds the speaker. He carefully chose the words which would create this feeling in his readers.

The mood of the poem could be changed dramatically with the substitutions of a few words:

> The watchman rings the bell of parting day
> The mooing cows trot swiftly o'er the lea,
> The farmer eagerly strides his homeward way,
> And leaves the world to starlight and to me.

The basic action is similar in the second version, but the reader has a warm and hopeful feeling about the story about to be told. This is due to the use of words that portray life, hope, youth, and promise: "rings," "trot," "swiftly," "homeward," and "strides."

Read the following passages first for content. Then choose the mood which most closely describes the feeling you get from the passage.

Excerpt from "Nurse's Song"
William Blake (1794)

When the voices of children are heard on the green,

And laughing is heard on the hill,

My heart is at rest within my breast

And everything else is still.

1. A. peaceful   B. desolate   C. mysterious   D. haunting

Excerpt from "Wakefully
by Nathaniel Hawthorne (1835)

Whether Faith obeyed he knew not. Hardly had he spoken when he found himself amid calm night and solitude, listening to a roar of the wind which died heavily away through the forest. He staggered against the rock and felt it chill and damp; while a hanging twig, that had been all on fire, besprinkled his cheek with the coldest dew.

2. A. serene   B. joyous   C. uneasy   D. angry

Excerpt from "The Sing-Song of Old Man Kangaroo"
by Rudyard Kipling (1902)

Nqong called Dingo–Yellow-Dog Dingo–always hungry, dusty in the sunshine, and showed him Kangaroo. Nqong said, 'Dingo! Wake up, Dingo! Do you see that gentleman dancing on an ashpit? He wants to be popular and very truly run after. Dingo, make him SO!'

Up jumped Dingo–Yellow-Dog Dingo–and said, 'What, that cat-rabbit?'

313

Literary Elements and Devices

Off ran Dingo–Yellow-Dog Dingo–always hungry, grinning like a coal-scuttle,— ran after Kangaroo.

4. A. light-hearted   B. gloomy   C. sinister   D. disturbing

AUTHOR'S TONE

We use a certain **tone** of voice when we say things. Our tone of voice shows our feelings about what we are talking about. Think of the many ways you can say "We have a double period of PE today." You might say it in a tone of voice that conveys an attitude of anger, excitement, or boredom. A writer must work a tone of voice into a piece of writing, just as we add a tone of voice to what we say. The author does this by the use of punctuation, by the choice of words, and by the way in which the words are used in a passage.

Following is a partial list of tones authors use to add emotions or feelings to their writing.

Examples of Tone				
angry	cold	dramatic	optimistic	sad
anxious	relaxed	fearful	pessimistic	formal
rude	hysterical	flippant	humorous	satirical
merry	expectant	lofty	threatening	serious
frustrated	apologetic	sarcastic	sympathetic	objective
polite	cynical	excited	relieved	biased

In the section on mood, you learned that the use of certain words is important in creating a mood. With tone, the particular choice of words is less important than *how* the writer uses the words. A writer can use the same type of words to convey very different feelings towards a subject.

Read the following two letters and see if you can identify the tone of each author.

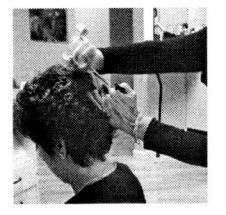

> Dear Customer,
>
> We miss your business! Our records indicate that you have received hair design service from our excellent staff of style artists in the past. But we haven't heard from you lately. Even if you are growing your hair long, we can still serve you with a fine array of hair care and hair coloring products. We now have an expanded staff of highly qualified styling engineers and color artists guaranteed to give you that dazzling look that will turn heads everywhere you go. We hope you have enjoyed our service in the past and look forward to seeing you in our salon soon!
>
> Your friendly *coiffeurs,*
>
> Buzzcut Hair Designs

> To Buzzcut Hair Designs:
>
> You may look forward to nothing more than my continued absence from your place of hair mis-care. I would sooner go to a landscape architect and have my hair cut with a lawn mower than set foot inside your shop again. The last time I graced your salon was just before the fall dance. I had come for some sun-catching highlights and an up-do. Little did I expect to walk out of there with blotches of brass-toned discolorations throughout my hair, which was piled on top of my head and held in place with pink clips and what can only be described as a glue-like substance. I certainly did "turn heads" at the dance, but not for the reasons you would like to think.
>
> Your ex-customer,
> Ms. Mary Smith

The first letter's tone is optimistic and cheerful. The second letter has an angry and somewhat flippant tone. The authors of both letters use formal language to express their ideas. However, the **tone** which each author conveys is very different.

Practice 3: Mood and Tone

A. Based on the list of different types of tone on **page ...** identify the author's tone for the following passages. Then discuss your answers with your class or instructor.

Making School Safe for Everyone

Today, police officers patrol school halls and principals enforce backpack rules to prevent hidden weapons on campus. These measures are taken to make students feel safe at school. But many students—up to 80 percent in middle schools—never feel safe at school. They are students who experience bullying. Bullying can involve physical abuse such as kicking or hitting a classmate. It can also be as simple as laughing at someone because that person dresses differently or eats different food at lunch. Bullying can leave a child with physical scars or with hurt feelings. Either way, it makes the whole school a sadder and more unsafe place for all students.

1. What is the author's tone in this passage?

   A. sarcastic B. objective C. sympathetic D. threatening

Literary Elements and Devices

Excerpt from "The Nightingale and the Rose" by Oscar Wilde

"What a silly thing Love is," said the Student as he walked away. "It is not half as useful as Logic, for it does not prove anything, and it is always telling one of things that are not going to happen, and making one believe things that are not true. In fact, it is quite unpractical, and, as in this age to be practical is everything, I shall go back to Philosophy and study Metaphysics."

So he returned to his room and pulled out a great, dusty book, and began to read.

2. What kind of tone does the author use in this passage?

   A. neutral   B. humorous   C. cynical   D. happy

B. Read the following passages and try to identify the mood of the passages by answering the questions which follow them.

Excerpt from "The Open Boat" Stephen Crane

There was a long, loud swishing astern of the boat, and a gleaming trail of phosphorescence, like blue flame, was furrowed on the black waters. It might have been made by a monstrous knife. Then there came a stillness, while the correspondent breathed with the open mouth and looked at the sea. Suddenly there was another swish and another long flash of bluish light, and this time it was alongside the boat, and might almost have been reached with an oar. The correspondent saw an enormous fin speed like a shadow through the water, hurling the crystalline spray and leaving the long glowing trail.

3. What kind of mood does the author set in this passage?

   A. pessimistic   B. anxious   C. casual   D. happy

Chapter 19

POINT OF VIEW

A story's **point of view**: is the perspective, or outlook, from which a the story is told. There may be a character narrating the story, or there may be an unidentified speaker describing the action and thoughts of all main characters. For example, Mary Shelley writes *Frankenstein* from the first person point of view, but she uses three different narrators to tell their own stories: Dr. Frankenstein, the creator of the monster; the monster himself; and Walton, the last man to speak to both.

THREE TYPES OF POINT OF VIEW

First Person	In the **first person**, a narrator tells the story from the "I" point of view. In *The House On Mango Street*, Esperanza tells her story as the main character. Likewise, in Shiloh, Marty Preston, the main character, narrates the story about himself and a dog.
Second Person	In the **second person**, the speaker is talking to you and uses the pronoun "you." This is not often used on its own, but the second person reference is fairly common in poetry, short essays, and songs. For example, the songs "You Are My Sunshine" and "You've Got a Friend."
Third Person	The speaker tells a story describing characters as "he," "she," or "they" as in *The Pearl* by John Steinbeck.
• **omniscient**	Omniscient means "all-knowing." In the **third person omniscient**, the narrator is capable of knowing, telling, and seeing all that happens to the main characters. In Guy de Maupassant's "The Necklace," the third person speaker describes all the story action, and the inner thoughts of the main characters.
• **limited**	In the **third person limited** point of view, the speaker tells the story knowing only what is seen, heard, and felt by the thoughts and viewpoint of one character, usually the main character. **[Example]**

Deciding what point of view the author is using to tell a story is a first big step in understanding how that story will work. When you determine what the point of view is, you are ahead in understanding how the frame for the story will be set.

The choice of narrator affects the **credibility of a text**. The credibility of a text simply means how believable the story is for the reader. Is the voice true to the character, the place of the story, and the time of the story? If the answer to these questions is yes, then the voice helps the story become believable to the reader. One example of a credible text is Phyllis Reynold's *Shiloh*. Naylor's narrator is a boy whose voice reflects the time and place of the story.

Literary Elements and Devices

A first person narrator who is very honest and clear-sighted, such as Naylor's Marty, may be well trusted in telling a story. This point of view, however, is limited to the narrator's experience and feelings only. The same holds true for the limited third person. For example, in Stephen Crane's *The Red Badge of Courage*, only one character, the young soldier, is understood completely. The third person omniscient is the most knowing position for a narrator. However, does this narrator simply give the facts and details to the reader and let the reader make decisions about the story, or does the narrator state an opinion and expect the reader to agree? A believable narrator will let readers decide what they think about a story. An example of this type of narration is John Steinbeck's novel *Of Mice and Men*.

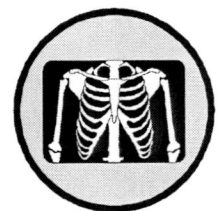

LITERARY STYLE

Literary Style refers to an author's choice and arrangement of words and phrases in a sentence or paragraph. Authors use different types of literary styles to produce a particular effect for a particular audience. Depending on the audience and the effect the author wants to create, a writer may use short sentences and common words, while another may use complex language and long, elaborate sentences.

There are two kinds of literary styles: **informal and formal**. Like wearing a gown or a tuxedo to a prom but jeans to hang out with friends, an author chooses formal or informal style depending on the context, the audience, and the effect he/she wants to produce. Informal style is casual and straightforward, sometimes consisting of slang terms and grammatical inconsistencies, short sentences, and a simple vocabulary. The following excerpt from Mark Twain's *The Adventures of Tom Sawyer* is an example of informal language:

> You don't know about me without you have read a book by the name of The Adventures of Tom Sawyer; but that ain't no matter. That book was made by Mr. Mark Twain, and he told the truth, mainly. There was things which he stretched, but mainly he told the truth. That is nothing. I never seen anybody but lied one time or another, without it was Aunt Polly, or the widow, or maybe Mary. Aunt Polly—Tom's Aunt Polly, she is—and Mary, and the Widow Douglas is all told about in that book, which is mostly a true book, with some stretchers, as I said before.

Twain's style in this excerpt is informal; it contains grammatical errors, slang, and a personal tone. Do not assume, however, that informal style *always* contains grammatical errors. Journalists, for example, often use informal style because it allows them to present information in a concise, brief manner but with little slang, misspellings or grammatical errors. Below is an example of how journalists use informal style in their writing to convey information quickly and correctly.

> Nonprofit organizations directing toy-drives for homeless children reported they are struggling to meet an increase in demand this Christmas. They are calling for both donations and volunteers to fill the growing need.

In this example, informal style allows the writer to cut through the frills or any unnecessary words and relies on the facts without directly appealing to the reader's emotions.

Formal style, on the other hand, may contain frills or unnecessary words, is grammatically correct, consists of a broad and interesting vocabulary, complex sentence structures, and rarely contains slang terms. Formal style gives an author's writing an entirely different feel than informal writing, even if the subject is the same. The example below is based on the same information as the toy drive article above, but it is written in formal style.

> As we lie snug in our warm down beds on a bitter winter's night, benevolent organizations strive to provide those who have no warmth, no shelter from the extremities of nature's elemental whim, a light of hope; a bright and shiny new toy, wrapped in joyful paper and topped with a whimsical bow, for Christmas. Toy drives are a means through which humanitarian societies empower the weak and humble to enjoy the generosity of Christmas; yet, these auspicious labors are being tried by mounting exigencies this year; to satisfy the burgeoning requests, officials are calling for minute yet meaningful acts of charitable assistance.

Below is another example, taken from Jane Austen's *Sense and Sensibility*, which exemplifies formal style.

> Elinor, this eldest daughter whose advice was so effectual, possessed a strength of understanding, and coolness of judgment, which qualified her, though only nineteen, to be the counsellor of her mother, and enabled her frequently to counteract, to the advantage of them all, that eagerness of mind in Mrs. Dashwood which must generally have led to imprudence. She had an excellent heart; her disposition was affectionate, and her feelings were strong: but she knew how to govern them: it was a knowledge which her mother had yet to learn, and which one of her sisters had resolved never to be taught.

Authors often use both formal and informal styles in their work. For example, an author who portrays many characters would include informal and formal styles to give each character a different and unique voice.

Practice 4: Informal and Formal Style

1. Look again at the toy drive examples given in formal and informal style. What differences can you see?

Read the following two passages. Which is formal style and which is informal style?

Passage 1

> Well, I finally made it back! After a long trip to Mexico I really looked forward to coming home. I never knew how much I liked my own bed! Even my annoying sister doesn't bother me. My cat, Fifi, still acts like I've betrayed her though. I think my sister must've annoyed her too!

Passage 2

> After an arduous journey through the exotic and beautiful landscape of Mexico, I've finally returned. The sights and sounds of home have taken on a new and refreshing aspect; almost as if I've arrived to an oddly new yet familiar landscape, a wonderful sense of rediscovering an old home.

2. Explain the key differences between formal and informal style.

Literary Elements and Devices

3. Write a brief letter to a close friend in informal style and then write it in formal style.

SYNTAX

Syntax is the study of the rules that govern how words, phrases, and clauses are combined to construct complete sentences. When you diagram a sentence, identifying the parts of speech, types of clauses or phrases, and the relations between these elements, you are studying the syntax of the sentence. For example, the syntax of the sentence *The captain steered the ship* can be broken down as follows: The subject is *captain*, the verb is *steered*, and *the ship* is the direct object of the verb *steered*.

Syntax varies from language to language. For instance, in the English language, adjectives come before the noun: "The beautiful house." In Spanish, however, adjectives follow the noun they modify: "La casa bonita" or "the house beautiful."

Practice 5: Syntax

1. Define syntax.
2. Diagram the syntax of the sentence *she cooked our lunch.*
3. Describe any syntactical variances from language to language that you may know.

Chapter 19 Review: Literary Elements and Devices

A. Read each excerpt in column A. On the line following each excerpt, write the letter of the word in column B which best describes the kind of literary device it is.

Excerpt	Literary Device
1. "Success is counted sweetest/ By those who ne'er succeed." – Emily Dickinson _____	**a. alliteration**
2. In "The Crisis," Thomas Paine describes King George as "a common murderer, a highwayman, or a housebreaker." _____	**b. hyperbole**
3. "The air was heavy, and cold with dew." – Stephen Crane _____	**c. imagery**
4. (allusion)	**d. onomatopoeia**
5. "All the world's a stage, / And all the men and women merely players." –Shakespeare _____	**e. metaphor**
6. "At last he heard from along the road at the foot of the hill the clatter of a horse's galloping hoofs." – Stephen Crane (sound device) _____	**f. rhythm**
7. "Love's stricken 'Why' is all that love can speak." _____	**g. simile**
8. Happy as a lark. _____	**h. allusion**
9. "But soft! What light through yonder window breaks?" – Shakespeare (sound device) _____	
10. "A mass of wet grass, marched upon, rustled like silk." – Stephen Crane _____	

B. Read the following passage. Then, answer the questions about literary devices that follow it. The passage takes place during the American Civil War, as a young soldier waits with his regiment for the enemy to appear.

Excerpt from The Red Badge of Courage
by Stephen Crane

There were moments of waiting. The youth thought of the village street at home before the arrival of the circus parade on a day in the spring. He remembered how he had stood, a small, thrillful boy, prepared to follow the dingy lady upon the white horse, or the band in its faded chariot. He saw the yellow road, the lines of expectant people, and the sober houses. He particularly remembered an old fellow who used to sit upon a cracker box in front of the store and feign to despise such exhibitions. A thousand details of color and form surged in his mind. The old fellow upon the cracker box appeared in middle prominence.

Some one cried, "Here they come!"

There was rustling and muttering among the men. They displayed a feverish desire to have every possible cartridge ready to their hands. The boxes were pulled around into various positions, and adjusted with great care. It was as if seven hundred new bonnets were being tried on.

The tall soldier, having prepared his rifle, produced a red handkerchief of some kind. He was engaged in knotting it about his throat with exquisite attention to its position, when the cry was repeated up and down the line in a muffled roar of sound.

"Here they come! Here they come!" Gun locks clicked.

1. What is the flashback in the story?
2. Where does the flashback bring the reader and the character?
3. How does the flashback compare with the present moment of the story?

C. Read the following poem and answer the questions about literary devices.

There is no Frigate like a Book

1 There is no Frigate like a Book
2 To take us Lands away
3 Nor any Coursers like a Page
4 Of prancing Poetry–
5 This Traverse may the poorest take
6 Without oppress of Toll–
7 How frugal is the Chariot
8 That bears the Human soul.

– Emily Dickinson

4. Which of the following lines from the poem contain a *simile*?
   A. line 1   B. line 4   C. line 6   D. line 8
5. Which of the following lines contains an example of a *metaphor*?
   A. lines 1–2   B. lines 3–4   C. lines 5–6   D. lines 7–8
6. Which of the following lines from the poem contain *alliteration*?
   A. lines 1–2   B. lines 3–4   C. lines 5–6   D. lines 7–8
7. Write down the words that *rhyme* in this poem.

8. Describe what the *metaphor* from question 7 is comparing.

9. **Short Answer.** Use your own paper to write your response.

   Explain what is being said about books in this poem and how the figurative language helps say it.

Chapter 20
Comparing and Contrasting

Louisiana Reading GLEs addressed in this chapter include:	
ELA-6-M1	Comparing/contrasting and responding to United States and world literature that represents the experiences and traditions of diverse ethnic groups (1, 4, 5)

Comparing and **contrasting** is the process of looking for similarities and differences between two or more objects, characters, or ideas. On the LEAP 8 Test, you may be required to read a literary passage. Then you may be asked to answer questions about similarities and differences between characters, events, settings, etc. You may also be asked to write responses in which you compare and contrast ideas, characters, or situations in a reading passage.

In this chapter, you will learn about comparing and contrasting as a reading as well as a writing skill. You will also practice answering questions about comparing and contrasting.

INTRODUCTION TO COMPARING AND CONTRASTING

One of the most important aspects of comparing and contrasting is to look for similarities or differences within the same category. A familiar way to express this idea is to make sure you are comparing "apples to apples" and "oranges to oranges" but not "apples to oranges." For example, consider the following sentence:

> This candy is tangy and sweet, but that candy is green.

This statement compares flavor and color which are two unrelated categories. We may be able to conclude that the writer likes sweet candy and does not like green candy, but we can't adequately compare the two candies because we don't know the color of the sweet candy, and we don't know the flavor of the green candy. Therefore, when comparing or contrasting two things or ideas, stay in the same category.

Comparing and Contrasting

COMPARING AND CONTRASTING IN A READING PASSAGE

Sometimes, finding similarities and differences that are described in a reading passage can be difficult. Two strategies that can help you with comparing and contrasting are the following:

1. Looking for signal words
2. Creating an H-map

As you review a reading passage in order to answer questions about comparing and contrasting, you can look for **signal words** that point to a similarity or a difference in the selection. Studying the following list of signal words will help you find similarities and differences in reading passages.

Signal Words for Similarities and Differences			
Similarities		**Differences**	
again	too	although	not as / not like
also	as well as	but	on the contrary
both	just as ... so too	contrary to	on the other hand
likewise	the same	despite	neither
once more		different from	regardless
similarly		even though	still
similar to		however	though
in the same way		in contrast	yet
like		in opposition	unlike
as		in spite of	whereas
in a related way		instead	while
parallel		nevertheless	conversely

Read the following passage which compares the United States (US) and the Union of Soviet Socialist Republics (USSR) regarding their involvement in World War II and the Cold War. As you read, notice the bolded signal words that point to similarities or differences.

Neither the United States nor the USSR had wanted to enter World War II. **Both** had been forced to enter the fighting because of sneak attacks. The Soviets were caught off guard when Hitler broke his non-aggression treaty and invaded the Soviet Union on June 22, 1941. **Similarly**, the United States suffered a surprise attack when the Japanese struck the US naval base at Pearl Harbor on December 7, 1941. From that time on, the two countries were allies in fighting the Axis powers of Germany, Italy, and Japan.

Both countries, **however**, had very different ideological systems. The United States had long prided itself as a strong democracy with an emphasis on free enterprise. **In contrast**, the Soviet Union was **still** under the strict one-party rule of the Communists, who exercised strict government control over the economy. The United States contributed vast amounts of hardware and technical superiority to the war effort **but** relatively few soldiers. **On the other hand**, the Soviets provided very little technical development **but** millions of soldiers. The Soviets lost over 20 million lives in the war, **while** 290,000 US soldiers were killed in World War II.

After the defeat of their common enemy, the US and the USSR battled over their ideological differences. The United States pushed for free elections and open markets, **while** the Soviets wanted "friendly" Communist governments installed in formerly occupied territories. During this conflict called the Cold War, **both** countries tried to use economic and political means to exert influence in different parts of the world. **Likewise**, **both** countries tried to gain superiority in the development of nuclear weapons.

After using signal words to identify similarities and differences, you can clarify your findings by **creating an H-map**. An H-map is a simple diagram shaped like the letter H. In the bridge of the H, you list the similarities, and in each column of the H, you list the differences. Make sure you label each column with the key concept you are comparing and contrasting.

Below is an example of a completed H-map based on the reading passage on the previous page. It shows the similarities and differences between the US and the USSR during World War II and the Cold War.

Differences US	Cold War Similarities	Differences USSR
• attacked Japan • democracy • free enterprise • contributed hardware and technical superiority • relatively few soldiers killed: 290,000 • in Cold War, pushed for free elections and open markets in many countries	• didn't want to enter WWII • forced into fighting by sneak attacks • allies against the Axis powers • used political and economic means to exert influence in other countries during Cold War • competed in nuclear arms race	• attacked by Germany • strict one-party Communist rule • government controlled economy • few technical contributions to war • contributed millions of soldiers' lives: 20 million lives lost • wanted friendly Communist governments installed in former territories

Practice 1: Comparing and Contrasting in a Passage

Read the following passage. Underline the signal words that indicate similarities or differences. Then create an H-map which highlights the similarities and differences between French and English colonization of North America.

The main interest of 17th century French colonizers in North America was trade in animal furs. Some furs were used for hats that were very popular in France at the time. The Native Americans were valuable trading partners to the French, supplying animal pelts from beaver, otter, muskrat, and mink. Consequently, the French saw no need to try to conquer them. Likewise, the French did not destroy the forests because they wanted to maintain the habitat of the animals they valued so much. Because the northern areas of North America, where the French colonized, were sparsely populated, epidemics took less of a toll. Similarly, the French tended to see native peoples as equals, and they accepted intermarriage. The Native Americans were also valuable to the French as allies in wars against the British.

In contrast, the English colonies may be called "colonies of settlement" where settlers tried to establish English society in the New World. They took control of the land and brought their own political and economic systems, as well as crops and animals. The English came to the New World in much greater numbers than the French, and they wanted control of more and more land, thus displacing great numbers of Native Americans. The Native Americans were not as beneficial economically to the English as to the French, so the English saw them, instead, as an obstacle to progress and a nuisance.

COMPARING AND CONTRASTING LANGUAGE AND TONE

On the SC HSAP Test, you may be asked to compare and contrast the language and tone used in two different reading passages. **Language** refers to the words a writer uses. **Tone** is the way the writer uses those words to convey a certain attitude or feeling to the reader. Language (what is said) and tone (how it is said) are often determined by the **author's purpose** and the intended **audience**—the person(s) who will read a text. For example, the way you ask someone for a favor is very different from the way you tell someone to leave you alone. Also, the language and tone you use with your friends in the school cafeteria probably would not be appropriate in the principal's office.

To see how language and tone can differ, read and compare the letter below with the e-mail that follows.

4-17-04

Sally H. Jones
621 Oak Ridge Rd.
Charleston, SC 29402

Dear Sir:

Because of my great love for animals, I am very interested in working at Purrfect Pets. I visit your store frequently as I purchase food and supplies to care for my several cats and dogs. I am always impressed by the cleanliness of your store and the care you show the animals.

During the school year I will need to work part time, but I will be available to work on nights and weekends as needed. Once school is out for the summer, I will be available to work full-time.

Please find enclosed my application and a list of references. I look forward to hearing from you soon.

Sincerely,

Sally H. Jones

Sally H. Jones

Hey Jack,

 What's up?! I'm really psyched about workin' at the CD Emporium with you. I mean I don't have the job yet, but why wouldn't they hire me? By the way, when you're at work this afternoon, can you pick up a job application for me? Thanks! You're the best!

 Does your sister still want to work at that stupid pet store? That would gross me out! Cleaning out all those cages with all the animal stuff in it. No thanks! Give me some cellophane-wrapped CDs any day. Catch you later. Thanks again.

T.J.

Did you notice the similarities and differences between the two letters? Both writers are seeking jobs. They also want to work where they enjoy what they are doing. The authors share a similar purpose, but their audiences are different.

Sally is writing to the owner of the pet shop where she wants to work. She has chosen the language of a business letter to address her potential employer. She avoids dialect and slang terms, and her tone is formal and respectful. The language and tone of T.J.'s e-mail, however, is very different because he is writing to a good friend and is asking a favor. Along with an informal tone, he uses slang terms and abbreviations that Jack will understand easily. Assuming that Jack will recognize T. J.'s style of language, T.J. uses neither his full name nor a salutation such as "sincerely" or "your friend."

Comparing and Contrasting

The type of language and tone used in a text greatly affects how the reader will interpret it. Be aware of the language and tone you use in writing and in speaking. Also, study the following types and examples of language and tone to help improve your reading and writing.

	Different Types of Language
Informal	**Slang** is very informal language that enjoys a brief popularity and then generally becomes obsolete. It is often confined to a limited group of people. Examples: crib, dis, psych, yo' mama, word, peace, my bad, cool, dude, etc.
	Colloquial English refers to words that are appropriate in dialogue and informal writing but inappropriate in formal writing. Contractions, short words, and clichés may be used. Examples: You bet I'll be there! He's in so deep there's no way out! The apple never falls far from the tree.
	Nonstandardized English contains grammar and usage that do not follow the standard rules for English. The pronouns or verbs are nonstandard.
Formal	**Standardized American English** is the English that is most widely accepted in the United States. It is the language of educated people. The grammar used in Standardized English becomes the model for all to follow.

Examples of Nonstandardized and Standardized English	
Nonstandardized	**Standardized**
He **done** all the work by **hisself**.	He **did** all the work by **himself**.
I **ain't got no** money.	I **don't have any** money.
You and **me talks** all the time.	You and **I talk** all the time.

Different Types of Tone				
angry	depressed	dramatic	optimistic	sad
anxious	lackadaisical	fearful	pessimistic	tragic
boring	hysterical	happy	formal	disgusting
calm	expectant	lofty	pensive	informal

Chapter 20

Examples of Informal and Formal Tone	
Informal	Formal
I'm so psyched!	I'm very happy.
How much are you gonna sell that car for?	I wanted to inquire about the car for sale.
Ain't no way I'm gonna work for you.	I regret to say that I must decline your offer of employment.

Practice 2: Language and Tone

You are running as a representative for your class on the student council. You want to write a short announcement to your friends and to the school faculty that explains why you are running for this office. How would your language and tone differ for these two audiences? Explain your answer. Then, write a short announcement for each audience.

COMPARING AND CONTRASTING AUTHOR'S WORD CHOICE AND SYNTAX WITHIN A TEXT AND IN TWO OR MORE TEXTS

WORD CHOICE

Word choice is one of the tools that an author uses when writing. By choosing words carefully, writers can build meaning into their work that goes beyond the actual words. In Chapter 2 you read about connotations and denotations of words. By carefully choosing an exact word, a writer can imply ideas or emotions to the reader. For example, if a writer is describing a character and wants the reader to have a positive feeling about the character, careful word choices can accomplish that goal.

Let's compare these two descriptions of characters: "Shirley was very slender and attractive, and she looked as if she had dressed quickly and casually without regard to the latest fashion dictations from New York." and "Ethel was very skinny but attractive; however, she looked as though she had thrown on any old thing in her closet without regard to any fashion sense whatsoever."

The first description implies Shirley is attractive and fashionable in her own way without seeming to care about the latest styles. She is someone to whom style comes naturally without any effort. The second one seems very similar on the surface, but if you read carefully, it gives a very different impression of the character. Ethel is also of a thin build; however, the author says Ethel is thin "but" attractive instead of "and" attractive. The word "but" implies that the two qualities don't usually go together. Shirley has dressed "quickly and casually" which implies with speed and disregard for formality, but doesn't say that she paid no attention to what she was putting on. Ethel has also apparently dressed in haste, but the phrase "thrown

Comparing and Contrasting

on any old thing in her closet" implies a greater haste and no conscious or subconscious planning at all. Shirley disregards the "latest fashion dictations from New York," but the reader has the sense that she has her own sort of style. Ethel apparently has no inborn sense of style, and she doesn't pay attention "whatsoever" to any recommendations about style. Even the conjunctions between the independent clauses of each sentence contribute to the sense of the two girls being opposites: Shirley is "attractive; and she looked. . . ," while Ethel is "attractive; however, she looked. . .." In Shirley's case, "and" implies the rest of the sentence is an extension of being attractive; but in Ethel's case, she was "attractive" but the conjunction "however" sets up the rest of the sentence to be in opposition to "attractive."

By looking carefully at an author's word choices, you can get clues about the author's attitude toward a topic or character. Comparing and contrasting an author's word choices and treatment of various aspects of a work should give you insights into the author's intentions.

SYNTAX

Syntax is the grammatical structure and pattern of sentences. In English, there is usually more than one grammatically correct way to communicate a thought. In some cases, one choice will be preferable for a particular reason; in other cases, the choices may be equal. Syntax is another of the tools that writers can use to focus attention on various parts of a text. By varying the focus of sentences, writers can call the reader's attention to certain parts of the writing.

If you have watched a Star Wars movie in which the character Yoda appears, you have probably noticed the odd way he speaks. His sentences are understood and are, for the most part, grammatically correct, but "odd they sound" compared to the syntax used by most speakers of English!

Writers tend to have a particular style of syntax. Even within a single piece of writing, they may purposely vary their syntax to suit different purposes. By noticing a writer's syntax and noticing shifts in the syntax, a reader can gain additional clues about the writing. In a work of fiction, a writer will have different characters speak differently. A character's speech style would include word choices, syntax, and degree of formality. By manipulating those elements, the writer indirectly tells the reader about the character.

In order to compare and contrast syntax, you have to look at the syntax in each section or piece of writing, try to determine the author's intentions in each case, and then make your comparisons and contrasts based on your findings.

Practice 3: Author's Word Choice and Syntax

A. Read the following pairs of sentences. Compare the word choices that have been made in each sentence. Explain how the word choices impact the meaning of the sentences.

1. It was a slow drive to the backwoods resort where we were supposed to stay.

   It was a leisurely drive to the country resort where we planned to stay.

2. My younger brother assured me that he had our parents' permission to go to the park.

   My little brother claimed he had an OK from our parents to go to the park.

3. I was truly embarrassed when I stumbled and dropped my entire lunch tray onto the floor.

   I was mortified when I stumbled and dumped my entire lunch tray onto the floor.

4. Days later, I got used to the dead silence of the farm at night.

   After a day or two, I became accustomed to the peace and quiet of the farm at night.

5. It may be a surprise, but I will be agreeable if my friends want to go and see *The Lord of the Rings* again.

   Believe it or not, I'll deal with it if my buds want to go see *The Lord of the Rings* again.

B. Rewrite the following sentences by changing the syntax to emphasize the part of the sentence that is bolded. The first one is done as an example.

1. Although he was my neighbor for 10 years, **I never really knew Mike**.
   I never really knew Mike although he was my neighbor for 10 years.

2. The dogs, **the ones that barked all night long**, live across the street from my Grandma.

3. I watched the national news on TV while **I did my homework**.

4. Today's weather forecast is for thunderstorms, so **practice is cancelled**.

5. **Very carefully watching the traffic**, Kayla crossed the busy street

COMPARING AND CONTRASTING UNIVERSAL THEMES WITHIN AND BETWEEN TEXTS

When analyzing and discussing (or writing) about literature, often you will need to compare and/or contrast the universal themes in a single piece of literature or in more than one piece of literature. Certainly the first thing to examine is the universal theme or themes present in each individual piece of literature. If you are discussing a single piece of literature, you need to consider each character and how that character is related to the plot and theme. How do the characters relate to each other? Sometimes, within a single piece of literature, one character may represent or be involved in one particular theme, while another character represents a different theme. By considering these questions, you will then have the points of discussion that will be your basis for comparison and contrast.

If you are comparing more than one piece of literature, there are additional questions to explore. What is the genre of each piece of literature? How might the form and characteristics of the genre affect the writer's treatment of the theme? What are the similarities and differences in the way the characters in each piece are related to the theme? Answering some or all of the preceding questions should provide you with material for comparison and contrast.

COMPARING CONTRASTING CONFLICT IN TWO OR MORE TEXTS

Sometimes you may be asked to discuss the conflicts in two or more pieces of literature or texts. The pieces may have many similarities, or they may be very different. In order to have some points to compare and contrast, you will want to look carefully at the conflicts in each text. Consider the types of conflict,

Comparing and Contrasting

internal or external, and the details about each conflict. Which characters are involved? To what extent does the conflict impact and affect the plot of the story? Once you have determined the facts about the conflict in each text, consider how the qualities of the various texts are related to each other.

Practice 4: Comparing and Contrasting Universal Themes and Conflict

Think about some of your favorite short stories, fairy or folk tales, movies, and novels. Choose at least three works and create a chart like the one illustrated below. One title has been filled in as an example.

	The Wizard of Oz	(Title of Work)	(Title of Work)
Universal theme and Main conflict	longing to go home man vs. man, Dorothy vs. Wicked Witch and others		
Work with same universal theme	*The Odyssey*		
Main conflict in above work	primarily man vs. man, Odysseus against various people he meets on his journey		
Additional works that are related by similar theme and/or conflict	*E.T.* (longing to go home)		

COMPARING AND CONTRASTING CHARACTERS IN FICTION

Writers can develop characters in several different ways, including **description**, **dialogue**, **action**, and **relationships with other characters**. A skilled fiction writer creates interest by developing strong characters with distinct personalities. A simple example is A. A. Milne's children's stories involving Winnie the Pooh. In each story, Pooh is usually optimistic, Piglet anxious, Rabbit self-centered, and Eeyore tragically pessimistic. Regardless of the situation presented, each character acts and reacts in a way that reveals his unique personality.

Sometimes authors use characters to represent or symbolize larger themes. For example, in the *Lord of the Rings* movies, Gandalf the White dresses in white, and through his words and actions, he represents honor, truth, and goodness. On the other hand, the nine Ringwraiths are cloaked in black and they are enslaved to carry out evil purposes–they are the incarnation of evil. The conflict between these characters in the story symbolizes the larger theme of the conflict between good and evil.

A classic example of contrasting characters is found in the story of "The Tortoise and the Hare." Though you are probably familiar with it, read the story carefully, noting similarities and differences between the two main characters.

The Tortoise and the Hare

Once upon a time, in a great forest, there lived a hare and a tortoise. Tortoise was slow in everything he did. Sometimes he ate his breakfast so slowly that it was almost lunch time before he had finished. He kept his house clean and neat, but he did it at his own pace, very slowly.

Hare, on the other hand, was quick as a wink in all that he did. He got up early in the morning, finished his breakfast, and went for a brisk walk in the forest before Tortoise had even gotten out of bed. Hare could not imagine how Tortoise could stand to be so slow all the time.

Hare was sure that he was the smartest, fastest, most handsome animal in the whole forest. And he never failed to tell his friends how splendid he was. "I think I look especially fine today," he would say to himself as he stood in front of his mirror.

Tortoise never bragged about himself. He knew that he was not particularly handsome and that he was very slow, but he did not mind. He was happy to spend his time working hard, painting his beautiful pictures at his very slow pace.

One day Tortoise was sitting beside the stream painting a picture of the pretty wildflowers on its bank. Hare came up and said, "You are such a slowpoke, Tortoise. You've been working on this same picture all week!"

"I'm not so very slow," protested Tortoise.

"Silly fellow," said Hare. "You're so slow that I could beat you at anything you can name. Just name something, and I'll win."

"All right," said Tortoise. "How about a race?"

What an idea! Hare laughed and laughed at the thought of running a race with Tortoise! Hare laughed so hard he thought he would explode.

On the day of the big race, all the animals in the forest gathered to watch. Tortoise and Hare stepped up to the starting line. Tortoise looked nervous when he saw all the animals. Hare smiled and waved to the crowd. He could hardly wait to show Tortoise a thing or two about running a race. Fox looked at both runners. He shouted, "Get ready. Get set. Go!"

The race was on! Hare dashed across the starting line. In a blink of an eye, he disappeared over the first hill. "Oh dear," said Squirrel to herself. "There goes Hare, out of sight already. Poor Tortoise hasn't even started!" Sure enough, Tortoise was just beginning to climb the steep path—very slowly.

Hare ran and ran until he was sure he would win. "This isn't even a race," he said to himself. "I think I'll lie down and rest a bit. Then I'll finish and still have plenty of time

Comparing and Contrasting

to spare. There's no way that slowpoke will ever catch up with me!" So Hare lay down under a shady tree and soon fell fast asleep.

Suddenly, Hare awoke with a start. He could hear cheering. He jumped up and started running as fast as his long legs would carry him. But when he saw the finish line of the race, he could not believe his eyes. Tortoise was about to win the race. Hare could not believe it. Tortoise was crossing the finish line!

The crowd cheered and cheered. They ran to the finish line to congratulate Tortoise. The wise Owl blinked his eyes and said what all the other animals were thinking. "Slow and steady wins the race!"

To compare the two characters, you may develop an H-map similar to the one below.

Differences Tortoise	Similarities	Differences Hare
• slow • humble • works hard • walks steadily • never gives up on race • wins race	• they are animals • they live in a forest • they have other animal friends • they run in race	• fast • boastful • works little • runs quickly • sleeps during race • loses race

In the story of "The Tortoise and the Hare," the author contrasts the two main characters, so the differences and similarities between them are relatively simple. On the SC HSAP Test, you may find more complex stories and characters. In this case, consider the aspects of character, listed below, to help you make your comparisons and contrasts.

Character Aspects		
gender	family situation	personality traits
age	physical appearance	thoughts and feelings
occupation	style of dress	role in the story (protagonist, etc.)
goals	way of speaking	relationship to other characters

Practice 5: Comparing and Contrasting Characters

A. The Tortoise and the Hare

Based on the H-map of the tortoise and the hare, write a one paragraph response to the following question: Which character appeals to you the most—the tortoise or the hare? Include 3-4 reasons for your response.

B. Character Experiment

Read Nathaniel Hawthorne's short story "Dr. Heidegger's Experiment." The characters all face a similar experience but react to it in different ways. Choose two characters, develop an H-map, and write a paragraph comparing and contrasting them. Share your paragraph in a small group with other students or with your teacher.

C. Other Stories

Review a novel or short story that you have read recently, and create an H-map comparing and contrasting two of the characters from the story. Possible choices may include Mark Twain's *Adventures of Huckleberry Finn*, John Steinbeck's *The Pearl* or *Of Mice and Men*, S. E. Hinton's *The Outsiders*, Harper Lee's *To Kill a Mockingbird*, Edgar Allan Poe's "The Cask of Amontillado," or Bret Harte's "The Outcasts of Poker Flat."

D. Business Card Design

Design a business card for two or more characters based on stories you have read. Each card should reflect the unique personality of each character. Ask for feedback on your cards from other students or from your instructor. See the sample business card below.

Sample business card for the Tin Man from **The Wizard of Oz**.

Friend of Oz, Inc.

♥ - Felt Help for Anyone in Need

Tin Man
Healer of Heartaches

Free Advice:
Squirts of oil
greatly appreciated

Toll Free 1-wiz-ard-ofoz
153 Yellow Brick Road
Land of Oz 12345

Chapter 20 Review: Comparing and Contrasting

Read the following two reports. Then, write constructed responses for the questions below.

Report 1

The County Government meeting broke up after a long debate. Bill Smith's supporters claim that he is the duly elected representative of the people and should be allowed to take his seat on the council. His opponents disputed this, saying that his previous protests of council activities disqualifies him from holding public office.

Report 2

We elected Bill Smith, and he's our man. His enemies are just jealous. They think they can throw some mud around and make it stick to Bill. No way! He's squeaky clean. There ain't nothin' they can do to make him look bad. He stood up for us before, makin' sure the council listened to us. Now those jokers say that's a bad thing. Stick by Bill. He stuck by us!

1. Compare and contrast the language and tone of these two reports.
2. From what type of literature do you think each report comes? Why?

Read the following scene from a 1906 story by O. Henry. Then, write constructed responses for the questions that follow.

Excerpt from "The Coming-Out of Maggie"

This scene from the story takes place at a private dance held by the "Give and Take" Athletic Association. Two young men are about to fight over Maggie.

Some fine instinct that Rome must have bequeathed to us caused nearly every one to turn and look at them—there was a subtle feeling that two gladiators had met in the arena. Two or three Give and Takes with tight coat sleeves drew nearer.

"One moment, Mr. O'Sullivan," said Dempsey. "I hope you're enjoying yourself. Where did you say you lived?"

The two gladiators were well matched. Dempsey had, perhaps, ten pounds of weight to give away. The O'Sullivan had breadth with quickness. Dempsey had a glacial eye, a dominating slit of a mouth, an indestructible jaw, a complexion like a belle's, and the coolness of a champion. The visitor showed more fire in his contempt and less control over his conspicuous sneer. They were enemies by the law written when the rocks were molten. They were each too splendid, too mighty, too incomparable to divide preeminence. One only must survive.

"I live on Grand," said O'Sullivan, insolently; "and no trouble to find me at home. Where do you live?" Dempsey ignored the question.

"You say your name's O'Sullivan," he went on. "Well, 'Big Mike' says he never saw you before."

"Lots of things he never saw," said the favourite of the hop.

"As a rule," went on Dempsey, huskily sweet, "O'Sullivans in this district know one another. You escorted one of our lady members here, and we want a chance to make good. If you've got a family tree let's see a few historical O'Sullivan buds come out on it. Or do you want us to dig it out of you by the roots?"

3. Create an H-map showing the similarities and differences between the two men.
4. Rewrite the scene so that O'Sullivan and Dempsey are two women fighting over a man named Mike.
5. Predict what will happen in the next scene of O. Henry's story, and then write the scene. Then find a collection of O. Henry's stories. Compare your scene with the actual next scene from "The Coming-Out of Maggie."

Read the following interview. Then, write constructed responses for the questions that follow.

Dating in Different Countries

American teen-age girls must find their own husbands, and no one else can do it for them.

This concept is very difficult for teenagers in India to understand as you can tell from the following interview with two Indian teen-age girls.

"Don't you want to be able to choose your own husbands?" I asked.

"No! Never!" the girls answered vehemently. Nisha, a very beautiful girl with wide, almond-shaped eyes went on to say, "I don't want to worry about whether I'll get married or not. I know I'll get married. I know my parents are a better judge of character than I am. I am too young to make such a decision. When my parents choose someone for me, I know it will be someone that will be able to support me, and someone that my family already likes and respects.

"What if I lived in America and I chose a boy my family didn't like? Before it was over, everyone might be against me. There might be bad feelings at home with my parents because of my choice, and if I argued with my husband, who would support me?"

It was Rasheed's turn. "It seems the American system would be very humiliating for me. I would have to spend a lot more time making myself beautiful and attractive and try to figure out ways to get boys to notice me. And if the boy I liked didn't notice me, maybe I would feel like a failure as a person. I would have to compete with other girls to be the prettiest—it seems so demeaning and stressful. And what if I were shy? Would I get married?"

"Possibly not," I answered honestly.

Comparing and Contrasting

Nisha asked the hardest question, "In America, does the girl get to choose? Isn't it the boy who chooses anyway?" A good question.

6. Compare and contrast how women and men choose a husband or wife for marriage in the United States and in India, based on the "Coming-Out of Maggie" story and the "Dating in Different Countries" article.

7. What are the strengths and weaknesses of each approach to finding a marriage partner?

8. Which do you think is the better way to choose a marriage partner? Why?

Chapter 21
Writing About Literature

LOUISIANA READING BENCHMARKS ADDRESSED IN THIS CHAPTER INCLUDE:	
ELA-1-M3	Reading, comprehending, and responding to written, spoken, and visual texts in extended passages (e.g., ranging from 500–1,000 words (1, 3, 4)

Sometimes, you will asked to write about literature. In this section, you can prepare to write such responses for classroom work, or standardized tests, by learning more about writing a response to literature. You may choose your own literature selection, or you may be assigned what to read. Your first step for an effective response to literature is to read the selection carefully. Be sure to **identify different literary devices** the author is using such as **simile, description, irony, characterization, personification, and conflict** as well as the author's **tone, point of view,** and **theme.**

You may be asked to write an **essay response to literature** for class or for exams. Like the other types of writing in this book, an essay response to literature requires practice so that you can become proficient and confident in writing this kind of composition. Although this type of writing may be challenging, you can prepare yourself for that possibility by learning more about writing a response to literature.

Sample Topics

Here are some sample questions that would require you to write a response to literature:

Describe a piece of literature you have read. Explain why you liked or disliked it. Use specific examples from this work of literature

What character in literature, TV, or movies most resembles you and why?

Books, movies, and television can offer opportunities to learn valuable lessons. Write about a lesson you learned from a book, movie, or television show that proved to be of value to you.

Writing About Literature

FORMS OF LITERATURE

To write a response to any of the above sample topics, you would need to decide on a **piece of literature, a TV show, or a movie** that you like. In addition, you would need to remember enough about what you read or saw to develop a satisfactory response to the topic.

Example:

> **HINT:** One way to prepare yourself to write a response to literature is to jot down, before the deadline, the titles of a favorite story, poem, novel, TV show, and movie. Then brainstorm about the characters, events, or details relating to these types of entertainment. Before starting your essay test, review and memorize the titles and as much of your brainstorming as you can to write an effective essay about literature.

WRITING AN ESSAY ABOUT A POEM

Robert heard from his teacher that his class would be writing as essay response to literature next week. To prepare the class for this assignment, Robert's teacher, Ms. Angeli, required her students to write an essay on the following topic:

Choose a favorite piece of literature. Explain what it means to you in your life.

Robert's favorite piece of literature is a poem by Emily Dickinson. Prior to the assignment, he read this poem several times:

> This world is not conclusion;
>   A sequel stands beyond,
> Invisible, as music,
>   But positive, as sound.
> It beckons and it baffles;
>   Philosophies don't know,
> And through a riddle, at the last,
>   Sagacity must go.
> To guess it puzzles scholars;
>   To gain it men have shown
> Contempt of generations,
>   And crucifixion known.
>
> Emily Dickinson (1830–1886)

Ms. Angeli then told her students to brainstorm and jot down details and thoughts about the piece of literature. Here is what Robert wrote about the poem:

Chapter 21

This writer says there is life after we die, our life on earth continuing into the next life. It's like music. We can't see eternity. It's very real like the sound of music. People talk about the life after death. It's really a mystery, hard to explain. Some people live like there is nothing beyond this life. Others would rather die, than give up their belief in eternal life.

I can relate to this poem. My friend, Todd, died in a car accident. It really affected me. He was one of my best friends in school. I really miss him. We all do. I believe he's not really dead. He's moved on to a better life in the beyond. Todd and I went to the same church, we were in youth group together. He had strong faith and stood up for his beliefs in eternal life. So I feel better, knowing that Todd isn't gone, he's in God's house now.

After her class took notes on their favorite piece of literature, Ms Angeli gave them time to review what they had written. Then she directed them to discard their notes and respond to the topic in a 400-500 word essay. Based on the topic, here is what Robert wrote about the Emily Dickinson poem:

My friend, Todd, died in a terrible car accident two months ago. Witnesses said he hit a guard rail and then rolled over several times before hitting the side of a mountain. He was dead before the rescue team got to him. This news devastated me because Todd and I grew up together and went to the same school and church. He was one of my best friends, and I miss him. I was very depressed, and even thought about death a lot. My counselor helped me and told me to read a poem by Emily Dickinson called "This world is not conclusion." This poem has become my favorite piece of literature because it helped me deal with the loss of my friend, Todd.

One of the reasons I like this poem is because the poet says in the title that "This world is not conclusion." Todd and I were in the same church and youth group together. Sometimes we would talk about death, and he would say, "Robert, God promises eternal life. We don't have to worry. Just love God and your neighbor." When I read this poem, I hear Todd telling me not to lose hope. There is a life after death.

Another reason I like this poem is because, without faith, philosophers are always trying to figure out how there is a life after death. Such a belief doesn't make sense knowing what happens to the body after we die. How can you prove we live forever? The answer is that our knowledge is not enough. God promises eternal life if we trust and believe in the resurrection of the body. This poem expresses this belief and helps me accept Todd's death better.

Finally, the poet mentions that sometimes people have to die because of what they believe. This may sound strange. In the United States, we are free to say and practice what we believe. However, not everyone has had this freedom. Some people would rather die than give up their beliefs in God and a life after death. Christ, for example, was crucified for what he believed. I could also imagine Todd dying for his faith. He would never give up his beliefs. So I feel better knowing that Todd died with a strong faith in God and life eternal.

I'm glad my counselor recommended that I read "This world is not conclusion" by Emily Dickinson. This poem helped me recover from the loss of my friend, Todd. The thoughts and beliefs expressed in this poem pulled me out of my depression. Now I can move on with my life.

Writing About Literature

After reading Robert's response to what this poem meant to her, Ms. Angeli wrote the following comments about Robert's essay:

> *Robert, you would definitely receive a passing grade on this essay. You respond clearly to the topic, and you explain in detail why this poem helped you recover from the loss of your friend. You include examples and reasons that support your main point. You also organize and connect your sentences effectively. In addition, your grammar, usage, and spelling are very good.*

WRITING AN ESSAY ABOUT A STORY

Carefully read and study the literary selection below based on the folk story, "The Crane's Reward." Then, <u>read</u> both the SAMPLE task and the SAMPLE written response that follows.

The Crane's Reward

Before the humans came and frightened away many of the animals, the lion was the king of Kisii. Sometimes the elephant thought that an elephant should be the king of Kisii, but then the lion would roar about what a tasty king the elephant would be. The elephant would agree quickly that lions were better at being king.

A great and fearsome lion went out hunting. It was not long before he caught and killed a zebra that was big enough for his lionesses and cubs to eat their fill, with plenty left over for himself. When he and his family were eating, a small bone got caught in the great lion's throat. He could barely squeak to his lionesses that a bone was caught in his throat.

One lioness tried to get the bone out with her paw, but she could not get her great paw far enough into the lion's mouth. The cubs could get to his throat with their little paws, but they were too clumsy to get the bone out. The lionesses tried to ask other animals to help, but they were all afraid of being eaten and ran away.

Soon the lion saw a crane sitting on a high branch watching him. "Crane," squeaked the lion. "Help your king. Your neck is long and thin and so is your beak. You can take this bone from my throat."

The crane was in no hurry. "Why would I do that? One bite and the bone and I will both be in your stomach."

"I shall reward you," said the lion. "I do not want you both stuck in my throat. Then who would help me?"

The greedy crane could not resist the promise of a reward. He flew down to the lion and ordered, "Open your mouth as wide as you can." With the lionesses and cubs watching, the lion opened his mouth widely. The crane stuck its bill down the lion's throat until

342

its whole head and part of its neck were in the lion's mouth. The bone was easily plucked out and dropped at the lion's feet.

"I'll have that reward now," said the crane.

"You already have it," said the lion. "Now you can tell the other animals that you gave an order to your king, and he obeyed. You can boast that you put your head into a lion's mouth and lived to tell of it."

The crane started to argue, but even the mighty elephant knew better than to argue with a group of lions. Amid the roars all around him, he stretched his wings and flew away to tell his story, as far from any lions as possible.

–Courtesy of the **Afro-American Almanac**

MODEL WRITING TASK: <u>**READ ONLY**</u>

> Writing Task
>
> In the folk story "The Crane's Reward," the author is teaching a life lesson or theme through the actions of the crafty lion and the greedy crane.
>
> Write an essay in which you discuss how the author communicates this theme. Include examples of the author's use of plot, character, and personification to convey this theme. Explain how the writer's use of literary devices adds meaning to the story and illustrates the lesson or theme.

SAMPLE Essay Response to a Literary Selection:

In the folk story, "The Crane's Reward," the author is able to teach a lesson or theme on how personal vices such as greed can be used against a greedy person. Those who are wise learn how to use these vices to their advantage. He uses two animals of Africa, the lion and the crane, to illustrate this life lesson. The characters of the folktale seem all the more relatable through the author's use of actions, character development, and personification.

The lion is described in the story as king of Kisii. He is the most powerful animal in the area, and all other animals are afraid of him. The lion even intimidates the mighty elephant. However, the lion soon finds himself in a vulnerable position when he gets a bone stuck in his throat. He is choking badly, and none of his family can get the bone out. The lion calls out to the animals to help, but they are too afraid of being eaten, all of them, except the crane.

The crane in this story is the only animal who has a beak long enough to pull the bone out of the lion's throat. He is also frightened about being eaten by the lion, but when the lion promises him a reward, he cannot resist. After taking out the bone, the crane immediately demands, "I'll have my reward now," exposing his true reason for helping the lion. The lion's crafty response about giving the lion orders, entering his mouth, and living to tell about it as a reward stumps the crane, and he flies away without the reward he was expecting.

Writing About Literature

This folktale draws on the personification of animals to make the characters' personalities more exaggerated. People keenly understand the power of the lion and the wisdom the lion possesses. The crane, on the other hand, is always flying around looking for an opportunity to score a quick meal. The storyteller draws on this personal knowledge to portray the lion as smart and the crane as greedy. At the same time, the folktale is an allegory describing a lesson for all humanity—a lesson of the folly of greed.

Notice that this student states the life lesson or theme in the first paragraph of the essay. Each of the other paragraphs explains how the actions and personalities of the lion and the crane convey the story's theme. This student also writes clearly and accurately about the story with minimal errors in grammar and usage.

Practice 1: Writing About Literature

Make a list of your favorite story, poem, novel, TV show, and movie. Review Robert's brainstorming and notes on his favorite poem. Then brainstorm and jot down details and thoughts about each of your favorites. Choose one of these favorite works of literature, and write a 400–500 word essay on why it is your favorite piece of literature. Use Robert's essay as a model.

Practice 2: Writing About Literature

Nick's favorite movie is The Wizard of Oz. He jotted down thoughts and details about the movie. Then he was going to review his notes as much as he could in preparation for writing a response about a lesson he learned from a movie.

Now review Nick's notes. What suggestions would you make to help him improve his notes about this topic?

Then write your own notes about The Wizard of Oz. or another favorite movie where you learned a lesson. Share your notes in a group or with your instructor so you can get some feedback on your work. Then, on your own, or in a group, write an essay and explain the lesson or theme the movie taught you. Use examples from the movie to support your views.

I like the Wizard of Oz. It's a grate movie, lots of action. This girl gets cute in a hurricane. Then her house blows away and she's in it. Her dog goes too and they wind up in Oz., a colorful land. She meets a scary crow and a tin man and a lion man. They have many adventures, dance and sing, and a which scars them sometimes. Then they meet the mean old wizard. He's a fake and afraid. The girl cries to go home so afairee wich wavs her wond and the girl end up back home with a big hedach but happy to be home.

I like this movie. Lots of ecsitmint. Lots of laffs, a whole lot of fun. See it agin And agin. I lerned a lot about the land of Oz and how to live a happy life.

Practice 3: Writing About Literature

Read and analyze one of the following poems. Brainstorm about it, make notes, and review them carefully. Put aside your notes, then write a 400–500 word response to this poem explaining how it relates to your own life. Use Robert's essay about his friend, Todd, as a guide.

The Sick Rose

O Rose, thou art sick!
The invisible worm
That flies in the night,
In the howling storm,

Has found out thy bed
Of crimson joy:
And his dark secret love
Does thy life destroy

–William Blake (1757–1827)

Loss and Gain

When I compare
What I have lost with what I have gained,
What I have missed with what attained,
Little room do I find for pride.

I am aware
How many days have been idly spent;
How like an arrow the good intent
Has fallen short or been turned aside.

But who shall dare
To measure loss and gain in this wise?
Defeat may be victory in disguise;
The lowest ebb is the turn of the tide.

–Henry Wadsworth Longfellow (1807–1882)

CHAPTER 21 REVIEW

1. To improve your ability to write about literature, read the following poem by George M. Horton. Horton was born a slave in North Carolina and went on to become a well-known black poet of the nineteenth century.

The Fearful Traveller in the Haunted Castle

George Moses Horton (1798?–1880)

Often do I hear those windows open
And shut with dread surprise,
And spirits murmur as they grope,
But break not on the eyes.

Still fancy spies the winding sheet,
The phantom and the shroud,
And bids the pulse of horror beat
Throughout my ears aloud.

Some unknown finger thumps the door,

From one of faltering voice,
Till some one seems to walk the floor
with an alarming noise.

The drum of horror holds her sound,
Which will not let me sleep,
When ghastly breezes float around,
And hidden goblins creep.

Methinks I hear some constant groan,
The din of all the dead,
While trembling thus I lie alone,
Upon this restless bed.

At length the blaze of morning broke
On my impatient view,
And truth or fancy told the joke,
And bade the night adieu.

'Twas but the noise of prowling rats,
Which ran with all their speed,
Pursued in haste by hungry cats,
Which on the vermin feed.

The cat growl'd as she held her prey,
Which shriek'd with all its might,
And drove the balm of sleep away
Throughout the live-long night.

Those creatures crumbling off the cheese
Which on the table lay;
Some cats, too quick the rogues to seize,
With rumbling lost their prey.

Thus man is often his own elf,
Who makes the night his ghost,
And shrinks with horror from himself,
Which is to fear the most

– Courtesy Academic Affairs Library

University of North Carolina

Chapel Hill

> **Writing Task**
>
> In the poem "The Fearful Traveller in the Haunted Castle," the author uses a personal experience to convey a theme or lesson about life.
>
> Write a 400–500 word essay about the theme or lesson in this poem. Use examples and images from the poem to explain the theme.

2. Locate the following short stories in your literature book, in the library, or on the Internet:

    Richard Connell's "The Most Dangerous Game"
    Bret Harte's "The Outcasts of Poker Flat"
    D.H. Lawrence's "The Rocking Horse Winner"
    O'Henry's "The Gift of the Magi"

> **Writing Task**
>
> Read 2–3 of these stories. Then write a 400-500 word essay about one of them. Explain why you liked or disliked this story. Support your viewpoint with examples from the story.

LEAP 21 Grade 8 Language Arts Post Test 1

The purpose of this practice test is to check on your progress in English language arts after reviewing the material in this book. The items and selections in this practice test are based on Louisiana standards for English Language Arts. Competency in these standards is required for promotion to ninth grade.

GENERAL DIRECTIONS

- Read all directions carefully.
- Read each question or example. Then choose the best answer.
- Choose only one answer for each question. If you change an answer, be sure to erase the answer completely.
- At the end of the test, you or your instructor should score your test. Then determine whether or not you are prepared to be tested on the real LEAP 21 Grade 8 in English Language Arts.

SESSION 1 — WRITING

On the real test, you will have extra pages for your prewriting and your rough draft. You will also have an answer document with two pages labeled for the final draft. In the real test, write your final draft only in the answer document.

For this practice test, however, you will use your own paper for each step. First you may take a few minutes to brainstorm or create an outline. Then write a rough draft. Be sure and label each page, identifying the steps. Then, write your final draft on two pages.

Post Test 1

WRITING TOPIC

Read the topic in the box below. Write a well-organized composition of at least 150–200 words. Be sure to follow the suggestions listed under the box.

> Your local school board is considering requiring all students to wear uniforms. You have decided to write a letter to your school board explaining how this change would affect you and your friends.
>
> **Write about why you support or oppose school uniforms.**
>
> Before you begin to write, think about the advantages and disadvantages of school uniforms. You can be in support of the change or against the change. How would wearing a required school uniform affect you?
>
> Now write a **multi-paragraph** letter to the school board **explaining** your viewpoint on school uniforms.

- Give specific details and explain why you think the way you do so that your readers will understand what you mean.
- Remember that your audience is the local school board; use appropriate language and explain your ideas clearly.
- Be sure to write clearly and to check your composition for correct spelling, punctuation, and grammar.

NOTE: On the real test, your teacher will read instructions to you and will hand out the answer documents. You will also be told that for this session, and this session only, you will be allowed to use a dictionary and a thesaurus.

Session 2—Reading and Responding

In this section of the test, you will read three passages and a poem. Then you will answer questions about what you read. This part of the test contains both multiple-choice and constructed-response questions. Answer these questions on the lines provided.

Many people are familiar with the general history of the United States but don't always know the history of a specific place. Read this article about this history of the island of Galveston. Then answer questions 1 through 8.

Galveston

1   The island of Galveston has a long and colorful history. Galveston is a barrier island off the coast of Texas in the Gulf of Mexico. Its history is chaptered with shipwrecks, buccaneers, outlaws, cannibals, and explorers. Some of the remarkable characters that have shaped the history of Galveston include the Karankawa Indians, the Spanish explorer Alvar Nunez Cabeza de Vaca, and the swashbuckling pirate, Jean Lafitte.

2   In the 1400s and 1500s, the island was inhabited by natives known as the Karankawa Indians. In Texas, the Karankawa are known for being cannibals. This label, however, is sometimes misunderstood. The Karankawa were a tribe of hunters and fishers. They lived in the coastal area of Texas between Galveston and Corpus Christi. They fished in the shallow waters along the coast and used long-bows to hunt. The long-bows were as long as the Indians were tall. And the Karankawa were a tall people: many were over six feet tall.

3   It is true that the Karankawa were known to practice cannibalism, but it was not for food. It was for superstitious reasons. The Indians believed it was a way of gaining power over enemies. A few eyewitness records of the Karankawa still exist. One account, by Alice Oliver, describes the Indians as a tolerant people who taught her some of their language when she was a child in the 1830s.

4   The Karankawa may have gotten their fierce reputation from the Europeans. These Europeans often tried to kidnap Indians and sell them as slaves. In those days, the slave trade was a large part of the world economy. In their travels as part of this economy, Europeans spread diseases which killed thousands of Indians. They also fought the Indians for their lands. For these reasons, the Karankawa, like many natives, were unfriendly towards Europeans.

5   One European landed on the island of the Karankawa without a slave ship or any other form of threat to the natives. His name was Alvar Nunez Cabeza de Vaca. He came to the island as a starving survivor of a shipwreck. De Vaca was a famous Spanish explorer. He had sailed from Spain and was out to claim territory for his king and his country. While he was in the Gulf of Mexico in 1528, a hurricane washed him onto the shores of Galveston Island.

6   The Karankawa Indians were generally friendly to de Vaca. He lived among them for four years. De Vaca learned about the Indians' way of life. He was able to understand them and communicate with them.

7   In 1532, de Vaca left Galveston Island and traveled across Texas in search of his fellow countrymen. He found some of them, but the meeting was a shock for his fellow Spaniards. After four years with the Indians, de Vaca looked more like an Indian than a Spaniard. De Vaca wrote of this meeting that the Spaniards he met "just stood staring for a long time."

8   De Vaca was a writer. In his day, many explorers of the "New World" kept written records of their travels. De Vaca's writings were important for two reasons. First, even today they give us a close-up look at the land and people of North America in the 1500s. The second reason is even more unique to de Vaca. At the time when de Vaca was exploring, European nations were trying to claim as much of the world as they could. Any native people that they met in their quest were considered to be obstacles. These natives were most often conquered, murdered, or enslaved. De Vaca, however, had come to know the natives as people. He was appalled by the way Europeans treated the natives. He wanted to let people know about these injustices.

9   When de Vaca returned to Spain in 1537, he wrote in graphic detail of the abuses that Europeans were inflicting upon the native people of the New World. His written accounts

of cruelty, torture, and murder make a shocking story. They enlightened many Europeans who then called for a better policy towards the natives. Alvar Nunez Cabeza de Vaca was one of America's first human rights champions.

10   About 300 years after de Vaca left Galveston, the island was adopted by another colorful personality. In 1817, the "gentleman pirate," Jean Lafitte, came out of no certain origin and arrived on the island. He hoped to set up a base of operation in the Gulf and continue his work of smuggling illegal cargo.

11   At the time, Texas was fighting for independence from Spain. Jean Lafitte did not become involved in the war. He considered himself a businessman, not a soldier. His shipmates were mostly criminals, and his business often involved illegal activity; but Lafitte's manner was, for the most part, refined. Many people found the handsome "privateer" intriguing. Lafitte set up a small village on the island. There were huts for his pirate friends, places of business, and a red mansion for himself. There was a lot of pirated wealth in the village and many parties as well.

12   The island people welcomed Lafitte because of the money, but they were uneasy about his friends. On a fall night in 1820, a U.S. government ship threatened Lafitte with death if he did not leave the island. The next morning, the village was in ashes, and Lafitte and his band had vanished. There is no record of what happened to Lafitte after that time, but he probably did not retire as a boot maker somewhere. Chances are that he joined the many nameless high seas buccaneers of the 1800s.

13   History still recalls the name of Jean Lafitte, as well as de Vaca and the Karankawa Indians as some of the more captivating chapters in the story of Texas. Today, Galveston's people and cultures are as diverse as ever. This "port of entry" for many immigrants to the United States continues to be a source of stories, legends, and vibrant history.

For questions 1 and 2, choose the correct answer.

Read this sentence from the article.

One account, by Alice Oliver, describes the Indians as a tolerant people who taught her some of their language when she was a child in the 1830s.

1. In this sentence, tolerant is closest in meaning to
    A. accepting of different views.
    B. able to withstand environmental challenges.
    C. not affected by a drug.
    D. financially generous.

2. The author included paragraph 9 in this selection because it helps the reader understand
    A. when de Vaca returned to Spain.
    B. what type of person de Vaca was.
    C. how de Vaca viewed the native people.
    D. why de Vaca's writing was important.

LEAP 21 Grade 8 Language Arts

Write your answer to question 3 on the lines provided below.

3. Write a short summary of paragraphs 11 and 12 of this selection.

_____

_____

_____

For questions 4 and 5, choose the correct answer.

4. From the information about the Karankawa provided in this selection, the reader can conclude that

   E. they were hostile toward newcomers.
   F. they were distrustful of the Europeans.
   G. they were involved in illegal activities.
   H. they were unable to communicate with others.

5. Which feature of the selection most strongly indicates that it is a work of nonfiction?

   A. It tells a story.
   B. It is told in third person.
   C. It includes factual details.
   D. It is divided into paragraphs.

Write your answer to question 6 on the lines provided below.

6. How does the history of the Karankawa Indians reflect the history of the other conquered ethnic groups? Give a detail from the passage to support your answer.

_____

_____

_____

For questions 7 and 8, darken the circle beside the correct answer.

7. Which statement from the selection is an opinion?

   A. Galveston is a barrier island off the coast of Texas in the Gulf of Mexico.
   B. The Karankawa may have gotten their fierce reputation from the Europeans.
   C. About 300 years after de Vaca left Galveston, the island was adopted by another colorful personality.
   D. In 1532, de Vaca left Galveston Island and traveled across Texas in search of his fellow countrymen.

Post Test 1

8. One way the characters in this article are different from those in many legends is that

    A. their exploits are exaggerated
    B. they led extraordinary lives
    C. they had exciting adventures
    D. they are based on historical fact

Read this story about a girl's holiday experience. Then, answer questions 9 through 16.

Family Time

1 The steam from the bread pan scorched Selena's face as she took it from the oven. She wiped her face with an apron after carefully setting the bread down. The day would not go well with her if she dropped the bread. Selena's mother had already scolded her for ruining a batch of cookies. It had been her fault, but how could she not go chasing after the late autumn butterfly? It would have brought her such luck to catch it today. She knew that butterflies are a symbol of this holiday season, the Days of the Dead. That is because caterpillars wrap themselves up as if dead. Then, they come to life again in bright new colors and in new butterfly bodies, able to fly. Selena had not moved fast enough and could only watch as this butterfly disappeared into the trees. Suddenly, she had remembered the cookies.

2 "A busy day like this needs to be broken up a little," her mother had said kindly after seeing the regret on Selena's face. Selena had not meant to let the cookies burn or crack. "But let's spare the food from breaking and burning. It's hard enough to keep the babies from taking bites out of all the loaves!"

3 Such words from her mother made Selena feel more of a part of getting ready for her favorite celebration. Most of the kids at school didn't understand how a celebration called the Days of the Dead, *Los Dias De Los Muertos*, could be joyful and fun.

4 "Well," Selena thought to herself as she buried a toy skeleton into the next loaf of bread she would bake, "for us this is just the best time of the year."

5 Selena wished that her grandparents lived closer. The drive to the countryside, where her great-grandparents had settled after arriving from Mexico and where her grandparents still kept house, seemed so far away. It was really hard to ride for hours smelling the *pan de muerto*, the special bread of this celebration of the dead, without being able to take a nibble. Selena also fretted at the lure of cookies and chocolates shaped as skulls, coffins, and skeletons which were wrapped so well that she couldn't sneak one out along the way to the cemetery. Besides the enticing aroma from the sweets, there were miniature silver bells and religious ornaments decorating the baskets full of food, teasing her hunger. They made jingling come-to-supper sounds. Once her family reached the cemetery though, everyone would be feasting and storytelling and cleaning the graves. Selena and her family would also place bouquets of fresh yellow marigolds, golden chrysanthemums, and favorite foods of the departed at the headstones.

6 Selena knew people who thought the idea of picnicking at a graveyard was disrespectful. She had explained to them it was done to include the members of the family who had passed on. It was a celebration of the people in final stage of this life, the dead, and a celebration of the people beginning a new stage of this life, the children. The chil-

dren would continue to gather in the memory of the ones who had lived before them until it was time for them to join the departed. This celebration would mark the eternal circle of the family. Some families in cities, however, had to create an altar, an *ofrenda*, in their homes. The families would decorate their altars, placing foods and flowers on them for the celebration. Selena was glad that her family could gather together out underneath the pale November sky.

7   As her parents pulled into the cemetery parking lot, Selena heard her name being called. She saw seven of her cousins racing over. They grabbed her by the arms and pulled her to the far side of the gates with them. They wanted her to see the *calacas* (skeleton doll) collection they had made. As she was the eldest cousin, she would judge each of the handmade dolls for her cousins. Selena couldn't decide which was the cleverest: was it the skeleton bride holding flowers, the skeleton cowboy holding a lariat, or the skeleton poet holding a book? As she thought about it, her cousins handed her one last *calacas* to add to the group.

8   "This is the cleverest *calacas* ever!" Selena announced with a merry smile lighting her eyes. She gently held up the doll, a small skeleton child holding a tiny butterfly net with a bright orange butterfly nestled inside.

For questions 9 through 12, darken the circle next to the correct answer.

9. In paragraph 8, Selena's choice of the cleverest *calaca* reflects

   A. her favoritism of one cousin over the others.
   B. her knowledge of skeletons and butterflies.
   C. her wish to have caught a butterfly that day.
   D. her preference for butterflies over moths.

10. Why is paragraph 6 important in this selection?

    A. It introduces the setting of the story.
    B. It provides background information.
    C. It reveals clues to how the story will end.
    D. It shows the traits of the main character.

11. From the information in paragraphs 2 and 3 of this selection, Selena's mother can best be described as

    A. forgiving.   B. difficult.   C. angry.   D. embarrassed.

12. Which sentence in the selection best supports the idea that the celebration of the Days of the Dead is an important event?

    A. This celebration would mark the eternal circle of the family.
    B. Some families in cities, however, had to create an altar in their homes.
    C. It was a celebration of the people in final stage of this life, the dead…
    D. Selena was glad that her family could gather together out underneath the pale November sky.

Post Test 1

Write your answers to questions 13 and 14 on the lines provided below.

13. Is this story told in third person limited or omniscient point of view? Identify one way you can tell.   1-M2

    _____

    _____

14. What ceremony or tradition does your family have and how could you teach others about it?   1-M4

    _____

    _____

For questions 15 and 16, choose the correct answer.

15. Which feature of the selection most strongly indicates that it is a work of fiction?   6-M3

    A. symbolic elements
    B. facts about the Days of the Dead
    C. expressed opinions
    D. plot, setting, characters, and dialog

16. In the future, what could Selena do to make sure the cookies don't burn?   7-M2

    A. She could tell her mother to watch them if she needs to leave the kitchen
    B. She could put skeleton toys in them.
    C. She could bake them at her grandmother's house.
    D. She could be quicker about catching the butterfly.

The following poem by Paul Laurence Dunbar is about someone who owes a debt. Read the poem below. Then answer questions 17 through 22.

The Debt

This is the debt I pay
Just for one riotous day,
Years of regret and grief,
Sorrow without relief.

Pay it I will to the end—
Until the grave, my friend,
Gives me a true release—
Gives me the clasp of peace.

Slight was the thing I bought,
Small was the debt I thought,
Poor was the loan at best—
God! but the interest!

—Paul Laurence Dunbar

Write your answer to question 17 on the lines provided below.

17. What universal theme does this poem express? Use an example from the poem to support your answer.

    6-M1

    _____

    _____

For questions 18 through 20, choose the correct answer.

18. What does "until the grave, my friend/Gives me a true release" in the second stanza of the poem mean?

    1-M3

    A. until he buries his debt
    C. until death sets him free
    B. until the person he owes has died
    D. until he has paid his debt off

19. What is the poet's tone in the poem and why did he choose it?

    7-M3

    A. The tone is optimistic to show that the speaker has a bright future ahead.
    B. The tone is humorous to highlight the funny quality of the speaker's situation.
    C. The tone is ironic to emphasize the quirks of fate the speaker has experienced.
    D. The tone is neutral to illustrate that there is little or no emotion in this poem.

20. Which of the following events is most likely not the cause of the poet's debt?

    7-M4

    A. falling in love
    C. buying something he couldn't afford
    B. studying for exams
    D. attending a party

Write your answer to question 21 on the lines provided below.

21. If you had some kind of debt to pay, who could you go to for help or advice? Name one resource you have and explain why it would be helpful in this kind of situation.

    7-M2

    _____

    _____

    _____

For question 22, choose the correct answer.

22. The speaker regrets his debt, just as Selena in "Family Time" regrets

    1-M4

    A. burning the cookies.
    C. losing the butterfly.
    B. chasing the butterfly.
    D. the long drive to the cemetery.

Though the wreck of the *Titanic* is probably the most well-known shipwreck, the fate of a ship called the *Portland* has also piqued people's interest. Read this article called "The Wreck of the *Portland*." Then answer questions 23 through 28.

The Wreck of the *Portland*

1   It has been called "New England's Titanic." The wreck of the great luxury steamship, the *Portland* was New England's greatest maritime disaster. In the years since it sank, it also became one of the world's most sought-after wreckages. Historians and surviving relatives of victims wondered where and how it had gone down, and how it might have been prevented.

During the summer of 2002, divers discovered the 104-year-old shipwreck. It was found 460 feet underwater, about 20 miles north of Cape Cod, Massachusetts. With the discovery of the sunken hulk came hope for answers to some of the questions surrounding this historic tragedy.

It was Saturday evening of Thanksgiving weekend in 1898. The waters of Massachusetts Bay were calm. The *Portland* was to launch at 7:00 p.m. from Boston Harbor. It would travel a short, 90-mile run to Portland, Maine. Before setting sail, the ship's captain, Hollis Blanchard, visited the offices of the Weather Bureau in Boston. Like any experienced captain, he wanted to be sure that weather conditions were safe for the voyage.

In the weather offices Captain Blanchard learned two important facts. The first fact gave him something to be concerned about. It warned him that a huge, cold weather system was traveling out of the west towards Boston from the Great Lakes in New York State. The second fact caused him little anxiety. A warm weather system was heading up the Atlantic coast. Captain Blanchard and the Weather Bureau took little notice of this second fact. They could not predict the havoc that would be caused when the two weather systems met.

Captain Blanchard thought about his options. Should he stay in port and wait out the cold weather front coming from New York? Or should he set out on the calm waters of the bay and reach his destination before the weather front ever reached Boston? Blanchard was a 30-year veteran of the sea. He was also knowledgeable in the new science of meteorology. He studied weather scientifically, something not all captains did at that time. Captain Blanchard was courageous and skilled. He also had a reputation as a storm-runner. He made his decision: the ship would sail. He was sure he would make landfall ahead of the storm. He was mistaken.

2   The *Portland* battled a raging blizzard that night. The tempest, now know as the Portland Storm, was something rarely seen and long remembered by the mariners and coastal people of New England. Winds reached almost 90 knots. Snow and wind halted train and ferry service from Maine to New York. The storm killed over 400 people. It tore up harbors. It damaged at least 350 vessels. The *Portland* was the most well-known of these vessels. In fact, it was the loss of the *Portland* that gave the storm its name.

3   Captain Blanchard handled the storm as well as any captain could. The *Portland* was not built to weather storms at sea. She was built to run rivers. She was wide, shallow, and top-heavy. The bell resting atop the ship weighed over 500 pounds alone. Yet, in spite of these challenges, Captain Blanchard managed to turn the ship around in the storm without

it capsizing. He tried to elude the storm, but it was too swift and powerful. At about 9:30 on Sunday morning, November 27, 1898, Blanchard lost the struggle. The ship went down, and all aboard went with it. There were 192 passengers and crew aboard. Only 38 bodies were ever recovered.

4   The wreck of the *Portland* was especially tragic for the African-American communities of New England. An unknown number of African-Americans rode as passengers on the ship. In addition, one-tenth of Boston's African-American population worked as part of the ship's crew.

5   Blame for the wreck has been tossed about. Some still blame the captain. Captain Blanchard was known for taking risks. After visiting the Weather Bureau, he had judged that he could outrun the Great Lakes weather front. The Weather Bureau was also blamed. The Weather Bureau apparently was not very concerned with the Great Lakes weather front and barely mentioned the Atlantic weather front. Records indicate that the front racing up the Atlantic coast was only "indicated," not predicted. So, little threat was seen in that approaching front.

6   The ship's owner, the Portland Steamship Company did not escape blame, either. The company was in chaos due to deaths and retirements. All the men in positions of responsibility in the company had been in their jobs for only a few weeks. They were therefore not well experienced. During the time when Captain Blanchard was deciding whether to sail or not, the company manager could not be contacted. He was attending a funeral, along with other company employees. Therefore, Captain Blanchard was left to make his own choices. It was the combination of all these circumstances that added up to the tragic event.

7   Video footage of the wreck of the *Portland*, taken during the summer of 2002, shows the wreck sitting upright on the ocean floor. Its hull is still intact, but much of its structure is gone. The video shows features that positively identify the wreck as the *Portland*. These features include the paddle guard, rudder assembly, and the paddle wheel hub. The overall length of the steamship also matches that of the *Portland*. Scientists discovered that the deck of the ship was ripped off. They surmise that this was probably caused by a great wave that hit just before the ship sank.

8   The wreck is located within sanctuary waters of the National Oceanic and Atmospheric Administration. The NOAA provides protection for the shipwreck. Sanctuary regulations forbid any moving, removing or injuring of any submerged cultural or historical resources. These historical resources include objects and pieces from shipwrecks. With this protection, the *Portland* can be researched. Perhaps some questions will finally be answered about that tragic night over a century ago.

For questions 23 and 24, choose the correct answer

23. The passage says that "He was also knowledgeable in the new science of meteorology." What does <u>meteorology</u> mean?

    A. fear of the weather
    B. time of the weather
    C. relating to the weather
    D. study of the weather

Post Test 1

24. What can the reader conclude from the information in paragraphs 9 and 10? 7-M1
   A. Captain Blanchard was an irresponsible person.
   B. The Weather Bureau had incompetent employees.
   C. Many factors contributed to the wreck of the *Portland*.
   D. The ship's owner was unconcerned about the *Portland*.

Write your answer to question 25 on the lines provided below.

25. What is the author's <u>main</u> purpose in this selection and why is it effective or ineffective? 7-M3

_____

_____

_____

For questions 26 and 27, choose the correct answer.

26. Which sentence in the selection best supports the idea that the *Portland* was doomed? 7-M1
   A. The *Portland* was built to run rivers.
   B. The *Portland* was wide, shallow, and top-heavy.
   C. The *Portland* battled a raging blizzard that night.
   D. The *Portland* was not built to weather storms at sea.

27. The author presents the information in this selection by 7-M3
   A. effectively summarizing several theories.
   B. relating events as they occurred.
   C. using facts to make a strong comparison.
   D. giving examples to illustrate an idea.

Write your answer to question 28 on the lines provided below.

28. Identify one way in which the narrator of Dunbar's poem "The Debt" is similar to Captain Blanchard and one way the two characters are different. 6-M2

_____

_____

_____

360

ESSAY

29. Both the Karankawa in "Galveston" and Selena and her family in "Family Time" have unique traditions. Compare and contrast how outsiders misinterpret or misrepresent the traditions of these characters. Use at least one detail from each passage to support your discussion

Session 3— Using Information Resources

Introduction: In this section of the test, you are asked to look at some reference materials and then use the materials to answer the questions on page .

Topic:

Suppose you want to write a report about how the French and English contributed to what Canada is like today. You will need to learn about Canada's history, as well as what Canada is like now. Three different sources of information about Canada are included in this section of the test. The information sources and the page numbers where you can find them are listed below.

1. Brochure

   VIA Rail Tour (page)

2. Excerpts from a Book, *Canada Today*

   A. Copyright Page (page)

   B. Table of Contents (page)

   C. Graphs (pages)

3. Article from a Magazine

   "The Canadian Constitution" (page)

Post Test 1

> Model bibliographic entries for different types of references are on page 20. These show acceptable formats for entries.

Directions: Skim pages 14 through 20 to become familiar with the information contained in these sources. Remember that these are reference sources, so you should not read every word in each source. Once you have skimmed these sources, answer the questions on pages 20–23. Use the information sources to help you answer the questions. As you work through the questions, go back and read the parts that will give you the information that you need.

1. Brochure

VIA Rail Tour

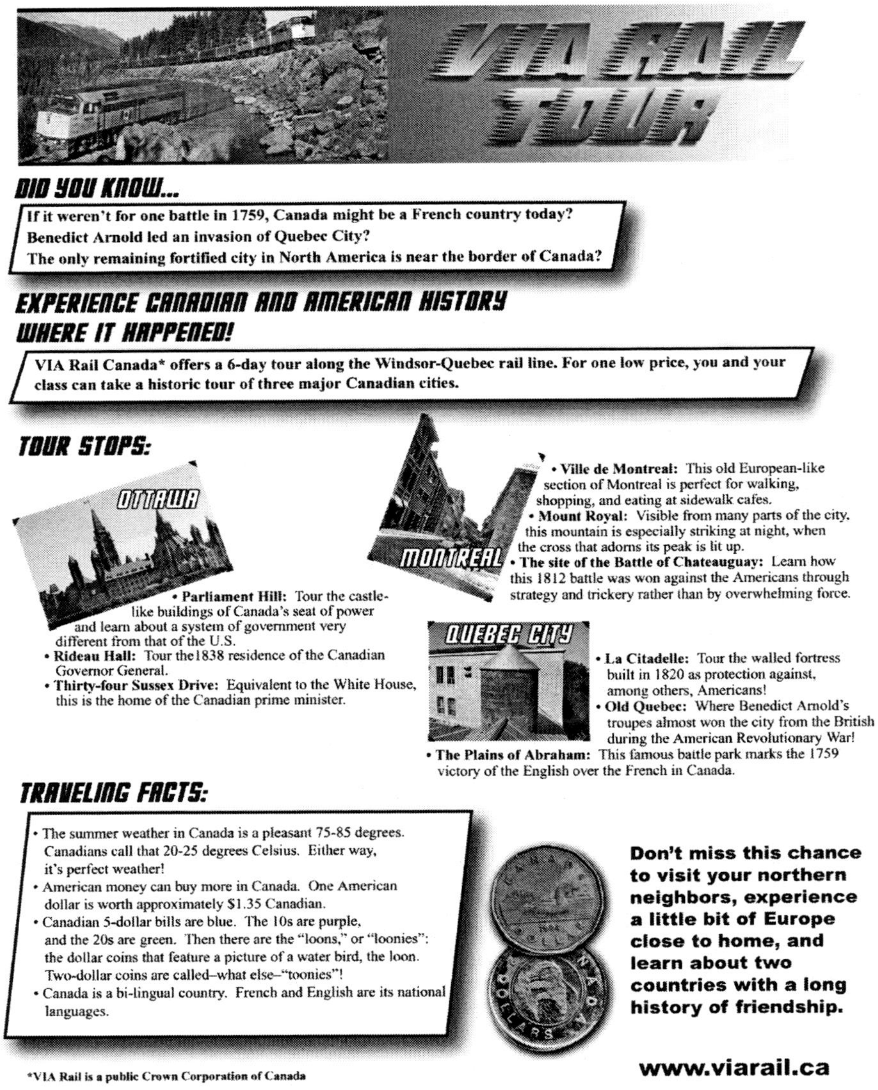

VIA RAIL TOUR

DID YOU KNOW...
- If it weren't for one battle in 1759, Canada might be a French country today?
- Benedict Arnold led an invasion of Quebec City?
- The only remaining fortified city in North America is near the border of Canada?

EXPERIENCE CANADIAN AND AMERICAN HISTORY WHERE IT HAPPENED!

VIA Rail Canada* offers a 6-day tour along the Windsor-Quebec rail line. For one low price, you and your class can take a historic tour of three major Canadian cities.

TOUR STOPS:

OTTAWA
- **Parliament Hill:** Tour the castle-like buildings of Canada's seat of power and learn about a system of government very different from that of the U.S.
- **Rideau Hall:** Tour the 1838 residence of the Canadian Governor General.
- **Thirty-four Sussex Drive:** Equivalent to the White House, this is the home of the Canadian prime minister.

MONTREAL
- **Ville de Montreal:** This old European-like section of Montreal is perfect for walking, shopping, and eating at sidewalk cafes.
- **Mount Royal:** Visible from many parts of the city, this mountain is especially striking at night, when the cross that adorns its peak is lit up.
- **The site of the Battle of Chateauguay:** Learn how this 1812 battle was won against the Americans through strategy and trickery rather than by overwhelming force.

QUEBEC CITY
- **La Citadelle:** Tour the walled fortress built in 1820 as protection against, among others, Americans!
- **Old Quebec:** Where Benedict Arnold's troupes almost won the city from the British during the American Revolutionary War!
- **The Plains of Abraham:** This famous battle park marks the 1759 victory of the English over the French in Canada.

TRAVELING FACTS:
- The summer weather in Canada is a pleasant 75-85 degrees. Canadians call that 20-25 degrees Celsius. Either way, it's perfect weather!
- American money can buy more in Canada. One American dollar is worth approximately $1.35 Canadian.
- Canadian 5-dollar bills are blue. The 10s are purple, and the 20s are green. Then there are the "loons," or "loonies": the dollar coins that feature a picture of a water bird, the loon. Two-dollar coins are called–what else–"toonies"!
- Canada is a bi-lingual country. French and English are its national languages.

*VIA Rail is a public Crown Corporation of Canada

Don't miss this chance to visit your northern neighbors, experience a little bit of Europe close to home, and learn about two countries with a long history of friendship.

www.viarail.ca

2. Excerpts from a Book, *Canada Today*

   A. Copyright Page

   CANADA TODAY

   Copyright, 2001, by Henriette Plunke. Printed in Canada. All rights in this book are reserved. No part of this book may by used or reproduced without written permission except in the case of brief quotations for use in critical articles and reviews. For information address The Press of Quebec, 256 High Road, Quebec, Canada.

   Cover photo, Claire Tryon: Parliament Hill, Ottawa

   Copyright © 2001 Henriette Plunke

   Maps copyright © 2001 Henriette Plunke

   First Edition
   ISBN 0-889-10345-1
   ISSN 2224-234

Post Test 1

2. Excerpts from a Book, *Canada Today*

   B. Table of Contents

Contents

Preface

    A Brief History of Canada's Past............................ 4

Chapter One—The Food

    What's French Got to Do With it?........................... 12

    Fish and Chips, Shepherds Pie, etc.......................... 20

    And Never the Twain Shall Meet?........................... 28

    Purely Canadian... 37

    Restaurant Reviews.. 45

Chapter Two—The Culture

    Arts... 56

    Architecture.. 78

    Entertainment... 90

    Music... 102

    What to do in the Winter................................... 114

Chapter Three—The Political Scene

    The Past.. 121

    Gaining Autonomy.. 135

    The Constitution.. 147

    The Role of Government................................... 155

    Political Parties... 162

Chapter Four—The Lay of the Land

    Getting Around.. 166

    Where to Visit?.. 178

    Facts and Figures—Weather, Festivals, etc.................. 182

    Graphs and Statistics...................................... 185

    Bibliography.. 189

    Acknowledgements.. 197

    Credits... 198

    Index... 199

2. Excerpts from a Book, *Canada Today*

   C. Graphs

BAR CHART OF POPULATION WITH *KNOWLEDGE* OF FRENCH: CANADIAN PROVINCES AND TERRITORIES, 1996

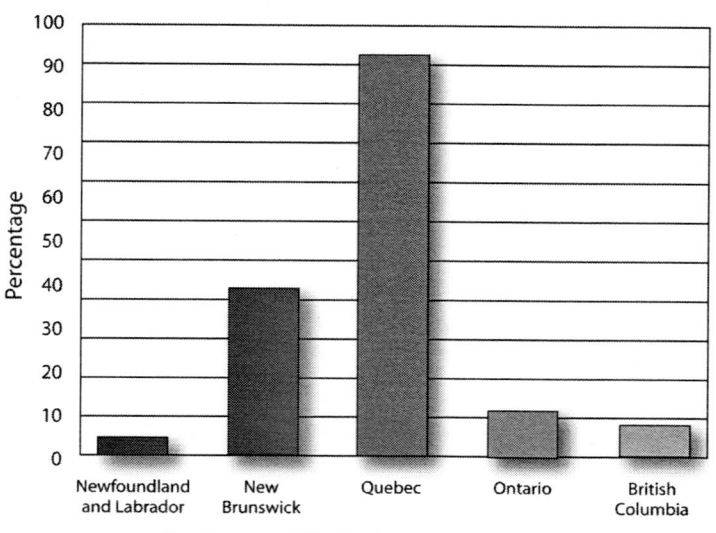

Province/Territory	Percentage
Newfoundland and Labrador	~5
New Brunswick	~40
Quebec	~92
Ontario	~11
British Columbia	~7

Source: Canada. Statistics Canada. 1996 Census.

BAR CHART OF POPULATION WITH *FRENCH MOTHER TONGUE*, CANADIAN PROVINCES AND TERRITORIES, 1996

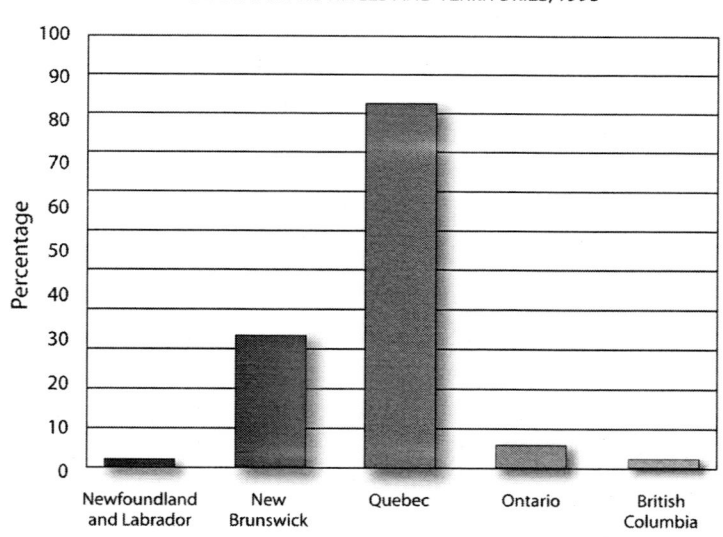

Province/Territory	Percentage
Newfoundland and Labrador	~2
New Brunswick	~32
Quebec	~83
Ontario	~5
British Columbia	~2

Source: Canada. Statistics Canada. 1996 Census.

**BAR CHART OF POPULATION WITH *ENGLISH MOTHER TONGUE*,
CANADIAN PROVINCES AND TERRITORIES, 1996**

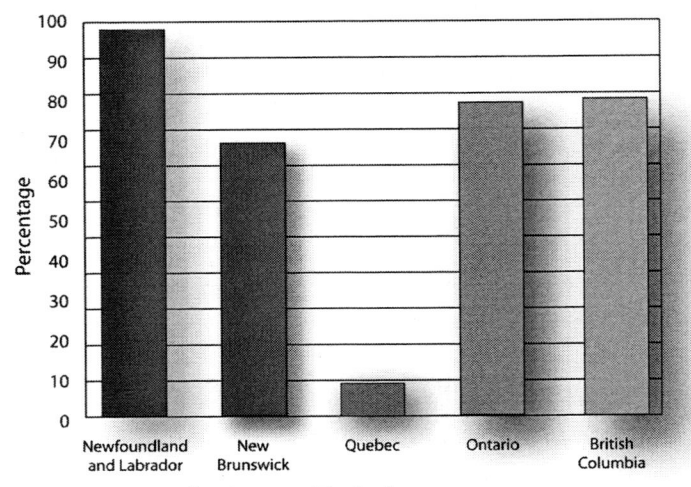

Provinces and Territories Source: Canada. Statistics Canada. 1996 Census.

3. Article from a Magazine

"The Canadian Constitution"

The Canadian Constitution

1 How does a country establish itself when it is already over 100 years old? This question has faced Canada since 1982. In that year, Canada finally took ownership of its constitution from the government of Great Britain.

2 Until 1982, the Canadian constitution had been housed in London, England. It was part of a British law called the British North America Act. Since it was a British law, only the British government could change it. Many Canadians did not find this acceptable. They felt that they should have complete control over their own constitution.

3 One Canadian who felt that way was the prime minister of Canada, Pierre Elliot Trudeau (pronounced Troo-dough). A popular young French-Canadian, Trudeau governed his country for a total of 16 years. Trudeau had two personal and political goals. He wanted to *repatriate*, or take back, the Canadian constitution from England. He also wanted harmony between the French and the English in Canada. Neither issue was a simple matter. In Trudeau's own province of Quebec, a political party called the *Parti-Quebequois* had been gaining popular support. The members of the P-Q were called separatists. They wanted the province of Quebec to separate from Canada and form its own country. Trudeau was against this break-up of Canada.

4 The repatriation of the constitution in 1982 was the finale of a long history towards Canadian self-determination. Why did it take so long? The answer may lie in the story of two rival world powers, France and England, who tried to build a country together. When France settled the land north of the 13 American colonies, she took control of an important part of the continent. Whoever controlled the St. Lawrence Valley, where Quebec City was built, could control much of Eastern Canada. Therefore, the British also wanted

Quebec City, and they fought for it. In 1759, in a place called The Plains of Abraham, the British defeated the French and took the city. This was a turning point in Canadian history. It is the reason why most of Canada is English today, and not French.

5   After this victory, England ruled Canada. However, the French-Canadians still kept their culture and way of life. In 1774, the British Government passed a law that recognized the unique culture of the French Canadians. It was called the Quebec Act. The law gave the province of Quebec more land. It recognized the Catholic Church as an important part of French life. It also allowed some French laws to govern Quebec citizens. This generous English law marked the beginning of an attitude of tolerance between the French and English in Canada.

6   The next milestone in the journey towards nationhood occurred in 1767. On July 1st of that year, Great Britain signed The British North America Act. The act made Canada a *dominion*, a member of the British Commonwealth of Nations. This was the birthday of Canada. July 1st is still celebrated each year in Canada, much the way the U.S. celebrates July 4th.

7   As a dominion, Canada had strong ties to Great Britain. A special member of the Canadian government, called the Governor General, represented the Queen in Canada. The Governor General signed all laws passed by the Canadian government. Still, this position was mainly symbolic. The real power of the government rested in the prime minister and the members of Parliament. These representatives were elected by the citizens.

8   In spite of ties to Britain, the Dominion of Canada was an independent country. However, Canadians wanted to be recognized as a country equal to any free government in the world. They wanted control over their own constitution. In 1982, the government of Canada passed the Canada Act. It requested the right to full ownership of its constitution. Queen Elizabeth signed the Act in Ottawa, Canada's capital. By signing the act, the Queen transferred all constitutional power from England to Canada.

9   Once Canada had power over its constitution, Canadians had to decide how it would be rewritten. One important element, added by Trudeau's government, was a Canadian Charter of Rights and Freedoms, or Bill of Rights. Until that time, the rights of Canadian citizens had never been written out as law.

10   Still, many parts of Canada had unique needs to be recognized. The old balance between the French and English cultures had to be considered. The French wanted to be accepted as a unique society within Canada. The Native people of Canada also needed special recognition. They required protection of their lands and treaties. The rights of women also had to be ensured. These and other issues had to be discussed as the 200-year old society struggled to define what kind of country it was.

11   The repatriation of the Canadian Constitution began a chapter in Canadian history that is not yet finished. Attempts have been made to amend the constitution to include the wishes of all members of society, but Canadian society is very complex. Proposals have been hammered out and then defeated by provinces or by citizens. The perfect solution has not yet been found. However, every Canadian citizen has been included in the search for it.

12 The Canadian Constitution may one day be amended to everyone's satisfaction. Meanwhile, it is at least owned by Canadians, and it, along with the Bill of Rights, defines a free and independent democracy whose people work together to guarantee equality for all segments of their diverse society.

Bibliographic Entries

The following five sample entries are based on formats from the *Modern Language Association (MLA) Handbook for Writers of Research Papers*. They show some acceptable formats for bibliographic entries.

A Book by a Single Author

Levy, Ellen. Bird Habitats. New York: Bunting Press, 1997.

A Book by More than One Author

Varick, William M., and Geraldine Abernathy. Endangered Birds of California. San Francisco: Wild World Publications, 1996.

An Encyclopedia Entry

"Extinct Birds." Encyclopedia Americana. 1998.

A Magazine Article

Alfaro, Lorenzo. "Exploring Off the Beaten Path." Natural Life 25 August 1997: 21-28.

Book Issued by Organization Identifying No Author

American Birding Association. Warbler Identification Guide. Chicago: American Birding Association, 1995.

For questions 30 through 34, choose the correct answer.

Read this portion of an outline of information from the article about the Canadian Constitution.

> A. Important Events in Canadian History
>   1. The French settle Quebec.
>   2. Canada becomes a nation.
>   3. _____
>   4. Rights of Canadian citizens become law.

30. Which information belongs in the blank?
    A. The British take Quebec City.
    B. England rules Canada.
    C. Queen Elizabeth signs the Canada Act.
    D. The Governor general signs all laws.

31. One reason a tourist might visit Quebec City would be to

   A. visit the cross on Mount Royal.

   B. learn about the 1759 victory of the English over the French.

   C. explore the 1838 residence of the Canadian Governor General.

   D. see a European-like town.

32. Chapter One of the book called *Canada Today* would be most useful for finding information about

   A. the nuances of French cooking.

   B. where to eat along the U.S.-Canadian border.

   C. how to prepare the national dish of England.

   D. how the French and English contributed to Canadian cuisine.

33. On which page of the book called *Canada Today* would you begin to look for information on skiing in Canada?

   A. 14   B. 166   C. 68   D. 4

34. Look at the VIA Rail Tour brochure. Which of the following most accurately describes why this brochure was probably written?

   A. to describe tourist attractions in Canada

   B. to give the reader a brief history of Canada

   C. to explain the differences between cities in Canada

   D. to encourage the reader to take a tour of Canada

Write your answers to questions 35 and 36 on the lines provided below.

35. Using information from the *Canada Today* copyright page, write a bibliographic entry for the book. Use the most appropriate format shown on page __ as your model.

   _____

   _____

   _____

36. What percentage of Canadians in the province of Quebec have English as their first language? In what source did you find this information?

   _____

   _____

   _____

Post Test 1

SESSION 4 — PROOFREADING

Read the rough draft of a student's story about her fascination with ballet. Read "Joining the Dance" and then answer questions 37 through 44.

Joining the Dance

When I was a little girl, I wanted to be a ballerina. I remember how it all began. It was (1)<u>Christmas 1997 my mother</u> took (2)<u>me and my little sister</u> to see a performance of (3)<u>The Nutcracker.</u> My sister was really (4)<u>too small</u> to enjoy the performance, (5)<u>and she started crying disturbing the people around her.</u> My mother had to take her out to the lobby. I couldn't leave. I was lost in the world of the dance. The dancers were amazing. It was (6)<u>as if they didn't</u> have to follow the rules of gravity. They seemed to float weightlessly over the stage. I sat frozen until the curtain came down.

The entire ride home I begged my mom to let me take lessons. Once she saw how serious I was about it, she signed me up at a local dance studio. She took me to the store to purchase (7)<u>my supplies, tights, slippers, leotard, and skirt.</u> I was a girl obsessed. I would dress in my leotard all the time, not just for lessons. I wouldn't walk across the room; I would dance. (8)<u>I never played outside any more.</u> I was always in my room practicing my positions. While all my friends were dancing to the sounds of Mariah Carey, I was dancing to Tchaikovsky. Ballet was my life.

Choose the correct answers to questions 3 through 44. Choose only one answer for each question.

37. How should you correct the error in number 1?

    A. change **Christmas 1997 my mother** to **Christmas 1997; my mother**
    B. change **Christmas 1997 my mother** to **Christmas of 1997, my mother**
    C. change **Christmas 1997 my mother** to **christmas 1997 my mother**
    D. There is no error.

38. How should you correct the error in number 2?

    A. change **me and my little sister** to **my little sister and I**
    B. change **me and my little sister** to **my little sister and me**
    C. change **me and my little sister** to **my little sister and myself**
    D. There is no error.

39. How should you correct the error in number 3?

    A. change **The Nutcracker** to **"The Nutcracker"**
    B. change **The Nutcracker** to *The Nutcracker*
    C. change **The Nutcracker** to **the nutcracker**
    D. There is no error.

40. How should you correct the error in number 4?

    A. change **too small** to **to small**
    B. change **too small** to **two small**
    C. change **too small** to **too young**
    D. There is no error.

41. How should you correct the error in number 5?

    A. change **and she started crying disturbing the people around her.** to **and started crying disturbing the people around her.**
    B. change **and she started crying disturbing the people around her.** to **and she started crying, disturbing the people around her.**
    C. change **and she started crying disturbing the people around her.** to **and began to cry disturbingly.**
    D. There is no error.

42. How should you correct the error in number 6?

    A. change **as if they didn't** to **as if they did't**
    B. change **as if they didn't** to **yet they didn't**
    C. change **as if they didn't** to **as if she didn't**
    D. There is no error.

43. How should you correct the error in number 7?

    A. change **my supplies, tights, slippers, leotard, and skirt.** to **my supplies: tights, slippers, leotard, and skirt.**
    B. change **my supplies, tights, slippers, leotard, and skirt.** to **my supplies, tights, slippers, leotard and skirt.**
    C. change **my supplies, tights, slippers, leotard, and skirt.** to **my supplies: tights, slippers, leotards and skirts.**
    D. There is no error.

44. How should you correct the error in number 8?

    A. change **I never played outside any more.** to **I rarely played outside any more.**
    B. change **I never played outside any more.** to **I hardly ever played outside anymore.**
    C. change **I never played outside any more.** to **I never played outside anymore.**
    D. There is no error.

Post Test 1

LEAP 21 Grade 8 Language Arts Post Test 2

The purpose of this practice test is to check on your progress in English Language Arts after reviewing the material in this book. The items and selections in this practice test are based on Louisiana standards for English Language Arts. Competency in these standards is required for promotion to ninth grade.

GENERAL DIRECTIONS

- Read all directions carefully.
- Read each question or example. Then choose the best answer.
- Choose only one answer for each question. If you change an answer, be sure to erase the answer completely.
- At the end of the test, you or your instructor should score your test. Then determine whether or not you are prepared to be tested on the real LEAP 21 Grade 8 in English Language Arts.

Session 1—Writing

On the real test, you will have extra pages for your prewriting and your rough draft. You will also have an answer document with two pages labeled for the final draft. In the real test, write your final draft only in the answer document.

For this practice test, however, you will use your own paper for each step. First, you may take a few minutes to brainstorm or create an outline. Then write a rough draft. Be sure and label each page, identifying the steps. Then, write your final draft on two pages.

Post Test 2

WRITING TOPIC

Read the topic in the box below. Write a well-organized composition of at least 150-200 words. Be sure to follow the suggestions listed under the box.

> Your Language Arts teacher has asked you to write a composition answering the following question.
>
> When you choose a friend, what qualities do you look for?
>
> Before you begin to write, think about how you choose friends. Think about the friends you have now. How did you choose them? What attracted you to them? What is it about these people that makes you want to be a friend?
>
> Now write a **multi-paragraph** composition **explaining** the qualities you look for when choosing a friend.

- Give specific details and explain why you think the way you do so that your readers will understand what you mean.
- Remember that your audience is your teacher; use appropriate language and explain your ideas clearly.
- Be sure to write clearly and to check your composition for correct spelling, punctuation, and grammar.

NOTE: On the real test, your teacher will read instructions to you and will hand out the answer documents. You will also be told that for this session, and this session only, you will be allowed to use a dictionary and a thesaurus.

Session 2—Reading and Responding

In this section of the test, you will read three passages and a poem. Then you will answer questions about what you read. This part of the test contains both multiple-choice and constructed-response questions. Answer these questions on the lines provided.

How much do you know about the speed of sound? Read this article about sonic booms and find out. Then answer questions 1 through 8.

Sonic Boom

1   A booming economy and rapid social change were not the only reverberations from the experience of World War I. In the 1940s and '50s, new flight technology enabled military fighter planes to fly faster than the speed of sound. This piercing of the "sound barrier," however, was an explosive and sometimes ground-shaking event. It used to annoy adults and startle infants, but it delighted young children. The sound of a fighter plane at drill, suddenly slicing through the air above their heads, would often stop children at their play. They knew what came next. They would cover their ears, yelling, "Here it comes!"

Then, *BOOM!* the skies would answer, and they would laugh with the excitement of such a display of speed and power.

2   Most of those children knew that the explosions were called "sonic booms." They also knew that the explosions meant that the plane had "broken the sound barrier." That expression had become part of household language, so fascinating was this science-fiction-like idea to Americans. What the children did not know at the time, though, was how basic and well established were the scientific principles behind this new development in aeronautics.

3   To understand how sonic booms are produced, it is necessary to understand the nature of sound and how it travels. Sound is really moving air particles. When we hear a guitar being played, we are really hearing the movement of the air particles caused by the vibrating movement of the guitar strings. This movement pushes the air particles that are around the strings. Once pushed, those air particles in turn push against the air particles next to them. In this way, the "push" moves, like a slinky toy, through the air. This is called a "compression waveform" because the air particles are pressing against each other and moving each other through the air.

4   Sound takes time to travel. It moves at different speeds through different materials. Through air, sound moves approximately 750 mph. Therefore, if a car approaches you at only 30 mph, the sound waves from that car reach you before the car does. That is fortunate, because it allows you to get out of the way of the car. Now, imagine a car that travels at 800 mph. That car would reach you before you heard it!

5   Cars cannot travel 800 mph, but rocket-propelled aircraft can—and even faster. Aeronautics professionals use "Mach" (pronounced "mock") numbers to describe speed. Named after Austrian physicist Ernst Mach, these numbers describe speed in terms of how it compares with the speed of sound. A jet at Mach 1 is traveling at the same speed as sound. At Mach 2, it is traveling at 2 times the speed of sound. Naturally, Mach 3 would be 3 times the speed of sound, and Mach .5 would be half the speed of sound. Any speed above Mach 1 is *supersonic* speed.

6   The sonic booms that stopped children at play in the 1950s were the early trials of the new flight technology towards achieving supersonic speed. In the earliest years of aviation, piston engines, like the ones in today's cars, drove the propellers that flew propeller airplanes. Later, jet-propelled engines enabled planes to achieve far more speed and altitude. Then, the development of rocket engines in the 1940s gave the needed thrust to send flight speed (literally and figuratively) into orbit!

7   Rocket engines are basically controlled explosions. More than three centuries ago, the great scientist Isaac Newton suggested that if an explosion were caused in a machine, and the energy from that explosion were channeled to the rear, the machine would be propelled forward at a great speed. Newton may not have envisioned that machine going faster than the speed of sound, but his theory is what formed the basis of rocket technology in the mid 20th century. This technology, in fact, has propelled "machines" up to *5 times* the speed of sound.

8   Why, though, are sonic booms heard along the flight path of these high-speed machines? Remember that if air waves are moved, they create sound. If they are moved

Post Test 2

gently, they create a gentle sound. If they are moved at "lightening" speeds, they move so quickly that they collide violently into each other. Then they crash into more and more air particles before those particles have time to move. Finally, the whole compressed collection of air particles wallops our eardrums all at once, sounding to us like an explosion.

9 A supersonic jet speeding across the sky can be compared to a boat cutting through water. If the boat is on a slow cruise, small waves of water move in a *V* shape away from the front of the boat. But if the boat crashes through the water at high speed, it causes something more like a tidal wave. In the same way, air particles crash in a *V* shape away from all sides of the nose of a supersonic jet, causing a "tidal wave" also called a "shock wave" of sound to strike our ears.

10 The breaking of the sound barrier was a milestone in transportation and military history. However, it has been hampered, so far, by this corresponding hazard of sonic booms. Because of the inherent force of sonic booms, which can damage buildings and bridges, supersonic air travel is banned over the continental United States.

11 The next challenge in supersonic flight technology is the development of a "boomless" supersonic aircraft. Flight engineers have made some progress in this area, but more development is necessary. If a quiet supersonic aircraft is finally developed, we may be able to travel from Los Angeles to New York in a matter of minutes, without disturbing anyone, either working adults or playing children, on the ground.

For questions 1 through 4, choose the correct answer.

1. The passage says that "Newton may not have envisioned that machine going faster than the speed of sound, but his theory is what formed the basis of rocket technology in the mid 20th century." What does <u>envisioned</u> mean?
   A. imagined   B. proclaimed   C. observed   D. believed

2. Which organizational pattern is used in paragraphs 7 and 8 in this selection?
   A. cause/effect   C. comparison/contrast
   B. chronological order   D. proposition and support

3. Which statement from the selection is an opinion?

   A. A supersonic jet speeding across the sky can be compared to a boat cutting through water.

   B. Named after Austrian physicist Ernst Mach, these numbers describe speed in terms of how it compares with the speed of sound.

   C. …We may be able to travel from Los Angeles to New York in a matter of minutes, without disturbing anyone…on the ground.

   D. The sonic booms that stopped children at play in the 1950s were the early trials of the new flight technology towards achieving supersonic speed.

4. Paragraphs 6 and 7 of this selection are mainly about

    A. the development of rocket technology.

    B. the effect of a sonic boom on children.

    C. the explosion caused by a rocket engine.

    D. the energy that is produced by an explosion.

Write your answer to question 5 on the lines provided below.

5. Is 'Sonic Boom' a work of fiction, nonfiction, poetry, or drama? Identify two features of the selection that support your answer.

_____

_____

_____

For questions 6 and 7, choose the correct answer.

6. The author included paragraphs 3 and 4 in this selection because they help the reader understand

    A. what the speed of sound is.   C. how sound moves through the air.

    B. when sound waves are heard.   D. why sound travels at different speeds.

7. In trying to create a "boom-less" supersonic aircraft, what must scientists do?

    A. find a way to build bridges and buildings so that the sonic boom doesn't harm them

    B. create an airplane that does not violently disturb air particles at high speeds

    C. build aircraft that don't go faster than the speed of sound

    D. experiment with watercraft instead of aircraft

Write your answer to question 8 on the lines provided below.

8. The children of the 1940s and 1950s knew the sound of a sonic boom well, but children from later generations aren't as familiar with this sound. Give an example of a technology that you are familiar with now that later generations may not experience.

_____

_____

_____

The people we meet either on or off a sports field aren't always who we expect them to be. Read this story about a football team with a unique team member. Then, answer questions 9 through 16.

What Goal Line Block?

1   The fall of 2003 was a time of crushed hopes, lost dreams, and diminished football attendance. Our team, the Southside High Saints, was on a downward spiral that seemed permanent. We needed a miracle to get us back on the winning track we'd achieved the season before: victory in the regional championship. How could we have fallen to such miserable depths? How deep was this abyss, you ask? After three games, our record stood at Saints 0, rest of the civilized world 3.

2   Now for the fourth game, I, the quarterback, decided to energize my team: "Guys, we have stunk it up long enough! What d'ya think we're doing out there? We're supposed to be playing football, not shuffleboard!" After admiring my sharp observations, the coach spoke his mind. He pontificated about reaching goals by having heart, team spirit, and camaraderie—yada, yada, yada.

3   We practiced daily after school for this pivotal game. We ran basic patterns and endurance trials. My passes were nailing receivers—I had the distance, I had the targets. Luckily, our offensive line kept the defensive team blocked an average of 14 seconds, so I could set plays. Simultaneously, our team's defensive unit fought to breech the line for a sack—on me! Our best player on defense, a star middle-line backer named Scottie, was as determined as I to take this game. Scottie and I had played together since 7th grade and knew each other exceedingly well. I often bragged that I could trust Scottie with, not just my life and my girlfriends, but with my football career.

4   Our game was scheduled to begin that Saturday at noon, but a late-season thunderstorm delayed the start. The opposing team, the Tri-city Titans, rumbled through our gates exactly at noon. They stalked across the field ignoring the storm, sneering at the lightning, and jeering at the decision to postpone: they thought they smelled blood.

5   The coin toss fell to them; the Titans chose to receive. The field was slick, the sky was overcast, and the fans were silent—ominous portents for a gridiron battle.

6   The Titans began their rush; Scottie stopped them. We, the Saints, took the field, and then we left the field. Back and forth went the fortunes of our teams with no scoring, until the second half when the Titans managed to score a field goal, crafted with a 40-yard punt return.

7   There were six minutes left. I called my play, scrambling for the goalposts off the line of scrimmage. At the thirty-yard line, I suffered blows from a ton of Titans. The first hit sent me sliding in the mud; subsequent hits sent me sliding under the mud like a hibernating dusky salamander. After resurrecting me from the sodden clay, my team scored a three-point field goal, tying the game. I wiped the mud from my eyes, as Scottie strode by and with a grin, slapped my helmet, saying, "This next tackle is for you, you *!#%* dog."

8   Four minutes remaining, our defensive line strategically aligned themselves against the Titans. The field dimmed into twilight; the management switched on massive light bulbs, but they required time to attain maximum brightness. Saint fans undulated restlessly, waiting for the feared blow to strike again. The Titan center snapped the ball. The quarterback fell back, and then scrambled in the same pattern I had. Demonically desiring to out-play me, he leaped, twisted, and dodged. The first tackle slid off; he spun around the next tackle, and now he was tearing down our sideline, nearing the Titan goal line, putting the yards behind him: 27 ... 25 ... 22 ... 20 ... a tackle! He was down! In

the next two seconds, most of the Saints and half of the Titans piled on with Scottie sailing atop the pinnacle, and a Titan leaping up after him. As those two clashed over the twisted mound of bodies, there suddenly appeared a single, solitary leg flying up over players still on the field—spinning knee over foot and foot over knee with a gentle arabesque motion, sharply illuminated by lights now glaring at full strength.

9   A tremendous silence shuddered through the stadium; then a collective gasp sucked the silence away. I swaggered over to the pile, and slapped Scottie's helmet poking out from under a Titan backside.

10   "So whazzup with that!" I kidded him, "You didn't screw ol' stumpy on tight enough?"

11   The Titans were in shock—hyperventilating and trembling. After we extracted Scottie and the rest of the players from the heap, he told the Titans how he had lost his leg when he was six, in a boating accident. While he was talking, our coach brought Scottie's limb back to him. Scottie stayed on the field putting the prosthesis back on. We bragged on him to distract the Titans. We told them how he was one of the first students with a prosthetic limb in the public school system allowed to compete in sports. He won permission with a perfect attendance record and an outstanding academic record, too. We were so used to Scottie's prosthesis that it was practically invisible. Sure, Scott used the fake limb as a prop for jokes occasionally, but that didn't work around old friends anymore.

12   I'd like to say that we let up on the Titans, but no, we schooled 'em. We made two touchdowns in the game's final three minutes. The Titans? Our defense, spearheaded by Scott, silenced them. They vanished into the deepening night, vowing, after congratulating us, to even the score the next time our teams clashed. They were wrong. Our goals had shifted; mental blocks, holding us back, evaporated. Instead of playing to protect our championship status, we played to make believers of people who doubted us, including ourselves. So, we won not just the regional championship again, but continued to victory in the state championship. That game with the Titans was our miracle. Like I'd told the team before; most goals can be achieved with heart, team spirit, camaraderie . . . and, by getting a leg up (in the air), stunning our opposition!

For questions 9 through 14, choose the correct answer.

Read this sentence from the selection.

> He pontificated about reaching goals by having heart, team spirit, and camaraderie—yada, yada, yada.

9. In this sentence, <u>pontificated</u> is closest in meaning to

   A. replied.   B. yelled.   C. demanded.   D. lectured.

10. The passage says that "Like I'd told the team before; most goals can be achieved with heart, team spirit, camaraderie . . . and, by getting a leg up (in the air), stunning our opposition!" What does the expression <u>getting a leg up</u> mean?

    A. making an attempt   C. having an advantage
    B. having control over   D. depending on someone

Post Test 2

11. Which sentence in the selection best supports the idea that the football game is an important event?
    7-M4
    - A. We practiced daily after school for this pivotal game.
    - B. Our game was scheduled to begin that Saturday at noon, but a late-season thunderstorm delayed the start.
    - C. Four minutes remaining, our defensive line strategically aligned themselves against the Titans.
    - D. A tremendous silence shuddered through the stadium; then a collective gasp sucked the silence away.

12. Which part of the plot is illustrated in paragraph 8?
    1-M2
    - A. the setting
    - B. the conflict
    - C. the climax
    - D. the resolution

13. The author's use of first person point of view helps the reader understand
    7-M3
    - A. the narrator's opinion about football.
    - B. how the Titans feel about the game.
    - C. the coach's attitude toward the Saints.
    - D. the thoughts and feelings of the main character.

14. Which statement from the selection best supports the main idea?
    7-M1
    - A. We made two touchdowns in the game's final three minutes.
    - B. Most goals can be achieved with heart, team spirit, camaraderie . . .
    - C. Our goals had shifted; mental blocks, holding us back, evaporated.
    - D. … We played to make believers of people who doubted us, including ourselves.

Write your answers to questions 15 and 16 on the lines provided below.

15. What is the <u>strongest evidence</u> to suggest that 'What Goal Line Block?' is a work of fiction?
    6-M3

    _____

    _____

    _____

16. What lesson can be learned from the events in this story? Use an example from the selection to support your answer.
    6-M1

    _____

    _____

    _____

The following poem by Li Ho was written in about 810 A.D. and is still widely read today. Read the poem. Then answer questions 17 through 22.

A Beautiful Girl Combs Her Hair

Awake at dawn
she's dreaming
by cool silk curtains

fragrance of spilling hair
half sandalwood, half aloes
windlass creaking at the well
singing jade

the lotus blossom awakes, refreshed
her mirror
two phoenixes
a pool of autumn light

—Stanzas I–III by Li Ho

For questions 17 through 19, choose the correct answer.

17. What is the woman being compared to in this poem?

    A. a mirror   B. a lotus blossom   C. a windlass   D. a phoenix

18. In the poem, "the lotus blossom awakes" means that

    A. the flower is waking up.   C. the girl is waking up.
    B. the flower is opening its petals.   D. the girl is going to sleep.

19. Which answer best describes the mood that the poet creates through word choice and image?

Write your answer to question 20 on the lines provided below.

    A. serene and lovely   C. bored and depressed
    B. lazy and quiet   D. neutral and emotionless

20. How is the author's use of language in this poem different from how it would be in a piece of nonfiction?

_____

_____

Post Test 2

For question 21, choose the correct answer.

21. Which of the following universal themes does this poem best express?

    A. beauty is only skin deep
    B. youth is beauty and beauty youth
    C. don't judge a book by its cover
    D. youth is not eternal

Write your answer to question 22 on the lines provided below.

22. What do you think the poet has left unsaid in this poem? Support your answer with a detail from the poem.

_____

_____

_____

Many schools throughout the United States have mascots. Often these mascots are animals, but there are many schools whose mascots are people. Read this article about mascots. Then, answer questions 23 through 28.

People as Mascots

1   "Go! Go! Go!" scream hundreds of fans. The quarterback barrels towards the goal line. Finally, the old stadium explodes into a riot of war cries and chants. Tomahawks wave. Buckskin-clad cheerleaders flourish turkey feathers and leap for joy. A war-painted mascot mimics an "Indian" dance. The score board chalks up another six points for the *Braves*.

2   So it has been for decades on Friday nights at Centerville High School. The games and the "Indian" rituals that go along with them are a beloved tradition here–as they are in many high schools throughout America.

3   Other Americans, however, while not as loud or boisterous as the screaming fans, are beginning to be heard above the din. They are the descendents of the nations of America's first peoples. They look on and see cartoons of their culture used in another culture's games, and they say, "This is disrespectful."

4   In most cases, these voices are stubbornly ignored. Just as stubbornly, however, they persist. In recent years, they have been joined by the voices of other American communities. In February 2004, the California Senate Education Committee began debating a bill to "eliminate racial mascots" in school sports. The Dallas School District has requested that Dallas schools not use "Indian" mascots and logos. All public schools in the district have complied with that request. Over the last 30 years, according to Jeff J. Corntassel, professor at Virginia Tech, "nearly 1,000 primary and secondary schools have traded their Indian mascots for non-racist alternatives." These and other organizations have begun to reject the use of Indian-based images in sports.

5   The quarterback and fans of Centerville High don't understand the controversy. Why is there a problem with what they feel is a harmless tradition, they ask. How do these "Indian" mascots affect Native Americans?

6   According to Barbara E. Munson, chair of The "Indian" Mascot and Logo Taskforce in Wisconsin, they have many effects. One effect is that they stereotype a race of people. Mascots and logos use the most basic symbols of a people's culture. This creates stereotypes. Stereotypes, according to Munson, reduce human beings to cartoon images. Representing the various cultures of Native Americans with one image of, for example, a fierce *brave,* is demeaning. It is as senseless as drawing all European-American people as loud-mouthed, ill-mannered, socially graceless image of the "ugly American," made famous by a book of that name.

7   Another affect these logos have, says Munson, is that they lock Native Americans in the past. Native American cultures are a living part of American society. Showing them as angry warriors is like showing all European-Americans as black-and-white-clad Puritan settlers.

8   "Indian" logos are blamed for making all Native Americans the same. Native Americans do not think of themselves as "Indians." They usually think of themselves first as Huron, Sioux, Cherokee, or any one of the roughly 600 different tribes to which they belong. Secondly, they think of themselves as Native, or indigenous, peoples.

9   Munson points out that mascots and logos use objects that are sacred to Native Americans. Eagle feathers, drums, and other cultural objects are part of a spiritual tradition. Using these objects in games, she says, is like waving crucifixes or menorahs to show team spirit. When Native Americans see an "Indian" medicine man used as a mascot, they feel that it is humiliating. It would be like other Americans watching fans in a different culture dress up as rabbis or the Pope, and dancing around at sports events.

10 Finally, according to Munson, these "Indian" sports logos use violent images. Waving tomahawks, screaming about scalping, and carrying huge pictures of scowling warriors ignores the reality of Native Americans. Native Americans are like most other North Americans. They are peaceful, hard-working, family people.

11 "But, it's all in the fun of the game," muses the Centerville coach. "No one means any harm. In fact, we are *honoring* the Native people by using images of them. Besides, we are including another culture in public schools and sports!"

12 Like the Centerville coach, most teams mean no disrespect by using "Indian" logos. However, to this, Native Americans reply that teams know very little about the culture they are mimicking. Therefore, they would not understand the importance these symbols hold for Native Americans.

13 As for teams meaning no harm, Munson remarks, "When someone says you are hurting them by your actions, if you persist, then the harm becomes intentional."

14 Non-native sports teams often think they are honoring Native Americans with their use of cultural symbols. However, Native peoples do not feel honored. They see it as an inaccurate use of their cultural images.

15   Finally, Native peoples say that "Indian" mascots and logos do not add to the cultural diversity in schools. They say that oversimplified images of a culture only put up barriers to understanding. Indian youths in these schools, says professor Corntassel, "see their culture mocked and trivialized daily." As Barbara Munson says, they feel "marginalized" from the more common culture of the public schools.

16   Throughout her history, the United States has attempted to become a tolerant nation. In this attempt, many groups have had to fight for their right to be understood. African-Americans and Asians, for example, used to be shown on television in comical and foolish ways. They had to fight against these images. They have largely succeeded, and the country has become better for it. Native Americans hope that soon, sports teams will understand the harm in using cherished symbols of a rich culture in play. Then, too, they say, the U.S. will become much better for it.

For questions 23 through 25, choose the correct answer.

23. The author probably wrote this selection to

   A. trace the history of mascots in school sports.
   B. persuade coaches to eliminate the use of mascots.
   C. argue for the value of mascots in sports.
   D. discuss the effect of "Indian" mascots on Native Americans.

Read this portion of an outline of information from this selection.

> A. Using Indian Logos
>   1. stereotypes a race of people
>   2. locks Native Americans in the past
>   3. makes all Native Americans the same
>   4. _____
>   5. does not add to cultural diversity in schools

24. Which information belongs in the blank?

   A. teaches people tolerance
   B. encourages respect for indigenous people
   C. adds excitement to sports events
   D. reduces human beings to cartoon images

25. From the information in this selection, the reader can conclude that

   A. most people believe that stereotyping is harmful.
   B. Native Americans enjoy seeing their images on playing fields.
   C. most teams will eventually use non-racist mascots.
   D. certain ethnic groups are stereotyped on television.

Write your answers to questions 26 and 27 on the lines provided below.

26. How are the quotations presented in this article different from quotations presented in fictional stories?

6-M2

_____

_____

_____

27. Imagine you go to school in a place with an Indian as a mascot. What are two things you could do to raise awareness about the potential problems with the mascot?

7-M2

_____

_____

_____

For question 28, choose the correct answer.

28. The author presents the ideas in this selection mainly by

7-M3

    A. clearly presenting accurate historical information.

    B. using poorly executed exaggeration to make a point.

    C. telling an exciting story to illustrate a confusing principle.

    D. concisely developing an argument verified by facts.

1-M4, 6-M1, 6-M2

---

29. **ESSAY**

In both "What Goal Line Block?" and "People As Mascots" how does new knowledge affect how people view Scottie and Indian Mascots. Compare and contrast how knowledge affects a person's perception of a situation. Use at least one detail from each passage to support your answer.

Post Test 2

Session 4—Using Information Resources

Introduction: In this section of the test, you are asked to look at some reference materials and then use the materials to answer the questions on page __.

Topic:

Suppose you want to write a report about different ways people have developed to tell time. You will need to learn about how the idea of time is dealt with during a single day, a year, and within history. Four different sources of information about telling time are included in this section of the test. The information sources and the page numbers where you can find them are listed below.

> 1. Article from a Magazine
>   "Keeping Track of Time" (page __)

> 2. Advertisement
>   Hourglasses (page __

> 3. Chart
>   World Time (page __)

> 4. Excerpt from a Book, *Clocks*
>   Table of Contents (page __)

Model bibliographic entries for different types of references are on page __. These show acceptable formats for entries.

Directions: Skim pages __ through __ to become familiar with the information contained in these sources. Remember that these are reference sources, so you should not read every word in each source. Once you have skimmed these sources, answer the questions on page __. Use the information sources to help you answer the questions. As you work through the questions, go back and read the parts that will give you the information that you need.

386

1. Article from a Magazine

    "Keeping Track of Time"

Keeping Track of Time

1   When you want to plan a holiday or event, what is the first thing you consult? Chances are, it's a calendar. Calendars allow us to plan the future and remember the past. Imagine trying to plan a summer vacation, remember your friend's birthday, or even describe when you were born, without a calendar. There was a time, though, when days followed each other, unnamed and unnumbered. How did the ancient peoples come up with formulas for naming and counting days in this nebulous flow of time?

2   The calendar followed today in most Western countries has taken on some peculiar incarnations in the past. Rulers, priests, and mathematicians molded, twisted, added, and deleted days and months, trying to get them to fit into patterns of whole numbers that could be counted. The problem, though, is that days, months, and years are not as simple as that. Their life spans measure in the very awkward realm of numbers with up to 10 decimal places. For instance, one year, from the beginning of spring to the end of winter, lasts approximately 365.25 days (rounding out the several decimals).

3   In ancient Greece, the farmers and rulers noticed that time was divided into patterns. It seemed natural to count using those patterns. One of the most obvious patterns was the rising and setting of the sun. Another pattern the ancient Greeks knew well was the waxing and waning of the moon. As well as these cycles, they also knew the cycle of the seasons.

4   The ancient Greek calendars measured the changes of the moon. It takes about 29 days for the moon to complete its cycle. This is known as a "lunar month." In one year, there are 12 lunar months—minus approximately ten days. In other words, a lunar year of 12 lunar months would end on December 21. Therefore, in order for the lunar months to fit the cycle of seasons, the Greeks would simply add a number of calendar days to the end of each year.

5   Unlike the Greeks, the ancient Egyptians ignored the phases of the moon. They based their calendar on the sun. They divided the year into 12 months of 30 days each. That made 360 days. They were still a little over 5 days short of a complete cycle of seasons, otherwise known as a "tropical year." This posed little problem to the Egyptians, however. They simply added five party days to the end of each year. For five days, they celebrated the birthdays of important gods. Then, they began their next calendar year.

6   Of course, the "whole number" problem remained. Remember, a year is 365 *and a quarter* (rounding out the several decimals) days long, not simply 365 days long. Do the math. Under this scheme, every four years the calendar year would end a day earlier. Did the Egyptians party for an extra day in those years? Apparently not. They were content to let the timely order of days slide—by about one day every four years.

Post Test 2

7   Meanwhile, in ancient Rome, the calendar was being organized around the phases of the moon, as it had been in ancient Greece. There were 12 lunar months to the year. But, since 12 lunar months only add up to a year minus 10 days (approximately), the Romans would throw in an extra month when needed. (It would be a short month.)

8   With all the adding and subtracting of months and days, the Roman calendar still went out of rhythm with the seasons. To correct this, in 46 B.C. Julius Caesar gave his people a gift of three months of extra time in their year. Back in step with Nature, Julius Caesar made a further change of adding a "leap day" to February every four years—an idea we still use today.

9   The Julian calendar, as Caesar's invention is called, still measured about 11 minutes more than the exact length of a tropical year. Therefore, spring, for example, would begin 11 minutes earlier each year. In 1582, Pope Gregory XIII designed a new calendar. He wanted the date of the Spring Equinox to be on March 21st each year. The only solution was to remove some days from the calendar so that it would catch up with the seasons and equinoxes. That is exactly what he did. On October 4, 1582, people went to sleep only to wake up on October 16, 1582. Ten days had disappeared overnight by Papal order!

10   Once the "Gregorian" calendar had performed an overnight catch-up with the tropical year, the Pope made other minor changes to keep the calendar year and the tropical year in synch. His new calendar was adopted by most European countries. Both England and France, however, were reluctant to accept a system designed by the Catholic Church. England, in fact, kept the Julian calendar for another 170 years.

11   The Gregorian calendar is used by most Western nations today. However, it is not the only calendar in use. Muslim countries, which account for 1/5 of the world's population, use the Islamic calendar, which is based on the phases of the moon. Like the ancient Greek calendar, the Islamic calendar consists of 12 lunar months, each about 29 days long. Each month begins with the new crescent moon. That moon must be *visually sighted* by a respected witness before the month can officially begin.

12   The Islamic calendar measures time from the year the Prophet Mohamed traveled to Medina. This journey was called the Hijra, and every year after it is classified AH, or Anno Hijra, meaning the year of the Hijra. The year the actual Hiraj took place was AD 622, as measured by the Gregorian calendar. Therefore, the year 2003 of the Gregorian calendar is the year AH 1424 for Muslim countries. That is because it is 1,424 years after the Hijra.

13   The calendar is one of our most useful cultural tools. Yet, over the last many centuries and through many modifications, it still has flaws. Today, proposals are still being made for a more perfect system for measuring time. Meanwhile, nations who follow the Gregorian calendar continue their best effort in imposing order on the changing patterns of Nature. If that means having days appear and disappear from the picture, it may just serve to add an intriguing counter beat to the inevitable rhythm of days.

2. Advertisement

   Hourglasses

What better objet d'art to grace your desk than a classic timepiece?

What better objet d'art to grace your desk than a classic timepiece?

Nothing is more classic than a Sandman's Hourglass!

Crafted of hand-blown glass and encased in polished cherry wood, this exquisite timepiece is heirloom quality.

Filled with your choice of white, tan, or black sand, this lovely piece will accurately measure an hour for centuries!

Order yours TODAY for only $99!
(with shipping and handling)

Sandman's hourglass
www.sandmanshourglass.com

3. Chart

   World Time

World Time

Helsinki	12:00 AM	Honolulu	12:00 PM
Moscow	1:00 AM	Anchorage	1:00 PM
Abu Dhabi	2:00 AM	San Francisco	2:00 PM
Islamabad	3:00 AM	Phoenix	3:00 PM
Dhaka	4:00 AM	New Orleans	4:00 PM
Jakarta	5:00 AM	New York	5:00 PM
Hong Kong	6:00 AM	San Juan	6:00 PM
Seoul	7:00 AM	Sao Paulo	7:00 PM
Brisbane	8:00 AM	Montevideo	8:00 PM
Sydney	9:00 AM	Azores	9:00 PM
Suva	10:00 AM	Casablanca	10:00 PM
Wellington	11:00 AM	Paris	11:00 PM

4. Excerpt from a Book, Clocks

Table of Contents

Contents

Preface	1
A Brief History of the Clock	4
Sundials	7
Shadow Clocks	9
Equatorial	12
Horizontal	13
Diptych	15
Equiangular	16
Capuchin	19
Water Clocks	23
Hour Glass	35
Candle Clocks	46
Eastern Mechanized Astrological Clocks	52
Modern Clocks	61
Pendulum Clocks	72
Quartz Clocks	80
Atomic Clocks	95
Information for Collectors	104
Clock Repairs	122
Illustrations	145
Bibliography	159
Index	167

More Bibliographic Entries

The following five sample entries are based on formats from the *Modern Language Association (MLA) Handbook for Writers of Research Papers*. They show some acceptable formats for bibliographic entries.

A Book by a Single Author

Levy, Ellen. <u>Bird Habitats</u>. New York: Bunting Press, 1997.

A Book by More than One Author

Varick, William M., and Geraldine Abernathy. <u>Endangered Birds of California</u>. San Francisco: Wild World Publications, 1996.

An Encyclopedia Entry

"Extinct Birds." <u>Encyclopedia Americana</u>. 1998.

A Magazine Article

Alfaro, Lorenzo. "Exploring Off the Beaten Path." <u>Natural Life</u> 25 August 1997: 21-28.

Book Issued by Organization Identifying No Author

American Birding Association. <u>Warbler Identification Guide</u>. Chicago: American Birding Association, 1995.

For questions 30 and 31, choose the correct answer.

30. When it is 7 AM in Seoul, what time is it in Casablanca?

    A. 9 PM B. 10 PM C. 7 AM D. 6 AM

31. Which of the following best summarizes the information in the article "Keeping Track of Time?"
    A. The article traces the development of the calendar.
    B. The article describes the purpose of the calendar.
    C. The article convinces the reader to use a particular calendar.
    D. The article informs the reader about inventors of the calendar.

Write your answer to question 32 on the lines provided below.

32. Which calendar is most similar to the Greek calendar? Where did you find this information?

Post Test 2

For questions 33 through 35, choose the correct answer.

Use the model bibliographic entries to answer this question.

33. Which of the entries below is an example of a correct bibliographic entry for a magazine article?

    A. Martins, Linda. "Correctly Positioning a Sundial in Your Garden." Gardening Life 12 June 2002: 14–16.

    B. "Correctly Positioning a Sundial in Your Garden," *Gardening Life*, by Martins, Linda. June, 12, 2002, pp. 14–16.

    C. Linda Martins. "Correctly Positioning a Sundial in Your Garden." Gardening Life. 12 June, 2002: 14–16.

    D. Martins. "Correctly Positioning a Sundial in Your Garden." Gardening Life. 12 June 2002: 14–16.

34. To locate additional resources on clocks, where should you look?

    A. the index of the book *Clocks*

    B. the website www.sandmanshourglass.com

    C. the bibliography of the book *Clocks*

    D. the table of contents of the book *Clocks*

35. Based on the information in the table of contents for the book *Clocks*, a diptych is a kind of

    A. atomic clock   B. horizontal   C. modern clock   D. sundial

Write your answer to question 36 on the lines provided below.

36. In what way might the information given in the advertisement about Sandman's Hour Glass be of use to you in gathering information for your report?

___

___

___

392

SESSION 4 — PROOFREADING

Read the rough draft of a student's report on how the Electoral College works. Read "Electoral College" and then answer questions 37 through 44.

Electoral College

Who chooses the President of the United States? (1)<u>If you said the voter's, you</u> are right, but not completely. When voters cast their ballots on Election Day, they are not voting directly for the president. They are actually voting for a group of presidential electors. These people have pledged to support the (2)<u>candidate</u> that wins the popular vote. This system is called the (3)<u>Electoral College, a group of people</u> who meet in their state capitals in December to vote for president. The electors cast a total of 538 votes. (4)<u>To be elected president, a candidate must</u> have at least 270 electoral votes.

(5)<u>Each of the states have</u> a different number of electors. The population of a state determines the number of electors. The electors are equal to the number of (6)<u>Senators and Representatives in Congress</u> who represent that state. The states with the biggest populations have more electoral votes than less populated states. This is why candidates running for president spend (7)<u>alot</u> of time in states like (8)<u>Florida, California and New York</u>. They hope to get more electoral votes and win the race!!

Choose the correct answers to questions 37 through 44. Mark only one answer for each question.

37. How should you correct the error in number 1?

   A. change **If you said the voter's, you** to **If you said the voter's you**
   B. change **If you said the voter's, you** to **If you said, "the voter's," you**
   C. change **If you said the voter's, you** to **If you said the voters, you**
   D. There is no error.

38. How should you correct the error in number 2?

   A. change **candidate** to **canidate**
   B. change **candidate** to **candidates**
   C. change **candidate** to **cannidate**
   D. There is no error.

39. How should you correct the error in number 3?

   A. change **Electoral College, a group** to **Electoral College, which is a group**
   B. change **Electoral College, a group** to **electoral college . . .**
   C. change **Electoral College, a group** to **Electoral College, people**
   D. There is no error.

Post Test 2

40. How should you correct the error in number 4? 3-M3

    A. change **president, a candidate** to **president; a candidate**

    B. change **To be elected president** to **To be president**

    C. change **To be elected president, a candidate must** to **A candidate must, to be elected president**

    D. There is no error.

41. How should you correct the error in number 5? 3-M4

    A. change **Each of the states have** to **Each state have**

    B. change **Each of the states have** to **Each of the states has**

    C. change **Each of the states have** to **Each one of the states have**

    D. There is no error.

42. How should you correct the error in number 6? 3-M5

    A. change **Senators and Representatives in Congress** to **Senators and Representatives in congress**

    B. change **Senators and Representatives in Congress** to **senators and representatives in congress**

    C. change **Senators and Representatives in Congress** to **senators and representatives in Congress**

    D. There is no error.

43. How should you correct the error in number 7? 3-M5

    A. change **alot** to **allot**

    B. change **alot** to **a lot**

    C. change **alot** to **alott**

    D. There is no error.

44. How should you correct the error in number 8? 3-M2

    A. change **Florida, California and New York** to **Florida, California, and New York**

    B. change **Florida, California and New York** to **Florida, California, New York**

    C. change **Florida, California and New York** to **Florida, California and, New York**

    D. There is no error.